S. L. Frank

The Unknowable

An Ontological Introduction to the Philosophy of Religion

Translated by

Boris Jakim

Ohio University Press
Athens, Ohio
London

Library of Congress Cataloging in Publication Data

Frank, S. L. (Semen Liudvigovich), 1877–1950.
  The unknowable.

  Translation of: Nepostizhimoe.
  Includes index.
  1. Knowledge, Theory of. 2. Religion—Philosophy. I. Title.
BD211.F713   1983   200′.1   82-22565
ISBN 0-8214-0676-0 (cloth)

Attingitur inattingibile inattingibiliter.

(The unattainable is attained
through its unattainment)

NICHOLAS OF CUSA

Contents

Translator's Preface   ix

Foreword   x

Introduction   xii

Part I   **The Unknowable in the Sphere of Objective Knowledge**

    I. The Unknowable For Us   2

       1. THE OBJECT OF KNOWLEDGE AS THE UNKNOWN AND UNGIVEN   2

       2. THE UNKNOWN AS THE UNKNOWABLE FOR US   13

    II. The Essentially Unknowable in Objective Being   21

       1. THE METALOGICAL NATURE OF BEING   23

       2. THE ELEMENT OF THE IRRATIONAL   30

         a. *The Irrational as the Substrate and Ground of Metalogical Concreteness*   30

         b. *Individuality*   33

         c. *The Transfiniteness of Reality*   36

         d. *Becoming*   39

         e. *Potentiality and Freedom*   41

    III. The Unknowable as Unconditional Being and Reality   48

       1. OBJECTIVE REALITY   49

       2. IDEAL BEING   57

       3. UNCONDITIONAL BEING   65

       4. REALITY   70

    IV. On Wise Ignorance (Docta Ignorantia)   77

       1. THE OVERCOMING OF NEGATION   77

2. Transcendental Thinking 87

3. Wise Ignorance as Antinomian Knowledge 92

Part II The Unknowable as Self-revealing Reality

V. The Unknowable as Immediate Self-being 100

1. Immediate Self-being as Being that Reveals Itself to Itself 101

2. Immediate Self-being as the Dual-unity of Immediate Being and Selfhood 109

3. Immediate Self-being as Subjectivity 118

VI. Outward Transcending: The "I-Thou" Relation 124

1. The Revelation of "Thou" 124

2. The Correlatedness of "I" and "Thou" 131

3. The Two Basic Forms of the "I-thou" Relation 137

4. The "I-thou" Relation as the Unity of Separateness and Mutual Penetration 141

5. Love 144

6. The Being of "We" 148

VII. Inward Transcending: Spiritual Being 156

1. Inward Transcending 156

2. Spirit as the Illuminating Ground 162

3. "Spirit" and "Soul" 168

4. The Mystery of the Person 173

Part III The Absolutely Unknowable: Holiness or Divinity

VIII. Holiness (Divinity) 182

1. The Opposition between the Outer World and the Inner World and the Problem of Their Inner Unity 182

2. Beauty 189

3. Primordial Unity as the Primordial
   Ground of Being   196

4. The Primordial Ground as the Primordial
   Foundation, Light, and Life   202

5. The Primordial Ground as Holiness (Divinity)   206

6. The Certainty of Holiness (Divinity)   212

7. The Essential Relation of Divinity to All Else   218

IX. *God and I*   224

   1. Divinity as "Thou"   224

   2. The General Revelation of God and Concrete-
      Positive Revelation   232

   3. God as "Thou" and Divinity   237

   4. God's Absoluteness and "I"
      as a Reality   243

   5. God-with-me as Love   248

   6. The Paradoxicality of Life as the Being of
      "I-with-God"   250

   7. God-with-me as "God-man" Being   257

X. *God and the World*   261

   1. The Concept of the "World" and the Problematic
      Nature of the "World"   261

   2. The Problem of the Ground or Origin of the World   266

   3. The Problem of the Ground or Origin of Evil
      (The Problem of Theodicy)   276

      a. *The Limits of the Validity and Solvability of the
         Problem of Theodicy*   277
      b. *The Essence of Evil*   281
      c. *The Problem of Responsibility for Evil*   286
      d. *The Meaning of Suffering*   293
      e. *Summary of Our Examination of the Problem
         of Evil*   297

   Conclusion   300
   Index   303

Translator's Preface

Simon Lyudvigovich Frank (1877-1950) was a leading figure in the fascinating flowering of Russian philosophical thought that spanned roughly the first five decades of this century. At the heart of this flowering were four philosophers: Pyotr Struve, the most important Russian Marxist before Lenin; Nikolai Berdiaev, the philosopher of freedom; Sergei Bulgakov, the economist and unorthodox theologian; and Frank, the great philosopher of "living" knowledge and ontological total-unity. These four thinkers walked together on a road that led around the stumbling blocks of revolution and exile, a road that led from Marxism to Christianity.

Frank was expelled from Russia in 1922 and worked in European exile until his death in London. His most important works are *The Object of Knowledge* (1915), an examination of the limits of abstract knowledge; *The Soul of Man* (1917), a work of philosophical psychology; *The Foundations of Social Being* (1930), a work of social philosophy; *The Unknowable* (1939); *The Light Shineth in Darkness* (1949), an exploration of the nature of evil in the world; and *Reality and Man* (published posthumously in 1956), a metaphysics of human being.

The Unknowable is Frank's most mature work and possibly the greatest work of Russian philosophy of the 20th century. It is a work in which epistemology, ontology, and religious philosophy are intertwined: the soul transcends outward to knowledge of other souls and thereby gains knowledge of itself, becomes itself for the first time; and the soul transcends inward to gain knowledge of God and acquires stable, certain being for the first time in this knowledge of God.

Frank's work was not intended exclusively for the professional philosopher or theologian. It was also written for the intelligent layman who aspires to a philosophical understanding of the practical problems of life and the world. The problem of evil in the world, for instance, is not a problem that concerns only the professional philosopher.

Frank is one of the best stylists among the Russian philosophers; his syntax is clear, his images are distinct, his explanations are lucid, his arguments are well-constructed and easy to follow. All translations are approximations. The translator hopes he has accurately conveyed the content of Frank's thought and given an idea of his style.

B.J.

Foreword

Every foreword is really an afterword and more necessary for the author than for the reader. The book must speak for itself, but in offering his book the author may be permitted his desire to address a personal word to the reader.

The present book is the result of a long philosophical development. The first exposition of my philosophical system appeared in 1915: *The Object of Knowledge: On the Foundations and Limits of Abstract Knowledge*. This book was published in French translation under the title: "La connaissance et l'être," (Paris, chez Fernand Aubier, 1937). In a series of later works, I developed the principles of my world-view in the fields of psychology, social philosophy, and the philosophy of religion. In the present work the final results of my thought are presented in a synthetic unity and in the framework of the philosophy of religion.

As much as possible I have avoided citing the views of other philosophers and giving a critical exposition of my attitude toward these views —this not from the conviction that my own views are completely original but only so as not to complicate the objective progress of my thought and increase the size of the book. Even so, it will be clear to the knowledgeable reader how much I owe the contemporary philosophical literature and, especially, the old philosophical tradition. New and creative work in philosophy is possible in general only insofar as old and forgotten ideas are reborn in a new form.

My entire thought is founded upon that *philosophia perennis* which I perceive to be the essence of Platonism, especially in the form (i.e., neo-Platonism and Christian Platonism) in which it traverses the whole history of European philosophy, from Plotinus, Dionysius the Areopagite, and Augustine to Baader and Vladimir Soloviev. In principle, philosophy coincides here with speculative mysticism. Among many great minds of this orientation, I wish to single out one thinker who, combining in a grandiose form the spiritual achievements of antiquity and the Middle Ages with the fundamental problems of the modern period, attained a synthesis that has never again been attained by the European mind. I mean Nicholas of Cusa. In a certain sense he is my only teacher of philosophy. And in essence my book is intended to be nothing more than a systematic development—on new paths, in new forms of thought, in new formulations of old and eternal problems—of the basic principles of his world-view, his speculative expression of the universal Christian truth.

To many readers, both of the philosophical and the theological camps, my book will probably appear to be an illegitimate, formless mixture of "premiseless" objective–systematic philosophy and theology born of religious faith. The book as a whole, the whole complex progress of its thought, is essentially an answer to this objection. I am powerless before anyone who thinks that this is not enough. I feel protected from this objection by solidarity with the great minds of the past who are my models.

I foresee yet another objection. To many readers my book will appear "difficult," "complex," "confused," and its terminology will appear "artificial." I tried as hard as possible to find clear and simple expression. But the accusation of difficulty and artificial complexity, invariably addressed to any original philosophical thought and its verbal expression, is totally unjustified. Does one demand that the ideas of higher mathematics be expressed in a form accessible even to those who know only the four operations of arithmetic? Penetration into the deeper connections of reality requires a concentration of thought that not everyone can attain, and new thoughts can find their essential expression only in new words. If anyone considers all this difficult and unnecessary, he is not obliged to read the book, after all.

One more thing: The author would have no right to consider himself a philosopher and would betray his own thesis if he thought his work anything more than a mere hint, a "babbling" indication of the truth of genuine, ineffable, unutterable Reality.

The book was first written and was to have first appeared in German. Its publication was hindered by the unfavorable political circumstances of the time. The Russian text contains a series of significant changes and additions. It is not simply a translation of the German text, but a newly written work. I would like to thank the Publishing Committee of Russkaya Nauchnaya Biblioteka for giving me the opportunity to publish this work.

La Favière, August 1938

Introduction

Our life passes in the reality that surrounds us, a reality we call the "world" or "objective reality." In order to preserve our lives, in order to attain the ends that are necessary for our lives, we must "orient" ourselves in the world, i.e., we must come to "know" the contents and connections of the world which surrounds us; we must take account of these contents and connections in such a way that we acquire the possibility of acting in a purposeful manner in relation to them, the possibility of following a path that is necessary and useful for the conditions and ends of our life. But since the world has an infinitely diverse and changing content, different at any given point in space and time, it follows that our experience, our knowledge of the data of reality could not serve the ends of practical orientation if we did not have the possibility of apprehending *familiar* elements in the new and changing. And it is precisely these familiar elements which make purposeful action possible. Such is the living, biological–psychological foundation of what we call *conceptual knowledge (begriffliches Wissen)* or *abstract knowledge.*

Such orientation in the world would be completely impossible, of course, if in some sense the world did not come to meet us halfway. Luckily, the world does come to meet us halfway. In spite of all its diversity and changeableness, the world contains resemblance and repetition, certain laws and regularities; and it is precisely this feature of the world which allows us to "recognize" familiar, habitual elements in the new and unfamiliar. To a certain extent the world is dominated by rationality and order, which allow us to subsume everything that is fluid and diverse in the world under "concepts," i.e., to find in the world identical "essences" or "elements" on the basis of which we can apprehend the new and altered as the repetition of the familiar. Genetically, this "familiarization" with the world, this "orientation" in it, occurs in such a way that, starting from the medium which surrounds us, from the familiar content of our environment, we attempt to acquire what is new and unfamiliar with the aid of familiar elements which are logically fixed as "concepts." True, this process always involves the learning of something new; the fund of what we apprehend as familiar always grows larger. Our ideas, adapting themselves to heretofore unknown facts, largely change their previous content, as a result of which new concepts are formed, new types of the "common" and "familiar." But the aim of knowledge as orientation in the world remains the same: to grasp in the new and unfamiliar the repetition of what is familiar and habitual; to apprehend the new as only "seemingly" new, as a variation of an essentially familiar theme. In essence this is what we mean by the act of "understanding" something in the world: to "understand" is to "recognize," i.e., to find the old and familiar in the new. The practical application of this principle serves as the foundation of our guiding assumption, without which we would be hopelessly lost, powerless, and unhappy: the assumption that even the infinite chunk of the world's being which is concealed from us and unknown to us, the part of being which we have never encountered and which has never been the object of our cognitive gaze, will, in the final analysis, be a repetition of what is already familiar and habitual.

This is the orientation of so-called "common sense" with respect to reality. We may define "common sense" as knowledge guided by interests relating to the preservation of life and the maintenance of favorable conditions of life. And we may add that the orientation of *scientific* knowledge does not differ fundamentally from the point of view of common sense. Even if we completely ignore the fact that the very posing of the questions (which posing must necessarily affect the results obtained) of scientific knowledge has as both its starting point and goal requirements relating to practical orientation in life and the conquest of the world—in other words, even if we consider scientific knowledge only as "pure" knowledge, which arises from selfless, disinterested *curiosity*—even then the aim of this knowledge would consist in the following questions: *what* is actually hidden in that which is hidden from me, and *how* (i.e., *as what*) must I understand this new phenomenon, which I encounter for the first time? All scientific knowledge is *conceptual* knowledge. In the new and unfamiliar, scientific knowledge attempts to find something *common*, common with what is already familiar. It attempts to subordinate the unfamiliar to what is familiar and habitual. Precisely this is the meaning of all scientific "explanation." Like common sense, science aims to know the world or objective reality as a system or aggregation of the least possible number of identical (i.e., repeating) elements, which precisely as "familiar" elements serve as reference points for our orientation. It is true that scientific knowledge supplements and corrects, often in a wholly radical manner, the fund of concepts drawn from ordinary life-experience, i.e., from what has for us the significance of the familiar and habitual. The difference between the system of concepts of scientific knowledge and practical life-experience is often so great that we are not in a position to embrace and combine the images of the world which arise from these two sources into a coherent picture. (Consider, for example, the Copernican world system, not to mention the latest research on atomic structure, and try to compare these achievements with the picture of the world which serves as the foundation of our relation to things and people in our practical life). But however great this difference, it is essentially of the same kind as the difference between what is given directly to the senses and what is merely conceivable in the world picture of our practical life; e.g., I cannot combine into a coherent picture the idea of distance between me and a city from which I am separated by many hours of rail travel. However distant and elevated its final ends and results, in the final analysis all scientific knowledge is nothing else but the expansion and improvement of the cognitive structure employed by practical orientation in life or even by every curious infant for familiarization with the surrounding world.

We can go further and affirm that even metaphysics in its usual form, what Kant called "dogmatic metaphysics" (the goal of which is to know the directly inaccessible, deepest essence of the world's being—the most general, eternal relations and primordial origin of this being) does not, in the final analysis, essentially differ from that orientation in the world to which both practical life-experience and scientific knowledge tend. Whether or not the goal of metaphysics is attainable does not concern us here. What does concern us is that here too the goal consists in the attempt to know reality in such a way that, in the concealed deepest core of reality, the core from which everything else arises and in which everything else is grounded, we attempt to find certain conceptually fixed elements which, having for us the significance of something "intrinsically understandable" (i.e., "familiar"), would make the rest of reality (i.e., the concealed part) also "understandable," "knowable," "familiar." For example, the concept of "substance" originates in the idea, borrowed from life-experience, of "base," "support," "foundation"; but no refinements have been able to eliminate this popular idea from the content of this concept as a *metaphysical* concept. Similarly, the concept of God as a metaphysical concept, i.e., the concept of God as the Creator and Lord of the world, is based on the idea, borrowed from life-experience, of artisan and builder as well as the idea of all-powerful lord and autocrat. We could show the same thing for all the other metaphysical concepts by means of which we attempt to find the ultimate "explanation" for the whole system of phenomena that make up the world and our life.

As a result of this tendency which dominates human life and the human spirit, the world and all of reality appear to be something that is familiar or that can become familiar. This tendency is based on two assumptions: first, that everything which is at present unknown, concealed, unfamiliar—everything that confuses and astonishes us—can be known and "explained," i.e., can be reduced to the familiar, the self-evident, the understandable; and secondly, that even if the structure of the unknown and unfamiliar is such that factually and practically it can never become known and familiar, nevertheless we have the right to recognize it as knowable and familiar in principle, i.e., reducible to elements that are familiar and understandable or that can become familiar and understandable.

Such is the prosaic, rationalized, "secularized" picture of the world, and our life and thought usually move precisely in such a world. This world is banal and unsanctified, a world without holiness, even if it happens to contain elements which are usually attributed to the "religious" consciousness. For everything that falls into the category of the familiar, known, and knowable is, as such, sober, prosaic, "secular," unsanctified. "Fear and trembling" is inspired only by the unfamiliar, unknown, and unknowable. Insofar as reality is known "clearly and distinctly" (to use Descartes' term) or is even conceived as knowable, i.e., as consisting of clear and distinct contents; insofar as reality is viewed by us as *the objective world*, as a unity of graspable, essentially "transparent" contents and data which stands open to the cognitive gaze and admits logical definition—it is frozen for us into the *familiar world*. Sober orientation is the only possible relation to this reality, and therefore this reality is one that lacks inner meaning, does not grasp us with intrinsic inner significance. When Aristotle apprehends the source of scientific knowledge in "surprise," in the fact that something appears to us as unfamiliar, strange, incomprehensible, he quite consistently adds that successfully attained knowledge eliminates surprise. What is known is no longer a source of surprise. What had seemed to be incomprehensible becomes self-evident. Aristotle cites the example of irrational numbers, whose possibility and presence in the world are at first a source of surprise, but which then become a simple and necessary concept.

But sometimes we have experience of a wholly different kind. From our childhood there rises in us the memory of a state in which every bit of the world, every thing and every occurrence appeared to us as an unknowable mystery, and the world was a world of mystery, inspiring joy, wonder, or terror. Was this state, which constituted the content of our lives then, only absurd, meaningless error, the fruit of ignorance and mental impotence, or did we perhaps feel a reality that slips away from us now? Certain remnants of this life-feeling of blissful childhood continue to live in us even now. Every experience of *beauty*—in the enjoyment of art or in the contemplation of the beauty of nature or the beauty of a human face—shakes us, if only for a brief moment, with holy trembling. In the face of events that shake us (be it the death of a loved one or the birth of a new human being), we feel that we stand before a kind of mystery: bearers of life seem to disappear into the unknowable distances or to rise out of the unfathomable depths. Great catastrophes in nature (earthquakes, floods, hurricanes) and great social cataclysms seem to us mysterious forces that suddenly grasp hold of our habitual, familiar, stable world. However firmly we have grown into the pattern of our ordinary, everyday life; however reasonable and responsible we consider ourselves to be; however interwoven we have become with our position in society, with the "role" we "play"; however habituated we have become to observing ourselves from outside and seeing our "objective" selves as others see us, nevertheless we sometimes, if rarely, feel something else. And this something else is something unknowable and mysterious, and we feel dimly that the genuine essence of our soul is something wholly other, something we have made a habit of hiding from other people and from ourselves. And what we strive to hide is not even morally bad. The censor that is our reasonable, everyday consciousness strives to stifle those feelings which we experience as elevated and holy, those manifestations of mysterious rapture and intimate joy we sometimes experience. This censor strives to stifle them because they do not fit into the framework of the generally accepted, rationally expressible moral consciousness. Embarrassment, a tendency to conceal, characterizes us not only in relation to what is bad in us but also in relation to what is best in us, in relation to everything we cannot express in ordinary words or generally acceptable, rational, habitual concepts. And if we are intellectually honest, we must admit that what is unknowable and incomprehensible in us— everything that, rising to the heights or sinking to the depths, does not coincide with the level of what is called the "normal" man—makes up our genuine essence. Therefore, not only the "starry heavens above me" and "the moral law within me" (as Kant thought), but also everything that is in general unknowable and mysterious "within me" inspires in us wonder, a kind of holy shudder of fear and trembling. True erotic love with all its rapture and agony, with everything that it includes, from "Sodom" to the "cult of the Madonna," is an astonishing mystery, a revelation of unknowably terrifying and blissful depths of being. And no cold, cynical analysis (not excluding "psychoanalysis") applied to this deepest layer of being can suppress the shudder of bliss or terror which the living human soul feels in this experience. Consider genuine religious experience (in contrast to the frozen, peculiarly clear and distinct world of theological *concepts*) and the particular experiences of prayer, confession, or communion, in which we suddenly feel ourselves miraculously liberated from the agonies of conscience, from overbearing care or inner turmoil, and transported to unknown pure heights where our souls attain peace. We feel the inflow of incomprehensible, supra-rational, grace-giving forces. We experience the presence of "other worlds," which mysteriously have dominion over our earthly existence, over "this" world. And forces from these "other worlds" penetrate into our sober, everyday life.

In all such cases it appears to us that we stand before something unknowable, which clearly differs from everything that is familiar, understandable, knowable in clear and distinct concepts. Behind the objective world and in its most unknown depths, we feel the unknowable, as a kind of reality which appears to lie in a dimension of being wholly other than the objective, logically knowable world which coincides with our usual environment. Furthermore, this dimension of being is such that its contents and manifestations appear to be simultaneously both infinitely removed from us and present at the most intimate center of our person. And when we become conscious of the unknowable, when we are submerged into this dimension of being, we suddenly begin to see with new eyes the habitual objective world and ourselves. Everything that is familiar, habitual, common disappears. Everything is reborn in a new, transfigured aspect, with new, mysterious, intrinsically meaningful content. Anyone who does not know this, anyone who has never experienced Goethe's "*stirb und werde*," this spiritual resurrection to life after "death," after a terrifying leave from the earthly world into mysterious depths, is truly (to use Goethe's words) "only a dim guest on the dark earth."

But is this not simply an error or illusion, a subjective psychic state which overwhelms us, thus seemingly proving the hypothesis that the germ of insanity is concealed in the depths of almost every normal man? Or in a more general form, is not the awareness of the unknowable something which can be understood in our everyday or scientific concepts and thereby incorporated into our habitual, familiar, knowable picture of the world, into the habitual, rationally explainable objective world, as the element of the "irrational" in our psychic life? Such is the objection of our sober, rational consciousness in relation to the states and experiences in which we appear to escape this consciousness and go beyond its limits. However convincing this objection might appear to anyone who has taken the side of the rational consciousness and is not in the habit of doubting the absolute superiority and infallibility of its claims, it is not difficult for the unprejudiced, truly philosophical mind to apprehend the methodological arbitrariness of this objection. This objection is based on the logical error of *petitio principii* or the error of *idem per idem*. No one is a judge in his own case. The absolute superiority of logical, rational explanation *cannot be proved logically*, for all proof is itself based on faith in the absolute, complete competence of purely rational thought. That experience of the irrational or transrational consciousness which appears to rational thought to be reducible to an illusion (or more generally, to be knowable precisely in forms of rational thought) remains (from the point of view of the experience itself) rationally unknowable, and we simply have a collision of two irreconcilable "points of view," of two primary "faiths" if you will. It follows that the problem under consideration cannot be solved in a genuinely convincing manner by this approach, the most accessible and simple for most people.

But this state of affairs can lead to another formulation of the problem, whose result will again be the denial of the objective validity of the experience of the transrational—unknowable element of being. That is to say, the doubt we considered above can be formulated in another way: Like skepticism, which pretends to possess particular breadth and freedom of thought, we can attempt to soar above these two antagonistic spiritual orientations and evaluate them impartially. In fact, it is easy to be tempted by the supposition that the entire argument and the entire difference have only subjective-psychological significance, that it is simply a question of two different psychological reactions to the same objective content (which itself is untouched by this difference): the cold, sober rational reaction, and the dreamy, emotional reaction which permeates our inner being. Depending on differences in psychic inclinations and predispositions, or on differences in temporary psychic states and moods, we can either just soberly "record" the given content of experience or experience it as something unknowable, mysterious, holy. This supposition is made more natural by the fact that one and the same objective content of being can indeed be apprehended by these two so different means.

At first glance this sort of broad skepticism seems particularly wise and "objective." But in reality it is a dishonest deception or a case of inconsistent thought. After all, the ultimate, most general axiom (an axiom that truly does not require proof) of all thought and all knowledge is the recognition that there really exists some objective truth, something that "really" *is*. Therefore, in appearing to affirm the equal rights of two opposite "points of view," skepticism faces a dilemma: *either* it really affirms with complete honesty only one truth, namely that everything in the world is illusion, a subjective state of the human soul, *or* (which is usually the case) it surreptitiously affirms the genuine objectivity of the rational, logical "point of view" and considers the "dreamy, emotional" reaction to be a subjective-illusory appendage to the "genuine" reality of facts. In the latter case, skepticism is reducible to the objection, already examined above, which is based on faith in the superiority of rational knowledge. Consequently, this case does not require further examination. But skepticism is essentially reducible to the same thing also in the former case, in which it considers *all* knowledge to be "subjective." In this case skepticism takes as its starting point the cold, bitter (and purely "rational") assumption that the world as it genuinely is is exhausted by the aggregation of errant human souls that live by means of all kinds of illusions. There is no need for us to examine the substance of this philosophical world-view. It is enough to affirm that it too, beneath a veneer of impartiality and spiritual breadth, admits only one kind of reality (though in a special form): the kind of reality that is accessible to the rational consciousness.

Thus, skepticism only appears to eliminate all the seriousness and responsibleness of the question we are examining, namely: What is the objective meaning of the experience of the mysterious, unknowable, and transrational compared with experience which can be expressed in clear and distinct concepts and which represents being in the form of the "familiar," "understandable," and "clearly and distinctly knowable" objective world, an objective world which therefore (because of its "familiar" and "knowable" nature) lacks inner meaning and significance? How can we separate these two forms of experience? What meaning, in the sense of *genuine* knowledge (i.e., knowledge of *what really is*), must and can we attribute to these two experiences? But since the point of view that attributes objective meaning to "rational" knowledge (the decomposition of being into a system of clear, self-evident universal elements which are graspable in concepts) is generally accepted and seems to force itself upon us—in other words, since the burden of proof lies on the opposing point of view—the question takes the following form for us: Can one affirm that there is really

nothing in reality which could not be included in the scheme of the familiar, understandable, knowable? Or, on the contrary, can one discover the
objective presence of the unknowable in the make-up of reality itself? Our
book attempts to answer these questions; here we can give only a preliminary clarification of their meaning.

To do this we must attempt to define more precisely the very concept of
the "unknowable" insofar as we can do this now without anticipating the
results of our later discussion. First of all, it follows from what we have said
that the "unknowable" is not something absolutely and unconditionally
unattainable, not something like Kant's "thing in itself." (We shall devote
a later discussion to Kant's concept and its relation to what we mean by the
"unknowable.") On the contrary, insofar as it is in general possible to
speak meaningfully of the unknowable, it must be accessible to and attainable for us in some form. Thus, in spite of its unknowableness, the unknowable must somehow be encountered by us in the content of our experience
(taking "experience" in the broad sense as the totality of everything that in
some form is "given" to us, is "present" before us, or is "revealed" to us).
If our experience did not contain what we mean by the unknowable, it is
evident that we could not form such a concept or even use the word
"unknowable."

If we take the unknowable in its literal sense, meaning a relation to our
cognition, namely the denial of the possibility of "knowledge," we are
dealing not with absolute unknowableness for our *experiential consciousness*
but only with inaccessibleness for our *cognitive consciousness*. Our further
investigation will examine what this means, whether it is possible, and, if
so, in what form. Here it is sufficient to take as our starting point the
logically fixed assumption (as yet hypothetical from the point of view of
real meaningfulness) that we can conceive of something as present in our
experience which is inaccessible to our *cognitive thought*. Since all knowledge that can be expressed in the form of a judgment (even that which
appears to be "given" immediately without the aid of thought) is conceptual knowledge, knowledge expressed in the form of concepts (these ideas
are explored in our book *The Object of Knowledge*), it follows that what is
inaccessible to conceptually knowing thought is "unknowable." In other
words, we take as our starting point the assumption that, in experience, in
the content of what in some manner stands before us or is revealed to our
consciousness, we can encounter the unknowable—something that cannot
be analyzed into the features of a concept, something that cannot be apprehended "clearly and distinctly" (to use Descartes' terminology), some-

thing that cannot be apprehended as a familiar, general, and therefore repeating content of being.

This inaccessibleness for cognition can signify two things. First, let us examine the easier assumption: the "unknowable," present before us as an experiential reality, may be "hidden" from us in its *content*. In other words, although completely ungraspable or indistinctly graspable in its content, the unknowable could be self-evidently present in our experience precisely as something "hidden," "veiled," "very distant." In another formulation, we could self-evidently have the unknowable without its being explicitly given to us, like the inaccessible core or inner content of a nontransparent, closed shell (see *The Object of Knowledge*, Chapter III). This is the usual, most widespread, and often the only meaning assigned to the concept of the unknowable.

However, a second interpretation is possible or at least hypothetically conceivable. It is possible to conceive of something which, though it is given explicitly, is by its intrinsic content, by its nature, such that it would be contradictory and logically impossible to apprehend it as familiar, univocally definable, knowable. Thus, the unknowable would be given to us in such a form that we could not "explain" it or take logical account of its content. If these two assumptions could be found to be really justified, the concept of the unknowable would be just as valid as the concept of the familiar, the habitual, the unknowable. We could then distinguish these two concepts of the unknowable by calling them "the unknowable for us" and "the unknowable in itself" (or "the essentially unknowable"). This means that in the first case the inaccessibleness for cognition would be determined by the factual weakness or limitation of our cognitive capacity, whereas in the second case it would be determined by the essence of the reality we attempt to know. And of course it is conceivable that the two cases could really coincide, that the "unknowable for us" could coincide with the "unknowable in itself." (We shall see later how this is possible.) The "unknowable for us" is much easier to analyze than the "unknowable in itself," and does not present as many difficulties, but it is also not as significant as the latter form. We shall see later that the "unknowable for us" is possible only in the context of *objective* knowledge, which scarcely exhausts our total knowledge. Therefore we shall concentrate our attention on the "unknowable in itself."

If the possibilities outlined here could be factually realized, we would have, along with sober rational knowledge in concepts, another knowledge: knowledge of the incomprehensible and unknowable, knowledge as "wise ignorance" (*wissendes Nichtwissen, docta ignorantia*). Along with rational knowledge, we would have another knowledge just as *objectively valid* or perhaps even more valid—a knowledge to which we may give the preliminary name of "mystical" knowledge. (There is no need to point out that here "mystical" means not arbitrary or foggy, but rather something that is objectively certain and, *in its own way*, completely clear.) This mystical knowledge would contain a fundamental justification of that extraordinary orientation with respect to reality which we discussed above: the orientation for which reality is something greater and other than the combination of familiar, understandable contents and connections; the orientation for which reality has not only the significance of the environment in which we must "orient" ourselves but also its own inner significance, which *essentially illuminates our life*.

We shall attempt to trace the element of the unknowable (something which is still only hypothetical) in three strata or spheres of being: (1) in the world which surrounds us or, speaking more broadly, in what is present before us as *objective being* (which we aim to explore in its roots and foundations); (2) in our own being as it is revealed, on the one hand, as the "inner life" of each of us and as it is manifested, on the other hand, in relation to the inner life of other people and in relation to the more profound, spiritual ground of our psychic life; and (3) in that stratum or sphere of reality which, as the primordial ground and total unity, somehow unites and grounds the diverse, heterogeneous worlds of 1 and 2. This is an outline of the work that follows.

Part I

The Unknowable in the Sphere of Objective Knowledge[1]

To know is not merely to see things but also to see how they are submerged in the Absolute.

AL-HUSSAYN IBN-MANSUR AL-HALLAJ[2]

Chapter I

The Unknowable For Us

1. THE OBJECT OF KNOWLEDGE AS THE UNKNOWN AND UNGIVEN

We take as our point of departure a statement of the basic condition of knowledge as it is explained in detail in my book *The Object of Knowledge*. All objective knowledge is expressed in the form of judgment. A judgment is an act of thinking in which we are directed at "something" and in which we somehow "determine" this something, i.e., catch something "definite" in its makeup. What we are directed at is the "object" of knowledge, and what we find in it and what we say about it is the "content" of knowledge. The object can be definite, i.e., already (partially) known; psychologically this case predominates in our knowledge. Or the object can be as yet completely indefinite. In the definite case we have the two-term judgment "A is B." It is evident that the judgment "A is B" does not mean that "A is identical to B," for the content of A is precisely A and is *not* B. Thus, the judgment "A is B" can mean only one thing: "where A is, there also is B," or "with A is linked B." The true meaning of this judgment appears to be that "what we have come to know as A (i.e., that in which we have found the content of A) also possesses the content of B." In the indefinite case, on the other hand, we deal with an object whose adequate grammatical expression is the so-called "subjectless" or impersonal sentence, e.g., "it is raining," "it is light outside," etc. A judgment of this sort is subjectless only in its outer expression; but actually it too is directed at some object (or "refers" to something) and says something about the subject. Only here the object remains indefinite, not designated in a concept. In some languages this indefinite object has a very appropriate designation in the third person pronoun (and this designation is especially successful in the third person neuter, if the given language, like German, has such a form): e.g., the German *es donnert*. In essence, this impersonal or subjectless judgment coincides with the so-called "existential judgment" (a judgment about existence). "Something is A" coincides in meaning with the judgment "A is."

"It is raining" means "rain is (now)." The distinction between the impersonal judgment and the existential judgment can lie only in the psychological accent, not in the logical meaning. If I say "it is raining," what is essential is that I feel or see the rain and define it as rain and no other thing in a situation that heretofore has been undefined. If I say "rain is," the accent falls on the thought that the definite content (what I call "rain") is not invented by me, is not my fantasy, but really belongs (now) to the makeup (hitherto undefined for me) of objective reality. In both cases we are dealing with the same thing: definite content is found and fixed in an indefinite object or in objective reality in general.

However, the difference between the two-term (synthetic) judgment and the one-term impersonal or existential (thetic) judgment is not essential for our basic theme, for the "A is B" judgment signifies that "that at which we are directed," "that which we have in mind" (and which is still indefinite as such), contains, along with and in conjunction with the content of A, the content of B as well. Therefore, we have the right to express this judgment in the impersonal form "there is an AB," which form is equivalent to the existential judgment "AB (or the belonging of B to A) *is*." Thus, all objective knowledge can be expressed in the form of the impersonal judgment "there is an A" (if in the composition of A we include the whole manifold variety of perceived and known content, that is, both A and B in our scheme). However varied and complex (and therefore differentiable) the content of a judgment may be, taken in its fullness it is a definite content which can be designated by the symbol A. And on the other hand, the *objective* meaning of a judgment—i.e., the object which is indefinite in itself, the domain of objective being in whose composition we find A—is expressed by "there is" or, in other languages, by such phrases as "*es gibt*," "*es ist*," "*il est*," "*il fait*," "*il y a*," etc.

It follows that all objective knowledge presupposes the directedness of the cognitive gaze at the "unknown," at some *x* in which the content of A is sought and discovered, and, moreover, in the sense that A "belongs" to the otherwise unknown object and is grasped in the composition or on the background of this object. Thus, the adequate formula for all objective knowledge is "*x* is A," which means, on the one hand, that it is possible to find or perceive some A in the composition of *x*, and, on the other hand, that this A belongs precisely to *x*, enters into its composition, and is grounded or rooted in it. The known content of A is delineated—precisely *as* known, disclosed, clear content—on its own dark background, but it is not detached from its background. Rather, it is known precisely on this background, on this basis, as something that inseparably belongs to it. Thus, all objective knowledge, taken in the fullness of its meaning, signifies that the unknown at which our cognitive gaze is directed is *partially* known and clarified as the content of A. However, this unknown is, *as the unknown*, a permanent ingredient of our knowledge; it is that at which our knowledge is directed and that within which all we already know is situated in its proper place.

Whatever new problems may arise in connection with this conclusion, only one thing is of essence for us: along with what is known, with what is defined conceptually, there stands—eternal and uneliminably stable in the world of our knowledge—the unknown, the unilluminated, the dark, that which is concealed in the symbol x and is the common background and ground of everything that is known. This can also be expressed in the following way: All knowledge (if not always psychologically understood in this way) is essentially an answer to a certain question. Every "A is B" judgment is logically preceded by the question "what is A?"; hence, the *primordial* judgment "x is A" (see above) is preceded by the question "what is x?" (or "what can we apprehend in the composition of x?"). The directedness of the cognitive gaze at the *unknown* is the condition that makes all knowledge possible. However far our knowledge may reach, this primordial directedness of the cognitive gaze cannot disappear, cannot be abandoned or overcome, for it is the basic condition of what we call knowledge. Our knowledge can never become absolutely perfect or finished, can never become fixed or static. Rather, our knowledge is always the movement of knowing, the effort of illuminating the "darkness" which surrounds us, the directedness at this "darkness." Therefore, knowledge presupposes a constant opposition to the darkness. The *unknown*—that at which our gaze is directed in the primordial question "what is x?"—is the primary and basic condition of *all* questions, the principle which defines the meaning of the questioning itself. Thus, the unknown as such is something absolutely undeniable and "unquestionable" (the German word is *fraglos*). As the condition of all questions, the unknown is undeniable to the utmost, self-evident, "unquestionable" in the literal and absolute sense of this word.

If one is interested only in the essence of the matter, i.e., if one disregards the purely human, psychological side of the problem, it might appear that there is no need to waste words on the absolutely self-evident, no need to break down an open door as it were. Nevertheless if we emphasize what is self-evident it is because most people do not recognize it as self-evident.

Most people do not even notice it. To most people, the "open door, " the door into the *unknown*, appears to be closed, and not even a door that leads to what is beyond, but rather an impenetrable wall or, more precisely, the absolute limit to what is accessible to us. No matter how this error arose, it is undeniably ubiquitous, and we are always psychologically inclined to commit it. Reasoning in the abstract, we all know of course that the world is not exhausted by what we already know about it, but is infinitely wider and more abundant. But insofar as it is a question of our practical cognitive relation to the world or even of our general orientation in being, we are all inclined to live as though the world were confined to the "habitual." That which we experience as the "surrounding world" (*Umwelt* or *Mitwelt*), that in relation to which our life passes, and the cognition of which is determined by our life-interests, is experienced practically as coinciding with the world in general. Our governing condition is that the world is known to us, and that the known, familiar, habitual world is for us the whole world. It would appear that one does not have to be a "scientist," a "thinker," or, least of all, a "philosopher" to know that every step of our life is a new experience, a finding out of something hitherto unknown. All of us have this experience, but almost no one understands its genuine meaning. There is no need here to discuss the origin of this strange error, this false idea, which is utterly opposed to things as they really are. It is clear that our practical life, the need to economize our spiritual powers, and to have an underlying feeling of stability and security, forces us to close our eyes to the dark abyss of the unknown which surrounds us. It is this practical need which requires of us this self-limitation and therefore *limitedness*. One thing is certain: the limitedness is a real part of us, and it becomes necessary, if not to break down an open door, at least to push our consciousness through it, to force our consciousness to see that the door is in fact open, that our "room" or our "house," the "little world" in which we live, is only a part of the boundless unknown world. How many arguments could be avoided if everyone could see and really feel that the "little world" of his neighbor is as real as his own. How many social and political tragedies would vanish by themselves if all the parties involved could step, in a concretely psychological way, out of their own particular "little worlds" and feel the narrowness and relativeness of these worlds and the validity of all the other "little worlds" inhabited by the other parties (let us recall that the word "party" is derived from *pars*, "a part"). This is not just the ordinary, "average-man" narrowness of simple, unsubtle, unthinking people. Politicians live in the "little worlds" of their ideas, determined by party views and interests; leaders of nations live in the "little worlds" of their nations; scientists live in the "little worlds" confined by the methods and interests of a given scientific program.

But if this is the case, it might seem absurdly and dangerously romantic to alter human nature in this connection, to attempt to become smarter than what the conditions of our life seem imperiously to demand from us. To re-educate ourselves in this connection might be to transform ourselves from people who orient themselves soberly in the surrounding world into empty, dangerous dreamers, whose gaze is lost in unnecessary boundlessness. But in spite of the fact that it is simply a question of the truth, of things as they really are (in this sense, the practical consequences must be a matter of total indifference for us, for he who attempts to know the truth must always be prepared to be guided by the principle: *pereat mundus, fiat veritas*), the problem also has a practical aspect. Within certain limits, it may be that the narrowness and closedness of the consciousness are the condition of its "soberness' and practical value. But this is true only within very narrow limits. Furthermore, the openness of our consciousness, its ability to open and expand infinitely, the fundamental state of an infinite expanse about our own known, habitual, familiar "little world"—is *also* a condition of the normal and even practical functioning of our consciousness and cognition. In fact, the extreme closedness of the consciousness is nothing but a principal sign of insanity. Whatever mania we consider (e.g., megalomania, paranoia, etc.), a man who suffers from such insanity always supposes himself the center of the world, perceives the world perversely because he does not take it in all its breadth, i.e., he does not consider those sides and domains of the world which have no relation to his own person, which do not enter into the sphere determined by his own interests; in other words, he does not see the world which transcends his own "little world." In identifying his own "little world"—that which is known and familiar to him, that which is important to him in connection with his own personal interests,—in identifying this sphere with the infinite fullness, richness, and complexity of the world in general, in identifying it with the world which is alien and unknown to him, the maniac inevitably comes to an utterly perverse idea of the world. If we were to compare the case of the maniac with what we said above about the limits of the consciousness or the consciousness of the limits of the reality of the "normal," "sober," practically oriented human spirit, we would arrive at the paradoxical but unquestionable conclusion that it is actually the so-called "normal," "sober," "average" consciousness that, to a certain degree, is close to the state of the maniac, is semi-maniacal as it were. On the other hand, the seemingly romantic demand for a clear and intense consciousness of the whole breadth of being beyond the limits of what is known and familiar is extremely significant even from the practical point of view, for it is the necessary condition of a genuinely unprejudiced relation to being, adequate to reality itself. It is also the condition of the genuine fruitfulness of our lives. Every new initiative; every ability to conquer what is new, unknown, but nonetheless useful; every art of right action in general, requires the ability *to see reality in its proper perspective*. This general and self-evident proposition is, of course, also applicable to what interests us: namely, the ability to see the presence of the unknown as such, to see the narrow sphere of the clear and the familiar surrounded by the infinite fullness of the unknown, to see the hidden, the transcendent, the non-given, given in experience. In practical life as well, this ability is the necessary first condition of a fruitful and purposeful relation to reality. As long as Bacon's proposition "knowledge is power" retains its force (there is no need to demonstrate this proposition here), the condition of our "power" or practically right orientation in life will be what we have seen to be the condition of all knowledge: namely, the apprehension of the unknown, which alone leads to a state of questioning and thus to knowing and knowledge.

But let us return to the heart of the matter. The aforementioned psychological state of the "limitedness" of consciousness has its theoretical expression in so-called "empiricism," the teaching that all knowledge can, in the final analysis, be reduced to an aggregation of "empirical data." If we take "experience" or "the empirical" to mean all forms of data, everything that is revealed to us, stands before us, or is experienced by us in any form or manner whatsoever, then the doctrine of empiricism would of course be completely undeniable. In this formulation we could reproach the doctrine with lack of content or utter indefiniteness, if precisely this indefinite breadth of formulation did not have great value as a corrective to the narrowness and inadequacy of more precise formulations. It is precisely this useful and adequate breadth that William James has in mind when he speaks of the method of "radical empiricism." Similarly, Husserl in his phenomenology subtly and incisely outlines the fruitful problem of a genuinely unprejudiced description of *everything* that really stands before us and is contained in the apprehended object.

Conventional empiricism, however, affirms something wholly different: it tries to reduce the content of knowledge (and of consciousness) to a definite finite aggregation of explicit sense data. We do not intend to crit-

icize here the *sensationalistic* aspect of this theory; the falseness of this aspect
has been sufficiently exposed by the current theory of knowledge. Only
one thing interests us here: the idea that everything which in one way or
another is directly accessible to us and is directly revealed to us can be
totally reduced to a finite, observable aggregate of "data" in the sense of
what is *clearly* present before us. Although at first sight this idea may appear
to be true, it essentially distorts the real relationship of things. If the foregoing affirmation were true, at each moment our knowledge would consist
of a complete, finished aggregate of contents which, at the next moment,
would be replaced by another aggregate of contents, just as complete and
finished. All the work and dynamics of *knowing*, of the penetration into the
unknown and the gradual disclosure of the unknown would be inconceivable in general. But it is hard to imagine a "description" less adequate to
the true essence of the matter. We cannot even call this a prejudiced description. It is rather an arbitrary construction, which crudely distorts the
facts. The true makeup of our knowing and knowledge consists rather in
the fact that everything that is given openly and explicitly is given only on
the background of the non-given, the inexplicit, the unknown. Although
not consisting of something explicitly given in the narrow sense indicated
above, the background itself is nonetheless "given" in the sense that it is
immediately and self-evidently present. Therefore, in the makeup of "experience" in the broad sense, we must distinguish between what is given
explicitly or openly and what is present as background but the content of
which is not revealed to us (see a detailed discussion of this in *The Object of
Knowledge*).

It is these two elements, forming the makeup of knowledge, which are
expressed in the two necessary elements of a judgment: x and A. The whole
of A (the whole combination of what is explicitly given) can be compared
to a small island surrounded on all sides by the ocean of the unknown, x. If
we attempt to trace, in a variety of directions, the presence of this x in the
makeup of immediate experience, it turns out that even this analogy of an
island surrounded by the ocean is not wholly adequate to the genuine essence of the matter. In contrast to an island, the combination of all things
that are given explicitly does not have definite "shorelines,"i.e., distinct
limits separating it from the ocean of the unknown, but, instead, has limits
that fade away and imperceptibly merge with the unknown and become
one with it. Similarly, our spatial field of vision is not like a framed picture,
which is distinctly separate from the "background" on which it is given.
At its edges, it loses its distinctness and imperceptibly merges with what

lies beyond it. Although this "beyond" is not "given" to us in the same sense that the visual field is given to us, we have not the slightest doubt that it is present with utmost stability and certainty even though it is "concealed" from our view. The same sort of certainty is associated with the presence of "distances" the vision cannot penetrate or with the "depth" of scenes obstructed by objects in the foreground. And in the temporal dimension, only the "present" (or, strictly speaking, only the mathematical moment of the present) is *given* to us. Nothing past or future can be given in the *same* sense that the present is given. The present is what "stands before us," *die Gegenwart*. Nevertheless, we have not the slightest doubt that the present is attached to the past and future, that it is a moment in the continuous, unbounded flow of time, and that we would not even be able to understand it *as* the present if we did not know with utmost certainty that it is the boundary between the past and the future. The past and the future are not "given" in their *content*. The past is either remembered with more or less accuracy or only guessed and reconstructed (as historians do it, for example). The future can, at best, be foreseen, guessed, predicted with more or less probability. The past and the future are unknown to us, at least in an important, dominant part of their content. Nevertheless, this "unknown" *exists* self-evidently and uneliminably, with this existence being, of course, in the appropriate forms of "was" and "will be." As for the present, its explicitly given content imperceptibly merges with the past, just as the future merges with the present. Hence, in spite of the clear distinction between these two types of the self-evident, there is no distinct boundary between what is explicitly given and what is present as the inexplicit background. Rather, there is something continuous and inseparable; the "island" imperceptibly merges with the "ocean" and becomes one with the latter. Finally, there is yet one more relationship, a genuinely all-embracing one, which exhibits the same makeup: namely the logical relation between every "this one" or "this kind" and every "other" thing. Whatever is explicitly given, when it is logically fixed, forms the content of a concept and, as such, is some "this one" or "this kind." But we know beforehand (and we know this with utmost certainty, though we do not explain to ourselves how we know this) that every "this one" is accompanied by "another," precisely by *everything that is other in general*. Furthermore, "this one" is conceivable only insofar as it means precisely "this one and not another," insofar as it means something that is constituted by a relation of *difference*, i.e., a relation to "another," a connection of negation with "another."

The relationship between "this one" and "another" is universal, i.e., it encompasses all other relations (including the spatial and temporal relations examined above). As a result of this relationship, every given definite makeup of "this one" or "this kind," i.e., of the explicitly given, never exhausts (regardless of what manifold variety it might contain) what is self-evidently present and stands immediately before us. For beyond the limits of "this one" or "this kind," there is "another"—everything that is "other"—which is presupposed by "this one" or "this kind." The genuine makeup of our knowledge always consists of what is of "this kind" and something else, which is "other," unknown. This genuine makeup is not expressible in any formula describing something finite and wholly surveyable: in the formula $a + b + c$, for example. Rather, this genuine makeup can be represented in the formula $a + b + c \ldots$, or more precisely (as we now know) in the formula $a + b + c + \ldots x$.

This leads to a simple and self-evident proposition, but one that is rarely distinctly remarked: The infinite is always present in the makeup of "experience" (in the broad sense of the word), and the finite is given only on the background of the infinite. Everything that is explicitly given, logically and distinctly fixed, is finite if only because, as "this one" or "this kind," it has a boundary that separates it from other things. Or, more precisely, it is constituted by this boundary. But it is always a *part* of something other. And this "other," either given dimly and indistinctly or not "given" at all but present precisely as the unknown, is infinite. For, here, the "other" means "everything that is other," and the constitutive feature of "everything that is other" is inexhaustible abundance. Of course, not everything that is indefinite and in this sense unknown—not everything that is other than given—is therefore infinite. Rather, we know, again with immediate certainty, that, beyond the limits of the empirically given, the world has an infinite variety of limited, finite "things," "beings," or, more generally, contents. But this knowledge refers not to the "other" or the indefinite as such but only to *something* other, *something* indefinite for us under the given conditions. In other words, in that which we designate by x, we foresee the presence of certain quantities A, B, C, etc., which are as yet unknown to us. And, of course, we know beforehand that, as such, i.e., as contents definite in themselves and indefinite only for us, they are finite, for finiteness, as we have pointed out, is a feature that constitutes a content as a definite content. But in this case we are dealing not with x as such but with contents that are concealed (given our current state of knowledge) in the depths of x and are invisible to us. We are dealing not with the "ocean" but with "islands" which are inaccessible to us. The "ocean" itself, x itself as such, in its essence as the unknown, the indefinite, is infinite or, rather, it coincides with the infinite. This does not mean of course that our consciousness *actually* embraces infinity. This would be the case only if we could distinctly survey the whole fullness of the content of infinity. Our consciousness *potentially* embraces infinity, which means that infinity is present in or for our consciousness as dark, unrevealed, nontransparent infinity.

The same relation can be clarified in another aspect. Every judgment, and thus every act of objective cognition, can be reduced, as we mentioned above, to the form of the existential judgment "A is." But what does this "is" really mean? What do we wish to express when we say that something *is*? The empiricist and the profane who generally agrees with the empiricist wish to assure us that this "is" means, in the final analysis, nothing more than that something "is given in our experience," "appears to us," "is the content of our idea." Let us refrain from discussing in detail certain other incongruities in this assertion: the incongruity, for example, that even what is not given directly to the senses—such as the atomic nucleus and other types of general connection—can be deemed to "exist" to the same degree as what is spatially and temporally definite, given concretely to the senses. Let us rather limit ourselves to the observation that the true meaning of the word "is," which always expresses the *objective, transcendent* validity of what is known, appears to have been lost here. "A is" means, always and in all cases, that A must be recognized as present completely independently of whether our cognitive gaze encounters it or not. That is, A must be recognized as present also in cases *where* and *when* our gaze does not capture it and it is not encountered in our experience, is not "given" to us. In this lies the objective validity of knowledge, which constitutes its meaning and without which we could not speak of knowledge.

But the objective validity of knowledge, i.e., the problem of "transcendence," conceals the paradox that we must know what, by definition, precedes all knowledge and is independent of it. As we explained in detail in *The Object of Knowledge*, the objective validity of knowledge presupposes that we must *see something without looking*. (It is precisely the awesome nature of this paradox which leads to the temptation of all kinds of "idealism," fruitless attempts that use all sorts of subtle interpretations to revoke, to declare non-existent, the transcendence of objective being.) There is no need here to explore the riddle of transcendence, i.e., the objective meaningfulness of knowledge (we did this in the *The Object of Knowledge*), but it is useful to concentrate on its genuine meaning.

The transcendence or objectivity of the content of knowledge means that knowledge, in its content, coincides with the existent in itself, i.e., with the existent as it is before knowledge has touched or illuminated it: with the unknown existent. In order for this absolutely necessary and therefore self-evidently true idea to be possible in general, we must in some manner "have" not only the known but the unknown as well; and we must have the unknown irrevocably and with utter certainty. Thus, all knowledge not only expresses the known but also contains an indication of the unknown. For the whole meaning of knowledge consists in the affirmation of the identity in content between the known and the existent—and thus the identity between the known and the unknown, that which does not enter into the makeup of knowledge.

The enigmatic "is" of every judgment appears to mean the same thing as "belongs to being," "enters into the makeup of being." But this "being" itself, in its primordial meaning of objectivity in general, is evidently nothing else but the unknown, the uncomprehended, the unfamiliar, taken as the all-embracing unity—that dark, boundless ocean which not only surrounds everything that is known but from whose womb the known rises like an island, and in whose depths the known is therefore rooted. Precisely this belonging to the unknown (as islands belong to the dark, all-embracing ocean) which, as the unknown, is given to us with uneliminable primordial certainty and is eternally present with or for us, is what we mean by the word "is," by the transcendent validity of knowledge. In contrast to all this seeming paradoxicality, we really *possess* being with complete certainty as the dark, all-embracing unknown *before* our gaze is directed at it, and therefore independently of what our gaze has been directed at, how long it has been directed, and what it has been able to discern. For how can we direct our gaze at something we do not have? How can our gaze penetrate distances that are not before us? Thus, the very *meaning* of knowledge, the transcendent which it presupposes, contains a self-evident indication of the presence of the unknown.

Let us return for a moment to the above-examined psychological aspect of the problem, which can now be illuminated from another point of view. Satisfaction with what is known, the pretension that everything that exists is completely exhausted by what is known and familiar—these are usually the sad privileges of an ignoramus, of someone who has no idea of the true essence of knowledge, someone who, for the most part, has acquired nothing by his own wits, but depends on the knowledge acquired by others and is satisfied with this knowledge. On the other hand, every truly knowing person is conscious (the greater the capacity for independent knowledge, the stronger this consciousness) that everything he knows is only an insignificant, infinitesimal fraction of the unknown; and that even this fraction is known only partially, remaining for the most part dark and unclarified. This tormenting, but fruitful consciousness of the inadequacy of all knowledge, this knowledge of one's ignorance,[3] is the determining feature of all knowledge. Only one who erroneously considers arbitrary "opinion" to be genuine knowledge, only one whose gaze is not immediately directed at the object itself, at the essence of the matter, can succumb to the illusion that he has complete, perfect knowledge, which does not require addition or improvement. On the other hand, one whose gaze is directed at the very object of knowledge always possesses, together with what is already known, the entire infinitude of the unknown. He always sees something like our image of the ocean with its unknown depths and distances. Newton, the great explorer of nature who discovered the laws of celestial mechanics and virtually solved the riddle of the universe, spoke so simply and beautifully in this connection: "I do not know what future generations will think of me. But I see myself as a child who found a few shells cast out on the ocean shore, while the ocean itself, in all its immeasurable, unfathomable boundlessness, is, as before, a great, unsolved mystery."

2. The Unknown as the Unknowable for Us

We might very well be asked: What connection does the whole foregoing discussion have to the basic theme of our investigation: the unknowable? For it is evident that the unknown, whose constant presence we discerned as the ground and background of all our knowledge, does not coincide with the unknowable. The unknown exists only to be known (at least partially) by us. This means that the unknown is the object of knowledge. As the unknown, the unfamiliar, it is precisely what is subject to being known. Knowledge of the unknown advances continuously. Our knowledge-acquiring spirit continuously conquers new parts of what was unknown to it; and that which is known thereby loses its darkness and alienness, is torn out of the abyss of the unknown as it were. And it would appear that there is no essential limit to the path of the spiritual–cognitive conquest and illumination of the unknown.

There appears to be another connection in which the unknown does not coincide at all with the unknowable. If we were to detach ourselves from the factual relative limitedness of our knowledge and our cognitive capacity and try to clarify the problem in a fundamental way, then all that is unknown would appear to us as at least potentially knowable, i.e., capable in principle of being known and even of being known completely and exhaustively. For, in itself, without reference to our practical cognition, everything that is unknown appears to us not as something essentially dark, but rather as an aggregate of completely univocal contents, as a precisely, i.e., inwardly clearly and distinctly, separated unity of diverse contents. Even though this separated unity of diversity remains unsurveyable and unclarified *for us*, nonetheless *in itself* it exists with complete, univocal definiteness. In the contrary case, our cognition would lack the objective meaning which is intrinsic to it—the meaning of capturing and illuminating *for us* what always was and is even without this illumination. For God, for some infinite consciousness and cognitive power, there evidently can be nothing unknowable, at least in this sense. On the contrary, in itself, as though viewed in the light of being itself, everything evidently exists with univocal clarity. Thus, the simple and undeniable fact that we are not all-knowing, that (using Goethe's words) *"vor unsere Nase gar bleibt viel verschlossen,"* in itself obviously does not give us the right to identify the unknown with the unknowable.

We can treat this latter objection in a suitable manner only later, when we discuss the possibility of the "unknowable in itself" or the "essentially unknowable." We remain here within the limits of the "unknowable for us" and confine ourselves to the first of the doubts mentioned.

That not every content of being which is unknown to us at a given moment is unknowable for us is, of course, completely undeniable and understandable. And since the unknown coincides with the object of knowledge, and since our knowledge can advance infinitely far, the unknown, it appears, coincides with the knowable and the known, and is therefore the direct opposite of the unknowable. However paradoxical this may appear at first glance, the notions of the "knowable" and the "unknowable for us" only seem to contradict each other. Indeed the knowable can also be the unknowable for us. Furthermore, it is obliged to be it. In fact, although it is not possible beforehand to set insuperable limits to the advance and expansion of knowledge, and in this sense knowledge is *potentially* limitless, nonetheless, our knowledge always remains *factually finite and limited*. Since, as we have seen, the unknown is essentially infinite, a portion (and even an *infinite* portion) of the unknown is preserved at every stage of the advance of knowledge. This is so even at the highest stage of knowledge or, rather, precisely because of the impossibility of the absolutely highest stage of knowledge. And in this connection the unknown evidently coincides with the unknowable.

This infinitude of what is unknown (and what cannot be known precisely because it is infinite) surrounds and permeates us. And only our practical habit of not paying attention to it makes us oblivious to it. First of all, there is a *spatial infinitude* which is always before our eyes, if only we have not forgotten (as, unhappily, city dwellers often do) how consciously to look at the sky; if, in fact, we have not forgotten about the existence of the sky in the course of our daily business; and if we have not forgotten about the existence of the stars which have vanished in the glare of the street lights. What is this infinitude which surrounds us, in the midst of which—clinging to a small, spinning clump called Earth—we are vanishingly small creatures? What is the meaning of our life, with all its sadness, alarms, and joys, in the face of that infinite expanse whose silence caused Pascal to tremble? And spatial infinitude is just as unknowable and frightening in the infinitely small. Can one understand concretely how all the events and phenomena of the world that are accessible to us and interest us, that form or touch upon our personal life, consist of the effects of almost imperceptibly minute atomic nuclei, electrons, and ions, expressible only in quantities of the order of a few millionths of a millimeter? Is it not wholly unfathomable that our fate, the happiness or unhappiness of our life, the features of our character, everything that we call our "I," are determined by the structure of almost imperceptibly small "genes" or "molecules"?

The unknowableness of *temporal* infinitude is revealed to us with the same awful certainty. First of all, we stand before the impenetrable future as before a dark abyss, whether it be the distant future of mankind and the world or only the near future of ourselves and our loved ones. What awaits us and our loved ones in the coming year or perhaps tomorrow? When are we or they to expect death? And where is the wise politician who can predict exactly, for example, the start of another world war and its consequences? What in fact do we know? What do even the most learned and wisest among us know about the future? If we do not count phenomena that are based on the most crudely general laws, phenomena such as a solar eclipse, for example (and that only under the assumption that a comet does not collide with our solar system and destroy it); and if we do not count certain elementary universal tendencies (such as the tendency of all living things to grow, age, and die) which can always be counteracted by forces that are unknown to us, we must admit that we know nothing about the future. The future is always the great "x" of our life, an unknown, impenetrable mystery.

The past is another matter, of course. Although the past is inaccessible to immediate experience, it is open to our knowledge. The past that we have experienced ourselves is open to our memory; the past that is beyond the limits of our life can be studied in all sorts of traces that it leaves behind. But what is the significance of the few thousand years of historical past that have been or can be studied compared with the entire immeasurably long past of mankind? What is the significance of everything that has been studied and is known in the historical past compared with the infinitude of everything that was in this past? What is the significance of all our limited paleontological, geological, and cosmological knowledge compared with the entire past (unencompassable by the mind) of our planet and of the whole universe, compared with everything that has occurred or existed? Out of the unknowable darkness of the infinite past, a brief, relatively surveyable interval of time emerges, like an illumined strip of land out of the unsurveyable ocean.

And if we turn to the inner dimension of being and view the life of our soul, this inner life appears to be surrounded even more awesomely from both sides of time (the past and the future) by the unknowable. Where do we really come from? Where were we and how were we before what we call our life began? Or is it that we did not exist at all, as it appears self-evident to our "common sense"? And what is the meaning of the "non-being" of our "I," our being for itself—a non-being which seems to contradict the very essence of the reality we have in mind? And what awaits us in the future? What will happen to us after death? Here, the abyss of unknowing is even more evident, the darkness of the unknowable is immeasurably more impenetrable. Who is bold enough to assert that he can acquire reliable knowledge of these things and express this knowledge in clear and distinct concepts?

Thus, the knowable world is surrounded for us by the dark abyss of the unknowable. But this is not all. It is not the case that we can know with perfect clarity one thing or even a boundless multitude of things, with an infinite portion of the unknown and therefore factually unknowable remaining outside of our knowledge. Since the unknown, as we have seen, not only surrounds the known but is mixed with and permeates it; and since (as we have demonstrated in detail in *The Object of Knowledge*) all knowledge is, in the final analysis, knowledge of the all-embracing whole (i.e., all particular knowledge is *partial* knowledge of the whole), it follows that everything that is known is only partially known and remains—in part and even in the infinitely greater part—unknown. Thus, our knowledge, in all of its states and in all the domains to which it refers, is not only accompanied by ignorance but is inwardly mixed with ignorance. Therefore, being is simultaneously knowable and unknowable—always and in all of its parts. *Everything that is known, habitual, familiar, does not stop being an unknowable mystery for us.* The deeper an object is rooted in the ultimate depths of being, or at least the more we are conscious of this rootedness (for example, we feel this rootedness in concrete reality more than in abstract contents; in living beings more than in inorganic bodies; in the human soul more than in a plant or an animal), the more clearly we feel the mysterious and unknowable even in that which we know clearly and that with which we are very familiar.

It is worth paying attention to the fact that our language symbolically represents this relation by words borrowed from space perception; "depth," "core," "distance," etc. We speak, for example, of the "inaccessible depths" of the soul or the "distance" between souls. But all other types of being can also have for us "depths" that are inaccessible to us, an "inner" makeup impenetrable to us, inaccessible "distances." All knowledge of something that was previously unknown is felt to be an "uncovering" or "opening" of what was concealed or closed to us, a penetration into the "depths," into the "core" of things, whereas we call "superficial" or "limited" that which does not satisfy our knowledge. In particular, the effort to know the most general and fundamental connections of being (what is called "metaphysics") produces in us an impression of penetration into the "depths" of the mysterious "core" of reality. In all these cases it is a question of the consciousness of a layer of reality that remains directly concealed or inaccessible for our cognitive gaze. Thus, it is a question of a reality about which we know with certainty that it *is*, but about which we do not know just *what* it is. And we recognize that everything, even objects that we know well and are most familiar with, contain a layer of being that is inaccessible to us or concealed from us. Of course, it is by no means excluded that, generally speaking, we shall some day reach these "depths," that the hidden will be uncovered, that our cognitive gaze will penetrate into what was previously inaccessible for it. But without mentioning the fact that an infinite portion of the unknown factually remains for every moment and state of knowledge, we can hardly consider it to be *self-evident beforehand* that our cognitive gaze is capable of actually attaining *everything* that is concealed or removed from it. It is always at least conceivable that, behind or in the depths of everything that is either given directly and explicitly or can be inferred indirectly from the given and by analogy with it, there is a layer of reality that is unconditionally inaccessible to us, remaining an unsolvable riddle for our *objective* knowledge. (The relation of other possible forms of knowledge to this problem is a topic for later discussion.) It remains possible that the potential infinitude of our knowledge does not coincide in size with the actual infinitude of reality. It remains conceivable that our knowledge grasps not all but only some of the dimensions of being. This latter supposition becomes necessary for us insofar as we have reason to consider the cognitive capacity of man not only quantitatively but also *qualitatively* limited.

Thus, there arises in us the basic idea of what Kant called the "thing in itself," *Ding an sich*. As our analysis progresses, it will become clear that the unknowable (in the sense we use this concept) does not coincide at all with Kant's concept of *Ding an sich*. However, we would like to direct attention to another aspect of the problem, namely to that which is legitimate in the concept of *Ding an sich* (although on a basis different from Kant's) and to that which is illegitimate and superficial in the usual objection to this concept. Insofar as the "possession" of an object, its "presence" for us or with us, is identified with knowledge of it; insofar as this possession or presence is recognized as possible only through our cognitive gaze touching or being directed at the object, the concept of the "thing in itself" (of a reality existent beyond the cognitive horizon) seems to be internally contradictory. However, as we have already pointed out, this identification contradicts the objective meaning of knowledge and must be rejected as false. The presence of the unknown, of what is hidden from the cognitive gaze, is, as we have become convinced, an evident fact. Its possession, its self-evident certainty for us precisely *as* the unknown and hidden is something wholly different from its cognitive acquisition (even if only partial) and even from the cognitive directedness at it. Insofar as this is the case, there is not the slightest contradiction in the idea of a reality that remains inaccessible not only to the given factual level of knowledge but also to every cognitive gaze directed at the object. And although this idea cannot be proved with certainty, it appears likely and probable. Of course, this does not prevent this kind of reality from revealing itself to us in a wholly different way, precisely in a way that does not involve objective knowledge. Kant himself notes that what is absolutely inaccessible to the "theoretical reason" reveals itself in some indirect way to the "practical reason." Here let us limit ourselves to the brief observation that, insofar as the human spirit itself belongs to reality and has an inner bond and kinship with reality, there can be no absolutely impenetrable barrier between the inner being of the human spirit and the total unity of being in that dimension which lies in the inner being of the human spirit. But if we ignore this inner bond, the following affirmation has meaning and validity: there are always depths and distances that are inaccessible to our cognitive gaze, directed at reality as at an object that stands before it; and the unknowable-for-us is self-evidently present always and everywhere in our experience (in the sense of *everything* that we have in some manner and *everything* that is present for us in some manner).

Insofar as we are conscious of this omnipresence of the unknowable-for-us, we take cognizance of an extremely significant universal fact that determines the entire relation of our knowledge to reality itself. We can formulate this universal fact in the following way: *Every thing and every being in the world is something greater and other than all that we know of it and all that we take it to be. Furthermore, it is something greater and other than all that we shall ever be able to know of it. What* it genuinely is in all its fullness and depth remains unknowable for us. Only dense philistinism can fail to see this fundamental fact. Anyone who has retained a genuine sense of reality always feels this. However wise, experienced, or learned a man may be, every particle of reality tells him of this—if only he is able to see this reality in its genuine essence, and not distorted and reduced by his blindness and pride. Poets tells us of this better than anyone. And there is no poet who has not taken as his starting point precisely this kind of apprehension of being. For to be a poet means, in the final analysis, to express in words and make us feel the unknowable and ineffable. The poet is afraid of ordinary human words. "They see and hear not, they live in this world as in darkness" (Tyutchev). "They speak of all things so distinctly; this is a dog, that's a house, here's the beginning, there's the end. They know everything that was and will be; no mountain is magical for them" (Rilke).[4] However, the poet knows: "But life is magical as always: in a multitude of places, it is born from its source, it is a play of pure forces which no one can touch who does not know how to bend his knee and be astonished; words gently come out of the unspeakable."[5]

Thus, taken in all the fullness and depth of its reality, the unknown (the partially revealed object of our cognitive gaze) always remains the unknowable for us.

NOTES

1. Part I is based on conclusions reached in my book *The Object of Knowledge* (*Predmet Znaniya*), Petersburg, 1915.
2. al-Hussayn ibn-Mansur al-Hallaj, one of the founders of Sufism, was one of the greatest mystics of all time; he was executed in the year 920. For his life and teaching, see Louis Massignon, *La Passion d'al Hosayn Mansour al-Hallaj*, Paris 1922; and Christopher Dawson's essay "Islamic Mysticism" in his book *Enquiries into Religion and Culture*, London 1933.
3. In the history of mankind, Socrates was the first to point out this type of knowledge. As is well-known, he stated that *he knows only one thing, namely that he does not know anything*, and he interpreted the saying of the Delphic Oracle that he is "the wisest of all Greeks" to mean that *others do not know even this*, i.e., their own ignorance.
4. Rilke. *Frühe Gedichte*.
   > *Sie sprechen alles so deutlich aus:*
   > *und dieses heisst Hund, und jenes heisst Haus*
   > *und hier ist Beginn, und das Ende is dort*
   > *Sie wissen alles, was wird und war*
   > *Kein Berg ist ihnen mehr wunderbar.*
5. Rilke, *Sonette an Orpheus*.
   > *Aber noch ist unser Dasein bezaubert; an hundert*
   > *Stellen ist es noch Ursprung. Ein Spielen von reinen*
   > *Kräften, die keiner berührt, der nicht kniet und bewundert.*
   > *Worte gehen noch zart am Unsäglichen aus.*

Chapter II

The Essentially Unknowable in Objective Being

Our task now is to determine to what extent there is legitimacy in the view, mentioned above, that the object of knowledge in itself, the object of knowledge in its essence or nature (which is the same thing as the object of knowledge for a hypothetical all-embracing, infinite knowing consciousness) cannot be unknowable; the view that, on the contrary, all reality is "explainable" *in principle*, i.e., expressible in "clear and distinct" concepts.

Insofar as we conceive the object of knowledge (the being that is unknown to us) in all its fullness as nothing but the aggregate (even if infinite and therefore inaccessible to us) of a univocally defined set of separable contents, it is by definition evident that we are *not* dealing with something *essentially unknowable*. We conceive this combined being as a sum of parts or an aggregate of terms, even if their number is infinite. And we cannot conceive it otherwise insofar as we identify everything that exists in its own being with the ideal of the exhaustively known and even with the conceptually known. This is the case because this ideal signifies the sum or system (even if infinite) of *determinations*, so that the unknown as a whole—*x* as *x*—must be conceived by us as consisting of the aggregate of definite contents ABCD . . . YZ. Furthermore, it is only because we apprehend being as an aggregate of such determinations—i.e., contents unconditionally and univocally defined in themselves though partially hidden from us and not defined *by us*—that reality first becomes objective for us. The fact is that the terms "object" and "objective being" or "objective reality" (for the present we use these terms synonymously) signify for us that which we conceive as existing with unshakeable stability and univocal definiteness: "that which is just what it is." And the task of knowledge as the ascent from obscure, incoherent, unconnected ideas to clear, distinct concepts, internally connected without gaps, is precisely the task of the clarification *for us* of the existing object in its definiteness. In this respect we understand "truth" to be just the *adaequatio intellectus et rei*, the coincidence of our concepts with objective reality in its existent definiteness.

Whatever the truth of this idea, it is perfectly evident that it does not exhaust the fullness and true meaning of what we call objective being. Even if objective being is conceived as *possessing* an aggregate of contents that are precisely defined *in themselves* (i.e., independently of our knowing them) and concealing these contents in its depths, objective being does not simply coincide with these contents. It "has" the contents but it "is" not simply their aggregate. Insofar as we keep ourselves from being confused by "idealist" prejudices and view the question in an impartial way, trying to get wholly clear about the true relation, it is perfectly evident that what we mean by "objective being" or "objective reality" (for the present we use these terms synonymously) is absolutely different from all logically or conceptually fixed content. If objective reality in itself were a content of this sort, it would be something like an "image" or "picture" existing in itself. But it is not an "image," it is precisely *being*. We immediately feel that we are dealing with something which, though difficult to explain, is self-evident to our experience, something that "permeates" all the logically and conceptually fixed contents of objective being and forms the essence of this being. Being is not *content* as the *contained* but as the *container*, or it is at least the unity of the one and the other. If we consider, for example, Berkeley's "idealist" contention that real bread, our life's daily bread, is strictly nothing more than an aggregate of "ideas" (regardless of whether they are concretely perceived contents or conceived contents), we immediately feel that this contention is a mockery of the true meaning of objective being. The bread gives us visual, tactile, gustatory, and digestive sensations, but—*pace* Berkeley—it is not identical with these sensations (even if these sensations are considered to be not psychic processes but the experienced contents themselves); the *giver* cannot coincide with the *given*. In objective being something "permeates" the contents of concepts (or of ideas and sensations), something that we can designate by the words "fullness," primordial inner unity," "concreteness," "massiveness," "livingness," etc.; all these qualities are absent in conceptual content as such. And it is precisely this excess, however difficult it may be to define precisely, that forms the essence of what objective being is for us. This excess is what "contains" or "has" the content; it is the "carrier" of the content.

But since in its essence this excess transcends all conceptual content (for it is not the contained but the container), it is something "transrational," something which (anticipating its more precise definition) we can call the "essentially unknowable."

If we focus our gaze on this elusive something which permeates all the logically fixed contents of objective being, we shall encounter it in a series of aspects or elements, each of which we shall now examine separately.

1. THE METALOGICAL NATURE OF BEING

In examining the first and most general of these elements, an element we call the metalogical nature of being, we can simply refer to the conclusions reached in our book *The Object of Knowledge*. Here we give a brief account of these conclusions insofar as they are essential to our theme.

That which we call abstract or conceptual knowledge, that which we usually express by the words "knowledge," "explanation," "understanding," contains or is based on two determining elements or aspects. These aspects are *definiteness* and *groundedness*. The *definiteness* of knowledge presupposes the differentiation of the content of being, which is immediately given to us in dim, inchoate ideas or thoughts, into a discrete series of determinations A, B, C . . . , each of which is univocally distinguished from the others and stands out from the common makeup. The *groundedness* of knowledge consists in the fact that these discrete elements, the parts into which being has been separated as it were, are combined by us into a systematic unity, such that we can grasp the *connections* among them. Let us consider these two aspects separately. For the sake of didactic clarity we shall begin with groundedness.

At first glance there appears to be nothing easier than to establish or apprehend a necessary connection between two phenomena or contents, regardless of what this connection may be. Consider a black rubber ball. We see its sphericity and blackness, we feel its softness and elasticity, we also "see" that these properties are interconnected, given together. The same thing appears to be true for all "connections" in general, even if, psychologically, we do not always apprehend them with the same immediacy and simplicity. Consider a triangle. If we did not see at once that the sum of its angles equals two right angles, we could ultimately learn to see this connection by drawing diagrams and examining the problem analytically, the result being a series of concepts. Or consider the constant, repeated connection in time of two phenomena: fire and heat. We come by observation to see the connection we call "cause": "fire gives off heat" or "burns."

If, however, we ignore purely random (spatial or temporal) juxtapositions of two phenomena (juxtapositions which cannot be strictly called "connections"), a more attentive examination will show that it is not so easy to ground what can be called a genuine "connection" or *necessary* "being-together" of two phenomena or contents, regardless of what this "being-together" may consist of: a causal connection (i.e., a lawlike temporal sequence or lawlike simultaneous spatial juxtaposition) or the necessary connection called "logical." Insofar as *real* connections (i.e., connections in space and time which cannot be demonstrated logically by analysis of content) are concerned, they are covered by the conclusion Hume came to in his unrefuted analysis of the causal connection. In experience we learn only of singular cases, which can at best be frequent and repetitive; but in the nature of the case no experience can give us knowledge of universal or necessary conformity to law. "Connection" is nothing but a figurative expression for what in experience corresponds only to contiguity or juxtaposition. The necessity or unconditional constancy of adjacency or juxtaposition can never be given in experience for the simple reason that experience refers only to what is factually encountered in it; that is, it refers only to what is singular and in the past, and it can never indicate the necessity of the repetition of the same thing in the future, in that which has not yet been an object. On the other hand, that a *real* connection cannot be grounded logically and does not follow from the general content of concepts is clear from the very nature of such a connection, insofar as it is a question precisely of a "real" connection and not merely a "logical" one. From the concept of "fire" it is impossible to deduce that fire burns; from the concept of a "material body," it is impossible to deduce that such a body has weight, and so on.

Something else appears to dominate the realm of logical connections, which "follow," as is usually thought, from conceptual content itself. Apparently it is sufficient to analyze attentively the concept "2×2" to know with certainty that this quantity is equal to 4. Apparently it is sufficient to analyze attentively the concept of a material body to know that it has extension. But this is not necessarily the case: a more profound examination shows with evident certainty that things are not so simple as we imagine and that we encounter the same difficulty as before, but in a different form. This can be shown in a purely schematic way for all types of knowledge: Every meaningful judgment, every judgment which teaches us something, from which we learn something, is always *synthetic in its logical meaning*; this means that the predicate of the judgment contains something new in relation to the subject. In the general scheme of judgments of the type "A is B," B is always something that is not contained in A as such: A as such (i.e., the content of the concept A) is precisely A only and not B. The judgment "A is B" always means that "A is connected to B," "B is linked to A." But if this is the case, it is not possible from the analysis or apprehension of self-contained A to deduce or apprehend its connection with B. Further, it is not even possible to deduce or apprehend a necessary connection from the *joint* perception of A and B if they are taken separately as self-contained entities. A is *only* A and not B; B is *only* B and not A. The fact that one is connected with the other is not "inscribed" on, or contained in, either of them.

Thus, if we start with conceptual knowledge, with knowledge already fixed in the abstract contents A, B, C, . . . *no* connection in general among these contents can be grounded or apprehended with necessity. But if this is the case, where does the groundedness of our knowledge come from? Where does our knowledge of the necessary connections among contents come from? There can only be one answer (which we discussed in detail in *The Object of Knowledge*). The real starting points of knowledge are not the separate contents A, B, C, . . . with the connections among them being only "added on" as it were. Rather, the real starting points are the integral complexes or unities *abc*, which are analyzed by us into the concepts A, B, C, . . . which are interconnected. Both conceptual contents and the connections among them (or the phenomena captured in them) are products of the analysis of an integral picture of being, in which everything is given or thought at once, i.e., in which there are as yet neither separate definite contents nor separate connections among these contents, but only an undivided, integral unity.

In order to understand the genuine meaning of this undivided, integral unity, it is necessary to consider one of the aforementioned properties of abstract knowledge, namely, its definiteness, i.e., its being differentiated and fixed in clear and distinct concepts. The definiteness of knowledge (its makeup as the aggregate of the logically fixed contents A, B, C) is based on the logical laws or principles of identity, contradiction, and the excluded middle. The form of the abstract content A means that: (1) A is itself, something that possesses inner identity ("A is A" is the principle of identity); (2) A is not something else, it is separate from everything else ("A is not not-A" is the principle of contradiction); and (3) this difference from everything else, this separateness, serves to univocally define A ("whatever is not not-A is A" or, in a more common formulation, "whatever is conceivable is either A or not-A, with a third possibility excluded" is the principle of the excluded middle).

In Chapter VI of *The Object of Knowledge* it is shown in detail that these logical laws or, more precisely, principles (which in indivisible union form the principle of definiteness) would be meaningless, incomprehensible, contradictory, and impossible if they did not signify a principle of analysis: the separation of a continuous whole into a series of separate determinations, i.e., the generation of an aggregate of determinations A, B, C, . . . from the undivided unity of being, which—in order to distinguish it from that which arises from it as an aggregate of determinations—we designate in lower case as *abc*. If this is the case, then this unity (the womb out of which emerges through the principle of definiteness the dismembered aggregate of separate determinations) is itself *not subject* to the logical principles or laws mentioned above, but transcends them or underlies them, forming a more primordial layer of reality. We call this layer "metalogical unity." Thus, the analysis of the definiteness of knowledge leads to the same results as the analysis of its groundedness. And the differentiability (the dissection into concepts) of knowledge—i.e., of its object—and its connectedness are both explainable by and originate from the very nature of being, from the indivisible inwardly-fused unity of being: from the nature of being as *metalogical unity*.

In being, everything is connected, or more precisely, intertwined, bonded together. Being in itself is not composed of parts that could be completely conceived separately, independently of the other parts. Being can be envisaged as a tangled ball of yarn—not a ball which can be unraveled into one simple thread, but a ball which is made up of a complex, mutually intertwined pattern. The beginning and the end of every particular phenomenon and content belong not to the phenomenon itself but lie in something else: in the final analysis, in the whole as such. It is precisely for this reason that all particular knowledge is partial knowledge of the whole. In order to see distinctly even the smallest part of the thread from which the pattern of being is woven, it is necessary (at least to some degree) to unwind the whole ball of yarn of being. But this "unwinding" presupposes an anticipatory or preliminary *possession* of what will later be given to us in an unraveled (though always only half-unraveled) way. This is the "metalogical unity" of being which we must have *in some way* in immediate experience prior to all "determination" and as the necessary ground of all determination.

As an explicit illustration of the foregoing discussion, we can say that all abstract knowledge, all knowledge expressed in concepts and judgments, is based on a perception of the "images" or "patterns" of being, the concrete "picture" of being. This is literally the case with regard to "knowledge through experience." All knowledge through experience presupposes a perception of concrete reality as such: a perception which not only psychologically but also logically precedes all the judgments in which we fix and express what is perceived. This is also the case figuratively when we deal with conceptual knowledge, of which mathematics is an example. The object of mathematical (and similar) knowledge is *concrete* in the sense that it cannot be adequately described by any separate judgment or even by any (always limited) system of judgments. That in abstract knowledge which is perceived and expressed as some sort of logical connection between A and B (e.g., some distinct law of numerical or geometrical relations, or even a set of such laws) exists in itself and is perceived by us in primary immediacy as a kind of unity which, on the one hand, is infinite and inexhaustible in breadth and depth, while, on the other hand, having the character of an organic (i.e., ultimately undivided and indivisible) wholeness. For this reason it is possible to penetrate deeper and deeper into an "object" (or "objective being") and to express it in a system of knowledge with ever-increasing accuracy without ever exhausting the object, without ever reaching its "end." In this sense, the object of thought (and thus the object of knowledge) is *concrete*, in contrast to the *abstractness* of all our concepts and judgments concerning the object. This means that being as such is metalogical and accessible to our perception precisely in its metalogical nature. And precisely this immediate perception of the metalogical essence or image of being as such is the primordial source of all objective knowledge.

We now arrive at a fundamental conclusion, which is highly significant for our basic theme. We have not one but two kinds of knowledge: (1) abstract knowledge about the "object" expressed in judgments and concepts—knowledge which is always of a secondary order; and (2) *immediate perception or intuition of the "object" in its metalogical wholeness and indivisibleness*—primary knowledge upon which abstract knowledge is based and from which it originates. Primary knowledge is expressed by us in secondary, abstract knowledge; and in this sense it is expressible in concepts and judgments. But this kind of "expressibility" refers to the ability to "reflect" intuitive knowledge, to "translate" it into the language of concepts. There is no relation of logical identity between what is expressed and the form of expression (i.e., between primary knowledge and secondary knowledge). There is only a relation we may call "metalogical correspondence" or "resemblance," and which, like all resemblances, presupposes difference as well. Of course, what is presupposed is not a logical difference in content (which is possible only in the case of a false judgment) but rather a "metalogical non-resemblance."

Thus, we come to understand that the source and ground of all our knowledge is—in itself, in its essence—something unspeakable and unknowable. And this is the case not because of some weakness or limitation of our cognitive capacities, but by the very essence of the thing. The concrete image of being is translated into a language of concepts the way a piece of music is represented in a score or the way a three-dimensional material structure is represented in a two-dimensional blueprint. Only in this way can we "take account of" the concrete image of being which is perceived through the senses or apprehended by the mind. But this "account" is not the same thing as the reality that it reflects or translates. Along with the account, we "have" the reality itself, in its own essence. To understand this, compare, for example, the living impression from a person with all that we can "express" about him in our judgments and concepts; or compare the concrete perception of a work of art with all that even the best and subtlest critic can say about it. Insofar as our judgments are true, there is a certain exact correspondence between their content and reality itself. But this correspondence is not an identity, but only a metalogical resemblance, for instead of concrete reality in all its fullness and unity we have—in our concepts—only frozen, partial sediments or fragments of this living reality which will never be fully interconnected. To (conceptually) "know" or "to take account of" reality is to express schematic propositions which are in some definite correspondence with the object of perception and to make this object accessible to a certain extent even without immediate perception or intuition. What we express in this schematic way is always something other than what we have in mind and other than the true makeup of the object that is "expressed." We usually do not notice this discrepancy because this "conceptual taking account" is generally the only form in which we can retrospectively "express" reality; however, with attentive observation we can learn to apprehend or feel the difference between reality itself (even in the form it takes in memory) and all that we can "express" about it. Only a literary artist has the ability not so much to speak about reality as to force us (to some degree) to see reality itself. On the contrary, the goal of our abstract knowledge is the closest possible approach to reality, its most precise reproduction. But it never completely attains this goal, just as no polygon inscribed in a circle or having a circle inscribed in it (no polygon with a finite number of sides or angles, however great this number) can coincide with the indivisibly simple figure of a circle in its qualitative uniqueness.

Thus, insofar as the word is a means of expressing thought or conceptual knowledge, reality itself remains unconditionally unspeakable and inexpressible in its living concreteness. We speak and think *about* reality, but cannot express and think reality itself. The intuitive knowledge that guides us here is what Goethe called *das stille bessere Wissen*. It is mute, silent, unspeakable knowledge. But this means that it is knowledge of the *unknowable*, of reality in its genuine, metalogical nature.

Reality in its concreteness (i.e., in its metalogical unity) is indeed unknowable, but not unknowable in the sense that it is inaccessible to us or concealed from us in such a way that we can know nothing of it. On the contrary, all our knowledge emanates from concrete reality and refers to it. The intuitive possession of reality is precisely the second form (the *first* form was that of "ignorance," for which the "object" is x) in which the object of knowledge (that at which our cognitive gaze is directed) is revealed to us. Intuition is *primary* knowledge, even though it is mute, silent, unspeakable knowledge.

Nevertheless, this domain of metalogical, supra-rational knowledge can be called the domain of the *unknowable*. Together with the *unknowable for us* (dark, concealed, only sought for), in metalogical knowledge we can catch glimpses of the *unknowable in itself*: of the unknowable as an explicit, clearly illuminated mystery, which does not cease being a mystery simply because it stands revealed to us and is open to our intuitive gaze.

That part of our consciousness which is guided by practical, utilitarian needs rarely takes account of this basic fact. Only rarely (in cases of esthetic or genuinely philosophical orientation) do we become distinctly conscious of the fact that what is present before our gaze—explicit, unveiled, immediately given to us—does not cease being unknowable, marvelous, mysterious. Furthermore, the unknowable and marvelous contain the very *essence of reality as such*, that which distinguishes reality from all our concepts of it. The greatest, most perceptive and best informed scholar in the world, one who knows all the contents and connections in the world though they remain mysteries for others, must (insofar as he has retained the ability to see reality as it is) regard the world with the same astonished, awed, and devout look with which an infant regards the world. Everything in the world, however much may be known about it, remains an eternally unknowable mystery, and not only in the sense (discussed in the preceding chapter) that it is always something greater and other than all we know about it, but also in the sense (much more profound and significant) that all reality in its concreteness is metalogical and therefore supra-rational and essentially unknowable. Thus, everything that is known and familiar is only the known and familiar side of reality, whereas the source and carrier of everything that is known—reality itself as such—is seen by our intuitive knowledge to be the essentially unknowable. Reality is unknowable, mysterious, marvelous not because of the weakness of our cognitive capacities, not because it is concealed from our cognitive gaze, but because its makeup, which is explicitly present before us, essentially transcends all that is expressible in concepts, and is something absolutely unlike conceptual content. Precisely in this sense is it the *essentially unknowable.*

It follows from the heart of the matter that this basic fact cannot be *proved* as an obvious deduction from accepted premises, from judgments and concepts. All we can do is present it, direct attention to it, and force people to see what is in front of their noses. Once this fact is noticed, it possesses utmost self-evident certainty and does not require special proof. This fact relies on simple reference to experience, but to experience which has not yet been rationalized, processed in the laboratory so to say, and dried out into concepts. It relies on reference to primary, immediate experience in all its "living juices."

2. The Element of the Irrational

a. The Irrational as the Substrate and Ground of Metalogical Concreteness

Let us go a step further. We ask ourselves: How can we more precisely define the element of the marvelous and unknowable in reality, perceived as a concrete object, as metalogical unity? This element consists first of all in the character of reality as an absolutely indivisible wholeness, as a primordial whole. This whole not only is conceptually unattainable for us in all its fullness and depth but contains—in itself, in its modality (i.e., in the character of its being)—something which differs from all conceptual content. Its concrete content can only be "expressed," "reflected," "transposed" into the contents of our concepts, but does not coincide with them.[1]

If we were to conceptually separate in the primordial whole that which corresponds to logically fixed contents from that which transcends such contents and does not belong to them, then—in this latter element—we would have (defined only in this negative way) the element of the *irrational*. We consider this "irrational" as a sort of substrate or *prima materia*. This "substrate" is what "has" logically fixed contents, and permeating and connecting these contents with its juices so to say, it gives them the character of a metalogical unity. This does not mean that concrete reality can be considered the simple sum of logically fixed contents and the irrational substrate. This sort of rationalizing hypostatization of the substrate leads to the unclear, internally contradictory notion of "substance." Nothing has brought more confusion into philosophical thought than the never-clearly-defined notion of substance. The point of view (governed explicitly by spatio-mechanical relations) that understands "substance" to mean the carrier, support, or base of the contents or qualities that it "carries" clearly contradicts the true relation that obtains: the "carried" is in reality inseparable from the "carrier," what is "supported" is inseparable from the "support." Substance wholly lacks concreteness insofar as it is sublimated in the rationalism of Descartes and Spinoza in the concept of "what exists (and is conceived as existing) in itself without requiring anything other than itself in order to be or to be conceived," in contrast to contents which, as qualities and relations, *are* and *are conceived* always in something else. Nothing in the world *is* or *is conceivable* which could exist in itself, apart from any relation to something else. Being is an all-embracing unity, in which every particular thing *is* and *is conceivable* only through its relation to something else. In this respect even the notion of God only seems to be an exception: strictly and precisely speaking, even God Himself does not possess the property to which scholasticism gave the name *aseitas*, i.e., God is not *ens a se*. Precisely because He is conceived as the "Primordial Ground," the "Creator," the "All-powerful Lord" of the world and everything else in general, He is not conceivable outside of a relation to His "creation." We shall discuss this in greater detail in another connection.

Here it is sufficient to emphasize the true character of what we are investigating: what we are investigating is the complete opposite of the idea of concrete reality as the simple addition of the "carrier" (the "substance") to the "qualities" or "contents" that are "carried." What is *primary* here is metalogical unity as the concrete, absolutely indivisible unity of the rational and the irrational. Only in thought is it possible to distinguish, retrospectively, these two elements as special and separate elements in reality. In the nature of things themselves, or reality itself, neither rationally or logically graspable contents (which are only abstract sediments of concrete reality that result from the conceptual dissection of the latter) nor the irrational substrate exist. The irrational substrate as something absolutely indefinable and contentless (by definition it is not a content or it is a "non-content") is something like an *existent nothing*, which can never be conceived as existing separately from its rational-qualitative component. All we can do is negatively define it as something that is not content, i.e., as something that is not qualitatively definable. In general, we grasp it by means of what Plato called *logismos nothos*, a sort of "illegitimate speculation." The fact is that we can never get a precise fix on it as such. On the contrary, directing our gaze at the rationally and logically graspable qualitative element of reality, we encounter the irrational on the periphery of our field of vision; through a sort of squinting vision we encounter the irrational substrate, which "has" ideal content or forms the background of this content. But since this substrate is in inseparable primordial unity with rationally definable contents, it gives these contents that continuity, fullness, and depth, that inner unity, owing to which they have the character of metalogical unity.

Through its inner connection with the irrational, reality is something which—though definable in the sense that we approach its concrete content (*Gehalt*) by grasping its abstractly definite contents (*Inhalt*)—does not itself coincide with any set of determinations. If by the term "definite" we mean that which is logically definite and definable, then concrete metalogical reality will always have for us the character of the "transdefinite." Even though the "transdefinite" is the final goal of our abstract knowledge, that at which our abstract knowledge is directed, it is a goal only in the sense of a "guiding star." The "transdefinite" can never be captured by abstract knowledge in a system of determinations. We always have to grope for the transdefinite: in confronting the transdefinite, we always have to expand, correct, complicate the system of our concepts; we always have to rectify and bend our system of concepts by whatever means possible in order to adapt abstract relations to the concreteness of the transdefinite. Insofar as they are determined by their rootedness in the irrational, relations between particular elements of reality (whether these be empirical relations that order external spatio-temporal phenomena or inner relations between contents themselves as such) never follow logically from abstract features and therefore do not coincide with any rational system of concepts.

Thus, our abstract knowledge is never (even in the domain of extratemporal connections among its contents) pure intuition in the sense of "reading" something that is immediately given. Rather, it is the hard labor, never fully completed, of "transposing" the unspeakable, the transdefinite into the definite; and the definite is always inadequate to the transdefinite in "tonal" quality. The transdefinite element of reality leads to a situation in which our thought, insofar as it serves precisely the cognition of reality, must always be dialectical, i.e., must always have as its motive force the consciousness of the inadequacy of its own rational essence; but nevertheless our thought must always try to overcome—through the mode of rationality which alone is accessible to it—the one-sidedness of all that is rational. (We shall discuss this in greater detail in another connection). Nevertheless we must face the fact that even the most subtle and exact theory is adequate to the transdefinite essence of reality only the way (to cite Goethe) that a "well-built cross" suits the living body that is crucified upon it.

The foregoing discussion has given us a more precise understanding of the nature of what we call the "essentially unknowable." Through its participation in the irrational and transdefinite, reality has the character of concreteness, i.e., the character of metalogical unity. Therefore reality is—in its essence and not only through the weakness of our cognitive capacities—something *greater and other* than all we can know about it. We can touch and we can catch the metalogical essence of reality. Precisely in this sense it stands revealed to us and is given to us. We can interpret it, which means that we can "know" it and "fathom" it, but we can never *possess* it with complete adequacy.

b. Individuality

What we have just clarified contains another idea which is highly significant. An indivisibly integral unity in its ineffable concrete content, reality is always something *unique*. This is the case not only for reality as an all-embracing unity but for each particular segment of reality as well. It is true that every particular segment of reality stands in a multiplicity of relations of resemblance or non-resemblance to other realities; but in itself, in its "eminent" essence, it is never a "particular case or example" of the "universal" which embraces it. There is no doubt that our abstract knowledge which subsumes the individual under universal concepts (i.e., represents reality in a complex system of genera and species) has objective validity. Its ground lies not in the subjective structure of our thought but in reality itself. The "universal" is an objective unity and not just a subjective unity; in this sense logical "realism" is undeniably true. Nevertheless, reality in its concrete content is in itself something wholly other than a net of concepts in which we try to catch it in our abstract knowledge. Thus, if we attempt to concentrate on the nature of reality as indivisible wholeness (i.e., on the inapplicability to its "eminent" content of the relations of partial identity and difference) we see at once that both the universal and the singular in reality are always *concrete*. From this point of view, genera and species are concrete unities perceived through the singularly concrete, which retains its full validity as something unrepeatable and unique. Plurality is absolutely absent in the concrete content of reality. From all-embracing unity to the smallest grain of sand, everything in reality is singular and unique. In this connection Goethe wisely remarked that if the gods speak, their language, adequate to reality itself, consists only of proper nouns. For the common noun has reality only as the particular case of something universal, as one of many, precisely as something that is inadequate to reality itself. The objective validity of plurality is its validity for that derivative, external sphere or aspect of reality which corresponds to the element of definiteness, to what can be captured by abstract knowledge in a system of concepts. Beyond these limits, i.e., in relation to reality in its concrete fullness, plurality is absolutely inapplicable and loses all meaning.

But all that is singular, individual as such, is absolutely ungraspable in concepts. It cannot be subsumed under a concept or "understood" or "known" in terms of concepts. It can only be felt or "intuited" as a mystery and a miracle, for in its essence it is something absolutely new and unfamiliar. For we know and understand only that which is repeated and can be "recognized," that which is apprehended by us as the "same thing as before." "Sober," rational observation, directed at the logical, conceptually expressible aspect of things, considers it self-evident and an empirically given fact that all things in the world repeat themselves or can repeat themselves. This is the basis of the possibility of soberly "taking account" of the existence of everything in the world. Even something which in itself is absolutely unknowable, such as the death of a man, is, for an experienced doctor or nurse, or for a soldier, nothing but one "case" among many, "one and the same thing," very familiar, which we can only register. For a biologist a given plant or animal is only an example of a particular genus or species; for an ethnographer a given Chinese or Negro is only a single representative of a particular race, embracing many millions of such representatives; for a military leader an individual soldier is only a unit among hundreds of thousands that form an army.

At first glance it appears, and this is the common belief, that this point of view is the only objective one. And it is maintained that the opposite view, namely that of love for the given individual creature as unique and unrepeatable, is burdened with subjective-emotional experience which distorts the objective makeup of reality, brings foreign elements into it. However, this latter view is the true one. The erroneous "sober" view distracts us from the individual as such, whereas the individual not only belongs to the objective makeup of being but forms the genuine essence of being in its concreteness. It is this neglect of what is infinitely great and significant that makes everything knowable and understandable for us, transforms reality for us into an "object of knowledge," limited to universal contents. We succeed at this neglect only because we deal not with the whole objective makeup of the phenomenon in question, not with its concrete fullness, but only with its abstract content, expressed in concepts. On the other hand, in relations, such as that defined by love, where we are directed at the concrete wholeness of reality, reality for us is always something unique and therefore unknowable. Although we calmly register the boundless number of "cases of death" among people in general, the generally known fact that human beings die at the rate of approximately one per second does not keep us from enjoying ourselves or arranging our affairs. It has become our habit to calmly read reports of mass killings, even of women and children, in international and civil wars. We know that these are habitual, familiar events, and that the dead will be replaced by the new-born. But when death takes a loved one, we know that no one and nothing in the world can replace him or her. Only this relation of love is genuinely adequate to the essence of reality, for it alone is directed at all the fullness of the concrete content of reality.

Thus, the absolutely "incomprehensible" (because conceptually ungraspable and therefore "unexplainable") essence of the singular and uniquely individual is the fundamental characteristic of reality in its concrete transdefinite essence. We usually distinguish between the notions of the "individual" and the "singular." Not all that is singular is individual. We tend to use the latter sparingly, saving it for those rare cases of genuine, qualitative uniqueness. But our deeper analysis, penetrating into the transdefinite essence of reality, has shown that all that is concretely singular is thereby "individual." This individuality, by definition "unexplainable" and "incomprehensible," is thus a clear index of the unknowable in the essence of reality.

c. The Transfiniteness of Reality

This scarcely exhausts the metalogical nature of reality, grounded in the element of the irrational. A doubt remains unresolved: insofar as the element of irrationality determines the metalogical nature of reality, the essence and effect of this element appear to consist only in the fact that it is a corrective to the limited character of all that is particular qua *definite*. But the definiteness of each particular segment of reality is determined by the principle of negation, as a consequence of which each particular element of reality differs from all else, becomes detached from all else, and is constituted as a determination. Thus, we might have reason to think that the above-examined modal difference between concrete reality and logically-conceptually defined content is significant only for *particular* elements of reality. In other words, it might appear that this difference is only a difference concerning the mutual relationship among parts in a whole reality. By belonging to the irrational, by being submerged in the substrate, each particular element of reality is linked by invisible threads to the whole, becomes inseparable from the whole. Thus, each particular element of reality becomes a carrier of fullness and depth which are not exhaustible in logical determinations—in contrast to the conceptually determined particular contents of abstract thought which are separated distinctly and univocally from one another. But this modal difference does not appear to refer to reality as a whole in its all-embracing unity. Reality in its all-embracing unity (including its irrational element) would appear to be *just what it is*; this means that its concept coincides with its real essence and is adequate to the latter. The foregoing analysis of the metalogical nature of reality would appear to indicate that the total unity of reality, even if does not possess the differentiation of a systematic unity is, as a whole, "something in general," i.e., a univocally defined "something." We could then say that this metalogical unity is subject to the principle of identity even though it is not determined by the principle of negation (the laws of contradiction and the excluded middle) and therefore is not differentiable, not decomposable into a separable set of contents A, B, C, ... And as a result of the principle of identity this metalogical reality is "something in general," a sort of "all-embracing content," i.e., a supratemporally identical and therefore univocally determined content. We can compare this unity to a work of art: for example, a painting, which is something greater and other than the aggregate of its particular contents, its separate colors and lines, and which can be grasped only as an integral unity, while retaining a completely definite content precisely as such a unity.

But can one actually grasp the genuinely all-embracing concrete whole as a *definite* whole? Or (which is the same thing) can one consider the principle of identity to be really separable from the other principles of definiteness (connected with the element of negation and expressing it) and conceive it as something independent of them? Let us again refer to our book *The Object of Knowledge*. All that is identical is a strictly closed or self-contained unity; it is given "all at once" as precisely "this thing." To be sure, it can embrace a manifold variety of things but it does so within rigid limits, thus becoming a strict unity, something like a numerical unit. But a "unit" is utterly inconceivable without a relation to something beyond the limits of itself, without a relation to a second something, another unit. Thus, the general form of "extratemporality" or "identity", though it can be abstractly distinguished from "delineation" or "distinction" as a special element, is so inextricably linked with the latter that it inexorably merges with it, i.e., assumes the character of *definiteness*. This is the deepest foundation for the fact that the intuition of concrete all-embracing unity is transformed—as if by itself, owing to some inner tendency—into a system of concepts, which is why this intuition can only function as a "potency" leading to abstract knowledge.

A very significant conclusion can be drawn from this. Only *particular* content, only something qualitatively particular or special (which is qualitatively particular precisely because it stands *apart* from all else) can be adequately understood as something completely definite. It is precisely for this reason that everything that is singularly concrete necessarily appears to be something identical, i.e., definite in itself, insofar as we grasp it as something completely autonomous, i.e., insofar as we detach our gaze from its connection with everything else. But if we attempt to conceive of some genuinely and absolutely all-embracing whole which really does not have anything outside of itself, which does not have any relation to something "other," we shall not be able to conceive it in the form of "identity" (i.e., definiteness in itself). Or, insofar as to "conceive" means to have something as a supratemporally identical unity, as a definite, unchanging "something of this kind," genuine all-embracing unity cannot be "conceived" in the usual sense of this term but must be given and accessible to us in some other form, namely a *metalogical* one. There is no hope of grasping the all-embracing whole, the metalogical unity, as something definite; to think this possible is to be led astray. In the final analysis the definite is always limited. But a metalogical unity is something limitless and in this sense *indefinite*. We can say in all seriousness that we are dealing with *de omni re scibili et quibusdam aliis*, with all things that we can conceive and with something else besides.

Reality as metalogical unity is not only transdefinite but also *transfinite*. Using a mathematical metaphor, we can say that reality is greater than any given (i.e., definite) quantity, however great and encompassing this quantity. This means that metalogical unity is something essentially unknowable—not only in the sense in which "knowing" is taken to mean "determining" and "grounding" but also in the sense in which it is taken to mean "conceptual grasping" or "encompassing" in general, the "embracing" of an extratemporal essence. Metalogical unity cannot be conceptually determined precisely because it is *indefinite in itself*, though (or rather because) it is the source of all definiteness. Although it contains all definite things as well as the very element of definiteness, total being, being as unity and all-embracing ground, is not something definite. It is not definite because it contains all other things too (i.e., indefinite things) and transcends all that is definite. The element of definiteness is contained in total being and is subordinate to it; but total being is therefore not subordinate to the element of definiteness. The essence of being as the transfinite consists in the fact that it is the unity of definiteness and indefiniteness: the difference between the two (like all differences) is a difference within the limits of being itself. Precisely in this (and not only in its unity and continuity) is the genuine concreteness of reality. The concreteness of reality consists in its "livingness," in its being a whole that cannot be completed and encompassed, but that always transcends everything that is definite and in this sense frozen and ossified. Since it is transfinite, being as an all-embracing whole is something *greater and other* than all its completed and finished forms. Transfinite being is reality as the possibility of what it is not. As such, reality is not only conceptually ungraspable, it is not even open to "intuitive" perception. It cannot be perceived, it can only be experienced. In this living possession of reality as the absolutely boundless, indefinable infinitude of the transdefinite, as something that always overflows its bounds, we have the genuine *essential unknowableness* of reality.

Someone may object, however, that all this may be just and valid as far as it goes, but it refers only to being as a whole, in its infinitude. This infinite being is perhaps the favorite theme of the philosopher, but it does not really interest anyone else. In life and in scientific knowledge we always deal with finite, particular things and realities. All that has just been said about the "transfiniteness" of reality is inapplicable to these particular realities. Thus, the whole theme turns out to be the object of a philosopher's idle curiosity and not significant for "real" knowledge.

However convincing at first glance, this objection is essentially illegitimate. Let us set aside the fact that the notion of the infinite, of the infinitely great and infinitely small, bears a close resemblance to our idea of the transfinite and plays an essential role in mathematics, where it has not only theoretical but also applied significance. Let us rather concentrate on the heart of the matter. "Transfiniteness" determines not only the "extensiveness" of being but also its "intensiveness." "Transfiniteness," that which overflows the bounds of all finished or definite existents, refers not only to the external dimension of these finished forms but also to their *inner depth*. Being is not only the common background which embraces all particular things or the common ground in which all particular things are rooted. It also permeates all existing things, is present as such in the smallest segment of reality. Therefore all that exists is, in its concreteness, permeated with the potency of being, for it is precisely this rootedness in being and this permeatedness by being which we have in mind when we speak of concreteness. It is for this reason that the overflowing, superabundant fullness of being or that depth of being in which this fullness transcends all finished forms and definite things, that which we call the "transfiniteness" of being, is present in every segment of being, in every particular reality, however small or insignificant in size or content this particular reality may be. The attentive gaze that penetrates into the genuine essence of things sees the immeasurable and indefinable abyss of the transfinite revealed in every point of being.

d. Becoming

This is revealed in a phenomenon whose utter incomprehensibility and unknowableness are usually not noticed only because it is a common feature of all our experience, the constant atmosphere in which our life is immersed. We are thinking of *time* or *becoming*. If we take the notion of the "concrete" in its specific and common meaning, namely as the opposite of the "abstract" qua extratemporal, we can say that the concrete is *in time* or occurs *in time*, is subject to *becoming*, i.e., to origination, change, and annihilation. This is not the place to discuss the problem of time in all its fullness and depth (for such a discussion see *The Object of Knowledge*, Chapter X). It is sufficient here to indicate the essential mystery, incomprehensibility, and unknowableness of what we call "time" or "becoming." "Before I ask the question 'what is time?' I know very well what it is, but as soon as I ask this question, I no longer understand anything," is St. Augustine's subtle remark in his *Confessions*. (We encounter the same idea in Plotinus, *Enn.* III, 7, I.) Where does this continuous flux come from, this flux which entrains us, permeates our entire life, and carries us with insuperable force to the abyss? Where is it going? And, especially, what is this unknowable something which we express in the obviously inadequate image of the "flux or flow of time"? Ancient Zeno, guided by the ideal of univocal conceptual determination, used the example of spatial motion to understand "becoming." His formulations were somewhat naive and helpless, but he was completely right in a certain sense when he proved that it is *impossible* for a body to move through a given space. This "motion" can be apprehended neither as the being nor as the non-being of the given body in the given space, and all attempts to *rationally* refute this argument remain without result. If science and rational knowledge can determine and measure motion and know becoming in general, it is only because becoming is viewed by science as what has already *become*, as what is given in the aspect of the *past* in a finished form. It is then the function of science to determine what is determinable in this finished aspect—for example, the length of a traversed path (for time itself is measured in terms of the distance traveled by the hand of a clock or by the sun across the sky) or the regular change of one state into another. But the essence of becoming as such—the element of dynamism in it, the element of something "happening," something "going on"—remains outside the field of view during scientific measurements.

Thus, rational thought can grasp and "understand" only things that are static or fixed. For conceptual thought, everything is a sort of extratemporal "content," something identical which, projected on the plane of time, appears to be constant, at rest. But this is precisely the reason why becoming itself, in its essence, must necessarily slip away from rational thought. Abstract thought simply misses the essential point of becoming and time. The essence of becoming as such cannot be broken up into separate elements nor can it be reduced to something identical or definite-in-itself. Although it has aspects in which something identical is encountered, aspects in which it can be grasped by conceptual thought (e.g., the order of material state changes and, in general, everything that remains constant in the variable), becoming as such is not essentially something identical but is precisely *change*. This apparently simple and universal phenomenon, habitual and familiar to the point of banality (first remarked by Bergson in our time), remains absolutely incomprehensible and unknowable. It has been called "unrest in itself" (Hegel) and "a troublesome essence which, unsated, always aspires to fulfillment" (Plotinus). These descriptions only tend to underscore the unknowableness of what is revealed to us. In all concrete existents, becoming exhibits (to be sure, in a special form whose peculiar features we have no need to describe here) an element of "overflowing the bounds," of "going beyond the limits of itself," which belongs to total unity, to being as a whole, and forms the essence of the unknowableness of such being. Time is as unknowable as eternity, for it is analogous to the latter. Plato called time "the moving image of eternity," and Angelus Silesius said that "time is the same thing as eternity and eternity is the same thing as time, if you yourself do not make a distinction between them." Time is analogous to eternity in the sense that both transcend what is finished and definite. It is as though the absolutely unknowable mystery of what we call the "creation of the world" has here on earth its image—albeit a distorted one—in the eternal creative unrest of becoming. Insofar as we are able to forget the feeling of familiarity, the habitual, everyday character of this phenomenon or rather of this all-permeating medium of all concrete being, insofar as we are able to clearly perceive its essence, we are seized with fear and trembling. For all that appears to exist, including ourselves, does not *really* exist, does not rest on solid ground. Plato said that the entire visible world (and we along with it) "only comes to be and passes away but does not really exist." Our existence passes as if in a whirlwind, as if in flight—flight from one unknowable abyss to another.

Thus, in becoming and time we find ourselves in that which exists concretely, and we stand, at every moment of our everyday lives, before the revelation of the *essentially unknowable* in being.

e. Potentiality and Freedom

Something else, something very significant, is also revealed in the structure of irrationality and thus in the metalogical nature of being which is determined by irrationality. Insofar as being is conceived not as given or present in a finished form, but as containing the element of becoming, being is *potentiality*, existent *potency*. This makes it clear that the concept of "possibility" is not (as is usually thought in the modern philosophy) a purely reflexive category, as if all that exists coincides with the "actual," with what is present in a finished form, and the idea of the "possible" belongs only to our subjective attitude, which performs cognitive and explanatory functions in relation to being. On the contrary, "possibility" is, as Aristotle thought, a constitutive category which belongs to the makeup of being itself. If being contains becoming, being is greater and other than all that is present in it in a finished form. Being is also that which *will* be or *can* be. The transcendence of self, the overflowing of bounds, the origina-

tion of what has not yet been (i.e., creation) is conceivable only if being in
its womb contains indefiniteness—indefiniteness which has the tendency
to generate something definite, to develop into definiteness. This is what
we mean by "potentiality" or "potency." In our present discussion (in
which we have to exclude a detailed study of many of the problems we
touch upon) we shall ignore the difference between passive and active
potentialities, between the possibility of a "raw material" assuming a definite shape under an external active force and the possibility of the formative force itself "conceiving" and "sculpting" this shape: the difference
between the possibility (using Aristotle's analogy) contained in the clay
from which the statue is sculpted and the "power" of the creative conception of the artist who sculpts the statue. Since in nature itself (or, more
precisely, in being) the artist or creator is found, as Aristotle says, "inside
the material which he shapes," we can ignore the foregoing difference and
limit ourselves to the general affirmation that the "unfinished" has the
capacity to become "finished," i.e., that in general there is being which is
"as yet unfinished," whether as "material" or as "creative conception."

To be sure, rational thought constantly succumbs to the temptation of
finding interpretations of being which deny the metalogical element contained in the transfinite essence of reality, the element which makes reality
essentially unknowable. This denial is realized in such a form that all newly
emergent things are conceived as wholly predetermined by that which
already exists or that which is present in a finished form. An attentive
examination of the notion of causality which is used in this denial will
easily convince us that the essence of the denial is an attempt to conceive
"becoming" and "origination" (i.e., the transition from the old, the already present, to the new, to that which is not yet in existence) in such a
way that they are wholly subordinated to the category of "identity" or
"definiteness-in-itself." It is maintained that only in this way can "becoming" be made understandable and explainable. The new, the newly emergent, is thus understood as nothing but the continuation of the old. This
idea not only determines the physical laws of the conservation of matter
and energy and the entire mechanistic orientation (by the way, now shaken
to its foundations and possibly destroyed) of the natural sciences in general;
not only is it clearly formulated in a number of new philosophical theories
of causality, but it was already clearly expressed in ancient philosophy: it
was important in the atomism of Democritus and especially Lucretius, and
it was contained as an embryo in the idea of *arche* of the Ionian "nature
philosophers."

This attempt at denial, however, contains its own refutation. If it is followed through consistently, it is reduced to the understanding of being as a "conservative system" (A. Riehl), in which essentially *nothing* changes. In other words, it is reduced, as it was for the ancient Eleatics, to a decisive denial of all change and becoming. "B follows from A" would then have to mean that A and B are one and the same thing. However, if B really follows from A, then at least one thing is clear in spite of the problematical character of this relationship: namely that B cannot be identical to A, and that it cannot be conceived as a simple continuation of A, otherwise it would not be B at all, but the original A, and nothing would follow from anything. This is one of those "explanations" which, unable to explain anything, prefers simply to reject what is to be explained. To refer to Schelling's clever metaphor, it resembles the doctor who, unable to heal the ailing member of the body, prefers to cut it off.

That from which B follows cannot in any case be A as a finished, pure determination. Nothing can "originate" from a determination, because its essence as a pure identity is incompatible with origination or change. Using the terminology we developed in Chapter I (it was developed in detail in *The Object of Knowledge*) we can say that B originates not from A as such but from Ax. This means that both A and B, or more precisely the connection A–B, originates from some x, with A preceding B in temporal sequence, so that B can originate from x only after A has originated from x. However, x is a symbol not only of the unknown or even of the unknowable-for-us but also a symbol of the unknowable in itself—i.e., of the transfinite essence of reality. Insofar as it is revealed in becoming, the transfinite essence of reality, conceived supratemporally, is potentiality, existent potency. We said above that everything that exists is something greater and other than everything that is in a finished form. This is evident in the fact of becoming and coming-to-be, which shows with self-evident certainty that everything that exists is also *that which it as yet is not*.

This sets strict limits to rational determinism and rational-causal "explanation." If all newly emergent things "follow" or "emanate" not from some previously existing *definite* being but from the transfinite essence of reality, if they originate in the dark (dark not only for us but also dark in essence) womb of potentiality, they originate "from themselves" and not "from nothing." They are not groundless but originate in the transfinite essence of reality, in indefinite and indefinable potentiality. It is evident that everything that is conceivable is not really possible at all times and under all conditions. Absolutely indefinite (i.e., infinite) potency belongs

only to the whole as such, only to being as all-embracing unity. The essence
of each particular element of being is characterized by the fact that it is
something definite. It is *particular* (i.e., a *part*) precisely because it differs, in
some manner and in some respect, from all else and is defined by this difference. Insofar as there is a causal connection between A and B (for the sake
of simplicity we ignore the problematic nature of this relation, i.e., the
extent to which it is generally valid to affirm the dependence of a phenomenon on a single cause), the phenomenon B follows not directly from an
absolutely universal and indefinable potentiality x, but only from a certain
potentiality which is specified and already partially defined by the presence of A. The phenomenon B follows from the A-branch of universal
potentiality, and this branch is capable of generating not all that is possible
in general, but only B. Only an oak, and not some other plant or living
creature in general, can grow from an acorn. But since such a specific
branch of potentiality is nonetheless rooted in universal potentiality as
such—since, in other words, reality as designated by A is not defined unconditionally and completely but contains indefiniteness as well—
causality here does not mean that the mature oak is "predetermined" in all
the details of its appearance and nature, that it is "preformed" in the acorn.
On the contrary, potentiality is directed toward a finished, *definite* condition only to a certain degree, or rather to a degree that can never be known
in advance. There is always something that remains indefinite.

Scientific thought, i.e., consciousness directed toward a systematically
connected and maximally complete abstract knowledge of the world, is of
course regulated by the principle that in the final analysis every phenomenon can be explained completely by consideration of all the definite fac-
tors and conditions associated with it. This postulate is legitimate and necessary for scientific thought; it is the motive force behind the progress of
science. But this postulate must not lead philosophical thought astray from
the true path. For philosophy this postulate must be no more than a working hypothesis or rather an auxiliary fiction, useful for scientific work.
Consciousness that is directed toward reality in its wholeness must always
be guided by the contrary postulate that an exhaustive explanation, on a
definite basis, of any concrete phenomenon is impossible. Such an exhaustive explanation is impossible not only because of the practical limits to our
cognitive capacity or (what is the same thing) because of the boundless
number of cases that must be considered, but especially because all concrete existents originate from the womb of the essentially indefinite and
therefore rationally indefinable potentiality of being. Science has the right

and obligation to "function" *as though* everything were rationally definable. This is the source of its creative pathos, and science does not have to raise the question of whether things are *really* rationally definable (it is even harmful). But once this question is raised, the only adequate, well-founded answer to it can only be *negative*.

But even if we ignore the essential fact that science is something different from philosophy, that science, guided by the basic postulate of the universal definability of phenomena, does not raise questions concerning the essential legitimacy of this postulate and therefore, as science, simply remains outside all conflict associated with the answers to these questions; even if we admit that there is a conflict between the scientific orientation which postulates the exhaustive knowableness of the world and the philosophical orientation which perceives transfiniteness and potentiality to be the source of the unknowableness of being in all its depth and fullness, we would still have to consider the following: In practice, science always resolves this conflict by ultimately taking as its object actualized, finished being. In other words, science always deals with the past, with being that is in the past. Even that portion of the present which we immediately experience belongs in this sense to the past. In the process of perception and apperception, the moment of the present has already become a part of the past, has become what *was* (if only *just*). "Minerva's owl" not only "flies out into the evening twilight" (as Hegel subtly remarked, criticizing the notion that cognitive thought itself forms reality), but it only sees what is already past: the contents of the day that has ended as they rest fixed in the glow of evening like immobile, incorporeal phantoms. *Ewig still ruht die Vergangenheit*, as the poet says, for the past is precisely nothing but what has already passed and what therefore no longer moves. It is frozen in a definiteness that no longer changes and is present before us as something utterly finished. As noted above, even when science studies processes, it analyzes not what *is* happening, but what *has* happened and what therefore lacks dynamism and stands before us as a finished, frozen picture. On the contrary, all concrete existents—in themselves, in their essences—are not finished things that are present before us in complete definiteness. Rather it is possible for them to *become* things which at the given moment are still logically indefinable, conceptually not defined. All concrete existents contain potentiality, have a certain core which in itself is something indefinite; and they *are* what they contain or have. However, this does not make it impossible to predict the future, which prediction is of course the key to all applied scientific (and ordinary, everyday) knowledge. But scientific pre-

dictions only touch on the *static* and thus rationally definable element of
being, expressed (in terms of time or temporality) in the repeatibility of
the definite aspects of phenomena. This is the key to the interpretation of
the future in the light of the past. But the future in all its concrete fullness
and form, the future precisely as the future (i.e., insofar as it has not yet
been realized), is not only indefinable but is essentially indefinite in itself).
This is the case because the future is that which is subject to realization and
therefore to the achievement of definiteness. From the point of view of
supratemporality, the future is potentiality itself, whose essence is
indefiniteness.

   This means that potentiality coincides with "freedom" in the most general sense of this term. The concept of freedom can have many meanings,
some of which will be examined later in other connections. Here we are
concerned with freedom in its most general sense, namely, freedom as the
phantom of all that is concretely real insofar as it contains the element of
dynamism. Dynamism—the element of happening, occurrence, becoming—consists in the fact that all newly emergent things cannot be viewed
as a simple continuation of what already exists, i.e., as originating from a
definite ground, but must be viewed as originating in indefiniteness, existent
in itself. We remarked above that possibility or potentiality can be either
passive or active. Let us briefly add that what we call "passive" possibility
(the flexibility, compliance, formability of the "raw material") is never
passive concretely in the absolute sense: in other words, it is never inert,
immobile, submissive. Everything that possesses concrete being has a certain dynamism. Everything that is formless in itself is not an inert, submissive mass, but rather the dynamic force of indefiniteness and formlessness,
the seething of chaos, that which Jacob Boehme called *Ungrund* and considered to be the primordial, ultimate depth of reality. On the other hand,
"active" possibility (i.e., creative conception and force) opposes this formless, "passive" stuff as a primary shaping power, as the work of determination performed on an indeterminate material.

   Thus, there is an element of dynamism in indefiniteness itself; there is a
dynamism of disorder, which complements the dynamism of definition, of
order. Without going deeper into the problematic nature of this primordial relationship, let us confine ourselves to the affirmation that it is precisely this indivisible dual-unity which contains the essence of potentiality
as primordial freedom, constituting the transdefiniteness and transfiniteness of reality. The irrational as the substrate of being is precisely not
passive, *is* not in a finished, though indefinite, form—if it is possible to

associate the ideas of "finished" and "indefinite." The irrational is dynamically active. It is a force that cannot be restrained, a chaotic urge thrusting out of itself towards formation, completion, realization. Insofar as being is already formed, already realized, already in a completed, finished form, it is ruled by necessity. And necessity is nothing else but the definiteness of being revealed in the definiteness of its connections. All things that are already in a finished form are necessary: a "necessary" thing is precisely "this" thing, it cannot be another. In the final analysis all necessity is reduced to a simple "this *is* how things are," the italicized "is" having the sense of an unchanging, immobile rock. But insofar as being is potentiality, i.e., the creative potency of *determination* occurring in the depths of indefiniteness, it is primordial freedom. Thus, being as a whole can be understood only as a transrational unity of rationality and irrationality, i.e., of necessity and freedom. And what has become frozen in pure necessity can only have the meaning of a dead, inert residue of the unknowable "livingness" of being. Being as a whole is not frozen and static; *it is not only what it already is*. On the contrary, it is *plastic*: it not only is, it is becoming; it is in the process of self-creation. It is growing, changing, being formed. And this is because potentiality, the potency to become what it is not, lies in the deepest core of being. This is what we call "freedom." Since all concretely existent things are rooted in the total unity of being and are permeated by the "juices" of the total unity, the element of primordial freedom is present, to varying degrees, in all concretely existent things. If naturalistic determinism does not wish to accept this situation, it is because of a prejudice, a prejudice that is ultimately based on the rationalistic belief that the essence of reality consists solely of the element of the rationally determinable, the element which forms the basis of our abstract or conceptual knowledge. This prejudice must be countered, decisively and categorically, by the self-evident perception of the element of the irrational, which is the source of the *essential unknowableness* of reality.

NOTES

1. The German language expresses this difference between concrete content and logically fixed content in the words *Gehalt* and *Inhalt*, respectively.

Chapter III

The Unknowable as Unconditional Being and Reality

In the preceding chapter we discovered the presence of the essentially unknowable, the presence of what transcends the principles of rational-abstract knowledge, in the makeup of *objective being*. We became convinced that in the "world," or "objective reality," or "objective being," which exists in itself, independently of us, a fundamental element is present owing to which "objective being"(which for now we take to be synonymous with the "world" and with "objective reality") contains something unknowable—unknowable not only *for us* but also *essentially*. But now a question arises: Is it possible to completely include the element of the essentially unknowable in the makeup of "objective being," or does this element contain something that shakes the foundation of the very concept of objective being and transcends it? Our analysis of the metalogical element and particularly of the elements of transfiniteness and freedom appears to indicate that the concept of objective being is indeed shaken by the inclusion of the essentially unknowable. By objective being we mean that which is *by itself*, that which stands before us as a stable, self-contained, closed autonomous whole. The etymology of the word "object," *objectum*, particularly the corresponding German word *Gegenstand*, points to something precisely defined and fixed, a goal or target that stands before our cognitive gaze like a solid body with which we collide. However, behind this well-defined, stable content, we have perceived a metalogical and irrational "layer" which can be compared, rather, to a mass in flux, in which one thing which lacks distinct limits flows into another, the whole mass appearing to overflow its bounds. Insofar as being is *indefinite in itself*, it clearly transcends what we call objective being. For in the final analysis objective being is necessarily conceived by us as the aggregate of all things that are *definite in themselves* and stand before us in all their univocal, uneliminable definiteness, which is independent of us. We shall now examine this problem in greater detail.

1. OBJECTIVE REALITY

Objective being is present before us and is apprehended most proximally by us as "objective reality." As yet we shall not attempt to define this latter term precisely. There is no need to define objective reality to be immediately aware of what we have in mind when we use this term. It is this immediate awareness which is our starting point here. Objective reality is that which distinctly and palpably differs from all "appearance" and "illusion," from the content of fantasy and dreams, from all types of "subjective" phenomena. Objective reality is that which is firmly grounded in itself, that which, in its inexorable and merciless factuality, opposes our dreams and desires. It is what we must take account of if we want simply to go on living. There is no need to philosophize to understand clearly and feel the impassable and frequently tragic chasm of difference which separates what is objectively real from all that we desire and dream about. There is no need to philosophize to understand, say, the difference between money that is really in my pocket and money that I only dream about, or the difference between actual old age and impotence that are objectively real and youth and strength that have vanished for ever and live only in memory. Objective reality is (as Dostoevsky's underground man says) a stone wall against which we break our heads and which therefore commands respect from most of us.

But what is genuinely objectively real? What enters into the makeup of what we call objective reality?

At first glance it appears that there is nothing easier than to answer these questions in a general way. All things that are inexorably and cruelly *factual* are "objectively real"; and objective reality is the combination of all the facts we must take into account, theoretically as well as practically, in our life and our acts as obstacles or reference points or as means to our ends. But here another difficulty arises which can easily confuse us. Along with the firm and solid, the irrevocable and enduring, there is much in the world that is pliant and plastic, transitory and changing. Along with what distinctly stands before us, there is much that is shaky, obscure, slippery, ungraspable. Above all, these latter features characterize our "inner life" and the "inner lives" of other people whom we encounter. A question arises concerning such phenomena as "opinions," "moods," "caprices" (ours and those of others), concerning the whole domain of what we call the "subjective" world: Do these phenomena belong to objective reality in the same sense as such things as houses, rocks, and mountains? On the one hand, these inner phenomena seem to be the direct opposite of objective reality, but on the other hand it is sometimes necessary to treat them as a very factually significant objective reality. Such phenomena as "bad moods," "caprices," "self-deceptions," and so on (my own and those of others) can often be obstacles more difficult for me to surmount on my life's path than all purely external obstacles, i.e., facts of the external world which hinder me. Such terrible "real facts" as world wars and revolutions which determine the entire historical fate of mankind depend concretely on "moods," "feelings," and "opinions," on apparently transitory, subjective phenomena in the consciousness of persons who are the rulers of states.

We can see that one and the same "subjective" phenomenon can simultaneously oppose "objective reality" and enter into the makeup of the latter. Sometimes, phenomena of this sort appear to us as transitory, subjectively determined events that are subject to our will. Yet at other times they appear to us as irrevocably and mercilessly stable facts of external objective reality. If, for example, a momentary caprice, temptation or urge becomes strong and solidifies, becomes a vicious character, a blinding, ruining passion or even an incurable sickness of the soul, then what we formerly considered to be the obvious opposite of objective reality becomes for us a mercilessly severe and bitter objective reality which we cannot overcome. Or consider the phenomenon of the political state. On the one hand it seems to be a creation of our own wills, but on the other hand—in the merciless severity of its demands, in its indifference to our personal lives—it often intrudes into our lives as a power much more severe, demanding, and influential than any phenomenon of nature and is sometimes felt to be (to cite Nietzsche) the "coldest of all cold monsters." Does the state belong to objective reality, to the objective world, in the same sense as phenomena of the material world? Thus, we see that the entire domain of psychic and spiritual phenomena does not fit easily into the usual scheme of objective reality, but contains something that makes the concept of objective reality indistinct and indefinite. Therefore, so-called "realists" (people for whom objective reality is the most important reality or even the only one) are, to a lesser or greater degree, "materialists" or "naturalists"; and by thus artificially limiting their mental horizon, they gain an equilibrium of mind and a seeming clarity of thought.

These preliminary and somewhat indefinite considerations are sufficient to allow us to draw two conclusions. First of all, what we call objective reality does not coincide at all with "being in general" or "reality"
(we use these terms synonymously for the present) but is only a sort of
segment of the all-embracing totality of the existent. For even everything
that we oppose to objective reality, even the "non-objective" or the purely
"subjective," *exists* in some sense or other. We are right when we deny the
claim of such phenomena to membership in the exclusive circle of reality
we call objective reality, but we commit the crudest of errors if we deny
their reality altogether. For everything that is experienced by us in some
way, everything that is given to our experience in some manner, *exists*
immediately in some sense. If I erroneously consider a ringing in my ears to
be the ringing of a doorbell, or if I consider the content of my dream to be
what takes place in "reality," I have the right and obligation to correct
these errors, to exclude these phenomena from the ranks of objective reality. But both the ringing in my ears and my dream are realities, even if only
of a subjective order. Objective reality can be compared to a building that
is constructed only of stones that are appropriate and satisfy a specific
criterion. But alongside the building there remains a chaotically strewn
heap of stones that were not used because they were not suitable for the
construction of the building. Thus, reality in its fullness is always wider
than objective reality. We agree with the poet who said: "As the ocean
embraces the earth, so our life is embraced by dreams." Continents, solid
ground—this is objective reality. The ocean which embraces the earth is
the "dreams," the "subjective" phenomena which belong to reality even
though they do not belong to objective reality. It is possible to observe two
erroneous tendencies with regard to this situation. On the one hand there
are the "romantic dreamers," who do not clearly distinguish the solid
ground of objective reality from the "ocean of dreams" which surrounds
it. Like inexperienced seamen, these dreamers sometimes attempt to cross
the ocean while ignoring shoals and reefs; they can easily perish. On the
other hand there are the "sober realists," who know perfectly well that
rough, stony ground must be crossed only on well-marked roads and only
on wheels. But in general they refrain from navigating the ocean and do
not even suspect that the islands and the continents are surrounded by it.
Both tendencies are equally erroneous and can lead to harmful results.

But this is not all. We now come to our second conclusion, which is even
more interesting and significant than the first. This division into "solid

ground" and "free, boundless ocean" is *not univocal*. Rather, depending on the point of view, one and the same phenomenon can be referred either to objective reality or to the world of "subjectivity." The division is conditional and relative in some sense (later this shall become clearer). Why is this so? It is not difficult to find an approximate answer to this question: Everything that stands before us as the *object of judgment*, having a definite content, turns out to be in some sense a part of objective being, i.e., of objective reality. (That the concept of objective being is broader than that of objective reality shall be discussed later; for the present the two terms are treated as synonyms.) And this accords with the fact that only judgments have copulas, i.e., only in judgments is the word "is" used. However, insofar as something is simply experienced, is given or is present in immediate experience, we do not yet say of it that it "objectively is," though every content of experience is therefore some "reality" in the general sense. A dream that I am experiencing or have experienced is *only* a dream and not an objective reality, but if I *think* the fact of having had the dream and say that "I have had such a dream," then in this respect I am already speaking about a fact that belongs to objective reality. Torn out of the immediacy of experience, this phenomenon becomes for me an object of thought and therefore a part of objective reality; it becomes something I must take into account as an uneliminable, unalterable *fact*. The whole material world is immediately present before us as an object of thought through the judgment that something "is." (There is no need here to examine why this is the case.) Psychic and spiritual phenomena, however, are most immediately perceived by us as contents of immediate experience and can become objects of judgments only later, in reflection, and always only partially. For this reason, psychic and spiritual phenomena are either referred by us to the sphere of "subjectivity," to that disordered "heap of stones" which only surrounds the building without being a part of it; or they are included (at least partially) in the "building," i.e., they are referred to objective reality. Let us briefly add that a phenomenon of experience becomes an object of judgment for us when our thought, our attention, perceives in this phenomenon a *definite* content: a content which owing to the principle of definiteness is constituted for us as some content A that is identical in itself and clearly distinct from other contents. Thus, the domain of objective reality coincides for us with the totality of phenomena in that aspect in which they form a connected system of determinations. (The necessary qualifications to this proposition will be presented later.) By a different path and in a different formulation, we arrive at the same conclusion as in the preceding chapter: Objective reality is only the segment of the *rational* (and rationalized by us), i.e., of the rationally knowable, in the makeup of reality. Beyond the limits of the rationally knowable, there stretches the dark ocean of the irrational and the unknowable, which is experienced only in the immediately given and transcends "objective reality."

In the preceding chapter we apprehended the layer of the irrational in the makeup of objective being. Here, we consider another aspect of the same problem. We see that everything that is irrational, everything that does not completely fit into a connected system of determinations, undermines the system of objective being or objective reality and transcends this system, without ceasing to be a reality in the general sense. These two conclusions, at first glance contradicting each other, are nonetheless compatible, for the object itself or (what is the same thing for us) objective reality itself, constituted for us as a system of objective, i.e., definite, contents, is also—as the *carrier* of this system—something greater and other than just the dark abyss of the unknowable, irrational, of that specific moment we call "being." Depending on which side of this relation is brought to the foreground, the irrational is either opposed to objective reality as something "subjective" or is perceived as the dark unknowable depth of the connected, ordered system of objective being. From this point of view, objective reality is not something finished once and for all, not a closed whole of definite dimensions, but rather something pliant and plastic, something that inwardly "breathes," expanding or contracting depending on from what side we approach it. The domain of what we call objective reality cannot be delimited definitely and univocally. This is the case not only because of the weakness of our cognitive capacities or the practical limits to our knowledge, but also because of the very essence of the *concept* of objective reality. Speaking paradoxically, objective reality as the sphere of everything that *objectively is* does not in itself have objective (i.e., precisely and univocally defined) boundaries. In other words, *although objective reality is the sphere of what objectively exists, it itself cannot be subsumed under the concept of the objectively existent*, for it lacks the chief characteristic of the objectively existent: namely univocal definiteness of content.

The same conclusion can be reached in a completely different way, namely, through an examination of the difficulties encountered when an attempt is made to clarify the relation of what we call objective reality to our consciousness of time.

Does objective reality contain only what *is* or does it also include what *was* and *will be*? Of course, what was was an objective reality *then*, in its time. And the future will some day *become* an objective reality. Thus, it appears that we must include in some sense the past and the future in the makeup of objective reality. But if we set aside the fact, examined above, that the future in a certain sense is not univocally predetermined, not determined in itself, but can occur in different ways, then we can say that the past and the future are not things we must take into account in the same sense that we must necessarily take into account the present. The past and future therefore lack the most essential feature of objective reality. True, the past as such is unchangeable for us, but it has faded away into the indifferent distances and has thus departed from the sphere of objective reality. The past is buried and no longer concerns us or concerns us only insofar as its consequences affect the present. On the other hand the future is, at least to some degree, precisely that which we create or construct ourselves, that which depends on our will, that which is the result of our own activity. In this sense the future appears to be the direct opposite of what we call objective reality. Even insofar as the future (in its cosmic content, for example) stands before us in a fateful, unchangeable form, it is still something that *is only yet to happen*, even though it is not something we make happen. In other words the past has passed and the future has not yet come. Neither "exists," both only "appear" to us. The past we can only remember or recognize only gradually with more or less probability from its traces; the future we can only guess about. Neither is "given" to us. Neither touches us in our experience or acts upon us as the present does, i.e., as that which inexorably is "objectively real."

At first glance it might appear that this problem is simply one of terminology. It seems that we have not one, but *two* concepts of objective reality. By objective reality in the narrow and "eminent" sense we mean the objective reality of the present, of what "stands before us" in experience, of what touches us, of what we perceive with our senses, of what alone is of practical significance for us. On the other hand, objective reality in the broader, more widespread sense encompasses all that ever was and will be. In the narrow sense of objective reality, the picture of the reality of distant geological and historical epochs and even the picture of our ancestors' lives seem unreal in comparison with the "palpable" objective reality of the present. However, in the broader sense these past epochs are included in the makeup of all-embracing cosmic and historical objective reality. The same point can be made about the relation of the objective reality of the present to that of the future. This distinction is similar to the one we make

in the spatial dimension of being between the "near world" which surrounds us and the "whole world" in all its fullness.

All this would be very simple if we could clearly distinguish between
these two concepts of objective reality. But we cannot. For in the strict
sense the present is nothing but an ideal boundary, lacking all duration,
between the past and the future; it is the moment at which the future,
which has not *yet* been, becomes the past which has *already* been. In this
strict sense the present evidently does not have objective reality. Everything that we are conscious of as the present has already, at the moment we
are conscious of it, become the past. Everything toward which our gaze
is directed, in cares or dreams, is the future, be it the near future of days or
years or only that part of the future which is the unfinished part of today. In
its concrete psychological significance, the "present" is for us the most
proximate segment of the past or future (what we can call the mathematical moment of the present). However, this notion of the most proximate
segment of the past or the future (the notion of "now") apparently can be
extended arbitrarily and is wholly relative. In one life-relation it can mean
"today" or this month, whereas in another relation it can encompass an
entire historical era, which in turn can amount to several decades or several centuries closest to us in time (as when historians begin the "modern"
period with the Renaissance).

From this point of view, only that which is time-encompassing is objective reality (a kind of all-embracing cosmic reality) in the strict scientific
sense, whereas all narrower, time-dependent "objective realities" would
have only the significance of indefinite, purely relative segments, conditioned by our psychology, of total objective reality. This conclusion is
essential for us, first of all, because, in contrast to what seems evident at
first glance, we must understand objective reality in this more exact sense
to mean something that is only "conceived" as such but not immediately
given to the senses. There is no objective reality in what is only immediately given to the senses. There is only a fleeting, formless, ungraspable
experience, i.e., something that cannot claim to be objective reality.

Total time-encompassing objective reality not only remains boundless
and unsurveyable for us in its content. It is even essentially inconceivable.
According to Kant's well-known (and unrefuted) antinomy we can conceive of reality neither as genuinely infinite in time nor as having a primordial, absolute beginning in time. Thus if by objective reality we mean only
all-embracing, total being, objective reality becomes for us a completely
impossible concept, precisely because it is inconceivable as a closed, self-

contained whole, and is then something infinite which vanishes in both directions (toward the past and toward the future), becomes lost in the abyss of the inconceivable, in the abyss of *nothing*.

Only one thing is of essence for us here. Total being evidently does not coincide with objective reality, for the simple reason that objective reality *does not exist* as a finished, self-contained whole. This confirms in another way the conclusion we reached above. What we call objective reality is, in essence, absolutely indefinite and boundless—not in the sense of actual infinitude but in the sense that it lacks all precise boundaries which would close and encompass it. Objective reality is necessarily diffuse and amorphous, and it can be larger or smaller depending on our interests and direction, on our point of view and sharpness of vision. And we are compelled to admit that this relative, amorphous quality belongs to the very essence of objective reality. Objective reality *does not exist* if we understand what "exists" or what "belongs to objective reality" to be something that is definite in itself. It is the *objectively real—something that is objectively real—* which undeniably exists for us. To deny this is to fall into dreamy idealism, which destroys the possibility of all real knowledge, the possibility of all activity based on sober orientation. The *objectively real*, indefinite in its size and limits, is present before us as a complex which is qualitatively definite in itself, and as such it is partially known by us. The objectively real is an "island surrounded by the ocean," and the shorelines of this island are not well-defined but merge imperceptibly with the ocean. And this is evidently so by the very essence of what we mean by objective reality.

The same thing can be expressed in a different form in the idea (clarified in the preceding chapter) that there exists no finished all-embracing objective reality which coincides with the totality of being, because everything that is objectively real is generated in the womb of the possible as real potentiality or existent potency. Even though potentiality or potency itself belongs to reality and forms the primordial depth of the latter, it cannot be called "objective reality." For the latter is a concept that is conceivable only in correlation with "possibility." That which actually *is* differs as such from that which *can be* and presupposes this "can be" beyond its limits. Thus, total being cannot be objective reality. It can only be existent potentiality, "giving birth" out of itself to objective reality, *potest* or *posse ipsum* as Nicholas of Cusa called it. It can only be the ground of being, embracing both the actually and potentially existent, what already is as objective reality and what only *can* be. Precisely because everything that is definite and therefore objectively real originates, strictly speaking, not from something other that is definite and objectively real but only from the indefiniteness of potentiality, there exists no all-embracing, connected whole or system of objective reality; there exists only the objectively real with indefinite boundaries which is generated in the womb of this primordial being.

2. IDEAL BEING

To this point our investigation does not yet allow us to affirm that we have gone beyond "objective being." So far we have used the latter concept as synonymous with "objective reality." We now must introduce an essential correction to make our discussion more complete. *The concept of objective being is broader in its content than the concept of objective reality.* The fact is that even existent potentiality can and—apparently even must—be conceived as *objectively existent.* This is revealed in the fact that what is only potential or possible in relation to concrete objective reality can also be present before us as a definite, clearly delineated content at which our cognitive gaze can be directed in the same way as at concrete objective reality. In this sense we can say that this "possibility" exists objectively, i.e., that it exists "in itself," independently of us. We have in mind ideal, extratemporal elements and relations between abstractly conceived "contents" or "essences." The modern theory of knowledge (Husserl is the principal proponent of this school along with the Russian philosopher Lossky) has explained with complete self-evidence (while setting aside all hypotheses of a "metaphysical" nature and considering only the purely logical aspect of the problem) that Plato's teaching of the "world of ideas" contains something absolutely legitimate and undeniable. Such elements of being as numbers, geometrical shapes, colors, sounds, and (going further) all universal, abstract contents of concepts, considered precisely as pure, essential *contents,* as well as such necessary extratemporal relations between these contents as "two times two equals four" or "red is a color," also evidently belong to the makeup of objective being, are in some sense independent of us, and are therefore genuinely existent realities. But since these realities lack all temporal determination, they cannot be considered concrete realities. They are not things or processes or essences, and in this respect they transcend what we call objective reality. This is precisely Plato's kingdom of the "genuinely existent" (*ontos on*) in contradistinction to what "comes into being and perishes" (*gignomenon kai apollumenon*). Of course there immediately arises the difficult problem concerning the relationship between these two "worlds," a problem that has constantly concerned philosophical thought from Plato's time to ours. However, this problem interests us here not in itself but only insofar as it is related to our basic theme, just as in general we discuss the entire problem of ideal being only in order to illuminate more completely and clearly the relationship between the rational element and the transrational (essentially unknowable) element of being.

The fact is that, at the very least, this reality of the ideal world can appear to us as the kingdom of what is unconditionally definite-in-itself, self-contained, present before us in a complete, finished form. In this case the entire problem of the concept of objective reality would have utterly no bearing on the kingdom of ideal reality, and we would then have in ideal reality a certain self-contained system of "objective being" in which everything in itself is rationally definite and therefore rationally definable. We would then have a sort of solid ground with distinct boundaries and well-defined inner structure, conceivable outside of all relation to the dark "ocean" of the indefinite and the unknowable. This is roughly Plato's conception in the middle period of his work, when he was first elaborating his teaching of "ideas" in a form that later became "classical" Platonism. (We know now that in his later works Plato came to understand the complexity which he had first failed to notice in this theme.)

Here we must again refer to the conclusions presented in our book *The Object of Knowledge*. In two respects, this kingdom of "ideas" or pure "essences" appears to us at first glance as autonomous, self-contained, inwardly unconditionally definite and therefore given to our thought as "objective being." First, every separate idea or essence (being that in reality which corresponds to the content of a concept) appears to be something self-contained, separable from everything else, free of all the "merging of one thing into another" which we remarked in concrete reality, and also free of all temporal change. Thus, every idea or essence is present before us objectively as it were as a sort of plastic, finished form. Second, taken as a *whole*, the kingdom of ideas appears to resemble an eternally fixed picture which in its essence, precisely as extratemporal being, is completely free of time-conditioned reality with its flux that binds us. This ideal being logically and (therefore ontologically) "precedes"—as prototype—concrete objective reality. This is why Plato depicted the world as having been created or ordered by a demiurge who used "ideas" as his models. Whether this kingdom of ideas exists "in itself" as Plato thought or whether it exists only in the "divine spirit" as Plotinus thought is not essential to us here in our preliminary discussion. In any event, this kingdom exists "in itself" (i.e., objectively) in the sense that it is independent of the time-conditioned concrete world, independent of the world in which it is "reflected" or "embodied."

It is not difficult to show that both of these propositions, however much truth they may contain (how much truth they do contain will become clear later in a wholly different connection), do not in any case exhaust the essence of ideal being and therefore do not adequately convey it. A deeper analysis will put the problem in a new perspective.

As for the first proposition, there is no particular need to repeat, after the discussion in the preceding chapter, that every separate content A (and therefore every separate "idea") has its genuine essence only in its relation to everything else (i.e., in the unity of A and non-A as well as in the unity ABCD . . .). The discussion in the preceding chapter referred directly to the *contents of concepts* and thus to ideal being; and only through the medium of ideal being did the discussion have meaning for everything that is conceivable in general. To the extent that an idea is conceived as what is identical to the content of a concept, it is absolutely self-evident in a certain sense that the idea is autonomous, complete, self-contained. But this is the case only because this affirmation is a tautology, a simple repetition of the meaning of the principle of definiteness. In this sense, any A is precisely only A and not something else; and A is not "concerned" with anything else. On the one hand this does not prevent every A from being constituted by a negation, i.e., by its relation to not-A. The separating "not" is also a connecting element or ground from which A first originates. On the other hand, A is conceivable only as a member of the set ABCD . . . , i.e., as derived from metalogical unity. Precisely insofar as we have in mind, for example, not the visible image of "red" or of a "triangle," and so on, but only its conceptually graspable "essence," this essence is revealed to us only in its "determination," i.e., in its reduction to something other and therefore in its unity with something other. Of course, the connections between ideas which are revealed here are in turn also apprehended (most proximally) abstractly, precisely in concepts of relations, i.e., in their "ideal essence." But in the final analysis the ultimate (or more precisely, the primordial) connecting elements are the "not" or "non" element which first constitutes definiteness as such and the "is" element which corresponds to the "copula" of a judgment. However, these two elements are not "ideas" but something wholly different, something we do not conceive plastically or in images (we shall discuss this in greater detail later). Ideal being exhibits the same set of problems which was revealed to us in the analysis of judgments and concepts and which led us to the discovery of metalogical unity. Thus, the kingdom of ideas can be conceived as "existent in itself" only on the basis of metalogical unity, i.e., the unity of what is undivided and indefinite, transcending all definiteness and limitation, and ultimately overflowing the bounds of itself. Ideal being is not spread before us, like a geographic map, as an aggregate of precisely delimited essences, as modern phenomenology in its classical orientation is inclined to assume. Ideal being is not only infinite, it has depth as well. Something in it remains hidden from us, and no analysis, however deeply penetrating, can completely explore this dimension of depth, can overcome the three-dimensional, "atmospheric" nature of this world and transpose it to a plane where it would appear before us as a finite set of independent essences. There are no magical means that can bare the mystery of being (this holds for ideal being too), with one sweep tearing off the veil of Maya as it were. Thus, the infinitude of ideal being is not only factually unsurveyable and thus unknowable, but also transcends everything that is definite-in-itself. Hence, this infinitude can scarcely have the character of an autonomous, self-contained world.

All this is pretty self-evident in the light of our previous discussions. It is more important to consider the inadequacy of the second proposition concerning ideal being, namely the proposition that ideal being is absolutely independent of time-conditioned concrete being and has priority over or "precedes" concrete being. Let us be direct: the common notion (alien to the subtle speculation of Platonism, devoid of rational argument, and totally inadequate in its formulation) that ideal essences are only abstractions from the fullness of concrete reality is, to some degree, closer to the truth than the abstract philosophical teaching of the objective existence of ideas. First of all, let us consider the simple fact that ideal being is extratemporal and is thus based on the *negation* of time, on the conceptual elimination of the element of time. But negation does more than separate. It also connects, i.e., it presupposes a negative relation to "something other" which is conceived in the negation and, consequently, a negative relation to the unity of the one and the other. Thus, extratemporal being presupposes beyond its own limits the temporal and temporality itself. And for this reason extratemporal being can be conceived wholly and exhaustively only in relation to temporality. True, this argument can be countered by the objection that this negation is present only in verbal expression or only in the psychological process in which the concept of extratemporality originates, but not in the essence of reality itself. Descartes did something similar when he took the "infinite" to be the product of the negation of the "finite" only in a verbal sense, while in fact he considered it to be something absolutely positive (i.e., "maximal fullness"). This objection, however, is not a serious one. That extratemporal being (universal content such as "redness," "the number two," etc.) is *conceivable* as independent of temporal being is evident only because this is a tautology, for to "conceive" precisely means to be aware of as extratemporal content. But if everything that is conceivable acquires genuine meaning for us not in the separate content of a concept but only in the judgment "A is B" (and ultimately in the judgment "x is A"), then here we have, along with the content of a concept, the enigmatic connecting and grounding "is" (or relation to x), which is not the content of a concept. True, it is possible to point out that this "is" is also extratemporal, since a judgment has extratemporal validity. But this is not completely the case. Strictly speaking, only a content that is identical to itself can be extratemporal. The form of extratemporality coincides precisely with the form of identity, with the categorial condition that constitutes definiteness. But the "is" element itself is neither a determination nor an identity. It is rather the link *between* determinations (or between a determination and the unity from which it arises), the *transition* from the "one" to the "other," that enigmatic and profound dynamic, living element of ideal being which Fichte called *Durch* (*Wissenschaftslehre*, 1804). Of course, this "is" element cannot be simply identified with the psychological act of linking or transition as with a real thought-process, for this would be an illegitimate confusion of categories. Nevertheless, this "is" element, as a link between determinations and as an element that grounds definiteness in being, contains something that transcends the pure extratemporality of definiteness and in some way resembles the concreteness of temporal being. This "something" is a unity that transcends all definiteness and in this sense is indefinite—what the later Platonists considered to be the "matter" of the ideal world. But if, on the one hand, this "is" element is not something abstract and extratemporal and, on the other hand, it essentially differs from all temporal processes and actions, then only one possibility remains: it must be concrete and *supratemporal* or time-encompassing. But such being of an "idea" in the all-embracing whole which itself is not an idea can be conceived in only one form: a form that involves not a separate temporal psychological act of thought but supratemporal *being in thought* and thus thought as universal *potency*, as potency that is no longer in the abstract-logical form of its content but has assumed the form of a kind of all-embracing concreteness. In this sense we must recognize with Plotinus, contrary to Plato or classical Platonism, that the world of ideas cannot be conceived except as existing in the "divine spirit"—in the all-embracing unity that is not abstract and *extratemporal* but concrete and *supratemporal*. But time and thus all of temporal being are somehow enclosed in this supratemporal unity.

The same conclusion can be demonstrated in another way. In relation to empirical, time-subordinated being, the kingdom of ideas, existing in the sense of having extratemporal significance, is the kingdom of "possibility." This significance which is independent of empirical objective reality means that the kingdom of ideas is that which is *possible in itself*, i.e., independently of its empirical realization. Thus, it might seem that behind and beyond objective reality there is an autonomous realm of pure possibility, independent of objective reality. We mentioned above that in the depths of objective reality there is a sphere of existent potentiality or potency. However, the concept of potentiality or potency should not be confused with the concept of abstract possibility which we encounter now. Possibility in this latter, abstract, sense means nothing but *noncontradictedness* or simply *conceivableness*. That possibility in this abstract sense is autonomous purely logically (i.e., is independent of all empirical objective reality or concrete realization) is obvious simply because this is in fact the meaning of the concept of possibility which we are discussing here. The truth "$2 \times 2 = 4$" would have meaning even if the world did not contain four concrete objects, for it only means that four objects (taken as two-times-two objects) are "possible," i.e., conceivable. The judgment "it may rain today" does not become false simply because it did not *actually* rain. It did not but it *could* have. All this is self-evident and almost a tautology.

This does not prevent us, however, from taking "possibility" to mean the possibility of realization. Let us admit that possibility in this sense does not yet mean the active, dynamic potency to realization. (The extent to which the kingdom of ideas in Plato's sense "coincides" with the kingdom of "effective forms" in Aristotle's sense is a problem which, having been mentioned in our previous discussion of existent potentiality, can now be set aside.) In any case, possibility would be a meaningless concept if it did not mean precisely the possibility (if not the necessity) of realization, the possibility of entering the sphere of objective reality. From this it is clear that the concept of possibility contains a *relation to objective reality* and is inconceivable without this relation. Even unrealized possibility is constituted by its relation to objective reality, if only as a movement to the latter that has stopped midway.

Here, the separating "not" or "non," the difference between the "one" and the "other" (in this case the difference between possibility and objective reality) upon which the definiteness of both of these concepts is based, is also a *linking* element. Even the complete "autonomy" of extratemporal ideal contents and connections with respect to empirical objective reality is only the specific form of their positive relation to objective reality (just as the autonomy of a sovereign state is determined by its international position). When applied to the concept of possibility, this means that the "conceivable," i.e., the *logically* necessary, does not—it is true—coincide with the objectively real, i.e., with the really necessary. But since logical necessity is *the necessity of the possible*, and since possibility in turn means *the possibility of realization*, it follows that logical necessity can be understood only as a partial element of unconditional or absolute necessity, outside of which this necessity is completely inconceivable in the full metalogical (and thus ontological) sense. This is the basis of the complete, exhaustive meaning of the copula of a judgment, of the word "is." The two partial meanings of "is," that which is present in fact and that which necessarily is in the sense of the inconceivability of anything else, are precisely only inseparable elements of its total meaning as an expression of unconditional supratemporal being in general. Only in a wholly conditional sense is logical realism, which affirms a kingdom of ideas existing in themselves, more correct than empirical realism, which does not recognize any reality except that of the concrete, the reality of singular things, subordinate to space and time. The legitimacy of logical realism consists only in the fact that the "logically necessary," taken in negating abstraction from the flux of time, is really "conceivable" as such. This logical necessity or "apodicticity" of extratemporal relations (just as the real necessity of the *categorical*, of "facticity" which empiricism identifies with the total fullness of being) is only a part of unconditional, supratemporal being, of concrete total unity. Both logical realism (i.e., "rationalism" and "idealism") and empiricism attain the genuine realization of their striving toward genuine reality only in *absolute realism* as *ideal-realism*, for which time and extratemporality are inseparably interconnected dimensions of all-embracing, concrete-supratemporal being. This is the only way to overcome the well-known difficulty associated with logical realism, the only way to find the way back from the kingdom of ideas to the kingdom of temporal being, the only way to explain how the latter originated from the former.

It follows from the abstract *conceivableness* of the extratemporally ideal that this domain has relative "autonomy," i.e., an inner conformity to law of the connections between ideal contents (just as there exists a relative "autonomy" of purely empirical connections in the makeup of objective reality). In order to be a good mathematician, that is, in order to orient oneself correctly in the domain of mathematical knowledge, there is no need to have experience of real things and relations. Ideal contents are "autonomous," or "intrinsically legitimate," "in themselves" as it were, without any relation to concrete reality. And this autonomy is what makes possible all sciences of ideal relations, the best example of which is mathematics. Here we are dealing, so to speak, with fragments of being that are freely hovering or "ungrounded" in the profound sense of "groundlessness." We "detach" ourselves from the relations of these fragments to the fullness of reality and tear them from the ground in which they are ultimately rooted. This groundlessness, this hovering in the sphere of pure possibility (in the sense of conceivableness), is what constitutes all being-in-itself, all the "autonomy" of such domains. (Mathematicians are very much aware of the "groundlessness" of their subject.) Nevertheless, the philosophical consciousness (i.e., the consciousness directed at knowing and capturing the world in its integral fullness) is compelled to search on round-about paths for threads connecting this "autonomous" domain with concrete total unity, with reality as such. The self-contained, "autonomous" character of the "ideal" world is not absolute, but only relative; this character does not signify the absence of all connections with the rest of being, but only the distinctive nature of these connections. For in general, nothing is conceivable as absolutely autonomous except all-embracing total unity itself.

We return here to our basic theme. If a more penetrating cognitive gaze, able to overcome abstract conceptual thought, sees ideal being only as an inseparable particular element of concrete total unity which has time-subordinated empirical being as its correlative element, then the concept of objective being even in the broader sense in which it does not coincide with the concept of objective reality becomes impossible as the concept of an absolutely autonomous, self-sufficient, self-contained reality. However, even in this broader sense objective being (as was the case with objective reality) turns out to be an "island surrounded by the ocean." Objective being grows, so to speak, out of the womb of *unconditional being* and is only conceivable as rooted in the latter. In this its supratemporal, concrete all-embracing total unity, unconditional being itself is not only not objective reality but it is not even objective being. Insofar as we conceive being objectively, it hopelessly splits apart into a time-subordinated reality of concrete things and processes and an extratemporally existent domain of ideal being. The form of definiteness—which is necessary for constituting "objectivity," the element of the "independence" of being from us, the presence of being before us as existent in itself (though "objectivity" is of course not completely exhausted by this element)—requires (insofar as it apprehends everything as a logically fixed "content") a sharp, totally unmoderated splitting of being into the temporal and the extratemporal. And within the limits of abstract knowledge, the limits of the apprehension of being as "objective," these "halves" cannot be harmonized; their ultimate inner connection, the real connection between them, cannot be completely perceived. They remain fragments, unconnected "chunks" of being. We cannot grasp their boundaries, where they touch each other and are inwardly connected. Insofar as we overcome this indefinite duality, which does not lend itself to conclusive "synthesis" within its own limits, and rise above the limits immanent to abstract thought, we transcend the limits to knowledge of objective being and ascend to the perception of unconditional being. Unconditional being (i.e., concrete total being) is not a reality that exists "in itself," is not "objectively" and externally present before our cognitive gaze. Unconditional being is not some "world," however broad and deep we conceive this latter concept. Unconditional being is neither an object of thought nor even an object of immediate apprehension. It is something wholly other, immeasurably more encompassing and deeper. And insofar as our thought has at all grasped, even if only darkly and indistinctly, the idea of unconditional being, the idea of concrete genuinely all-embracing unity, we have an intuition (even before all attempts to "explain" or "understand" this being) that unconditional being is something like a boundless ocean whose depths are dark and unexplored.

3. Unconditional Being

But what can be deeper and more encompassing than all of objective being in all its fullness? At first glance there appears to be only one way out of this quandary: idealism. If the whole fullness of objective being is rooted in something other than itself and is conceivable only as arising from this "something other," then it would seem that this "something other" can be nothing but "thought" or "consciousness." And what appears to us as objective being can only be the immanent content of this "thought" or "consciousness."

Later we shall discuss the element of truth contained in this conception.

Here we shall only emphasize that all "idealism" is not a simple, unprejudiced description of the genuine relation of things, but an artificial construction forced upon the facts and therefore erroneous. In our book *The Object of Knowledge* we demonstrated in detail the erroneous and contradictory character of "idealism." Here it is sufficient to note that "thought" or "consciousness" also "exists" in some sense and therefore also belongs to being and is subordinate to it. Therefore "idealism" is a form (although a very limited one) of *realism* and is based on *absolute realism*. For this reason it cannot be used to explain the latter. *Being* or *reality* is more profound and more primordial than the concept of "thought" or "consciousness."

But we can go further and make the general statement that all attempts to more precisely define unconditional being by clarifying its general content or its qualitative definiteness contain an internal contradiction. Every "what" (*chto*)[1]—be it "spirit," "thought," "consciousness," "will," "force," "matter," or anything else at all—is only conceivable as the content of some "indefinite something" (*nechto*) which as such is not a "definite something" (*chto-to*). If all abstract knowledge (knowledge in concepts) is expressible in the judgment "x is A," then it is essentially meaningless and contradictory to pose the question "what is x itself, as such." It was shown in a previous discussion that x *itself* is absolutely self-evident in the sense of being *unquestionable*, i.e., in the sense that it is meaningless to pose *questions* in relation to x. Furthermore, we are dealing here not with x as the "unknown" or "unknowable for us" but with x as the symbol of metalogically transfinite and thus essentially "indefinite" being. Thus, concerning unconditional being, we can say only that it is an "indefinite something" (*nechto*) which, though it contains every conceivable "definite something" (*chto-to*), is itself not a "definite something" (*chto-to*). However, this does not make it a contentless "nothing" (*nichto*).

A number of languages have a figure of speech which is usually employed without an awareness of its true meaning but upon attentive examination turns out to be a direct expression of ancient folk-wisdom that grasps the point we have just attempted to clarify. To express any affirmation (and in the final analysis all knowledge is an affirmation) or presence of something, German uses the words *es gibt*, French uses *il y a*, and English uses *there is*. This "it" or "there" which "has" or "gives" us something (in the final analysis it "gives" us everything in general) is hardly a meaningless word. All that we know or affirm originates in the fact that we have some sort of relation to "it" or "there." And this "it" or "there" really "has" or "gives" us every separate "this" or "that," enriching us with endless gift-giving, with all that "it has." And all these gifts remain unshakeably and inseparably rooted in this "it" or "there" even when we cognitively take possession of them. But this "it" and this all-embracing place called "there" are not something like a "world," are not, in general, some sort of "objective" or "definite" being. This "it" or "there" is nothing else but "something in general" or the unity of "everything in general; it is the indefinite-in-itself, though it contains and generates everything that is definite; it is always superabundant, overflowing the bounds of itself. It is creative, *unconditional being*. It is the dark maternal womb in which what we call the objective world is conceived and generated, both in its extratemporal ideal content and in its temporal flux.

In other words, what we have understood as unconditional being is precisely nothing but the *essentially unknowable* as the *transrational*, which differs by an irrational remainder (forming its essence) from everything that is definite and conceivable in concepts. That which is added to "content" and distinguishes the "real" and "existent" from the merely "conceivable," i.e., that which we mean by the word "is" in an existential judgment, is nothing but the *essentially unknowable*. Indeed, the ultimate error of all "idealism" is that it unnaturally and forcibly equates *reality* (which in its very *meaning* coincides with *transrationality*, with the *essentially unknowable*) with rationally conceivable "contents" which abstract thought is capable of grasping. As (explicit or implicit) *rationalism*, all idealism turns out to be unfounded owing to the transrational essence of reality, owing to the fact that total or unconditional being is in itself an "indefinite something" (*nechto*) or "all," which, indefinite in itself, is essentially something *wholly other* than any "definite something" (*chto-to*), any "this" or "that." The giddy question, nearly bringing us to the edge of insanity—what do we mean by the word "is," do we mean that something is, or do we mean that everything in general is—answers itself if we note that *the transcending of all that is conceptually knowable and expressible is precisely the essential defining characteristic of what we mean by reality.*

Being as such (i.e., in its absoluteness) and *mystery* are simply *one and the same*. Here we take "mystery" to mean not some riddle that requires solution (though this solution were a factual impossibility for us) but the "mysterious" in its very nature, i.e., the transrational, that which essentially opposes all that is knowable. The only reason we fail to notice the "mystery" of being is that it is the absolutely all-embracing background and all-permeating "atmosphere" of all our experience. And this background or atmosphere (like everything else that is absolutely familiar, unchanging, omnipresent) naturally escapes our attention. But when we perceive it *as such*, when we open our eyes and see it, we feel the eternal and ubiquitous presence of the absolutely unknowable mystery in all our experience and all our life.

The transrationality and thus the unknowableness of being have a two-fold meaning or "content." If we take being as such, as distinct from all that is contained in it, it is an absolutely indivisible, primordial, simple unity—an "indefinite something" (*nechto*) that is *not* a "definite something" (*chto-to*). The essence of being as such—*what* (*chto*) it is— simply coincides with its presence, with the fact that it *is*. In comparison with every content-carrying "what" (*chto*), being as such is "nothing" (*nichto*). As such an indivisible unity, devoid of all features, being as such can only be *experienced* in the sense of presenting its being to us and being possessed by us. But it cannot be explained by any sort of conceptual analysis. On the other hand this unity is also the unity of *all*. Not only does it embrace and contain *all*, it also completely permeates *all*. And being in *this* sense is not what remains after all else has been subtracted. It is rather the unity of *all* in general, the unity of every "what" (*chto*) *and* of its being. But since being as such is *all* in this sense, precisely *as unity*, all in being itself *is* unity. All togetherness, all contiguity, all connection of variety in being is the *merging* and *coincidence* in transrational identity of what is different. As a result, unconditional being is *coincidentia oppositorum*, a coincidence of opposites. Since being is all that it has and contains, peaceful coexistence in being becomes an antinomian coincidence of opposites. Insofar as we attempt to rationally express this relation in concepts and judgments, this is possible only through the affirmation that those things which are essentially incompatible with one another when taken in themselves nevertheless become compatible in unconditional being, and compatible not in a relation of difference (as may be the case in the reality of particular things) but compatible *unconditionally*, precisely because it is a question of unconditional and indivisibly simple being. Unconditional being transcends all that is knowable and logical and definite not only in the sense that it is metalogical, transdefinite, and transfinite, but also in the sense that it is transrational *qua* unknowable in the strict sense of unknowableness (i.e., incomprehensibility). This will become clearer in the following chapter.

However, the transrational or essentially unknowable is not remote or hidden from us. Since it coincides with unconditional being, it is present with ultimate, absolute self-evidence in all consciousness of reality if only we have eyes to see it. That which is most habitual, that which surrounds and permeates us, that in which we live and move, that which we are—reality as such—coincides with the unknowable. And all that is knowable and understandable, all that can be grasped conceptually, is rooted in the unknowable and has meaning only in relation to the unknowable.

But it is precisely for this reason that the conceptually knowable is inadequate to *reality itself* even if the contents of being are grasped with full adequacy. This contains the profound and completely legitimate meaning of skepticism. Only in its crude and helpless form is skepticism reducible to the affirmation that being, conceived here as definite in itself and therefore subject in principle to exhaustive conceptual knowing, is for ever screened from us, as it were, by a thick, impenetrable veil that we cannot raise or move aside. As is well known, this affirmation can be refuted by pointing out its internally contradictory character. Insofar as skepticism is presented as a reasoned theory and pretends to genuine truth, it is a metaphysical knowledge, an attempt to penetrate into the profound nature of things. The skeptic would have to touch the veil and even look behind it if he wants to be certain of the impenetrability of the veil and of the presence of the being hidden behind it. The fact is that this is precisely what the skeptic has in mind, though he is usually not distinctly aware of it and thus expresses his thought poorly. Even so, the skeptic knows a mystery that eludes the metaphysician with his arrogant intention of conceptually knowing everything. But what precisely does the skeptic know? Why is he so smug in the awareness of his superiority, as though he had stumbled upon something, had seen something with his own eyes, about which others can only construct inadequate theories and hypotheses? He has come to "know" the unknowableness which is immanently present in being itself. He has come to "know" it through experience and thus sees what the dogmatic philosopher does not want to see and cannot see: namely the transrationality, unexplainableness, and unspeakableness that form the very essence of reality. And the skeptic knows with certainty that in the face of this transrationality all human judgments and theories are absolutely inadequate. All judgments and theories touch only the surface of being, its "veil," and not the reality concealed behind it. True, this reality itself is also given to us and can be grasped by us with self-evident certainty (this is what the skeptic usually forgets to mention in his "theory"), but it is given and can be grasped precisely as the *essentially unknowable*. The wise, knowing *ignorance* that the skeptic preaches is a more profound *knowledge*.

4. Reality

The essentially unknowable as unconditioned being has yet another aspect in which its concrete makeup can be explored. Insofar as the essentially unknowable does not coincide with the conceptually knowable and insofar as it transcends all objectively conceivable being, it cannot coincide with any "perceived" being. For the "perceived" presupposes outside of itself the existence of perception itself and of the perceiver. To some degree the "perceived" is analogous to objective being as something which is present before us in some way and which we approach in an effort to grasp it with our cognitive gaze. But genuinely unconditional being must be conceived as the genuinely all-embracing unity and ground of everything else in general. There can be nothing outside of this being.

We have just seen that the basic drawback of all idealism is that it does not grasp the fact that "thought" or "consciousness" is also something that exists, i.e., that "thought" or "consciousness" also belongs to unconditional being. But if this is the case, if "thought," "knowledge," and "consciousness" also belong to being, then this judgment can be reversed, and we are obliged to emphasize that we can genuinely grasp unconditional being only insofar as we can take account in it of the elements of "thought," "knowledge," and "consciousness."

Above, in our analysis of ideal being, we came to a point where we could not be satisfied with only the "conceivable" in the sense of the *objective*, where we noticed with self-evident certainty the traces of something else in the "conceivable": namely, *thought* itself—not as a human "psychic" process but as the universal "potency" of thought. It is hardly accidental that the word "idea" has the twofold meaning of that which "is thought" or "found in thought" and that "essence," existing in itself, which is only grasped in or revealed to thought. The debate which has continued for centuries between logical realism and nominalism or conceptualism (those who are truly familiar with the history of philosophy know that this debate, which began in the time of Socrates and Plato, continues to trouble minds even to the present day), the debate whether "ideas" exist only in "thought" or "consciousness," or whether they must be recognized as a reality which exists even outside of thought, this debate originates in the fact that an "idea" simultaneously presupposes both of these alternatives, in the fact that an "idea" is a reality that stands on the threshold between "being in thought" and "being in itself." But since ideal being is an uneliminable element of unconditional being, it is not possible to orient oneself in unconditional being, to grasp it in its wholeness, if one does not take account of the potency of "thought" or "knowledge."

Conceived as a *special* reality, this element of "knowing," of the ideal "possession" of the content of being, is usually designated by the term "knowing subject"—this latter concept in some sense being identified with the concept "I." It is well known that Descartes (and St. Augustine long before him) in the truth *cogito ergo sum* apprehended the ultimate self-evidence of being precisely in this reality of the "knowing subject." The meaning of "I" (or rather the meaning of "I am") will be discussed later in another connection. The "theory of knowledge" as it evolved from Descartes' conception to German idealism and neo-Kantianism demonstrates that the identification of self-evident immediate being with the "knowing subject" and the identification of the "knowing subject" with "I" are associated with many uncertainties and difficulties. Even Descartes was forced to grapple with these difficulties and to recognize the primordial self-evident truth of God (as unconditional infinite being) as the necessary condition of the being of the limited "I." Following Descartes, German idealism and neo-Kantianism were compelled to replace "I" with the "absolute," "spirit," or "consciousness in general." Without penetrating into the depths of the problem as a whole, we shall limit ourselves to the simple affirmation that in all this the element of unconditional being was found to be present with undeniable certainty in the potency of "thought," "knowledge," or "consciousness." And this element was found to be present not in the form of "*es gibt*," "*il y a*," or "there is" (a form which, as we showed above, indicates the depths from which objective being emerges), but in the wholly other form of "givenness-to-itself" or "possession." The form of "givenness" obviously presupposes the one *to whom* something is "given" as well as the fact of "possession." Thus, unconditional being is "being for itself," for it includes not only everything that is given but also the one to whom it is given and the very relation of givenness or possession. This does not mean of course that unconditional being must be conceived as some sort of all-embracing consciousness along the lines of individual consciousness, that is, as some sort of "universal soul" or "universal I." Unconditional being contains precisely only the *potency* of thought or consciousness. And in this sense it also contains the element of "subjectivity," but one cannot determine in advance in what form and at what concrete points of being this potency will be revealed and realized. A correct understanding of the problem yields only one certain fact: unconditional being is not something that must be revealed and illuminated by something *outside* of it, for what can be outside of all-embracing, unconditional being? On the contrary, it is a being that *has itself* in such a way that it is the primordial unity of the "haver" and the "had" or the unity of being as *being-for-itself*, as the "ideal" *possession of itself*.

Before evaluating the significance of the foregoing considerations for our basic theme, let us briefly affirm that we find *the key to the solution of the problem of transcendence* precisely in the knowledge of the "haver" element of being, i.e., in the element of "subjectivity" as an inseparable, integral element of unconditional being. We showed in Chapter I that the true meaning of the relation of "transcendence" consists in the fact that our knowledge presupposes our "having" or the "presence with us" of the unknown (i.e., x) as that at which our cognitive gaze is directed and in which it discovers known contents. But we did not answer how or why this "having" or "possession" itself is possible. We now see that this "possession" has its ground in unconditional being. "I am" is not a closed, self-contained, self-sufficient, autonomous sphere of being. It is rather the *self-revelation* in us of the element of "having" or "possession," which itself belongs to unconditional being. Thus, every "I am" is immediately accompanied by "it (the being of the object) is" as the second, correlative element of being—not *my* being but total, all-embracing being. This all-embracing being is always and inseparably *with us* and *for us*, independently of the limits to what our cognitive gaze "reveals" or "illuminates" in this being at every given moment. And this is the case precisely because *we ourselves are in this being*, originate in it, are immersed in it, and are conscious of ourselves only *through its self-revelation in us*. Unconditional being—and thus the being of all that is outside of us—is present with maximal certainty and inevitability in every act of our self-awareness.

This clarification of the riddle of transcendence (developed in detail in *The Object of Knowledge*) is necessary for our basic theme only insofar as it leads to a better understanding of what we mean by unconditional being. But since most of us have the involuntary and ineradicable tendency to understand the word "being" in the sense of the being of that which "is in itself" and "independent of us," this word is little suited to designate what we have in mind. From now on we shall call this unconditional all-embracing being "reality", thus distinguishing it from "being" in the usual sense. (Later we shall see that in doing this we have not yet attained the true, most profound, genuinely all-embracing and all-grounding meaning of reality.) Only reality has the feature of *absoluteness; genuine total unity* is attained in concrete total unity, existing for itself, which not only embraces all being but also contains the latter as only one of its elements together with its self-revelation, and its givenness to itself or its cognitive possession of itself. Reality as the unity of *being* and *truth* (the unity of the being we are conscious of or experience and the very element of consciousness or life) is *immediacy* itself as the absolutely inexpressible, ineffable essence of what reality ultimately means for us. Only in this layer is all objective knowledge (and therefore all objective being) conclusively overcome, and it is overcome precisely because it is replaced here by the immediate *self-knowledge of reality revealing itself to itself.* We have now penetrated still deeper into the essence of reality as the essentially unknowable. We now see that it is not possible to affirm anything about reality not only in the aforementioned sense that it is *x itself*, which as such is always a subject and can never be a predicate, i.e., can never be expressed in a concept as the content of a judgment; moreover, reality is not only the ground of all conceptually graspable contents, a ground which is perceived beyond the limits of all abstract knowledge. The meaning of reality in its absoluteness goes still deeper. It is not possible to "affirm" or "express" anything about reality also in the sense that "affirmation" or "expression" is a completely unrealizable concept in relation to reality. It is unrealizable not only as a judgment with logically definite content but also as apprehension in general relating to something other outside itself. This reality is not "given" to us; *it is given only to itself*, and *to us* only insofar as we ourselves are this reality. This reality is not an object of perception, examination, or reflection. It "expresses" itself only mutely in silent, ineffable experience. In this sense it is analogous to the "I am" form of being, to the self-evident reality of this form of being which also, after all, *expresses itself.* However, in contradistinction to all idealism, this reality is not exhausted by the "I am" form of being but is realized or revealed only in the absolutely primordial and unspeakable unity of "am–is."

Here, all words are inevitably inappropriate. They can only hint at what one has in mind or they are only able to call men to make the attempt to catch the ineffable essence of this self-revealing reality through conscious participation in it. Here, there are neither questions nor answers, there is neither knowledge nor ignorance. The absolutely unknowable essence of reality as true all-embracing unity is revealed the way God is revealed, to those who do not seek and do not ask, for those who seek reality assume it to be far away, somewhere outside; and thus they do not find it, just as we would not find our eyes if we sought them somewhere apart from our body. The unknowable essence of reality is revealed only to those who, without seeking, simply have and experience it; to those who themselves exist in this reality and are able to keep their eyes open.

This reality is what was revealed to Indian thought as *Brahman*, as that which is known not by one who knows but by one who does not know, and which also coincides with the bottomless depths of our own inner being —with *Atman*.

But we can see that the impatient reader has for a long time had a purely practical objection. Why should we, living human beings, be concerned with this most profound and all-embracing essence of reality? Do we really have anything to do with this Indian Brahman, in which all the concrete, singular things that make up the genuine meaning and content of our lives hopelessly sink and dissolve? In reflecting upon the genuine essence of reality, we seem to have climbed to such heights of abstraction that it is impossible to breathe. We seem to have left far below us the whole concrete world of things and living creatures among whom our life passes. However natural such an objection may appear to be, however easily it may arise in our consciousness, it is *false*. It is as false as the common opinion that philosophy in general deals with "abstractions" and is removed from the concrete. Just the contrary is true: reality as it has revealed itself to us here is something of maximal *concreteness*, compared with which all else that is usually thought to be concrete is only an abstraction. And though the *general essence* of reality in this sense does to some extent touch upon the Indian concept of Brahman, it is hardly the case that this reality is present only in the experience of the detached and self-immersed reflective consciousness. Rather, it also forms the very heart of the everyday and "every-moment" experience of each of us. Let us attempt to briefly show this.

In our foregoing discussion of the concept of objective reality, we came to the conclusion that objective reality does not exhaust the entire makeup of our experience, but is only a sort of well-made, ordered "building," beyond which realities remain that are not used (like a heap of stones that lie in disarray at the construction site) in its construction; for this reason we call these latter realities "subjective." But this metaphor, fully suitable for elucidating the concept of objective reality, turns out to be utterly inadequate insofar as we attempt to completely describe with it the structure of our immediate experience. Insofar as we perceive reality in its full concreteness, i.e., insofar as it is given to us in immediate experience, it does not "split apart" into an abstractly conceivable, ordered "objective reality" and chaotic fragments of unused raw material that surround the "objective reality." Reality does not split apart into an "external world" and "subjective, inner experiences" that surround and accompany this "external world." On the contrary, this reality in all its concreteness, and not only reality as all-embracing unity but any particular content of experience as well, is immediately perceived and experienced by us as a certain *concrete fullness and organic unity*. When I delight in a beautiful landscape, feel the sun's rays, see the blue sky and the blue sea, or smell the fragrance of flowers; when I enter a room and survey, with a long, sweeping glance, the decor, the style formed by the entire combination of things which it contains and sense the "fluids" which the room has absorbed from the people who live there; when I am with another person and experience his outer appearance and inner essence along with his words and actions—in these and innumerable other instances, *immediate reality*, concretely given to me and experienced by me, is not *objective* reality, is not an *objective* being external to me, but is the *integral* unity of consciousness and what we are conscious of, the unity of experience and the content of experience. This immediate reality—in relation to a limited, particular segment of being— is that same ineffable reality (whose general essence we described above) which reveals itself to itself and is conscious of itself. In this sense, reality simply coincides with *life* in the fullest and most concrete sense of this word. However, it coincides not with *my life* (which I oppose to something other, to something external in general) but with *life in general*, of which I too am a part; it coincides with universal life in its given particular segment. The sight of the starry sky, its enigmatically intricate pattern of glittering and twinkling points, the mysterious silence of the dark cosmic abysses, the awe which fills me when I feel my loneliness beneath this sky and my kinship with it, all this, taken together as an indivisible unity, is a reality *to a greater degree* than the objective reality presented to me in astronomical theory (which, at least in its details, is questionable).

In essence we always live simultaneously in two planes: in the plane of orientation in "objective reality" as that part of reality (a part which always remains indefinite in its size) which we abstractly delineate and rationally express in concepts; and in the plane of immediate reality in its all-embracing and all-permeating concrete fullness. "Objective reality" is that which is *knowable* in reality (though in its makeup, too, we encounter the element of the essentially unknowable, and this because objective reality is not a self-contained, autonomous whole, but is submerged in the dark "ocean" and, at its boundaries and in its depths, merges with the ocean). But *reality itself*, from which "objective reality" emerges, is the *essentially unknowable*, precisely because it coincides with concreteness itself. We can have reality, we can participate in it, or rather we are obliged to participate in it. And its essence as "living life" (to use Dostoevsky's marvelous term)—not being the object of thought, not being present before us as an object, but only flowing into us and flowing out of us—coincides with the essentially unknowable. It is the eternal mystery in which and by which we live. It is not distant and concealed, but what is explicitly perceived or experienced: reality revealing itself to itself but revealing itself in its eternal, essential mystery. And we have this reality. It is scarcely the case that reality reveals itself to us only at the rarefied heights of philosophical speculation, directed at all-embracing total unity, for total unity would not be total unity if it were not present as a whole in every particular point of being, even in the smallest segment of being. In this case philosophical reflection (to use Socrates' immortal metaphor) plays the modest role of a midwife who assists at the birth of verbalized forms of that which we always have ineffably in us and with us; of that which is in us and for us every moment of our lives; or, more precisely, of that which is the very *essence* of what we mean by the word "is"; or, still more precisely, of that which we mean by the ineffable unity "am–is," which is reality itself. And those who do not understand the self-evident certainty of reality in its unknowableness, those who do not understand the radical difference between *reality as such* and *objective reality* are simply born blind.

It might appear that in attaining this concept of reality in its all-embracing sense which transcends all that is usually meant by "being" we have exhausted our theme, namely the clarification of the "unknowable." But this is not the case. Having captured reality in its immediacy and concreteness as the self-revealing, experienced, and living unknowable, we stand only on the threshold of the attainment of true reality in the concrete forms of its manifestation and revelation. But before crossing this threshold, we must reflect on the *methodological* nature of what we have attained so far.

Notes

1. Translator's note: Throughout this paragraph Frank plays on four words: *chto* ("what"), *nechto* (an "indefinite something"), *chto-to* (a "definite something"), and *nichto* ("nothing").

Chapter IV

On *Wise Ignorance*
(Docta Ignorantia)

So far we have traced the unknowable in a number of spheres or forms in which it is revealed. But what does this mean and how was this possible? It would appear that by definition nothing can be affirmed or expressed about the "unknowable" except that it is unknowable. Nevertheless, in the course of our discussions, it has seemed that we have indeed come to "know" clearly the unknowable as such, have found in it a number of different aspects or elements, without it thereby ceasing to be the unknowable. And we cannot even say that we have encountered this difficulty as if by accident, due to some oversight, and were alone in encountering it. On the contrary, in this regard we share the fate of all contemplative, philosophizing mystics. All such mystics affirm about God that He is unknowable, unfathomable, ineffable, unspeakable; and then they proceed to tell us in detail about this mysterious and ineffable essence of God. It appears that there *is* a possibility of knowing and defining the unknowable *precisely as such*. But how are we to understand and clarify this possibility?

1. The Overcoming of Negation

Let us again attempt to understand what we mean by "to know." The fundamental condition of all knowledge is *differentiation*, and the tool or instrument of differentiation is *negation*. Something is known insofar as we recognize it to be a certain "this." And something is "this" because it is not "other," because it is "different" from all "other." And it is not the case that the "other" precedes "this," but that both arise simultaneously precisely through this mutual difference, through separation from each other. Furthermore, the element of "identity to oneself," the element of "remaining one and the same," which characterizes everything that is known turns out to be inextricably linked (see Chapter II) with this constitutive form of "non-otherness." "To know" means to determine, to grasp as a determination; and the form of determination has its origin in negation. The "enormous power of negation" (Hegel's phrase) consists precisely in the fact that it is the universal instrument of knowledge.

The unknowable, that which is inaccessible to knowledge, must evidently lie beyond negation. But in this case how can the unknowable be determined and known *precisely as the unknowable*?

The most immediate answer to this question is as follows. If all determination and knowledge are based on negation, this must evidently be the case here too. Only here the negation evidently must emerge and function as *negation raised to a higher power*, as *negation of negation*. For when we say that the unknowable lies *beyond* negation, that negation is *not* applicable to the unknowable, and even when we simply express the unknowable using the word "*un*-knowable," we determine what we are thinking by the element "not." But in this case this "not" is directed at "not" *itself*. The truly boundless power of negation consists in the fact that it retains its force even when it is directed at itself, at the element that constitutes it. And if the negation of some single negation (i.e., of some negated separate content, involving the summation of two negations as expressed in judgments of the type "A is not not-A") does not—in accordance with the principle of the excluded middle—lead to anything new but only completes the genuine, ultimate *positiveness* of the content which is first constituted precisely by the negation of what its negation contains (such that A is precisely that which not-A is not), then the negation of negation itself, the negation of the very element of negation—negation raised to a higher power—leads to an utterly new sphere of being.

Furthermore, the one and the other, the double negation which constitutes determination and the negation of negation itself (negation raised to a higher power), are closely linked. If in Chapter I we became convinced that determination itself originates (precisely through double negation, because it is perceived as "this and not another") from metalogical unity and is inconceivable except in relation to this unity, now we can express the same relationship in another form: The determinate as "this and not another" presupposes the categorial form of "non-otherness" (the *non aliud* in which Nicholas of Cusa apprehended the highest formative principle of knowledge and being). But this "non-otherness" is nothing else but the unknowable revealing itself to us, which we grasp and know precisely by negating negation in relation to it. It is precisely in this way that the unknowable is known as such, and the indeterminate determined precisely as the indeterminate. If everything that is determinate as such is grounded in the principle of "either–or" (*aut-aut, entweder-oder*), in the choice between "the one and the other," in the rejection of "the one" in favor of "the other," now we *negate* this "either–or" and replace it with the principle of "both the one and the other" (*sowohl-als auch*). We then have the unknowable as *all-embracing fullness*, as the infinite, in contrast to the determinate which as such is the *limited*, that which excludes all "other" from itself. In this idea of the unknowable as infinite all-embracing fullness, the unknowable appears to us not in an empty, contentless sense, about which nothing can be expressed, but in *its full positive significance*. And what seemed to us simple ignorance turns out to be a special kind of knowledge, the most profound and adequate knowledge.

Since, as we have seen, the true ground of abstract knowledge is the perception of the metalogical unity that transcends this type of knowledge, it follows that every "either–or" which forms the essence of a concept is rooted in the principle of "both the one and the other." Setting aside the popular meaning of negation, i.e., negation taken simply as the rejection of error (a meaning that has tempted many philosophers; we shall return to it later), we repeat that in its logical or objective meaning negation signifies differentiation—the perception in reality of the different and the distinct. But the differentiation between the "one" and the "other" evidently presupposes the presence of both the one and the other as well as a connection between them, and thus the higher, metalogical unity of the two. Thus, if the principle of "either–or" (the decisive and explicit affirmation of the "one" through the equally decisive negation of the "other") has universal significance for all abstract, conceptual knowledge and for all practical orientations determined by this kind of knowledge, one must nevertheless keep in mind that the healthy, reasonable, realizable meaning of the "either–or" relation presupposes a wider perspective and a vision that is spiritually more encompassing, expressed in the principle of "both the one and the other." This is not only a practical commandment, the commandment of tolerance and spiritual breadth, the commandment that we must not be intolerant even to what is alien and unacceptable to us (this is the spiritual atmosphere which must permeate every clash of ideas, so that this clash does not deteriorate into a senseless, life-destroying fanaticism). It is also a fundamental, purely theoretical, ontological truth. Thus, all negation, forming precisely the essence of the "either–or" principle, intrinsically presupposes the *negation of negation*, as a result of which the sphere of action of the principle of "both the one and the other" is revealed to us. If negation is in general the principle of determination and knowledge, we determine and know negation itself also only through negation, precisely through the negation of negation itself. *The negation of negation is the positive perception of the ground and meaning of negation.*

Since we have taken the path of the perception of the unknowable as the sphere of the negation of negation, we must follow this path to its end and bring the argument to a consistent conclusion. However, we encounter a special difficulty. First of all, the categorial form of "both the one and the other" turns out to be inadequate to the metalogical framework in which negation is overcome. The principle of "both the one and the other" presupposes the presence of both the "one" and the "other," the presence of variety. The whole or the all-embracing fullness is then a sort of sum or aggregate of all its particular contents. But reality in its metalogical essence is undeniably something wholly other than the simple aggregate of its separate, particular contents. These contents are "separate" in general only insofar as they are *already determinations*, that is, insofar as they are subordinate to the principle of definiteness and therefore to the principle of differentiation, i.e., the principle of negation. In presupposing both the "one" and the "other," the categorial form of "both the one and the other" evidently presupposes the "either–or" form (which precisely constitutes reality as the "one" and the "other") to the same degree that the latter presupposes the former. The "both-the-one-and-the-other" form and the "either–or" form simply turn out to be correlative elements which lie, as it were, on one and the same level, in one and the same plane of being. Thus, with the "both-the-one-and-the-other" form, we have not yet penetrated into the depth of being that we are seeking.

Insofar as we really strive to penetrate, through the negation of negation, into a deeper layer of being, to penetrate precisely into the metalogical unity of being, the principle of "both the one and the other" is just as useless as the principle of "either–or." This deeper layer, being primordial unity, must be something absolutely simple, inwardly one (though it is the unity of unity and diversity, and all differences between particular contents originate in this layer). In this sense the unknowable is *neither* "both the one and the other" *nor* "either–or." It is "neither–nor," or, more precisely, it is based on a third principle, namely the principle of "neither–nor." The unknowable is absolutely detached being, not all-embracing fullness but "nothing"—the "quiet desert" (*die stille Wüste* of Meister Eckhart). The unknowable is absolute unity which (even though it grounds and generates all diversity) in itself, precisely *as* pure unity, surpasses all diversity. In this sense Nicholas of Cusa is right when he says that separate determinations pertain to the Absolute *neither disjunctively* (in the form "either–or") *nor conjunctively* (in the form "both the one and the other"). The Absolute is "non-otherness" itself, *non aliud* itself, the *unspeakable*. Thus, before our eyes the unknowable is suddenly transformed. A moment ago it seemed legitimate to define the unknowable as all-embracing fullness. But now, compelled to apprehend it more profoundly through the principle of "neither–nor," we see it as *nothing*. And our knowledge of it is knowledge of some *nothing*, and in this sense our knowledge of it is pure *ignorance*. It appears that only in this form can we succeed in penetrating into the unknowable, in understanding it as the absolute precisely in its unconditional detachment.

However, we are caught again in an antinomy. On the path of the negation of negation, we somehow arrive, without noticing it, at the *affirmation of absolute negation*. In attempting to overcome all separation and the very principle of separation, we affirmed something absolutely separate, detached, isolated. All the words we used in this process—*de*-tached, *without diversity*, *nothing*, the object of *ignorance*—contain the sense of negation. It is not hard to understand how we arrived at this paradoxical conclusion. It is true that we negated negation, but what we did was precisely to *negate*. In order to overcome negation, we used negation, the very principle we wanted to overcome. And this principle took revenge. Let us admit something very obvious: the negation of negation is also a negation. It is also subsumed under the general concept of negation and thus it also contains the element of limitation or exclusion of the "other." It is precisely in *this* negation (which we call "negation raised to a higher power" not by chance) that the "enormous power of negation" is first transformed into an all-destroying force. For even if ordinary negation determines and colors all things, constituting and permeating everything that is conceivable by the element of *limitation*, this ordinary negation precisely discloses all the richness of *positive* content in all its diversity. But when we attempted to overcome negation through its negation, it grew into a monster of all-destroying, all-devouring negation. Thus, that which we sought, the positive meaning of the unknowable, was disclosed to us as *nothing*, as existent negation as it were. But if it is nothing and if it is nothing but *nothing*, it has everything else, the whole fullness of positive being, *outside of itself*. But then it is not the Absolute, not the all-embracing fullness and total unity which we sought.

This is how we are punished for our intention to overcome negation by a new negation, that is, by the power of negation itself. In other words, insofar as negation is the constitutive principle of logical or abstract knowledge, it is unsuitable, even in the form of negation of negation (negation raised to a higher power), for knowledge of the supra-logical, the transrational as such. In other words, when, negating negation, we replaced the "either–or" principle with the 'both-the-one-and-the-other" principle, we became subject to another "either–or." That is, we took a position where we had to *choose* one of these two principles (by choosing the principle of "both the one and the other" we rejected the principle of "either–or") and thus became subject to the very principle we had chosen to reject. Precisely for this reason, the principle of fullness (to the extent we attempted to grasp it in its *pure*—logically delimited, detached— essence) faded before our eyes into the principle of "neither–nor," into pure *nothing*. It appears that the "either–or" principle disclosed its truly limitless force just when we were attempting to evade it, for in our attempted evasion we were pursued by it, propelled by its force. The unknowable as the absolute was then placed in sharp opposition to the relative, was perceived only as the non-relative. This appeared to be the only possible way to conceive and determine the unknowable: that is, in accordance with the fact that all conceiving and determination are based on negation, on the rejection of all that does not belong to the given object and contradicts it. But here it was disclosed that the *concept* of the absolute—the absolute as conceptualized, as conceptually known—contradicts the very *essence* of the absolute.

How can we overcome this difficulty? Must we, by further raising the "power" of negation with regard to the absolute, *negate* the negation of negation as well in its turn, i.e., attain a sort of third power of negation, negation-cubed? At first glance this scheme might be tempting, and the fact that it is analogous to Hegel's dialectic, which culminates in synthesis in its third stage, seems to indicate that we should try it. This "negation-cubed" might appear to lead to something positive and valuable in relation to the absolute as the unknowable. In fact, the essence of the absolute would then be known in such a way that in it both the one and the other would be simultaneously retained, *both* the principle of "both the one and the other" *and* the principle of "either–or." That which appears contradictory to abstract thought—namely, the *joint action* of the principle of "both the one and the other" and the principle of "either–or" (in other words, both the principle of unity and the principle of diversity)—in this case too must evidently be affirmed through the courageous transcending of definiteness and of the law of contradiction that conditions definiteness. Hence, the unknowable as the absolute transcends the opposition between separation and connection, between reconciliation and antagonism. In itself, the unknowable is neither the one nor the other, but precisely the unknowable unity of the two. Thus, the unknowable is simultaneously detached from everything *and* embraces everything. It is *both* nothing *and* all. It is truly absolute in the indivisibly dual sense that it is that which is *not* relative and also that which has the relative *not outside* of itself but embraces and permeates it. The unknowable is the ineffable unity of unity and diversity, and not in such a way that this unity embraces the diversity from outside like something new and alien, but in such a way that it *is* and acts in the diversity itself. In this aspect the unknowable is the ineffable unity of *both* absolutely contentless (as though pointwise) unity *and* infinite all-embracing fullness—and this coincides with our perception of the essence of unconditional being (see Chapter III, 3).

All this, we repeat, may appear to be very tempting and likely at first glance. It is not difficult, however, to see that this path does not lead to our goal. If we recall the dead end we reached on the path of the negation of negation, it should not be difficult to soberly realize that the negation to the third power is also negation and thus contains all the limitation that is a necessary feature of all negation as such. This simple consideration makes it clear to us that we have been trapped in a vicious circle. If we wish to remain on this path, we would be forced to negate in turn the negation to the third power in order to overcome the limitation that it contains.

Thus, we could show that the unity of unity and diversity, of simplicity and fullness, must not be taken only as a simple, abstract unity, but must also be understood—through this new negation—as the *difference* of these two aspects. But this path must and can lead us infinitely far. We would be compelled to pass through negations of the fourth, fifth, sixth powers, etc., *ad infinitum*. And each new power of negation, however much mental effort must be expended, would have for us a graspable and intelligible meaning. For each new stage of negation would mean the correction or revocation of the limited character of the negation immediately preceding. The task of each new negation would be to remove the absolute, rational-logical function (trapped in the frame of abstract concept as it were) of the preceding negation. But this process leads to the conviction that we are trapped in a vicious circle, that all succeeding negations essentially attempt to express what we attempted to express in the first negation of negation of negation and what was to have been the genuine meaning of this attempt: namely, the overcoming of conceptual abstraction, the attainment of genuine concreteness. This series of successive negations does not enable us to escape the *limitation* that characterizes all negation as such and that constitutes the very meaning of negation.

Thus, we must direct our mental gaze back and try to clearly understand what we meant by the first negation of negation and what we attempted to accomplish by means of it. We can now say that its purpose was to eliminate only the destructive or absolutely divisive effect of ordinary negation, not to eliminate the *positive* aspect of negation. Its purpose was not to destroy the *unity of diversity* which is the source of the manifold richness of things, but to preserve and strengthen this unity. These two opposed aspects of negation, however closely they may be connected, must be clearly distinguished. Negation must not be negated insofar as we take this second negation to mean pure annihilation, the irrevocable and absolute expulsion of negation from the ranks of reality as this is expressed in the cruel principle "either–or." On the contrary, if we wish to truly overcome the "either–or" principle, we must preserve the positive ontological meaning, the positive value of negation. It is precisely the abstract conception of negation which denies its ontological meaning. According to this abstract conception (which we briefly examined above), the function of negation consists exclusively in the *rejection of what is false*, the rejection of what has no right to exist in being, of what has crept illegitimately out of our subjectivity into objective being. In sweeping this falsity out of being, negation has performed its function, and reality now contains only what is positive. Negation here is like a broom, which is used to sweep rubbish out of a room, but which, after the job is done, is not left in the room as part of the furniture. On the one hand this view attributes to negation the power of absolute annihilation. But on the other hand it considers negation to be something improper which, in its turn, is marked for annihilation.

In contrast to this view, we re-emphasize that the true meaning of negation consists in delineating *differences* in being, in perceiving the differentiated character of being as its *positive ontological structure*. What is negated is not expelled from the sphere of reality. Rather, its definite place in reality is indicated through its negative determination. Whether negation has the meaning of immediate differentiation as pure logical determination ("A is not B" in the sense of "A as such is something other than B") or the meaning of the affirmation of oppositeness, antagonism, incompatibility ("A is not B" in the sense of "A is incompatible with B" or "where A is, B cannot be"), in both cases negation determines the true place of A and B *within the limits of being* by means of differentiation (either as the simple setting of boundaries between two contents as pure determinations or as the indication of the necessary *distance* between these contents). In both cases that which is negated is not annihilated, not cast out of total being. Both simple differentiation and oppositeness or incompatibility are real, positive ontological relations or connections. Thus, "negation" or, more precisely, the "negative relation" belongs to the makeup of being itself and in this sense cannot be negated.

Here we arrive at an extremely significant conclusion which we briefly examined in our discussion of the relation between the principles of "either–or" and "both the one and the other," and which we can now formulate clearly. Insofar as negation is not simply the rejection of what is false, but is orientation in the relations of reality itself, every negation is both the affirmation of a real negative relation and the affirmation of the negated content. In capturing the true meaning of negation and thus transcending it, we affirm reality *in the form of negativeness as well*. We ascend to the universal "yes," to the total all-embracing acceptance of being, which encompasses both the negative relation and what is negated as legitimate and uneliminable reality.

This point of view is not merely the only legitimate *logical theory*. It is also the only adequate *spiritual* state, the only state which is adequate to the essence of reality as all-embracing fullness. This point of view is the perception of the compatibility of the different and the heterogeneous, of the deep harmony and reconciliation in the fullness of all-embracing unity of all that is mutually antagonistic and empirically incompatible, the perception of the relativeness of all mutual antagonism, all disharmony in being. This point of view is the necessary correction and addition to the common belief (determined by the abstract understanding of being and a practical relation to the latter) for which the negation of something is its absolute rejection ("a fight to the death") and which dreams that after the triumphant annihilation of what is rejected there will be established in the world a pure harmony, smooth and absolute, no longer soiled by the struggle between antagonistic principles.

Just as the abstract-logical theory of negation attributes to negation the significance of absolute rejection, the function of expelling false things from being, while assuming that the carrying out of this function exhausts the entire meaning of negation, so the common spiritual orientation that is in inner kinship to this theory combines unlimited ferocity directed toward the annihilation of everything that is antagonistic with naive faith in the attainability of absolute harmony, of a "kingdom of heaven on earth" after the work of annihilation is completed. But bitter life-experience teaches that the goal of such a spiritual orientation is unattainable, that the orientation itself is a false one. The most radical and ferocious annihilation cannot destroy the roots of what is unlawful, illegitimate, disharmonious in being. Reality remains reality, and the new order toward which the destroyers aspire can never be a perfect harmony, the absolute agreement of all things, but must be full of the hostility of opposites, the conflict of antagonistic principles. The logical theory and the spiritual orientation determined by the theory commit the same error: Both the theoretical clarity of differentiation (i.e., the establishment of distinct boundaries between different contents, the putting of heterogeneous things in their proper places) and the practical struggle against that which is illegitimate and has usurped a place in being that does not belong to it—both this theoretical clarity and this practical struggle are legitimate and necessary, for they are in accord with both the differentiated character of being and the univocalness of its "normal" (i.e., ontologically grounded) structure. But both the one and the other mean not the absolute annihilation of what, theoretically or practically, is negated or rejected, but rather the ordering of our knowledge of being or the ordering of being itself. Furthermore, both the one and the other must flow from an awareness that both the negative judgment and the position of struggle and mutual antagonism that correspond to the very structure of being can never disappear without a trace, to be replaced by smoothened, conclusively reconciled positiveness. Even the principle of "either–or" is legitimate only in its proper place, i.e., precisely in conjunction with the principle of "both the one and the other," or (in relation to the absoluteness of its claims) with the principle of "neither–nor." As we have made clear, negation itself cannot be negated in the absolute sense, but must be overcome in its absoluteness, with its positive meaning preserved.

Let us now return to our basic theme. The "negation of negation" was, from the outset, only a false and crude expression for what we really had in mind. It was for us only the preliminary, imperfect instrument which we employed in order to free ourselves from the confining bonds of abstract knowledge and to adumbrate the task of attaining *the absolute as the unknowable*. Our real task is not to *annihilate* negation but to *overcome* it in such a way that, having transcended it, we can apprehend its true meaning. In this true meaning, negation is preserved as a constituent element of being, but loses its sting which has limited the cognitive horizon and made us blind to that which was negated. This is the genuine overcoming of negation—an overcoming that opens our eyes to the unknowable as metalogical and transrational reality.

2. TRANSCENDENTAL THINKING

Let us now attempt to examine our problem in another aspect, which will allow us to confirm in a more general form the results we reached earlier. All thinking is judgment, the capturing of reality in logical determinations, i.e., is constituted by a certain rationalization. How then is the thinking apprehension of the unknowable as the *transrational* possible?

We answer that this is possible because thinking is directed here at the basic condition of itself, namely at the principle of rationality. This type of thinking is thereby different from objective thinking, i.e., from thinking directed at an object as at a reality already rationally formulated. Objective thinking uses rationality as its instrument but does not notice that it is using it. Without knowing it, objective thinking gives rationality the power to influence the final result of thinking and to appear in its contents. On the contrary, thinking directed at rationality itself is *transcendental*. This transcendental thinking directs its gaze at the *universal conditions of rationality* as the result of thinking; i.e., it has as its object the very *depths* from which thinking (or the possession of reality through thinking) emanates. This difference between the two types of thinking was illustrated for us in the above-examined difference between the unreflecting, "abstract" use of negation and the illumination of the very *essence* of negation.

As is well known, Kant considered the genuine task of philosophy to be the "critique of reason." If we ignore the specific characteristics that determine the content of Kant's system and consider only its methodology, what we see is the same turning (which we have just described) of the cognitive gaze from already-formed objective reality to the basic conditions that constitute and create "objectivity" itself. In particular, in his "transcendental logic," in the "categories" and "fundamental postulates," that correspond to them, Kant attempted to reveal the "a priori" of objective knowledge and of objective being that is correlative to this knowledge. We repeat that it is not our intent to discuss the special structure of Kant's system; our attempt to clarify the systematic relationship which interests us can do without such a discussion. We would simply like to emphasize two aspects in which it is necessary for us to go beyond what appears illegitimate and arbitrarily limiting in Kant's conception.

The first aspect has already been mentioned above in another connection. This aspect is the falseness or the insufficiency of idealism *qua* "subjectism." (We use this unusual term to avoid the ambiguity of the usual term "subjectivism.") Having revealed the basic conditions of objectivity in the structure of knowledge itself, Kant—on the basis of artificial, scarcely univocally convincing arguments, which in turn are based on a number of prejudiced postulates—arrives at the conclusion that these conditions of objectivity must be referred to the sphere of the knowing subject, which is conceived by Kant as being outside the sphere of reality itself. Not to mention that Kant does not avoid confusing the "subject" as a concrete knowing being (the human being who knows) with the *potency of knowledge*, it is the case that knowledge is itself a real potency, a potency that belongs to reality. Thus, thinking orientation in "knowledge" or "thinking" is, despite Kant's view, orientation in reality itself. The elements from which the objectivity of being arises or from which it is created originate not in the detached, closed, self-contained sphere of subjectivity, but in the depths of reality itself. It is not the knowing subject (the human being who knows) that creates the objective world, the objective appearance of reality. And this objective appearance is not an illusion (not even a universal and necessary one) created by human thinking. This appearance is not due to the subject's looking at the world through colored glasses, so to speak, and involuntarily painting it in the colors of his glasses. Rather, objectivity, the objective form of being, is "created" by the reality itself in which objectivity is rooted. Thus, "transcendental logic" must not be the analysis of the subjective conditions of thinking, but *the logic of being itself*. Although transcendental logic is the self-awareness of thinking, it is also the illumination of the very foundations of being. Thus, every philosophy is essentially an ontology, for outside of reality in its broadest, most all-embracing sense, there is nothing. Transcendental logic goes beyond ontology only in the narrow sense, i.e., the ontology of *objective* being, and this is the case precisely because reality embraces something much broader and deeper than only objective being. Philosophy is orientation in the infinite atmosphere of being as it were, the universal background on which objective being is delineated and the characteristics of which determine the very objectivity of this being. Philosophy can be compared to the "plein-air" school of painting, to the art of perceiving and representing not separate objects without regard to their appearance when they are immersed in air, but the "air" itself. More precisely, philosophy perceives and represents the concrete whole, in relation to which "objects" are only particular elements conditioned by this whole. As such, philosophy is not a "critique" and not an analysis of "reason" detached from reality, but rather (to use a contemporary term) "fundamental ontology" or (to use Aristotle's good, old, simple term) "the first philosophy."

Let us now consider the *second* aspect. In Kant's transcendental logic the relation of "categories" themselves to the logical forms of thinking (i.e., to the elements that constitute rationality) is unclear. In spite of the well-known "deduction" of the "table of categories" from the "forms of judgment," and in spite of the fact that such formal determinations as "unity," "diversity," "being," etc., are referred to the makeup of categories, it appears that the formal elements of thinking (e.g., "identity" and "difference") do not have any sort of inner connection to the categories that constitute "objectivity." In other words, the fundamental logical elements of rationality are untouched by transcendental logic in its Kantian form. Kant's distinction between "transcendental" logic and "formal" logic was legitimate, but his belief that it is possible to construct the former without reference to the latter was illegitimate. As for formal logic, he believed very naively that since Aristotle this type of logic "had not dared to take a step back and was not able to take a step forward."

There is no particular need to explore in greater detail the relation between logical principles and "categories" in the Kantian sense, as we must in general keep from complicating our discussion with historico-critical investigations. It suffices to re-emphasize that the principles of definiteness, and thus the principles of rationality, have fundamental significance for the makeup of objectivity. It follows that the genuine "transcending" of the objective world or (which is the same thing) the perception of the conditions of objectivity—namely, the perception of the primordial depth of reality in which and owing to which objectivity itself arises—presupposes consciousness of the principles of rationality. And since consciousness signifies the transcending of what we are conscious of, thinking in this potentiated form, forming the true essence of philosophy as the "first philosophy," is thinking that transcends rationality and draws its conclusions from the sphere of the *transrational*.

But this transcending of rationality is thinking of a wholly special kind. The expansion of the cognitive horizon which it involves does not consist simply in our spatially extending the field of our vision so to speak and seeing *before* us a new object at which our gaze must now be *directed*. On the contrary, the sphere of the transrational which is attained in this transcending can never be "given" "objectively" to thinking (though we can perceive glimmers or reflections of this sphere in objective being, as we saw in

Chapter II); and thinking cannot immediately direct itself at this sphere. For everything that is objective as such is already rationally formed; and as we have seen, the transrational as such is not objective. The same thing can be expressed in another form: The common, banal affirmation that the unknowable cannot be "known" undeniably contains a certain truth: namely, that it is not possible to grasp the unknowable as such in thinking by directing at it the cognitive gaze. This is the case because it is contradictory to attempt *to determine the transrational*. Thus, transcending is not the attainment of something transcendent, but rather consciousness of the *transcendental*; and precisely for this reason it is "transcendental thinking." Consciousness of the ground of rationality makes indirectly visible, as it were, the "atmosphere" in which rationality originates and which is itself transrational. There is no need (and it is even impossible) for us to go beyond the limits of this "atmosphere," to take a position "outside" of it, and then to direct our gaze at it and see it. On the contrary, living in it, breathing it, and constantly keeping open our mental gaze, we become convinced of its presence immanently, through experience and self-revelation; and only in this form does it become certain for us. In order to attain the absolute, the transrational, the unknowable, we must not abandon the relative, the rational, the knowable. On the contrary, the former precisely *shines through* the latter, is given immanently and together with the latter, and is accessible to us only in this form. Furthermore, this is the only form in which we can meaningfully conceive it. "Transcendental thinking" is not objective knowledge. It is immanent self-knowledge, a retrospective, logically shaped account (which we give to ourselves) of the transrational reality that is revealed to us immanently through the sphere of the rational and logical.

Something else also follows from this. Objective knowing in all its aspects is something like the opening of what has been closed; the penetration into an originally unknown, concealed depth; the solving of a riddle; the pursuit of a prey that keeps escaping us. Objective knowing is guided by curiosity. It must answer the questions: "What, strictly, is hidden here?" "What is reality like when you attain it and take off the veil that protects it?" In attempting to logically formulate this, we must repeat that objective knowledge is realized in judgment, the most general formula for which is "x is A." In x (the unknown object), a certain A is revealed, exposed; and x itself is then determined "as" A; precisely this sates our curiosity. It is precisely along these lines that all dogmatic metaphysics (rational-objective metaphysics, as we can now define it more precisely) thinks that it can guess the ultimate essence of things and satisfy our insatiable curiosity, that it can solve the ultimate and deepest mystery of being. But this is a vain and internally contradictory intention. As we saw above, *x* as such (the essentially unknowable, the transrational) cannot be solved like a riddle, for this type of solving means "rational determination"; but this determination contradicts the very essence of *x* as such. Thus, there is no judgment that can immediately touch upon *x* as such. Since the unknowable is undeniable in the sense of being "unquestionable" (*fraglos*), there is no place in it either for questions or for answers. There is no place in it for the need, governed by curiosity, to open or reveal something, to penetrate into the hidden. On the contrary, the knowledge which is attainable here is a kind of *chaste possession without desire*, achieved without effort or seeking on our part and given as a gift. It is not a prize earned but a pure gift. Here knowledge is not judgment, but pure *contemplation*. And even this contemplation is not the contemplation of something that is present before us and can be observed, but contemplation through experience. We have reality here because it is in us or we are in it, because of the immanent self-revelation of reality precisely in its unknowableness. Since all judgment and determination here is essentially impossible and inappropriate, the knowledge of the unknowable is, as such, *ignorance*. But since here the unknowable itself is revealed to us, this ignorance is precisely *wise, knowing ignorance*. The rejection, essential here, of judging, determining knowledge is not forced resignation which dooms us to cognitive poverty, to the rejection of the dream of attaining the ultimate truth we desire. Necessary intellectual *humility* which consists in the recognition that our usual cognitive aspiration (guided by curiosity and a thirst for discovery) is illegitimate and meaningless when applied to this domain—this intellectual humility gives us the only adequate, full possession of the truth. It is precisely in wise ignorance, through the overcoming of the restlessly seeking and curious knowledge which is directed at objects, that our gaze first becomes open to the perception of all the fullness and positiveness of reality. This is precisely what Goethe had in mind when he said that one should not try to look for anything *behind* phenomena, but that one should learn to be content, like children, with pure experience, for pure experience is the truth. The same sort of situation arises in our relationship with a living human being. The genuine essence of a person slips away from us insofar as we try to know him as an "object," to expose his inner essence in a set of determinations. The true mystery of a person is illuminated only in love and trust, which are alien to all "spying" and incompatible with it. And only in love and trust do we gain living knowledge of the unknowable reality that forms the essence of a person. We shall become convinced later that this is more than just an analogy.

3. WISE IGNORANCE AS ANTINOMIAN KNOWLEDGE

But this is still not sufficient to answer the questions we have posed; i.e., how can the unknowable nonetheless be known by means of philosophy, and (the same question in another form) how can the transrational be grasped in thinking, the essence of which contains rationality? On the basis of our preceding discussion, we can also formulate these questions in the following way: Since the unknowable as such is revealed only in living knowledge (life-knowledge) and since abstract knowledge, realized in judgments, is totally inapplicable to the unknowable, how then can the unknowable be known in transcendental thinking, which as thinking can also be expressed, it appears, only in judgments? On the basis of our discussion in its entirety, it is clear, first of all, that *no* thinking in general can be an immediately adequate expression of the intuitively experienced unknowable, and what we have instead is a sort of transposition of immediately self-revealing reality into another tonal dimension, which is essentially inadequate to the reality, something like the simplifying, approximate piano score of a complex symphonic work. But how is this transposition itself possible? How is it possible for thinking to immerse itself in the "atmosphere" of the transrational, to breathe in this atmosphere, and thus to orient itself in it?

First of all, let us refer to some of our earlier conclusions. Any judgment (i.e., all knowledge that consists in the predication of logically, conceptually determined content) is absolutely inadequate to the very essence of the unknowable. Furthermore, in relation to the unknowable any judgment is contradictory and meaningless in this sense. Let us attempt to express this conclusion in a general logical form: Any judgment the subject of which is the unknowable and which affirms something about the unknowable, i.e., every judgment of the form "A is B," where A is the unknowable, must be rejected. This rejection is evidently carried out in the form of the negative judgment "A (the unknowable) is *not* B." Insofar as this negative judgment does not claim to be anything other than the rejection of the false affirmation that "A is B," it appears to be utterly legitimate. Thus, for example, in theology the perception of the unknowableness of God is expressed in the rejection of all conceivable predicates that can be attributed to God. (This

type of theology is called negative theology.) But the difficulty or inconvenience associated with this is that the rejection in turn has the form of a
judgment. And every judgment claims to be knowledge; that is, it claims to
express something about reality itself. If the *immediate* meaning of the
aforementioned negative judgment consists only in the rejection of the
opposite positive judgment, this rejection can be based—in accordance
with the very essence of abstract knowledge—only on the perception of
the corresponding *real* relationship. That is, the rejection of the judgment
"A is B" is based on the perception that A *itself* as a *reality* (in this case the
unknowable itself) *is really not* B. We saw above that negation has an ontological meaning, belongs to the very essence of reality. But in the present
situation the negative judgment not only rejects the false judgment but also
affirms something about the unknowable, has the meaning of negative
predication, negative definition, in relation to the unknowable. But in this
case the negative judgment must itself be judged by the principle which it
expresses and on the basis of which it arose, namely the principle that any
judgment about the unknowable, the predication of any logically definite
content in relation to the unknowable, whether in positive or negative
form, is internally contradictory and impossible.

The affirmation "A (the unknowable) is not B," taken as a full-fledged
judgment, evidently presupposes the principle of contradiction: "A either
is B or is not B" (more precisely, "A is either B or not-B"). But we
already know that the "either–or" principle does not hold in relation
to the unknowable as the absolute. We approach the essence of the unknowable only by overcoming this principle: first, through the principle of
"both the one and the other"; secondly (and more intimately) through the
principle of "neither–nor"; and finally and most adequately, through the
merging of these latter two principles, through the overcoming of negation. Thus, insofar as we take the statement "A is not B" to mean a negative judgment about the unknowable itself, it is as false and contradictory
as the correlative positive judgment. The only thing that can be expressed
about the unknowable is that on the one hand it is *both* B *and* not-B and that
on the other hand it is *neither* B *nor* not-B. Dionysius the Areopagite writes
about this in Part I, Chapter II of his *Mystical Theology*: "In the first cause of
being one must affirm everything that is affirmed anywhere in what exists
and attributed to it as a quality, for the first cause is the cause of all this. But
all this must also be negated in the first cause, for it transcends all this. But
do not think that here negations contradict affirmations, for the first cause,
transcending all limitations, surpasses all affirmations and negations."

But we have seen that this negation of negation is in essence infinite and never leads to the goal that is sought. This is precisely the basis of the perception that the unknowable as such can be grasped in *no judgment*. Insofar as it is necessary for us that knowledge of the unknowable be realized in judgment (for we cannot *think* in any other way) or, more precisely, that the unknowable be represented in the plane of judgment, this is possible only in one form: in the affirmation of the ineffable and unknowable but self-evident *unity of the positive judgment and the negative judgment*, this unity transcending (as we indicated above) both the principle of "both the one and the other" and the principle of "neither–nor" as well as all possible combinations of these logical forms of conceptual connection. The representation of the immediate perception of the unknowable as self-revealing transrational reality in the dimension of *judgment* (i.e., *thinking*) is therefore realized through the perception of an absolutely unresolvable *antinomism* in the essence of the unknowable, an antinomism that cannot be overcome by any new or higher concepts. There can be no adequate expression of this knowledge in the form of judgment. But if one takes into account the fact that the ontological meaning of all judgments (positive and negative) consists in the affirmation of a logically graspable relationship of things, in the perception of something positive, one must then arrive at the conviction that the form of expression of this transrational unity which best suits abstract knowledge is the dual affirmation involving both the *positive* and *negative* relations. This form is the form of *antinomism*.

Thus, we arrive at the conclusion that thinking, precisely as transcendental thinking which becomes conscious of the conditions of rationality, can capture the *image* of the unknowable in the form of *antinomian knowledge*, though this thinking is never adequate to the unknowable itself. Precisely this form of knowledge is the form of wise, knowing ignorance. The element of *ignorance* is expressed in the antinomian content of the affirmation, and the element of *knowing* is expressed in the fact that this knowledge is nonetheless in the form of *judgment*, namely the form of two mutually contradictory judgments. Here one must withstand the natural temptation (which from the point of view of abstract knowledge seems to be forcibly imposed on us, given to us with full certainty) to express these two mutually contradictory judgments in the logical form of a conjunctive judgment in accordance with the principle of "both the one and the other." For this again would be an expression of the pretension that transrational truth can be adequately expressed in a logically fixed form. Antinomian knowledge as such is expressed only in the "hovering"—which cannot be overcome or transcended by anything—*between* or *above* these two logically unconnected and unconnectable judgments. Transrational truth lies precisely in the inexpressible *middle*, in the unspeakable unity between these two judgments, and not in any connection between them that allows logical determination.

Transrational truth is the unknowable, logically inexpressible unity of knowings which are absolutely incompatible and unharmonized in the sphere of abstract-logical synthesis. From the point of view of the claims of abstract thinking, this means that we consciously humble ourselves, give ourselves to resignation. Our thinking rejects all logical synthesis in which it could be liberated from the unstable "hovering" between "thesis" and "antithesis." Abstract knowledge, which is habitual for us, views this demand for humility as cruel and unbearable, for consistency and transparent logical connection are absolutely necessary postulates of abstract knowledge, and any contradiction is a defect of knowledge, an unclarity of thinking. But this is the essence of the fundamental difference between knowledge of the transcendent, the absolute, the unknowable, and all knowledge of the particular contents of being. In the latter type of knowledge, the oscillation between two mutually contradictory judgments is only an expression of our impotence, for "in reality," in the nature of things we see the triumph of "either the one or the other" and do not have the right to reject the demand that we overcome or exclude contradiction. On the other hand, in the sphere of wise, knowing ignorance our "resignation" is completely *conscious* and is founded on the perception of its inner persuasiveness and legitimacy. And it is not a question of impotent oscillation or vacillation, but rather of *free hovering*, founded on firm decision and self-evident perception, in the middle or in the unity of two knowings. And ultimate truth is revealed precisely to this "hovering." Furthermore, this transrational position is completely stable and is rooted in the very ground of reality, though it is a "hovering" between or above mutually contradictory abstract knowledges. About it Nicholas of Cusa says that "it is a great thing to be firmly rooted in the unity of opposites" (*Magnum est posse se stabiliter figere in coniunctione oppositorum*).

We must underscore this conclusion with especial force. *Every ultimate synthesis that fully captures reality and is adequate to reality can never be rational but is always transrational.* This is not only a synthesis of which we have obscure intuitions and about which we can make obscure conjectures. It is also a synthesis that possesses the highest degree of self-evident certainty. But this certainty is absolutely inexpressible in word and thought. The synthesis remains unspeakable and is attainable only through a sort of mute contact, through a sort of *ineffable inner possession by it*. And this is not a draw-back but a great advantage. *We* cannot speak of ultimate truth and express it in our concepts, but this is only because ultimate truth *itself* speaks, word-lessly, for itself and of itself, expresses and reveals itself. And we have neither the right nor the possibility to fully express through our thinking this self-revelation of ultimate truth. We must be silent before the magnif-icence of truth itself.

This is the final result of philosophical self-awareness, outside of which philosophy is a vain endeavor, unrealizable in its arrogance. In its initial intention, philosophy (whether in its phylogenetic development in the his-tory of human thought as a whole or in its ontogenetic development as an embryo in every human consciousness that is filled with the passion of philosophizing) is an attempt to adequately express in a coherent system of concepts all of being without remainder. But as soon as philosophy attains an awareness of itself, a clear perception of its significance in relation to reality (historically, this perception was attained with full distinctness by Socrates, but essentially it was already possessed by his astonishingly wise predecessor, Heraclitus; it is also evident in the wisdom of the Upani-shads), it learns with self-evident certainty that its original intention is unattainable. But it is precisely in this knowledge of failure that *the genuine intention and the genuine high calling of philosophy are first attained*. For only in this way does philosophy lead human thought to its highest and ultimate desti-nation: the state of wise, knowing ignorance, the ignorance that is the highest and fully adequate knowledge. For the awareness that the deepest *thought* precisely *as thought* has its immanent ultimate boundary, only beyond which living, full-fledged reality is revealed to us—this *thought that overcomes all thought*, for it is based on the perception of what transcends thought—is precisely the ultimate and only adequate achievement of hu-man thought. This is the eternal meaning of Socratic "irony," manifested in the smile of pity at the error that lurks in *all* human thought insofar as it claims to be absolute truth and in the loving tolerance with which this error is exposed. In the face of Socrates' irony all the proud structures of philosophical systems that consider themselves to be absolute truth topple like houses of cards. The only true philosophy that deserves the name is the *philosophical overcoming of all rational philosophy*.

What we have just clarified—namely the simultaneous antinomian va-lidity, in relation to the unknowable, of mutually contradictory judg-ments—is but another aspect of what we had clarified earlier; namely, the necessity, in relation to the unknowable, of not negating negation in the usual logical sense, but of overcoming it—by becoming conscious of its essence—in such a way as to preserve it in its proper place in being. Insofar as negation is differentiation, separation, while the negation of negation is "non-otherness" as simple, undivided, undifferentiated unity, we can say that the metalogical overcoming of negation, which is the rejection of both terms of this alternative, leads to the unity of *separation* and *undivided wholeness* (or *mutual penetration*). And it is precisely in the form of this unity that we must perceive the content of the antinomian, "hovering" knowledge of the unknowable. If we use A to designate some concretely apprehended content of transrational reality and B to designate another content correlative to the first, then A is not B, is in this sense separated from B by the boundary "not," but it is not isolated, for the negative relation in its transrational significance is also a positive connection. On the other hand these two separate contents coincide, for in the sphere of antinomian knowledge the judgment "A is not B" is opposed by the equally legitimate judgment "A is B." The only way we can express this is to say that A and B are bonded together or have a relation of *mutual penetration* to each other. The separate which as such forms a *duality* is also *one*. Further, it is not a question of the rationally knowable and in this sense self-evident dual—unity of the two terms of the relation but rather of their genuine mutual penetration, which is expressed in "non-otherness."

"The great miracle is that out of one God made two, and that nevertheless these two remain one" (Jacob Boehme).

With this we arrive at a conclusion of the greatest significance; namely, that the only adequate ontological framework for wise ignorance, insofar as it is expressed in antinomian knowledge, is *antinomian monodualism*. It does not matter what logically graspable opposites we have in mind: unity and diversity, spirit and flesh, life and death, eternity and time, good and evil, Creator and creation. In the final analysis, in all these cases the logically separate, based on mutual negation, is inwardly united, mutually permeating; in all these cases the one is *not* the other but it also *is* the other; and only with, in, and through the other is it what it genuinely is in its ultimate depth and fullness. This makes up the antinomian monodualism of everything that exists; and in the face of this monodualism every monism and every dualism are false, simplifying, distorting abstractions, which are not able to express the concrete fullness and concrete structure of reality.

But insofar as we have the right to understand as a special higher principle (after all we have said it is hardly necessary to mention that this "specialness" is not an ordinary, i.e., logical, "otherness") the transrational

unity of unity and duality, identity and difference, indivisible wholeness
and separateness, this antinomian monodualism acquires for us the character of a *triadism* or *trinity* of reality. This contains the most profound and
general reason why human thought constantly arrives—in its most diverse
religious and philosophical expressions—at the idea of trinity as the expression of the ultimate mystery of being. But in this trinity (we repeat that
here we are completely opposed to Hegel's philosophy) the third or highest
stage, "synthesis," is absolutely transrational, expressible neither in judgments nor concepts, and is, so to say, the very embodiment of the unknowable. The *positive meaning*, the *positive essence*, of this synthesis is accessible to
us not in its fixed determination but only in the free *hovering* above contradiction and opposition, i.e., above antinomian monodualism—in hovering
that reveals to us the horizons of transrational unity.

The concrete manifestations of this fundamental ontological principle
of transrational antinomian monodualism will become clear to us in the
course of our further discussion.

Part II

The Unknowable as Self-revealing Reality

*Prius sibi ipse homo reddendus est,
ut illic quasi gradu facto inde
surgat atque attollatur ad Deum.*

St. Augustine

Chapter V

The Unknowable as Immediate Self-being

After the methodological discussion to which the preceding chapter was devoted, we now return, enriched, to the essence of our problem. In the final analysis we came to know the unknowable as an absolute reality which consists of the unity "is–am"—the unity of being as such with the element *for* which being is or the element which *has* being. As such a unity, unknowable reality is a *reality that reveals itself to itself.* If not for the fundamental fact that the unknowable itself, precisely in its unknowableness, reveals itself to itself and thus to us insofar as we participate in it, the unknowable would be absolutely unattainable and unfathomable for us in the sense that we could know nothing at all about it, could not even notice its presence. As we have mentioned, this does not mean that reality is something like a "world soul" or "absolute spirit." On the contrary, we have retained the right and obligation to more precisely define how this *being-for-itself* of the unknowable, the self-revelation of the unknowable to itself, is realized.

Without for the present commencing a systematic study of this question, let us note first of all that there is a form of being which discloses to us what we mean by the self-revelation of the unknowable (which we have attained through great effort and by a difficult path of increasingly more profound reflections on the essence of reality and its absoluteness) with the self-evident certainty of a fact of everyday experience. This is the form of being we usually call "inner": the being of the "soul" or "psychic" being. But henceforth, so as to avoid the traditional associations of such terms as "soul" and "psychic," we shall call this form of being "immediate being-for-itself" or, even less definitely, "immediate self-being" (in German this is *unmittelbares Selbstsein*).

1. Immediate Self-being as Being that Reveals Itself to Itself

The sphere or form of being that is given to us in immediate self-being lies beyond the limits of all objective being. Further, in a sense we have yet to clarify, this sphere lies beyond the limits of *reality*, at least in the sense we have discussed. On the path of our investigation, on which we appeared to have attained reality in its fullness as the unity of *all in general*, we somehow passed by the sphere of immediate self-being, without noticing it. And we did not notice it precisely because it is what is closest to us or, more precisely, because it coincides with ourselves and therefore is so little known to us and often goes unnoticed.

Why is it that we usually do not notice immediate self-being in the *form of being* that is characteristic of it and in which it is immediately manifest? Our consciousness is so full of objective being, so chained to the latter, that it tends to perceive everything that is revealed to it as a component of the objective world. This tendency is met half-way, so to speak, by immediate self-being itself: immediate self-being has a natural form of manifestation or revelation (which is immediately apparent) in the objective world. This is precisely the form of "inner" being which we designate as "psychic" being or the being of the "soul" in contrast to the outer spatial-physical world and also in contrast to all "ideal being." As *this* type of being, immediate self-being is of course well-known not only to the philosophizing consciousness but also to every man. Such realities as good or bad moods, feelings, desires, dreams, and so on, clearly differ from "outer" being. In contrast to the latter, "psychic" being appears to be "inner" because it stands in opposition to what is "outer" (i.e., spatial being) and because it appears to be located somewhere "inside," apparently somewhere "inside" the human body, though it is usually not noticed that these two determinations—nonspatiality and location inside the body—are essentially incompatible. The definition of psychic being as inner being does not remove it from the objective world but rather locates it within the latter. This definition makes psychic being a small, relatively insignificant, subordinate part of the objective world. The naive mind, insofar as it philosophizes, is inclined to have a materialistic or naturalistic point of view (in the most general sense of these concepts). For the naive mind, the visible and palpable (i.e., material) world always seems to be more primary and substantial, something massive and fundamental which is the ground and common background of everything else. From this point of view, "psychic" being presupposes as its ground all of organic and inorganic nature and is manifested only in animal life and particularly in the life of the human body. Moreover, it appears to be manifested as a sort of "appendage" or (to use a current technical term) an "epiphenomenon" of the body. The total, all-sided conditioning of psychic being by physical and physiological being is immediately apparent. A blow to the head strong enough to fracture the skull or the injection of one drop of cyanide into the body can destroy the richest psychic life. A simple flow of blood away from the brain causes faintness and thus an interruption of psychic life. Physical states and processes of all sorts exert a powerful influence on our psychic life. There appears to be nothing more powerless, insignificant, fragile than psychic life. Against the background of physical being, psychic life appears to be a sort of glowing ember, which under certain conditions flares up and is blown by every gust of wind only to be blown out in the end. It appears to be an insignificant, subordinate detail: a weak and fragile plant, growing in the soil of physical nature.

Many philosophers too consider objective being (though with an expanded composition) to be the common and all-embracing ground of all that exists. For, as we learned above, everything that is *conceivable* is an object or an objective content; and it would appear that nothing can be accessible to us outside of the form of conceivableness. From this point of view (quite widespread in philosophical circles and even among thinkers who have passed through the school of Kantian criticism), "philosophy" is nothing but the study of the most general qualities and relations of objective being, for "being" is considered to coincide with objective being. From this point of view, "inner" or "psychic" being appears to be (even if in a more refined or complex form) a part of objective being and is studied precisely in this form of its manifestation. Further, this point of view does not even suspect that philosophy in general, and thus knowledge of the genuine essence of so-called psychic being precisely as immediate self-being, begin only where we go beyond the objective.

Compared to this point of view, even the ordinary, unreflecting self-awareness turns out to be richer and more adequate. If in its first attempt at philosophical reflection the ordinary, everyday consciousness is almost inevitably trapped in a naturalistic scheme, nevertheless every man in his immediate self-awareness, outside of all philosophical reflection, has the feeling or experience of immediate "inner" being as something which belongs to a sphere wholly other than all "objective" reality. This is the sphere of inner, psychic life—not as it appears from outside to dispassionate observation and interpretation but as it is immediately revealed from within through experience. Then the whole boundless objective world appears to be something that has meaning and significance only in relation to this hidden inner world, which is the only true center of being, the only genuine being-in-itself. Thus, the objective world is that from which our inner world draws its material, that to which it must adapt itself, or that which it must overcome as an obstacle. Every man lives alternately in two worlds so to speak: in a "public" objective world, common to all, visible to all, in which his own being is only a small, insignificant, subordinate part of reality; and in an "intimate" inner world, invisible from outside, of dreams, joys, suffering, and desires, in the world of everything that makes up the true essence of human life, its true center, and in comparison to which the objective world—visible to all and accepted by all as if intended for universal "consumption"—has only derivative, utilitarian, purely relative value. Poets and novelists describe this intimate, inner life precisely in its essence as it reveals itself immediately in experience prior to all interpretation. But it is astonishing how rarely people fully take account of their distinctive inner being, that is, know it distinctly as a genuine, immediate *reality*. Compared with objective being, which often wholly embraces our consciousness and appears to us as the only genuine, grounded, stable, inexorably "objective" being there is, the inner world appears to us as the sphere of the "subjective," the sphere of everything that is unreal and imaginary, the sphere of dreams and illusions: in other words, the opposite of true being or "objectivity." We shall see later that there is some truth in this point of view, but that it is perversely grounded or interpreted. Let us make one preliminary comment: a special spiritual concentration is necessary in order to see the true nature of this fleeting, amorphous, dreamlike being, to see it precisely as a kind of *being*, a *reality* that is immediately revealed and thus inaccessible to negation and doubt. To cite the subtle German philosopher Lotze: "the soul" *is* just "what it passes itself off as."

Philosophical reflection—insofar as it takes account of this duality between the outer, objective world, accessible to us through objective knowledge and thinking, and the inner world, revealing itself immediately to itself from within—has tended, at least since Descartes, to interpret this inner being as "subjective" being, as the being of the knowing subject, the being of the one who (or that which) is directed at the objective world and is the carrier or the starting point of knowledge. Thus, inner being is compressed into a single point, as it were, into a pure, contentless "knowing subject." Everything that makes up the diverse living content of this inner world appears as something that is "given" to the inner gaze; and this "given" is usually interpreted to mean "objectively given." Insofar as the content of being is identified with the content of objective being, beyond the limits of the latter there remains only the pure "knowing subject," beyond the limits of known contents there remains only knowing itself— the cognitive gaze directed at existent contents, a contentless point of being the essence of which is exhausted precisely by the fact that it is the starting point of knowing, or the unknown "someone" correlative to the act of knowing and the content of knowledge. Descartes' view that immediately and primordially certain being is contained only in the knowing or "thinking" consciousness, in *cogito*, and that this *cogito* exhausts all of *sum*, is a view that has not yet been overcome, in principle and in essence, with full clarity in the philosophical literature. This view is essentially a profound, fatal error that has done immeasurable harm not only in the theoretical self-awareness of philosophy but also (in the form of "intellectualism") in the overall spiritual life of European man.

True, it is completely undeniable that the enigmatic sphere of inner being is *also* the point from which the cognitive gaze is directed at the objective world. In other words, the one who (or that which) is immediate self-being for himself (or itself) is also the one who (or that which) knows everything else—the one for whom (or that for which) objective being is revealed in knowing. This is not a coincidence of course, but an expression of a profound relation in being: the self-revelation of reality as total unity occurs in the sphere of immediate self-being, and this is evidently due to an inner kinship between total unity and immediate self-being. Nevertheless the "knowing subject" is in some sense precisely a *point* that lies *inside* immediate self-being. The function of knowing is associated with immediate self-being, occurs within it or emanates from it. But this "point" does not exhaust inner being and does not coincide with it. If we take the knower as an aggregate concrete reality which performs the function of knowing or from which knowing emanates, then on the one hand this reality is not an abstract contentless point but something very complex and rich with content; and on the other hand this reality is one whose form or character of being does not have knowing as its essential defining feature.

Insofar as we use the word "I" to designate the inner character of immediate self-being (we shall see later to what extent this designation is legitimate), it is necessary to emphasize that the use of the same "I" to designate the knowing subject is wholly inappropriate. Conceived as the knowing subject, an abstract point—the starting point of the cognitive gaze—cannot coincide with any fully concrete, real "I." Cognitive intentionality is a universal feature of all "consciousnesses" in general. Taken as "pure thought," this intentionality is something of utmost impersonality in personal being. Furthermore, taken in its pure essence, it is not exhausted by its presence in a multitude of concrete consciousnesses but appears to us as some *one* all-embracing entity—"consciousness in general," "logos," the "cognitive light." When human life is wholly immersed in pure thought and consciousness, is dissolved in it, so to speak, personality is then extinguished and seems no longer to exist, as is the case in the typical spiritual orientation of Indian philosophy. The pure "ego," as it is conceived in Descartes' "*cogito ergo sum*," has nothing in common with living human personality, with individual inner life. If we attempt to locate the process of knowing in the makeup of living personal being, we shall find that this process is adequately expressed only by the dative grammatical construction of such expressions as "knowledge is given *to* me, and "it is revealed *to* me," while the expression "I know" is wholly inadequate. The individual psychic life can only *aspire* to knowledge and make an *effort* to know. The very act of *realized knowing*, however, is a pure *gift*, received by the individual from outside: the act of the communion of the individual with light existing outside the individual.

Even the attempt to understand the sphere of inner being or immediate self-being as "consciousness" does not lead to the desired goal, because of the many meanings of the word "consciousness." "Consciousness" has a precisely defined meaning only if we understand it as the ideal "possession" of something which as "possessed" is distinct from the act of possession, i.e., if we understand it as intentionality, the directedness at a reality which "is present before us." Even though this "possession" or directedness precedes cognition in time and in essence, it is, like cognition, an "objective" framework, a framework for which the "possessed" is an object. It is not important whether the gaze is directed at some "outer" (i.e., "physical" or objectively "ideal") being or at man's inner being. For precisely beneath this gaze everything that is "inner" is transformed into the "outer," into something that "is present before us." The undeniable fact that immediate self-being contains the "unconscious" or "subconscious" is evidence that immediate self-being as such coincides neither with what is "known" nor with what is "possessed" or with what we are "conscious" of. Even more significantly, immediate self-being does not even coincide with the process or state of "possession." Everything we have just said about the fact that the knowing subject does not coincide with immediate self-being also holds with regard to the concept of "consciousness" as "possession" or "directedness." On the contrary, what is essential for immediate self-being as such is precisely the absence in it of the difference, the opposition, between the "possessor" (or "possession") and the "possessed," the difference between "subject" and "object." For it is evident that immediate self-being as such (i.e., precisely in its immediacy) coincides neither with the secondary, purely intellectual framework of "self-observation," "inward perception," "psychological knowledge," "self-analysis," "self-knowledge," nor even with that particularly intensified psychic framework which can be called "self-consciousness," characterized by the heightened and clear consciousness of one's "selfhood," one's "I." Immediate self-being precedes all these frameworks, which are derivative in relation to it. These frameworks can be realized or even conceived only if immediate self-being is present as such in the primordiality of its elementary essence. In whatever form we consider "consciousness," it contains the element of reflection, bifurcation, the directedness of something at something *other*; that is, it presupposes as its ground something more primary and immediate.

Therefore, if we wish to grasp adequately the essential character of this form or domain of being, we must say that it is a sphere in which "being" and "possession" (and thus the object of possession and the possessor) coincide, i.e., are not present as separate elements but dissolve in immediate and inseparable unity. True, we could have called this form of being a "consciousness," namely, consciousness as an *inner state* in contradistinction to the intentional–objective consciousness. But not to mention the inconvenience and drawback of employing a word with a firmly established traditional meaning in a new sense, and not to mention the fact that the significance of the "unconscious" or "subconscious" in immediate self-being would not be properly taken into account, we must affirm that the word "consciousness" (even in the sense of some "inner state") notes and emphasizes not the full concrete reality of immediate self-being but only *one* of its aspects. For immediate self-being is first and foremost a kind of *being*. True, it is a form of being to whose essence belongs the fact that it "has" itself (more or less clearly), but—along with this element of possession and inseparably from it—it is also a reality that "is that which it has." In other words, the essence of immediate self-being is not exhausted by the fact that it is a self-illuminating *light*. It is also the *darkness* that is illuminated by this light, and we can even say that the root or primordial source of this light is the darkness. Precisely as pure being (being as such), immediate self-being is a darkness, though the element of light and "illuminatedness" is also a necessary part, if often only to a minimal degree, of the essence of this being. Therefore it is inappropriate to identify immediate self-being as such, in the fullness of its concrete reality, with "consciousness" even in the modified and refined sense of this word. More appropriate is the word "life" in the most primordial sense of being as immediate experience of itself, as the unity of "experience" and the "experienced." Only one thing is of essence: we must grasp and understand immediate self-being as *being-for-itself*, as *being revealing itself to itself*, or existing in the form of *self-revelation to itself*.

Here a question arises: *What* reality is revealed to us in immediate self-being? In attempting to answer this question it is necessary to remember one thing: All qualitatively determined or determinable contents of immediate self-being are always only something that is encountered or occurs in this being, only something that this being carries or embodies, but not something that forms the essence of this being. In its essence, immediate self-being is not "content" (or the "contained") but the "container." It is not a *domain* of being that can be defined in terms of its qualitative content (as such, i.e., as psychic being, it is manifested only in its projection in the objective world) but precisely a *kind, mode*, or *form* of being, and thus a form of *being*, of *reality* as such. But all the words we use to define being as such and to define the various forms or modes of being can at best only be symbolic indications of what we mean, for all human words originally have an objective meaning, express conceptual content, and thus are necessarily inadequate to the *form* of being under consideration, which as a form of *being* cannot be covered by any logically fixed, conceptual content.

Nevertheless, in spite of all its inexpressibleness, this form of being is something wholly explicit and evident once we have succeeded in inwardly perceiving and grasping it. Immediate self-being is simply being as it is immediately revealed to us (and ultimately *to itself*): *being in the form of immediacy*. But we have seen above that being as the transdefinite and transfinite, as the ineffable unity of "eminent" *nothing* and all-embracing fullness, coincides with the transrational, with what was disclosed to us as the essentially unknowable. Thus, in immediate self-being we have *the unknowable in its immediacy*, for it reveals itself without the aid of clarifying thought. What we attained in the first part of our investigation by a concentrated effort of thought now simply reveals itself to us. Furthermore, we would never have attained it through thought in the first place if we did not have it in this form prior to and independently of all thought. Here we *have* the unknowable in the sense that we *are* the unknowable.

But this means that precisely the clearest knowledge of what we are discussing here leads to knowledge of its unknowableness. Only wise, *knowing ignorance*, conscious and distinct *seeing* of the unknowable as such is adequate to what we are discussing. All "psychology" which really *sees* its object and really takes account of its peculiar character must be "negative psychology" (by analogy to negative theology), i.e., it must be conscious of the fact that the essence of its object is expressed precisely in the inadequacy of all qualitative definitions, in "that which it is" ("not this and not this," as it is said about the Absolute in the Upanishads). Everything that psychology reveals as positive definitions and connections in the makeup of psychic being refers not to the character of psychic *being* itself but only to phenomena associated with and manifested in it. All these revelations of psychology would not only be useless but would lead to wholly false conclusions, distorting reality, if they were not accompanied by the awareness that, behind all these phenomena, immediate self-being itself as the unknowable is present—not as the passive and indifferent background of these phenomena but as a concrete, full-fledged, determining active force.

But knowledge of immediate self-being is more than wise ignorance, more than a perception of the genuine, precisely unknowable essence of being. Since the subject coincides here with the object or, more precisely, since neither the subject nor the object exists here (they are only introduced later by secondary reflection and verbal expression), wise knowing ignorance is also *ignorant knowing*. As experience and the self-revelation of being as the unknowable, it is *ignorance* which derives *knowing* out of itself, out of the depths of the unknowable with which it coincides.

There is only one verbal expression that is adequate to this ignorant knowing, for this expression represents the form of immediate self-being in contradistinction to all being that we objectively possess. This expression is "I am" or, more precisely (for that which is designated by the word "I" is still problematic for us), the simple word "am" (whose grammatical form already self-evidently implies the element "I"). *Immediate self-being is the am-form (Bin-form) of being.* This is the best expression of the form of being as the self-revelation of being to itself, the form which makes up the essence of immediate self-being. The "am-element" which we encountered previously (after a long and difficult search) as an element in the makeup of the unknowable reveals itself here with the complete immediacy and self-evidence of indivisibly continuous experience.

2. IMMEDIATE SELF-BEING AS THE DUAL-UNITY OF
IMMEDIATE BEING AND SELFHOOD

If the "am-form" of immediate self-being is the form of the being and revelation of the unknowable, a question arises: Are we really speaking about the same unknowable that was disclosed to us in metalogical unity and unconditional being in its total unity? In accordance with the considerations developed in our previous discussion, it would appear that there can be only *one* unknowable: the unknowable *as such*. But in stating that immediate self-being simply coincides with the unknowable as such, we appear to affirm, in a two-fold relation, a risky and unfounded proposition: on the one hand we appear to affirm that the essence or content of inner human being is equivalent to reality as such in all its absoluteness; and on the other hand, we appear to affirm that the total reality of being must be understood and interpreted in the spirit of a kind of "panpsychism."

This doubt can be adequately clarified only on the basis of a result achieved in our discussion of the logical character of the unknowable and reality as such. Specifically, let us recall that the categorial relation "either–or," which lies at the base of our doubt or question, has in general no validity with regard to the unknowable. In other words, the unknowable in its transdefinite and transfinite (i.e., transrational) essence lies *outside* the categories of *identity* and *otherness*, and is expressible only in the antinomian unity of both the one and the other of these categories. Thus, the question we raised above does not admit one definite answer. On the contrary, we must affirm that immediate being is *both* the *same* thing as the unknowable in the sense of absolute reality and something *other* as well. Or that it is *neither* the same thing *nor* something other. On the one hand it follows from the essence of the unknowable as such that it cannot be conceived as plural but only as *singular*. In this respect everything that exists is, without exception, a participant in *being as such*, its manifestation or concrete expression. In this sense immediate self-being too is precisely nothing other than simply *being itself*, i.e., the unknowable itself in its immediacy, in its self-revelation. Those who have not yet become convinced of this, those who still cling to the notion of the psychic sphere as nothing more than a component of objective being and do not see a deeper reality beneath it, cannot be convinced.

Furthermore, it follows from the transdefinite and transfinite essence of the unknowable as absolute reality that the unknowable is *never one and the same*, i.e., something unchangeably identical to itself. On the contrary, the unknowable transcends all identity, and thus at every moment and in its every concrete manifestation it is something absolutely new, unique, unrepeatable. An essential conclusion which follows from this is that there can exist different *modal* forms of being, different means or degrees of the self-revelation and self-realization of being. Thus, the "am-form"(the form of being of immediate being) is one of the various modalities of being (modalities which we shall consider later). In this sense the "am-form" is something other than the unknowable as absolute total unity; or it is the same unknowable but in another mode. Here we have our first concrete example of antinomian monodualism, which we discussed in our examination of methodology: a primordial unity manifests itself in a duality of otherness without ceasing to be itself, i.e., a unity. In the face of this antinomian transrationality of being, it is just as erroneous to absolutize human "inner being"(as Fichte did, for example, when he identified "I" with the "absolute") as to conceive human being as *unconditionally* opposed to the absolute (as we do, for example, when we subsume this being under the concept of "creature"). The only adequate formulation here is as follows: man in his inner essence, in his immediate self-being, is *neither* absolute reality as such *nor* something unconditionally (in the logical sense) other. Or (what is the same thing) he both *is* and *is not* absolute reality. Here the *hovering above* or *between* mutually contradictory definitions, the attainment of transrational unity between them, is the only form of thought in which the true relation is revealed to us. The unknowable as absolute reality as such is differentiated and gives birth—precisely in the "am-form" of immediate self-being—to something that opposes it. Nevertheless, both the one and the other remain in inner unity, so that in its *ultimate depth* immediate self-being does somehow coincide with absolute reality, without ceasing to be an independent form of being. Or (expressing it in a formulation we developed above) the relation between immediate self-being and absolute reality as such is conceivable only in the form of the *unity of separateness and mutual penetration*.

But now let us go beyond these general-methodological or formal-ontological considerations and explore more deeply the genuine structure of being as immediate self-being. Our verbal designation of this mode of being as "immediate self-being" already contains a certain *dual-unity*: namely the dual-unity of being as pure *immediacy* and *selfhood*.[1] Let us now attempt to describe both terms of this unity more precisely.

Immediate self-being has states or features in which its essential kinship or unity with the unknowable as undivided, undifferentiated total being stands out with complete self-evident certainty. One of these is the twilight-dreamlike state of the psychic life, when it is submerged in itself in senseless torpor, or when it passes from consciousness to complete forgetfulness in a dreamless sleep. Tyutchev describes this state with astonishing expressiveness and profundity of thought in his poem "Gray shadows have merged." In this state the "soul" (i.e., immediate self-being) simply merges with being in its totality and immediacy into an inseparable, boundless whole: "all is in me and I am in all." But there is also a state of a seemingly opposite kind in which we experience the same essential kinship with the chaotic totality of being. When passion—joy or suffering, fright (panic fear) or wrath, love or hate—possesses us to such an extent that we are "beside ourselves" in a state of "ecstasy" and step outside the objective reality that limits our "I," it is then that our "self-being" appears to sink and vanish in the turbulent flux of all-embracing chaos. This is the life-feeling Tyutchev has in mind when he describes how in the night wind he hears a beckoning call to which the chaos in our soul responds ("what are you howling about, night wind?"). Before the "sea" of inner being which can overflow its banks gradually and slowly, spreading boundlessly everywhere—or which can be a flood of turbulent waters, also covering everything everywhere—we have a vague sense of the essential kinship of our inner being with the dark infinitude of all-embracing reality. In both cases (the dreamlike state and the passionate state) the boundary is erased between the reality of the objective world (distinctly visible, rooted in itself, present to us from outside) and that which we are conscious of—in opposition to the objective world—as our inner being; both the one and the other merge in the chaotic, unbounded unity of formless being in general. Such states are evidence that something in us originates from the dark infinitude of primordially immediate being in general and forms a unity with it. This unity is in some way experienced in every mystical ecstasy. It is most clearly expressed in the Upanishads, in which Brahman, the absolute, is identified with Atman, the deepest ground of the soul. The fact that our discussion is concerned with certain exceptional, relatively rare states is not in itself an objection against their ontological importance and instructiveness, for it is precisely in exceptional states that one can find revealed something essential and of universal significance.

On the other hand it is obvious that such states are characterized by the weakening or even the loss of our "selfhood," which is one of the essential parts of what we designate as immediate *self*-being. In these states, "selfhood" vanishes, dissolves as it were, and leaves behind it only the *immediacy* of being, which then coincides in some way with the undivided boundless unity of unconditional being in general. The two indistinguishably merge into an impersonal "it" or "something." By selfhood we mean neither a "subject" nor "I" as the carrier or substance of immediate self-being nor (especially) "personality." All concepts of this sort would have to be founded upon assumptions which are too specific and definite, assumptions which we have not yet examined or the obscurity and arbitrariness of which have already been disclosed to us. But even if we eliminate all the more specific features of these concepts, we find that immediate self-being is nonetheless something wholly other (in a certain sense) than the unknowable as undivided, undifferentiated, boundless, all-embracing, total unity. The specific element of being as *self-being* is contained precisely in this otherness, which is often expressed in *opposition* and counteraction to everything else, in stubborn *self*-affirmation. Self-being is precisely "my own being." It contains the element of the stubbornness of the singularly existent in its consciousness of its own self-being. (In German, the notion of stubbornness is expressed in *Eigensinn—Sinn für das Eigene*, a feeling for, or will to, that which is my "own" being or emanates from it.) Selfhood is a painstakingly protected, separate sphere of being, "belonging to me." And we always attempt to decisively oppose its alienation or its mixing with the "external," with all that does not belong to it. Selfhood is always realized in solitude, in isolation; and it cannot be exhausted in any kind of communion, communication or self-revelation; it cannot find total realization, expression, or resolution in them. Insofar as we are really conscious of our immediate self-being (which is rarely the case), we are conscious of ourselves as "not of this world" in the most precise sense of this expression. We are conscious of ourselves as mute and inaccessible to everything else, as a sphere of being that is precisely only *for its own self* and not for anyone else.

However, this selfhood in its essence is being which inwardly, *for its own self*, is something absolute or, more precisely, the absolute itself. It is unique, the ground and center of everything else, for everything else exists precisely *for* selfhood, acquires graspable reality, meaning, and value only in relation to selfhood. As such, selfhood is an infinity, an immeasurable all-embracing kingdom, a kind of cosmos for itself, which in its essence is boundless and all-embracing. For its own self, selfhood is eternal, for immediate self-being is precisely pure *being* and cannot conceive itself as nonexistent. In its ultimate depth, selfhood is conscious of its immediate bond, its essential unity, with the absolute; it has itself as the absolute. But on the other hand selfhood is not total unity but stands in opposition to the latter, is separated from total unity, and has itself precisely only in this difference and separation. Selfhood is a kind of total unity, one of the total unities, but it is not total unity in general (total unity as such). For this reason it has itself precisely outside of total unity in general.

If we attempted to fix in a concept this dual essence of selfhood, we could say that this most general meaning of self-being evidently consists in the fact that it manifests itself as the *limitless* in the form of the *limited*. Embracing infinitely much, self-being is nevertheless finite, limited by something else. It is something that in some sense is *all*, while at the same time being only *singular*. "The soul is all in some way," says Aristotle. But it is all only "in some way," for at the same time it is not all but only singular. *All, the total unity of being, taken as singular is precisely what we mean by immediate self-being*. Although it is in some sense the all-embracing absolute, it is a kind of absolute which separates itself from all else and has this "all else" outside of itself. It is compressed and squeezed into itself so to speak, and precisely in this reduced, compressed form of being, precisely as only one among much else, it has itself, it is being-for-itself or self-being. And every self-being is not only "one among much else" but is also something absolutely "other": i.e., unique, unrepeatable, irreplaceable. Precisely for this reason every self-being is absolutely solitary in a certain sense. It cannot totally exhaust, express, or realize itself in any revelation to another, in any communion. It contains and is something—namely the element of selfhood—which always remains ineffable and mute *in its own self*. But precisely in this respect it is similar and inwardly kindred to the Absolute itself, to the absolutely unique. This is why the attraction of the human soul to the Absolute, to God, is (to use Plotinus' apt phrase) "the flight of the unique (solitary) to the unique (solitary)."

Below, in another connection, we shall clarify the meaning of this relation according to which self-being, which is unique and for itself a kind of absolute, primordial center of all else, is nevertheless conceivable only as *one among much else that is similar to it*. Precisely this will make it clear that what we call "I" and what we have just now described as "self-being," being in the "am-form," is in the final analysis unrealizable without the transcending of its own limits, that is, without an immanent bond to what is called "thou," without a bond to the "art-form" of being (*Bist-form*) which is correlative to the "am-form." Without yet examining this conclusion, we wish only to note the universal ontological meaning of what we have just clarified in relation to what was clarified earlier.

In immediate being, the element of *separation* or *separateness* is realized, which lies in the essence of the Absolute as the unity of separateness and mutual penetration. Only at first glance can the unknowable as the Absolute be identified with the inseparable, indivisible, limitless, formless fullness of total unity, with "Brahman." Only at first glance is it that which is revealed to us in the pure immediacy of our self-being. On the contrary, the transrational essence of the unknowable presupposes in the unknowable a "monadic" form of being. For total unity is not simply the undivided, homogeneous background or all-encompassing space that uniformly and indifferently embraces and absorbs all diversity. Total unity as the Absolute is not, to cite Hegel, "a night in which all cats are gray." For if it were such and only such, it would not be total unity, because in this case that which is perceived as diversity, as the joint being of the many and the separate, and which, given to us in primordial immediacy, also *exists* in some sense—would be *outside* of total unity. On the contrary, total unity as a true unity is, as we have seen, the unity of unity *and* diversity: a unity which not only embraces all its own parts and points but also inwardly permeates them in such a way that it is also contained as a *whole* in each part and point. Thus, each point of being, though it has all else outside of itself, nonetheless in its place and in its way is the whole itself, total unity itself. Being something singular *together* with all else, all existents are constituted by their *separateness*. But having all in themselves and also being connected to all else, all existents have *all* immanently in this double sense: in themselves and for themselves. All existents are permeated by all and permeate all.

Thus, the unity of separateness and mutual penetration as it is concretely manifested in immediate self-being, precisely in the element of selfhood, is the revelation of reality as such—precisely as the unknowable. Precisely that element in immediate self-being owing to which the latter separates itself from the all-absorbing unity of absolute being and opposes itself to this unity, i.e., the element of selfhood, is the most adequate expression of the deepest essence of the unknowable as concrete total unity. Keeping in mind everything we have said about the unknowableness and transrationality of the Absolute, we nevertheless have the right to say that in a certain sense concrete total unity is the *kingdom of spirits*. In defining it in this way, we do not rationalize it, for both of the elements through which we define its essence—the element of "kingdom" and the element of "spiritual" being—are themselves transrational and essentially unknowable. We can see that the *am*-element (the element of self-being, self-revelation to itself, being-for-itself) which belongs to total unity itself is realized in this unity in a multitude of mutually exclusive and mutually connected "selfhoods." One all-embracing "consciousness" or one all-embracing "selfhood" is conceivable only in the sense that this all-embracing being-for-itself generates a multitude of separate, mutually connected, and mutually limiting particular selfhoods.

We encounter the same transrational unity of separateness and mutual penetration when we examine the *inner* relation between the elements of "immediacy" and "selfhood" in the makeup of immediate self-being itself. In order to perceive this we must first attempt to more precisely define immediate self-being, the "am-form" of being. This can of course be accomplished only in concepts that are themselves expressions of wise ignorance. (In the present case these concepts take the form of "negative psychology.") As Bergson aptly described, immediate self-being is essentially process, "doing," dynamics, living duration, "temporality," or (what is the same thing) *freedom*. All these words signify that immediate self-being in its concrete content is not something that is fixed in a finished form, not something definite and complete, but something essentially unfinished and potential, something that is being born or created—being in the form of becoming, potency, striving, and realization. It is existent potentiality or potency, something we have already encountered in our examination of the roots or the substratum of objective being, something we have in immediate experience only in immediate self-being, in which this potentiality reveals itself to itself.

Since we use the word "freedom" to designate this potentiality or spontaneity, it is essential to remark (in connection with our earlier discussion of potentiality and freedom) that here we are dealing with two kinds or forms of freedom. Hegel defined freedom as "being-in-one's-own-self" (*Bei-sich-selbst-sein*). This definition is accurate only insofar as we take the element of "one's-own-self" in the broadest sense in which it coincides with immediacy, with intimate inner being, with being-for-itself in general. But if we conceptually abstract the element of selfhood from immediate being in its concrete wholeness, then freedom as "being-in-one's-own-self" can only mean the highest form of freedom, but not freedom in its universal essence. Freedom in its primordial sense can be expressed in general only in some negative manner: we consider it to mean the *un*-finished, the *in*-complete, the *un*-connected, the wavering, the oscillating, the ground-*less*, pure potentiality, the absence of foundation and determining ground (*Ungrund*), all this conceived as a *dynamics*, an inner unrest, an agitation, an attraction. Precisely this element of *un*-restraint, *an*-archy, forms the primordial, elementary essence of immediate self-being, that "chaos" which, according to Tyutchev, "stirs" in the depths of the soul. The essence of this element as the common substrate of psychic being was deeply felt and expressed in all its significance and intensity by Dostoevsky. The true essence of immediate self-being as the deep substratum of human existence as it is given to itself consists precisely of pure irrationality, unreason, groundlessness, and ungroundedness—and all this as a dynamic, living force. All that is *meaningless* in the depths of immediacy, all caprices and wild passions, all self-deceptive willfullness, is an expression of this primordial freedom as the substratum of inner self-being. Furthermore, one perceives here a certain inner dialectic which emanates from the inseparable, antagonistic dual-unity of immediate self-being and "self-hood." It is precisely under the unlimited reign of this blind, primordial freedom that man becomes *unfree*, for then he is "moved" or "driven" by this freedom and is not *himself* the moving or guiding force. Blind freedom is the impersonal element, the *it*-element, in inner life which destroys or imprisons our selfhood, that in us which we call "I myself." It is in this blind freedom that we experience the reign of a wild, unrestrained force of expansion, which pushes and drives us to go beyond the limits of our own selves, to stop being our own selves. And this blind force of expansion escapes the guidance of the embracing, formative, and guiding element of selfhood. Primordial, unrestrained, anarchic freedom is not being-in-one's-own-self but precisely *being-outside-one's-own-self*. It is a freedom which is also inner slavery, exile from the homeland of selfhood.

This primordial freedom in which we are driven by forces of our own inner being and which enslaves us is opposed by another, higher freedom which emanates from our selfhood. Selfhood as the guiding and formative principle of immediate self-being attains or at least seeks to attain the true freedom and spontaneity of our inner self-being in the struggle against the blind, primordial force of passions and urges. It seeks to attain freedom as the active principle of self-formation, as genuine being and stability "in one's own self" or, more simply, as "oneself." The blind stubbornness of primordial freedom, the feeling of "this is the way I want it" (expressed in German by "Eigen-sinn") which as such is alien to both the selfhood (*Eigen*) and the meaning (*Sinn*) of self-being and threatens to dissolve our selfhood in non-selfhood, to drown it in the common, indefinite "it"—this stubbornness of primordial freedom can be overcome by selfhood and thereby transformed into genuinely "self-sufficient" and "meaningful"

being. Thus, this freedom is realized through *self-overcoming*. Of this freedom Goethe says, *"Von der Gewalt, die Alle Wesen bindet, befreit der Mensche
sich, der sich überwindet"* (i.e., to overcome oneself is to triumph over the
forces that bind nature). This is not yet the ultimate and highest freedom,
genuinely "true" freedom which can never emanate from man's inner being alone, from immediate self-being as such in its separateness. (We shall
examine this "true" freedom in another connection.) This is not yet *complete* freedom, for it is freedom only in the form of *struggle*, the constant
counterattack against an attacking enemy, the defense of a besieged for-
tress. But it is nonetheless true freedom insofar as it is *self-overcoming*.

The paradox that *self-definition* can be realized only through *self-
overcoming*[2] is only partly resolved by the fact that "selfhood" is used here in
two different senses. The selfhood that is overcome here is, strictly speaking, only "immediacy" and as such differs from the true, formative selfhood that does the overcoming. However, these two aspects cannot really
be separated but are an inseparable unity: namely, the unity of immediate
self-being in which immediacy belongs to self-being just as much as self-
being belongs to immediate being. The two freedoms (the lower freedom
and the higher freedom; the blind, unrestrained freedom and the formative
freedom) described above are really one freedom in the final analysis: freedom in general as potentiality or potency. These freedoms are one not only
in the sense that they are different forms of one general concept of freedom
(which would be a simple truism) but also in the sense that blind, primordial freedom is already the initial, elementary activity of *self*-being and that
secondary (in sequence, not in importance), formative freedom includes all
the immediacy of blind "passion" and is precisely the ultimate expression
of the immediacy of our inner being. In other words, the unity of immediacy and selfhood is so intimate and unbreakable that selfhood cannot be
disclosed and spring into action except in the very substratum of primordial freedom and except through the forces of this freedom. Any attempt
to set aside this substratum, to overcome it in only an external way, not to
use it as the medium of all our activity, leads to the annihilation of *genuine*—
precisely genuinely *immediate*—selfhood. Furthermore, any such attempt is
even utterly impossible, for immediacy as primordial freedom is a basic
premise of *all* inner self-being. Selfhood, the counter-element to primordial freedom, can be attained, can flare up, only within the latter, and
therefore can overcome primordial freedom only through this very freedom. *"Zwei Seelen leben, ach! in meiner Brust,"* is something that every man
can say about himself. Nevertheless, every man is also conscious that these

"two souls" are really only *one soul*, that not only are they outwardly inseparable and inextricably linked, but that they are also inwardly rooted in
such a deep and intimate unity that either of the two can realize itself only
with the aid of the other, only in the soil or element of the other. Thus, here
too the transrational unity of separateness and mutual penetration is revealed: the principle of antinomian monodualism that regulates all of concrete reality and that here, in the intimate depth of our inner being, reveals
itself in the constant dramatic paradoxicality of our life.

3. Immediate Self-being as Subjectivity

Our discussion of the nature of immediate self-being was based on the
fact that both the ordinary consciousness and the philosophically oriented
consciousness tend not to see immediate self-being as a genuine reality.
Instead they tend to see either its reflection and manifestation in the makeup of the objective world or its function as the knowing subject. We demonstrated the falsity of both of these views and emphasized that immediate
self-being is essentially a special form of genuine reality in its own right
and that it is also the immediate revelation of reality in general as such. But
now we must direct our attention at an aspect of immediate self-being
which we have not yet discussed, an aspect which reveals that the prevailing opinion concerning immediate self-being is nevertheless partly legitimate (though for a reason wholly different from the one it supposes).

This prevailing view is psychologically explainable only partially by the
fact that human consciousness is usually subject to the overbearing influence of the objective world (or, in an "idealist" framework, directs its
attention primarily at the function of cognition). This view is also partially
an expression (though incorrectly grounded) of the primary and, in some
sense, self-evident feeling or consciousness that immediate self-being is not
yet "real," "genuine," full-fledged reality, but is something which acquires fullness of being only in relation to some other, more genuine and
more deeply grounded reality. The ordinary, usually half-conscious or instinctive justification of this feeling—namely that inner, psychic being, the
sphere of our dreams, feelings, moods, and desires is only "subjective"
compared to objective reality, that it is only apparent reality, a kind of
illusion or error—involves, of course, an extremely crude error of
thought. Only our opinions and judgments can be "subjective" in the sense
of falsity and error or incompatibility with objective reality. Moreover,
not the opinions and judgments themselves as facts are false but only what
is affirmed in them insofar as it claims to be a correct perception or reflec-

tion of objective reality. But no fact, nothing that is given, is present, or exists in any form whatsoever can, as such (i.e., in its simple inner make-up), be "false" and in this sense "subjective." But even if this kind of justification is utterly false and even meaningless, the immediate feeling which lies at the base of this judgment nevertheless contains a grain of truth.

In a previous discussion we perceived the element of dynamicity, potentiality, instability, incompleteness, striving, to be the essential defining characteristic of immediate self-being. It is evident from this that all becoming, all activity, within immediate self-being must always be without result, for here the dynamism of striving or becoming cannot eliminate itself by the ultimate attainment of the goal of striving: namely the positiveness and peace of possession. It is evidently this fundamental relation that Schopenhauer had in mind when he described the basic hopelessness of the "will to life," which can never attain its goal but can only be compared to the snake that, curling up in a ring, bites its own tail. The characteristic form of the being of immediate self-being is the form of potentiality, potency, becoming (which of course must not be confused with the creative actuality of reality). It is being in the form of *the striving to be*. But precisely in this, if it is correctly understood, lies its "subjectivity." Immediate self-being stands, as it were, on the threshold between being and non-being, and in this sense it can be compared to a "shadow" or a "dream." Shakespeare expresses it concisely and brilliantly when he says that "we are such stuff as dreams are made of." Or, referring to an ancient poet, let us consider that our existence is only a shadow seen in a dream, "the dream of a shadow." This form of being as "illusory" being that stands on the threshold between being and non-being is a specific transrationality that belongs precisely to immediate self-being as such. It is transrational and essentially unknowable precisely because it can be expressed only antinomianly as something which exists *but is not being* or as something which exists and does not exist at the same time. Thus, this specific character of immediate self-being is enigmatic from the ordinary point of view, slips away from the consciousness, which is guided by the criterion of rationality.

Immediate self-being has the property that within the limits of itself it cannot realize or fulfill itself despite the fact that it is scarcely something insignificantly small that has meaning only as an "appendage" of reality, but is, in itself, an immeasurably great and content-rich reality, a kind of special universe infinite in itself. Therefore it cannot remain within itself but by its very essence needs fulfillment, needs to lean or rest on something other than itself. And it can attain its goal, its true essence, only in this *other* or by leaning on this other. In its essence, immediate self-being is the instrument or medium for something other than itself, and only in relation to this something other does it fulfill its function and thus attain genuine being. If we take the notion of the "apparent" not in the sense of falseness or error but in the sense of "apparent being" as unstable, illusory, shadowy being that stands in contrast to true, genuine, fully existent being (*ontos on*), then immediate self-being is not true, fully existent being but a kind of groundless, hovering, illusory being. In this lies the meaning of its "subjectivity." When man, in opposition to nature and meaning, remains within the limits of immediate self-being alone (that is, when immediate self-being closes on itself and ceases to perform its function as a medium for or a way to *objectivity*), we then have sickness: namely insanity.

Thus, the essence of immediate self-being has *transcending* as a necessary feature: the passing beyond the limits of self, the crossing of the boundaries of one's own sphere of being. For immediate self-being acquires stable ground only when it attains something other and finds support in this other. Only then can its potentiality acquire its genuine goal: the stability of actuality. Here we see revealed with especial force the most general meaning of the saying that only he who sacrifices or loses his soul for something other than himself will save his soul.

But there are different forms or modes of this transcending. The first and most general form, which in a certain sense and to a certain degree (we refrain from discussing this here in detail) forms the general frame or background for all the other forms of transcending, is transcending in *cognitive intentionality*, in the "ideal" directedness of the "gaze" at reality, which thereby becomes our ideal possession and is known objectively by us. If above we rejected the prevailing view that cognitive intentionality is the determining feature of the intrinsic *form of being* of immediate self-being, then on the other hand it is nevertheless perfectly obvious that cognitive intentionality is an essential feature of its *mode of functioning*, its activity. The functioning or activity of immediate self-being is realized on the basis of the fact that something is "given" to it, that it "stands before" something, that it "encounters" something at which it is "ideally directed" (in a form that does not permit further analysis) in such a way that the "content" of what is given to it in this manner is "revealed" to it, "clarified" for it, or "known" by it.

But this mode of transcending is not "real" transcending of immediate self-being as such, precisely because of its "ideality" and in spite of all its necessity. That which "transcends" in the pure cognitive intentionality, in the cognitive directedness at an object, is not, in essence, immediate self-being as such but only a pure ray of "light" that emanates from this being or traverses it and attains the object. It is possible to be conscious of or even to distinctly know the world which surrounds us, while remaining utterly "indifferent" to it, remaining closed in one's own "psychic" life, remaining within the limits of immediate self-being, "stewing in one's juices" as it were. As an extreme case it is possible to imagine a clear and distinct knowledge of the surrounding world which—because there is no active or emotional participation in it—represents this world as a dream or a theatrical spectacle, which does not have the slightest effect on one's inner life. It is very possible that insane people, apart from their obsessions, have this kind of indifferent, unparticipating cognition of the world and thus remain locked in the worlds of their immediate self-being.

But this pure cognitive intentionality in its proper form of indifferent, unparticipating contemplation or observation is, in its detached form, a rather exceptional and even pathological phenomenon in the functioning of immediate self-being. Usually from the very beginning the cognitive intentionality is linked, through the function of "attention," to the intentionality of "feeling" and "wanting," to the intentionality of "interest." We not only "know" an object but also "feel" or "want" it; we are "interested" in it, even if only in the negative form of avoidance or repulsion. In most cases the cognitive intentionality is even guided in practice by the concrete intentionality of emotion and will. It is only this concrete intentionality that gives to things their "significance" and "importance," gives them "meaning," and makes them "for us" in a practical sense. And only this gives rise to the eminent meaning—precisely the *practical* meaning—of what we call "objective reality." In this sense objective reality is that which *acts* upon us. Furthermore, during this action the dynamic element of immediate self-being is directed outward. And the opposition in immediate self-being between its own, inner limitlessness and outer limitation is manifested in the aspiration of immediate self-being to absorb the "outer," the "other," into itself, to subordinate the "other" to itself, either to find support in the other and rely on it, or to battle against it, to defend itself against the other. Thus, immediate self-being is also *being-in-the-world, being-with-the-world*. And this bond with the world, this being with the world, is so dominant and determining in the concrete realization of immediate self-being that it usually obscures the genuine inner essence of immediate self-being as such.

But even this living intentionality of emotion and will is only a kind of intermediate stage, a kind of transition between purely ideal transcending in the cognitive intentionality and the genuinely *real* transcending of immediate self-being as such. For even though this living intentionality is a genuine form of the revelation and activity of immediate self-being, the genuine reaction of the latter as such to the world, it is still not the genuine transcending of immediate self-being itself. Although in this intentionality immediate self-being is really directed at something outside of itself and other than itself, nevertheless it does not pass beyond the limits of itself, does not acquire a genuine ground for itself in the other. On the contrary, immediate self-being remains within itself, within its "subjectivity," and is satisfied with sending out "feelers" into the surrounding world. Immediate self-being contains an internal contradiction or antagonism which consists in the fact that although it is "all" in its own self, it is "all" only in a potential and hidden way, and that—factually, externally, in its concrete realization—it is limited, only "one of many." And this contradiction or antagonism cannot be overcome in the concrete intentionality of emotion and will. Objective reality, even in its eminent sense examined above, remains only the external medium, only an obstacle or an aid, for the essence of human life as immediate self-being, which as before remains closed in its limitedness. Even in the most favorable and interesting environment, in the midst of full and successful outer activity, man can be inwardly alone, closed in himself, and continue to suffer from the contradiction between his inner claim to infinite fullness, a claim that forms his very essence, and his limitedness and alienation from everything that is other.

The real transcending of immediate self-being, its genuine bond and merging with the reality that surpasses it, the genuine attainment of stable ground for its own being, and therefore the real overcoming of its subjectivity, is realized only when it encounters and acquires—beyond itself—a reality that in some sense is *essentially kindred to it*, with which it can somehow merge, or on which it can solidly base its inner essence. This can occur in two directions: "outward" and "inward." The first form of transcending, i.e., outward transcending, is the real transcending of immediate self-being into another "I," into another "am," into another selfhood, into something which, though it has a form of being kindred to that of immediate self-being, is not *this* immediate self-being but "another" one. This is transcending in the "I–thou" relation. The second form, that of inward transcending, is transcending into pure *objectivity* in the sense of inwardly self-evident, self-grounded, not potential but actual being, which, however, is kindred in its content to immediate self-being, is—like immediate self-being—a being-for-itself; in other words, it is transcending into the true, solid, actual ground of immediate self-being itself. This is transcending into the reality of *the spirit.* We shall examine these two forms of transcending separately.

NOTES

1. In the following discussion we shall summarize certain ideas presented in our book *The Soul of Man. An Introduction to Philosophical Psychology (Dusha Cheloveka. Vvederie v filosofskuiu psikhologiiu),* Moscow 1917.
2. Translator's note. Here Frank plays on the words *samoopredelenie* ("self-definition") and *samopreodolenie* ("self-overcoming").

Chapter VI

Outward Transcending:
The "I–Thou" Relation

1. THE REVELATION OF "THOU"

We pointed out above that through outward transcending in the intentionality of emotion and will the objective world is transformed for us into an eminent, *practically* existent "objective reality"—be it a pleasant and beneficial objective reality that attracts us or a harmful and dangerous objective reality that we try to avoid. In this sense objective reality coincides with *my* world, with the outer reality of *my* life, with a reality that stands—with respect to *me*—in some relation essential for *my* life, with a reality that is essentially connected to *me*.

One might think that this element of "my" and "to me" already presupposes the concept of "I." From the point of view of abstract-logical analysis this presupposition is quite natural and even self-evident in a certain sense. But transcendental thinking, which penetrates into the "atmosphere" in which all categorial relations originate, finds the matter to be more complicated. Until now we have avoided the use of the word "I." We have avoided calling immediate self-being by the name that seems most appropriate for it. We have done this intentionally, for (contrary to the widespread, seemingly self-evident, view) immediate self-being in its inner, detached essence (as we have studied and described it until now) does not yet coincide with "I"—with "me"—in the full actual and concrete meaning of this word. Although we had to refer to the "I am" form of being in our analysis of the knowing subject, this usage was only preliminary. We saw that "I" as the knowing subject does not coincide with what we mean by the concrete "I." And to designate the form of being given in immediate self-being we preferred the verb form "am," not delineating in it, as an independent subject, "I" as a special reality. What is the true meaning of "I" and how does "I" arise from that potential reality we have called immediate self-being? These are questions we now examine for the first time.

Let us make the preliminary remark that the elements "my," "to me," "with me," etc. are more primordial than "I" in a certain sense. Psychogenetically this can be shown with complete certainty using the example of an infant's spiritual development and his use of words. In a certain sense "my," "to me," "with me," etc. are "I" only in its potential, not fully realized state. This is the form in which immediate self-being has itself in relation to objective being and *first begins* to reveal and actualize itself in this relation. But this is precisely only incomplete, half-finished, imperfect actualization. In this imperfect actualization, immediate self-being perceives not its own essence but only its self-revelation in its relation to that which is other—in relation to objective being. Objective being taken in its relation to self-being—what Fichte called "non-I" and what we can only call "non-selfhood"—is still too indefinite and therefore insufficient to bring "I" to complete revelation and genuine actualization. The complete actualization of immediate self-being, namely its blossoming or development into "I"—occurs only in relation to the mysterious, enigmatic, miraculous reality of "thou."

The well-known epistemological problem of how "I" can know "thou" or even another "I" or "another consciousness" in general, how "I" can encounter in experience this "other I," cannot be solved in this formulation for the simple reason that no complete or finished "I" exists prior to its encounter with "I," prior to a relation to "thou." Innumerable difficulties and absurdities arise when we attempt to use as a starting point (so habitual and seemingly self-evident a starting point) the isolated "I" which is thought to exist in itself in a finished form. The very concept of "another consciousness" taken as "another" or "second" "I" is wholly absurd, even apart from all difficulties associated with the problem of how we can come to perceive this "other I" if we start from our own isolated "I." In the precise and absolute sense of the words, there can be no other or second "I" (if for the present we ignore the possibility of ghostly doubles, a possibility we shall discuss later). For me, "I" is essentially something unique: namely "my I." Or more precisely (to avoid the logical error of *idem per idem*), "I" is given to me only as a component of the concrete "I am," and this "I am" is essentially unrepeatable and unique in relation to everything else. Philosophers who speak of some "I" which supposedly "is" betray the inadequacy of their thought to reality itself in the grammatical error in which the *first*-person pronoun is matched with the *third*-person verb form. It is an error not only in grammar but also in essence to say: "I is." Only "I am" corresponds to the truth, and it is evident that this "I am," as well as the "I" that is one of its components, is essentially *unique*. Or more precisely (so as not to commit the distortion of reality we have just discussed), "I *am* essentially unique." In this sense the word-combination "second I" is an obvious contradiction, something like a square circle. That which I call "another consciousness" is not the absurdity of a "second I" but simply "he." Furthermore, the only reason I can in general arrive psychologically at the unnatural, inwardly distorted notion of "many I's" is that in reflection I can have *myself* not in the primary form of "I am" but in the derivative, objective form of "he is" and then conceptually transfer this relation to another "he" or to other "they."

But, strictly speaking, "he" is already "thou," "thou" that was or will be. "He" is a possible "thou" that we perceive at the given moment not as a full-fledged concrete "thou" but as an attenuated, obscured, faded "thou," as a "thou" that for us is submerged in the impersonal and objective form of the being of "it." "He" is "thou" in the sphere of "it." But the very concept of "he"—the concept of "another consciousness" insofar as it is taken as such, precisely as a finished form—is an unsolvable riddle. For the "soul" (or "inner being") that I know objectively and encounter from "outside" should, it appears, be absolutely hidden and inaccessible for me. It should even be utterly incomprehensible for me how I can arrive at the concept of "another soul." We can neither see nor touch "another soul." There can be no question of perceiving it with our senses. And to postulate "supra-sensory intuition" would be to simply affirm that "another consciousness" is somehow accessible to us in a "supra-sensory" manner without attempting to explain how this is possible. On the other hand it is not difficult to show that all attempts to explain the "knowledge of another soul" as indirect, mediated knowledge are trapped in a vicious circle and presuppose what is to be proved. Further, the hypothesis of knowledge through "analogical inference" (through an analogy with "my own I") and the hypothesis of knowledge through "*Einfühlung*" both presuppose (apart from all the other difficulties that are encountered here) the very concept of "another soul," that is, they presuppose our knowledge of the being of something analogous to us. In analogical inference, it is possible to transfer a feature of a concept from one object to another object that resembles the first, but it is not possible to ground and define a wholly new concept. And that which is called "*Einfühlung*"—a special awareness of reality which is outside of me in being but which resembles me in content, an awareness realized in feelings which I experience as "not mine" but forced on me from outside—can transcend my "I" not as an illusion, not as a state of my own "I" (though a state that is alien to me), but as the ability to *know* another reality outside of me only under the condition that the appropriate reality is already given to me in some way even prior to "*Einfühlung.*" I can of course "feel into" alien psychic states, but only under the condition that I already know that "other souls" or "other consciousnesses" in general exist.

Furthermore, "thou" signifies something wholly other and much greater than "another consciousness." If we attempt to understand "thou" as an "object of knowledge," then it is such "another soul" that not only is the passive object of my cognitive gaze but is also known by me as being *directed at me myself.* But even this is not sufficient; I must also be aware that the "other soul" in its directedness at me is aware of my directedness at it and is also aware of my knowing it as knowing me as knowing it, and so on, *ad infinitum.* As two mirrors placed opposite each other give an uncountable number of reflections because a ray of light, reflected in them, crosses the space between them an uncountable number of times, so the knowledge of some "thou," insofar as we interpret it as objective knowledge, must contain an infinite number of reflected rays of knowledge, traversing the space between "I" and "thou," which of course is wholly unrealizable and contradicts our immediate, simple perception of "thou."[1]

But there are other difficulties. We are dealing with facts that are wholly opposed to the common psychological idea that we are immediately given only separate psychic processes or phenomena, but not their carrier. The fact that I encounter a "thou," that the gaze of "another being" is directed at me, that I stand before the presence of some "other soul," some "other consciousness," is given to me in a much more primary and immediate way than the knowledge of what precisely occurs or is contained in another soul. True, this general presence of "thou" is given to me together with a certain perception of its psychic state at a given moment or, more precisely, together with the qualitative character of its directedness at me. "Thou" "gives me knowledge" of itself, of its being, in a hostile or friendly look, in the severity or the gentleness of its directedness at me, in appropriate gestures, facial expressions, and so on. But beyond this the content of this alien psychic life is accessible to me only very imperfectly and with great difficulty. True, independently of the philosophical problem that is involved, we can to some extent know the "content" of this reality, penetrate "into" another soul. But this knowledge is somewhat uncertain, inaccurate, shaky, more or less obscure. "The soul of another is a darkness," according to the old Russian saying. This means that the immediate content of "another soul" is impenetrably dark for us. Even our closest friend, whom we think we know quite well, can sometimes astonish us with something we could never have expected from him. Thus, although in principle partly knowable, the inner content of "thou" is unattainable and unknowable for us in its essence and concrete fullness. But precisely this enigmatic, unknowable reality precisely in its unknowableness as pure reality as such is somehow "given" to us in complete immediacy. Here again we encounter the fundamental fact (which refutes all rationalistic theories of knowledge) that we know—with complete certainty and self-evident immediacy—of the existence of something the content of which is, at least immediately, concealed from us. However, this relation cannot be simply identified with the simple "possession" of an object, which possession precedes cognition of the content of the object (see Chapter I). For it is not a question of an absolutely indefinite reality, which I have in such a form that it mutely is present before me and passively gives itself to my cognitive gaze, as though passively waiting to be discovered by me. Rather it is a question of a reality that is revealed to me precisely because it is directed at me and touches me like the ray of a living, dynamic force. It is a question of a reality that I can have in no other way than by entering into an ineffable communion with it as with something that is essentially kindred to me.

Thus, it is completely evident that "thou" is not an object of knowledge, neither of abstract, conceptual knowledge nor even of the intuitive, contemplative knowledge that precedes and grounds abstract knowledge. "Thou" "gives" us knowledge of itself, touching us, penetrating into us, entering into communion with us, "speaking" to us in some way and arousing in us a living response. All knowledge is preceded not by simple "possession" (as we possess dead things) but by some form of living interaction or communion, by a mutual exchange of activity, the starting point of which is "thou" itself, the reality itself that reveals itself to us here. There is only one concept that corresponds to this relation: the concept of *revelation*. Until now we have used the term "to reveal oneself" both in the general form that signifies that reality as total unity is immanent to itself, is for itself, and in the form that signifies the determining concrete characteristic of immediate self-being. In both cases it is a question of "self-revelation," of the "revelation of itself to itself," of "being for itself." But the concept of "revelation" acquires a definite and precise meaning only as *revelation for another*, which actively emanates from what reveals itself and is directed at another self-being. As is well-known, this "directedness" at another is realized in the external means of "expression": look, facial expression, mimicry, word. In opposition to all naturalistic habits of thought, it is extremely important to understand that here the relation between "inner" and "outer," between *that which expresses itself* and *that in which it is expressed*, should be interpreted neither as "psychophysical causality" nor as "psychophysical parallelism." The former is contradicted by the simultaneity, the being-together, of the "expressed" and the "expression"; the latter is contradicted by the explicit, uneliminable *activity* of the process of expression as a dynamic striving or *movement from inside outward*. This process of "self-expression" in which something "inner," some self-being, breaks through to the outside, making itself explicit in the "outer," is a process *sui generis*, which does not fit into any of the categories applicable to the objective world. It is a process that cannot be compared to anything else; it is unique of its kind, primary. This is precisely the self-evident yet enigmatic and miraculous phenomenon of *revelation*.

It is obvious that "revelation" in this sense does not coincide with "revelation" in its theological usage. We shall discuss later how the general revelation we have described manifests itself and acts in the sphere of religious life. In view of the domination of human thought by traditional associations of words, we direct the attention of our reader to the fact that we are employing the word "revelation" not in the ordinary sense but in a much broader and more general one. This *general* sense of the concept of revelation is determined by *two* essential features. First of all, there is the active self-disclosure emanating from the self-revealing reality itself, directed at me, and constituting and revealing to me this reality as "thou." In this respect knowledge based on revelation sharply differs from the ordinary kind of knowledge, from knowledge determined by the activity of the knowing subject, which involves cognition emanating from the subject and directed at the object. Second, this is, above all, the revelation of reality as such and not of its content; for this reason it is the revelation of the unknowable. That which is "revealed" here does not cease being—even after "revelation"—the unknown and the unknowable. Rather it is revealed precisely *as* the unknown and the unknowable. The fact that the unknowable assumes for us the character of "thou" does not in any way signify knowledge of its content, but simply coincides with *self-revelation* or with revelation in the sense we have described. "Thou" is nothing else but that unknown "essence" which reveals itself to us in this form. "Thou" is the concrete revelation of the unknowable, which does not simply "stand before us," or "surround us" or even embrace and permeate us, but which *intrudes into us* from outside. That which we call "thou" or that which stands in the relation of "thou" to us is the *essentially unknowable* mystery of a living reality that is revealed to us in such a form that it touches us, intrudes into us, is experienced by us through its active effect upon us. All this is already given in another's gaze directed at us, in the mystery of living human eyes directed at us. And this is immediately and inseparably connected with the opposite activity that emanates from us. All knowledge or perception of "thou" is a living encounter with it, the intersection of two gazes. The intrusion of "thou" into us is simultaneously our intrusion into "thou," however outwardly unnoticeable, modest, muted, and restrained this intrusion. The encounter of two pairs of eyes, the intersection of two gazes, that which marks the beginning of all love and friendship as well as all enmity, that which is at the heart of the most fleeting and superficial "communion," this most ordinary and commonplace of events is also, for one who has thought deeply about it at least once, one of the most mysterious events of human life, or rather the most concrete manifestation of the eternal mystery that forms the very essence of human life. A genuine miracle occurs in this event: the miracle of the *self-transcending* of immediate self-being, the mutual self-revelation to each other of two carriers of being in other respects closed in themselves and existing only for themselves. And there is another miracle: through the revelation of "thou" and the correlative self-revelation of *me* to "thou," immediate self-being encounters and recognizes *its own self*, as it were. It encounters its own self beyond the limits of itself, precisely in the "other," in the living, dynamic reality of immediate self-being, which proceeds in the direction opposite to the ordinary one: *from outside inward*. Precisely this encounter reveals that immediate self-being has, besides its own center "inside itself," something correlative to itself outside itself, in "outer" reality. The dynamic "extrusion" from out of myself coincides with the *intrusion from outside* into me of something "me-like," something or rather someone who is essentially connected to me in the sense that he is something "I-like" beyond the limits of "me." And in this sense this someone can be called (in abstract language which is inadequate to the concrete relation) by the unnatural name of "another" or "second" "I."[2]

2. THE CORRELATEDNESS OF "I" AND "THOU"

This phenomenon of encounter with "thou" is precisely the place where "I" itself arises for the first time in the genuine sense. This is precisely where that potential being we designated as immediate self-being and have heretofore examined in its unfinished, imperfectly realized form is actualized and has itself as "I" for the first time. Experiencing itself as surrounded by some broader external atmosphere which nonetheless is kindred and permeating, an atmosphere in which it recognizes its own essence, immediate self-being attaches for the first time the element of "my" (which acquires particular intensity through contrast with the "other") to its own being (and not only to things and phenomena with which it is practically connected). Hence, "I" arises (or rather, *I arise* as "I") simultaneously with "thou" as a point of reality correlative to "thou," the two correlative elements forming the unity of "we."

Thus, the "I–thou" relation does not involve the external encounter of two realities that existed "by themselves" prior to the encounter: the realities of *fully formed* "I" and "thou." All the difficulties, discussed above, of apprehending the possibility of such an encounter and such a relation are the result of an erroneous formulation of the problem. The truth is that no fully formed "I" exists prior to the encounter with "thou." It is the revelation of "thou" and the correlative transcending of immediate self-being (if only in the accidental and fleeting encounter of two pairs of eyes) that first give birth simultaneously to "I" and "thou." They are born, so to speak, from a common circulation of blood, which from the outset flows about and permeates this kingdom of two mutually connected, kindred immediate beings. "I" first arises for me warmed and illuminated by the rays of "thou." The "am" form of being, which we discussed above, becomes genuine, full-fledged "I am" only insofar as it has itself in inseparable-unmerged unity with the correlative "thou art" form of being.

At first glance this conclusion seems to be a great paradox, a defiantly crude distortion of the genuine essence of the reality we are discussing. Is not what we call "I" something intimate and inner to the highest degree, something whose essence and being do not depend on anything outside of it—something autonomous and sovereignly existent in its very own essence?

However, despite its seeming persuasiveness, under closer examination this objection turns out to be inconsistent, and inconsistent for two reasons. On the one hand there are real facts and relations that shake the certainty of this objection. On the other hand even if the positive idea upon which this objection is based were true, the objection still would not achieve its aim, for it only appears to contradict our affirmation concerning the "I–thou" relation. Let us examine these two inconsistencies, starting with the latter, which is the more significant.

The fact that the form of being which we experience as "I" and call by this name is in some sense something sovereign, self-sufficient, dependent on nothing external, is, in itself, utterly true. But from the point of view of transcendental thinking (which must be used to survey the reality we encounter here) we do not have the right to be satisfied with a mere assertion of this "sovereignty" or "independence." We are obliged to clarify the *meaning* of these characteristics, i.e., to clarify the *categorial-constitutive* element that forms them. First of all we must recall that "sovereignty of being" in the sense of *absolute being out of one's own self (aseitas)* is characteristic in general of no particular thing but only of absolute total unity or its primordial ground. (We shall see later that this proposition has only relative validity.) In any case, "I" as the carrier of singular, particular "immediate self-being" exists (or rather "I" *exist*) not as some absolutely self-sufficient divinity, but only as an element in the makeup of all-embracing, total being. The "sovereignty" of *my* being is a relative sovereignty. It consists in the fact that I stand in a relation of "independence" to "other" "me-like" beings, that I possess my own special being, i.e., a being separate from these "others." But this separateness or independence is a *negative connection* to that from which I am conscious of being separate, just as the sovereignty of a political state is determined by its international position. "Autonomy" is constituted by a characteristic *negative relation* to that which is "outside of me," to that which in relation to me is a "being outside of me." But this negation is not a purely logical negation (which constitutes the simple "difference" between one thing and another) but a *living* negation in the sense of rejection, repulsion, self-defense against intrusion from outside. But this "external something" through the struggle against which I affirm my independence, the sovereignty of my "I," is precisely nothing else but "thou." Thus, the sovereignty of "I" in relation to every "thou" is a real connection (though of negative content) to "thou." Later we shall see more precisely how "I" arises from this very position of self-defense against "thou," in struggle with "thou."

Perhaps the objection will be raised that the sovereignty or autonomy of "I's" being has, besides the negative significance we noted in it, a purely positive significance as well, namely the immediacy of *my* rootedness in unconditional being, in reality as such. In itself this affirmation is wholly valid. But a "transcendental" analysis of its *meaning* leads, by another path, not to the refutation of our thesis but to its confirmation. That unconditional being in which we know ourselves to be immediately rooted is here being as *being-for-itself, reality revealing itself to itself*. But in this aspect reality presupposes the entity of "subject," the one *who* "has" or is "conscious" of reality, the one *to whom* reality is revealed. Who is this "subject"? If we answer "I myself," we commit the logical error of *idem per idem*, the tautological and false affirmation that "I's" being is rooted in "me myself." It is clear that we only have the right to say that the being of my "I" is its rootedness in the "kingdom" of "being-for-itself" as such. But this kingdom is unimaginable and inconceivable for us except in the form of a mutually connected *polycentric* system, in the form of a kingdom of "spirits" or concrete carriers of immediate self-being. Thus it turns out that the being of "I" is its rootedness in the being of "we," something we shall clarify more precisely later. But "we" is "I" and "thou." Thus, on this path too, we reach the same conclusion. Regardless of the aspect in which we consider this problem, the essence of "I" in all the sovereignty and immediacy of its being is revealed as its specific relation to "thou." Concretely, that which is legitimate in this consciousness of the sovereignty and independence of the being of "I" is reducible to the consciousness of a certain freedom, spontaneity, and thus "primordiality" of "I" and to the essential "equality" of *all* "I's" in this respect. Despite all the immediacy of this consciousness, it is constituted by a relation to another, a relation to "thou." Later, when we examine the relation between "I" and "God" we shall become convinced that the dialectical relation due to which the "primordiality" and "autonomy" of "I" is not its inner, immanent feature, but precisely an *expression* of its connection to the "other" can be revealed in yet another way.

This general fundamental clarification can be supplemented and indirectly confirmed by a number of considerations of a *real* order. Considering the problem psychogenetically for the case of an infant, we can say that consciousness (later expressed in reflection by the words "I am" or simply by the word "I"), the having of oneself as a special entity, as an inner center of life dynamically directed outward, is born in a general, vague undifferentiated life-feeling the moment the infant experiences the loving or the threatening look of his mother and responds to this dynamic, inward-directed ray of life with a corresponding living dynamics directed outward. In this our first life-experience, the element of "thou" (or "thou art") is just as primary as "I" itself; "I" is simply inconceivable without "thou." And if, from this chronologically primary and essentially embryonic state of our life-feeling, we rise directly to the heights of the most subtle and sophisticated analytical thought, we shall find that the history of philosophical thought indirectly confirms the conclusion we have just reached. Is it not astonishing that even though "subjective idealism" (the doctrine that subject is dominant in relation to object, that the world is "our idea") is so widespread and influential not one important, serious thinker has espoused solipsism: the doctrine that denies the reality of "other consciousnesses," the reality of "thou" and "we"? And this in spite of the fact that, from the purely logical standpoint, a consistent subjective idealism should end in solipsism. Berkeley, for whom the concept "to be" is equivalent to the concept "to be perceived" (*esse* = *percipi*)—and for whom the thought that the bread with which we nourish ourselves is something other than only a simple association of ideas appears to be only a "metaphysical fog," clouding a simple and self-evident relationship— Berkeley accepts without wavering, as something self-evident, the existence of a multitude of "spirits" or "souls." Similarly, when Kant (known as the "all-destroying," *der Alleszermalmende*, though it would be more accurate to call him the "all-verifying") reduces all of objective reality to a certain picture that is created by the subject on the basis of innate "forms of consciousness," he does not even pose the question concerning the ground of our faith in the real existence of "other consciousnesses," but simply shares this faith silently, and unconsciously takes it as the ground of his theory of knowledge (for "universal obligatoriness" as the criterion of truth signifies obligatoriness *for all*, i.e., presupposes the presence of many consciousnesses). It appears to me much easier to imagine a "subject," i.e., "me," without an "object," i.e., the real existence of the whole world, than it is to imagine the existence of "me" without the "thou" correlative to "me."

Psychogenetic experience and psychological experience lead to the same conclusion. As is well known, the world-perception of both the infant and the primitive man is characterized by the fact that they are always and everywhere conscious of themselves as surrounded by powers of a "thou-like" nature, that for them the world is full of "spirits," animate forces with respect to which both the infant and the primitive man stand in an "I–thou" relation. Bergson, in his *Deux sources de la morale et de la religion*, masterfully showed (in opposition to Lévy-Bruhl) that all of us, in spite of our "enlightenment," are "infants" and "primitive men" in our immediate, instinctive life-situations. He showed that here it is not a question of an ontogenetic or a phylogenetic stage of human spiritual development, but of a permanent, fundamental tendency of the human spirit. Rational-objective consciousness—replacing the kingdom of the spirit in which we participate by the world of things in which we soberly and detachedly "orient" ourselves, transforming all "thou" into "it"—forms a surface layer on the primary, instinctive life-situation and masks it, but is scarcely able to exclude or annihilate it. At the highest levels of spiritual develop-ment, in the religious life of such a genius as St. Francis of Assisi, for example, not only wolves, birds, and fishes, but even the sun and wind, even death and one's own body become "brothers and sisters," are expe-rienced as "thou."

Of course, the "enlightened" consciousness has the ready objection that all this is purely a psychological phenomenon, a delusion to which man tends to succumb. It is self-evident that one cannot ground a concept by reference to the fact that it is psychologically widespread or even that it is natural or inevitable. And in the present case it is necessary to concede at the very outset that man has the tendency to err in relation to what he imagines as the revelation of "thou." Man has the tendency to accept a *seeming* revelation of "thou" as authentic, to accept an experience of a "thou-like" character as an experience of the authentic reality of "thou." But, first of all, a question arises in the unprejudiced mind: does not the "sober" consciousness which is directed at the objective perception of real-ity have the tendency to commit the opposite error, i.e., to blindly pass by the authentic revelation of "thou," to deny "thou" even where it factually exists and reveals itself, to take the authentic revelation of "thou" to be an illusion? In certain cases (e.g., the common attitude of "civilized" man towards animals and even towards people of "inferior" races) this sort of error is obvious. Thus, one cannot deny out of hand the possibility that the infant, the primitive man, the poet penetrate more deeply—in their "ani-mation" of the world—into the genuine, deep, hidden essence of reality than our sober, prosaic, scientific consciousness.

From the more general, purely philosophical point of view, this possibil-ity becomes a certainty if we consider the general proposition, clarified above, that the "unknowable" as the genuine essence of reality is concealed behind all objective (i.e., rationally conceivable and rationally formed) reality, and that it is precisely this unknowable which immediately reveals itself to us, though in a special form of being, in immediate self-being. It then becomes clear that every experience of "thou"—in spite of all the

possible errors associated with this experience, in spite of all naive or prejudiced errors leading to quick generalization—contains, in the final analysis, a "grain" of the genuine experience of reality.[3] As we said above, the
total unity of being is a *kingdom of spirits*. In this sense the experience of the
reality of "thou," in spite of all the possible particular errors of its interpretation, has a universal significance.

In its general meaning, however, this metaphysical conclusion is not
important for our thesis. The important thing is not whether *every* "thou-
like" experience has real validity, not whether an authentic "thou" is in
fact contained in *every* concrete existent of reality. The important thing is
that, at every moment of its being, "I" stands (or rather, "I stand") in a
relation to *some* "thou," and that the very being and self-awareness of "I"
are inconceivable outside of this relation. And in this relation *the psychological experience as such* (even if in individual cases it is in error from the point of
view of the rational-objective definition of reality) coincides with the
purely phenomenological description of the corresponding reality that we
call "I" and is immanently self-evident. The fact of the universal preva-
lence of "thou-like" experiences, the fact that the very essence of the
experience of "I" is inconceivable without them (we shall clarify this in a
later connection) is evidence of the strict, inseparably intimate bond between "I" and "thou," the necessary correlatedness of these two forms of
reality.

Completely apart from its intrinsic significance, the objection we have
just considered is important because it directs us to something we have not
yet considered, namely to a possible differentiation in the makeup and
meaning of the revelation of "thou." Since this differentiation is significant for the further clarification of the nature of the unknowable as it is
concretely revealed in the form of "thou," we must devote to it a detailed
analysis. The makeup of the revelation of "thou" can be apprehended and
experienced in such a way that it discloses some element that is correlative
only to me, conceivable only in relation to me. In this case "thou," although in its essence it stands "outside" of me, is something whose meaning is exhausted by its function of "thou" in *my* life. Here "thou" coincides
with the *being-for-me* of "another," and the transcending that occurs in this
case means the attainment of "another," but precisely only as *existent for me*.
But the revelation of "thou" also contains something wholly other if and
insofar as it gives us a perception of "thou" as a reality *existent in itself and for
itself*. Even though the meaning of the concept of "thou" consists essentially in the fact that it is a reality that has a relation *to me*, is directed *at me*,

this relation and this directedness can be experienced in such a way that they appear to us as the revelation and the action of a "thou" that is *existent in itself*, of a genuine reality that is independent of me in its makeup. In order to clarify this highly significant distinction, we shall now consider the possible forms and aspects of the "I–thou" relation.

3. THE TWO BASIC FORMS OF THE "I-THOU" RELATION

The fact of the matter is that the "I-thou" relation as such, i.e., in its general essence, must not be confused with such things as sympathy, love, the giving of oneself, mutual intimacy, etc. We must, on the contrary, distinguish *two types* of the "I–thou" relation.

First of all, "thou" in its primary immediacy appears to me or is experienced by me as something alien, frightening, and threatening—something I feel to be frightening and threatening because it lies on the same level, in the same sphere of being as I myself. It is "thou," i.e., immediate self-being, and in this sense it is kindred to me or equal to me. But more than this, it is "other"—not because it is different from me in content or at least not only because of this, but precisely because of the intrinsic form of its being, namely its form as "thou," a second "I," which, contradicting the uniqueness of my "I," is *not my* "I" (that is, it has all the frightfulness of a double). "Thou" is not "I myself"; it is not that ineffable, unique root through which absolute being becomes self-being and is revealed in *me*. But arbitrarily and illegitimately, "thou" pretends to the significance of "I," wants to be like "me," demands for itself a place as "I," and copies my "I," copies *me*. My immediate self-being—having itself as infinite in its potentiality, being surrounded and permeated by its own element—feels itself confused and threatened in this its self-sufficiency *at the precise moment* when it first becomes a genuine "I" through the "I–thou" relation. At this moment it recognizes its limits and therefore sees danger. It is true that even outside of the "I–thou" relation immediate self-being has limits and encounters opposition from objective being, from simple "non-I." But since in this case immediate self-being stands in a relation to something absolutely other than itself, something that lies on a wholly other plane, the limits are only indistinctly felt. Furthermore, objective being does not actively intrude into my immediate self-being, but is experienced only as an external medium, an obstacle, and, in the worst case, as a purely *external* danger, an enemy that besieges me from outside but cannot break into me. On the contrary, "thou" contains the danger of an enemy who may intrude into me and constrict the *inner* fullness of my immediate self-being as such. Meanwhile, "I" experiences fear of a wholly special, eminent kind: the fear of inner insecurity. Therefore "I" retreats deep into itself, and because of this retreat becomes conscious of itself as *inner* self-being for the first time. "I" closes into itself in order to defend itself against attack. Perhaps the most revealing and universal concrete expression of this is shyness. A pair of alien eyes directed at me, the first immediate action upon me of "thou," throws me into a state of unfreedom in which my immediate self-being is paralyzed and its inner life is distorted. But the consciousness of "I" arises for the first time precisely in this situation. Moreover, "I" is born here as an actualized being *in itself* and *for itself*.

We have already seen that the fundamental consciousness of the inner, autonomous, independent character of the being of "I" is an expression of self-protection, self-defense against intrusion from outside by conceal-ment "inside," behind trenches and walls so to speak. Like some peaceful, unorganized primitive tribe which, on suddenly encountering an external foe, immediately organizes itself, closes ranks, groups itself around a leader, and which therefore for the first time becomes conscious of itself as an externally delimited unity with inner solidarity, as a collective whole that can be said to be the protophenomenon of a political state—immediate self-being achieves inner integration, loses its indistinct limitlessness, closes ranks about its center, its "I," and thus becomes "I" for the first time. And this "I," as the highest central agency, is then the "representa-tive" of the whole. Thus, "I" is immediate self-being that has retreated inside itself, closed itself in fear, and mobilized itself, so to speak, for the purpose of attack, sorties, battle. Its alienation and closed character are wholly determined by its directedness towards "thou," its obsession with "thou" as an enemy and threat. "I" arises and exists only *in the face* of "thou" as the alien, fearfully enigmatic phenomenon of "me-like non-I," which confuses and terrifies with its unknowableness. The reality of "thou," which as reality as such coincides with the unknowable in general, is revealed here in the aspect of its incomprehensibility and alienness. Or, to use Rudolf Otto's term for one of the determining features of the religious experience, "thou" is revealed as *mysterium tremendum* (the mys-tery that arouses trembling).

But precisely in this aspect, i.e., as that which is *alien*, "thou" is a kind of "it." The "other," insofar as it is for me *only alien* is therefore *something alien*. Insofar as I do not yet experience "thou" as a "second I" that is ontologi-cally equivalent to me, I am conscious of it only as a "me-like" (but not *my*) element directed against me, an enemy and threat—"thou" is for me an element of objective being, a kind of "it." "Thou" as alien stands at the boundary of "it." As my rival or enemy, "thou" can be my prey, my slave, my tool, or something subject to destruction. Insofar as "thou" is not perceived as equivalent to me, is not for me a legitimate "other," a legitimate other "I," it becomes some "it." ("He," as we have pointed out, is "thou" submerged in the sphere of "it.") It is true that "thou" cannot *wholly* become an "it"; otherwise the "I–thou" relation would be destroyed. Even the most intense repulsion from "another," even the most furious hostility and hatred is still an "I–thou" relation, though it borders on the absence of the relation. Only contempt leading to total indifference, to the non-being of "thou" for me, can transform "thou" into an indifferent "he," thus destroying the "I–thou" relation itself.

This orientation toward "thou" as alien can be considered (though only in a conditional and limited sense, as we shall see below) the genetically primary and fundamental form of the "I–thou" relation on which all that follows will be based, including the second form of this relation. "Thou" can of course have for me a *wholly other* meaning. It can contain an element directly opposed to the one we have just described. That is, immediate self-being can recognize in "thou" the soothing and comforting reality of a kindred soul, a kindred something that is like my homeland, a reality that, though outside of my immediate self-being, is inwardly identical to the latter. In encountering this kind of "thou" or in capturing this element in the makeup of "thou," I stop feeling that I am unique and alone. Outside of me, I have found something "me-like," existing in my image and likeness. "Non-I," without ceasing to be "thou" (i.e., without ceasing to be not "me myself") is "I" outside of me myself—and not in the frightening, unnatural, unlawful sense of a double but in such a way that, without losing or shaking the uniqueness of my "I" as such, I find in the external world a being full of the same element that makes up my own inner being. This is a sensitive and understanding "I–thou" relation that penetrates into "thou" and reveals "thou"; and it is precisely here that this relation is constituted for the first time in its full actuality. This is not a frightening and threatening but a comforting and joyous mystery: not *mysterium tremendum* but *mysterium fascinosum*. We shall return later to the essence of this mystery as the mystery of *love*. Here we shall emphasize only one thing: If one considers (we repeat, only in a conditional and approximate sense) that the consciousness of "I" and therefore the self-being of "I" as such arise for the first time in reaction to "thou" as the alien and threatening element of the "other," in reaction to an "I-like" being outside of me, then on the other hand "I" as such takes inner form for the first time, acquires solid reality, perceives the uniqueness, legitimacy, and comprehensibility of its essence only when it sees itself in the light of a "thou" that is essentially kindred and identical to it. In other words it takes inner form only when it finds its being confirmed outside of itself as a reality that is given from outside, is revealed from outside, and in this sense is "objective." Without respect for "others," without respect for "thou" as a self-evident, inwardly legitimate reality, there is no fully formed self-consciousness, no inwardly solid self-being of "I."

But here we must note that it is not so much a question of two different types or forms of the "I–thou" relation as of two different elements which to a certain degree and in a certain proportion are immanently present in all concrete "I–thou" relations. The difference between these two concrete forms of the relation is essentially reducible to the relative significance, or the degree of our awareness, of these two elements. If we call these two types of relations *negative* and *positive* "I–thou" relations, we can say that every concrete "I–thou" relation is simultaneously negative and positive. Even the most hostile orientation, the orientation of "I's" self-defense against "thou," or "I's" attack on "thou," conceals the experience of a certain "belonging-together," a certain kinship of "I" and "thou," for something absolutely alien and other could have no relation to me, and its being would lie in a sphere of reality wholly foreign to me. There must be "interest" between "I" and "thou," the consciousness that the two share the same *kind* of being. And this is potentially an element of closeness and unity. In the extreme case a "struggle to the death" is of course conceivable; and not even in the sense of an even-handed battle but in the sense of a hunt that ends with the death of the prey. But in this extreme case the "I–thou" relation has been lost completely and replaced by a pure "I–he" relation, which is equivalent to an "I–it" relation. On the contrary, all even-handed battle implies a minimum of "respect" for the enemy, a minimum of perception of him as a "me-like," "me-resembling" "thou." On the other hand every "positive" "I–thou" relation—however much love, mutual trust, sympathy, and understanding it may contain—always conceals a certain amount of "alienness" and "otherness" which cannot be overcome. And in every "thou," even one who is loved by me and kindred to me, there is something which terrifies me and which I cannot understand, precisely because in the final analysis I am nonetheless absolutely unique and alone for myself, and there can be no question of absolute, boundless, unqualified kinship between me and some "thou." Therefore, enmity and hate can be the expression of secret, unfulfilled love, just as love and hate in general are bonded together in some mysterious manner. Furthermore, erotic love, which aspires to the most intimate unity of "I" and "thou," presupposes harsh, sometimes tragic conflicts between its participants. Tyutchev calls "the union of a soul with its sister soul" their "fateful duel." Thus, in its essence the "I–thou" relation is, like the religious relation as it is described by Rudolf Otto, a mysterious, unknowable, and transrational unity of *mysterium tremendum* and *mysterium fascinosum, the unity of the mystery of fear and enmity with the mystery of love.*

4. THE "I–THOU" RELATION AS THE UNITY OF SEPARATENESS AND MUTUAL PENETRATION

The infinite diverse fullness of concrete phenomena and forms of relations which develop in the common ground of the "I–thou" relation has not yet been subjected to anything like complete scientific investigation. We can say that scientific (philosophical, psychological, and sociological) thought has scarcely begun this investigation, because (with such rare exceptions as Max Scheler, Martin Buber, Ferdinand Ebner, and to some extent Georg Simmel) it has not yet acknowledged the "I–thou" relation as a special, primary *form* of being. Only poets, novelists, and playwrights draw their themes from this sphere. We are not concerned here with the concrete, differentiated manifestations of the general "I–thou" relation as they are determined, for example, by the elements of domination and subordination, activity and passivity, the degree of closeness or intimacy in a relationship, restraint and intrusion, freedom and inhibition, etc. For us the essential thing is to clarify the general categorial *form of being* of the "I–thou" relation, and that only insofar as it has meaning for our basic theme.

"Thou" is "not-I" *par excellence*. It is constituted by the element "not" which is added to "I." However, we are not dealing with a purely logical "not" in its general meaning as an element constituting difference or opposition in the sense of abstractly, logically graspable incompatibility. Rather, we are dealing with a concrete "not," experienced or revealing itself as a *real living* relation. In accordance with the two forms or elements (i.e., negative and positive) of the "I–thou" relation we have just examined, this "not," this *separateness*, can have two meanings. On the one hand separateness can refer only to the reality of "I" and "thou." But on the other hand it can also refer to their inner makeup or essence. In the former case, in the case of an "understanding" "I–thou" relation based on "sympathy," "thou" is essentially only numerically "another," something like a real "second I," an immediate self-being located *outside* of me, but approaching me, revealing itself to me, and experienced by me. In the latter case the separateness also refers to the qualities, makeup, and essence of "thou" itself. "Thou" is "another" not merely in the sense of a "second I" but also in the sense of an "alien" being, in the sense of a self-being that is foreign and heterogeneous in relation to me. But since, as we have indicated, these two forms are two correlative, integral elements of every "I–thou" relation, it follows that the full, exhaustive meaning of this separateness lies precisely in the unity of both of these elements. "Thou" is *not* "I." "I" as such *am* absolutely unique and can think of myself only in the grammatical singular. And in this sense every "thou" is something wholly other than "I." But "thou" is also another, a second "I" or "me-like" being, located outside of me and connected to me, entering into my life. This antagonistic dual-unity of the terrifying and the intimately dear makes up the enigmatic essence of "thou."

But there is an inner connection between separateness and *mutual penetration*. The essence of the "I–thou" relation cannot be subsumed under the concept of a purely external relation, such as the relation between two separate bodies. On the contrary, the "I-thou" relation is a "communion." But the word "communion" conceals a riddle the meaning of which can be guessed only through the antinomian concept of *mutual penetration with separateness, the mutual penetration of the separate.* In some sense the "I–thou" relation contains the element of encounter, converging motion from two different points, the intersection of two dynamic potencies that meet on opposite paths. On the other hand we have already seen that this encounter would be impossible if "I" and "thou" did not originally belong to each other, if they were not originally *one with the other.* This being of *the one with the other* is not simple adjacency and interaction, even if we take these relations as inwardly experienced, self-revealing, existent *for* themselves. The effect upon me of a rock that strikes my body and causes pain and irritation is something *wholly other* than any (even the most antagonistic) "I–thou" relation. For the rock that strikes me is experienced in the form that the effect upon me "from outside" has as its consequence certain processes "inside" of me (i.e., in my immediate self-being) which have nothing in common with the "outside" reality that acts upon me. In other words the difference between "outside" and "inside" is maintained in all its force. Two bodies (and generally speaking, two objective realities) always remain, however intimate or deep their interaction, two separate, mutually external, *mutually non-penetrating* realities.

We have something wholly other in the "I–thou" relation as it reveals itself to us immediately in its genuine essence. The essential feature of the "I–thou" relation consists precisely in the fact that, in spite of a strictly maintained, never-disappearing *separateness*, the relation is dominated by a certain genuinely *inner* unity. This unity is essentially a *dual*-unity. The loss of this duality (as for example in the ecstatic-mystical immersion and dissolution in the absolute) means the loss of the "I–thou" relation. But this dual-unity is also profoundly inward, genuine *unity*. Here, the being of the one *with* the other, the action of the one *upon* the other, is the being of the one *for* the other. And this being of the one for the other is therefore, in spite of the separateness, the being of the one in the other. The very reality of the "other," "thou" itself, penetrates into me. "Thou" itself *is* for me, is experienced by me, is revealed to me *inside of me*, though as a reality that is *outside* of me. Or on the other hand, I transcend "myself." I experience "thou" as a reality *outside* of me; but because I *experience* it, it belongs to *my* life, to my immediate self-being (even though in my immediate self-being it is "other than I myself," precisely "thou"). Only insofar as I view "thou" in an objective-spatial way as an "alien body" that is joined to an "alien soul" can "thou" stand with univocal clarity *outside* of me in the literal, the precise sense of "outside," in the sense of "another place" than I. But taken in this sense it is no longer "thou" but at best only "he." But as "thou," as a content of immediately experienced self-being in which another reality, existing outside of me, is revealed to me—it is also located *inside* me. As we indicated at the end of the preceding chapter, this is something wholly other than transcending in the cognitive intentionality, for in the latter I am only the source of "the ray of light" which emanates from me and "illuminates," "reveals" for me a certain reality that is univocally existent *outside* of me, while in all other respects I as an immediate self-being remain *inside* myself (just as objective reality remains outside of me). Only *from outside* do I touch objective reality through my "gaze," through the "cognitive light." But here, on the contrary, we are dealing with the *real* transcending of immediate self-being, its real transcending of itself and its real penetration into the "other" (into "thou"). And this transcending also means the real penetration into me of the reality of the "other."

Thus, in the "I–thou" relation the transrational essence of reality—the essentially unknowable in reality—is disclosed with particular certainty as *the unity of separateness and mutual penetration*. That which an examination of the essence of reality in general and of immediate self-being in particular revealed to us as a certain kind of hidden essential feature of concrete reality, attainable only through penetration into the depths, namely the concrete unity of separateness and mutual penetration, here becomes immediately evident to our gaze. This unity of separateness and mutual penetration forms the very *essence* of the "I–thou" relation as a primordial *kind of being*, in which this unity is completely actualized in perfect equilibrium (although the equilibrium is always unstable). This coincidence of "inside" and "outside," of "I" and "not-I," with all the oppositeness preserved, is the most expressive disclosure of the coincidence of opposites, of the unity of two, of antinomian monodualism. The "I–thou" relation as "I–thou" being is thus revealed as a *primordial* form of being, as *the revelation of the inner structure of reality as such*—and precisely in its *unknowableness*—beyond all conceptual knowledge. Here we are dealing with what is absolutely unknowable for logical thinking determined by the principle of negation: namely the *real, inner, existent-for-itself mutual interwovenness and mutual permeatedness* of the "one" and the "other." And insofar as we have attained the metalogical unity of reality as concrete total unity, the unity of unity and diversity, the unity that is present in all its wholeness in every part and permeates every part—we can say that *in the "I–thou" relation genuine concrete total unity in its transrational, unknowable essence is revealed for the first time precisely as living being*. The fact that all-embracing unity is omnipresent, that it is present as a whole in all of its parts, is revealed to us here in all the livingness of this relation. It is revealed to us in the fact that singular being as self-being is not a closed, isolated, lonely being but—as "I"—is linked to "thou" and is a being that realizes itself as "I–thou" being. All immediate self-being becomes "I," i.e., realizes itself, only when it goes beyond itself, transcends itself into "thou." *Being is the kingdom of spirits*, and the kingdom of spirits consists precisely in the fact that *the one* always exists *for the other*, that, transcending itself, the one affirms itself only by abandoning itself for the other.

5. LOVE

The transrationality and unknowableness of immediate self-being as they are revealed in *the being of the one for the other* is disclosed in its ultimate depth in the phenomenon of *love*, in which the "I–thou" relation is realized in all its fullness for the first time. The riddle of the "I–thou" relation has not yet been completely solved by all we have said above. There remains one thing yet to be clarified. We have already seen that the possession of "thou," the transcending to "thou," can have a double meaning. A distinction must be made between the simple possession of some "thou" (i.e., the experience of the presence in my immediate self-being of a dynamic activity directed from outside and somehow analogous to my self-being) and the perception of "thou" as a *genuine reality, existent in itself and for itself.* The kingdom of self-revealing reality as it is disclosed in the "I–thou" relation is a being that has many correlative centers, a being that is *polycentric.* For immediate self-being itself as a concrete "I," these centers cannot be equivalent. *My* "I" is something absolutely unique for me. That deep, primordial point of being which I call "I," thanks to which I am for myself precisely "I am," has an absolute significance for me, a significance incomparable to anything else. In this sense *I am unique.* And all else— compared to this "I am," this self-illuminating point of light and love, this point existent for itself, through which all else can be *for me* for the first time—belongs, in the final analysis, to another, subordinate sphere. Of course, this should not be understood to mean that every man in his essence is an "egotist" in the common, everyday sense of the word. Such a view is based on dim, uncertain thinking that helplessly confuses conceptual categories. This vulgar, intellectually helpless theory is largely based on the confusion of our "I" as the subject of consciousness and knowledge with "I" as an immediate self-being in all the complex and unpredetermined makeup of its life. But even though immediate self-being is in itself undoubtedly something other than the subject of knowledge or even consciousness, it is nevertheless true that the ideal point called "subject"—the point at which the light of consciousness and knowledge originates—lies within immediate self-being. And in this sense it is true that, according to the ontological structure of his being as self-being, man is literally an "*egoist*" in his primordial makeup, i.e., he is a being who has as his absolute center that ineffable something which is called "ego" or "I." Thus, "thou" is precisely "thou-for-me": a reality which I possess in its action *upon me*, in its significance *for me*, and the essence of which consists for me precisely in this mode of its being. I cannot get out of my body and have "thou"— which in its essence is *not* I myself—with the same primordial immediacy with which I have myself. Thus, even though the possession of "thou" is possible for me precisely as *my* possession of "thou," it appears that I can never possess the genuine being of "thou" as a self-being that is absolutely independent of me; that I can never possess the element "art" in the judgment "thou art" in all its fullness and depth, in which "art" is another "am," which reveals itself to me. But the ultimate, genuine mystery of "thou" lies precisely in this "art," i.e., in a reality existent in itself, independently of me, in which the unknowable miracle of another "I" is revealed to me together with "me myself."

This miracle is realized for me in the phenomenon of *love*, and precisely for this reason love is a miraculous phenomenon, a kind of mystery. Love in its essence is not simply a "feeling," an emotional relation to another being. The primary meaning of the phenomenon of love consists in the fact that it is actualized, perfect transcending to "thou" as a genuine "I-like" *reality* that exists in itself and for itself; that it is the revelation and the perception of "thou" as this kind of reality and the attainment in "thou" of an *ontological point of reference for me*. The unattainable is attained here. Here I really "get out of my body": immediate self-being, without losing its unique center, becomes genuinely *bicentric*. Together with its center "I," immediate self-being now possesses the center "thou" as its *own* point of reference. Here "thou" is not merely my *possession*, not merely a reality *only in relation to me*, not merely a reality that is in *my* possession and which exists only within the limits of *my* self-being, in its action upon *me*. I do not "absorb" "thou" into myself. On the contrary, I myself step into "thou," am "transferred" into it, and "thou" becomes *mine* only insofar as I *myself* am conscious of belonging to it. It is a question of the existent transcending to the reality of the "other" as such. And insofar as the reality of the "other" is revealed to me in such transcending, knowledge *from inside* (through co-experience) of "thou's" otherness and *uniqueness* is thereby attained for the first time. And this knowledge is the recognition and acceptance of "thou." Only on this path, through love, do my eyes open through the perception and acceptance of the otherness of the "other," of "thou"; and "thou" becomes for me a "second I."

Common "wisdom" says that love "blinds." This seeming wisdom contains a grain of truth only in the sense that love, if it destroys the possibility of "sober," dispassionate orientation in objective reality, can lead to erroneous *comparative* judgments and evaluations; that is, we tend to take the side of our "loved one" to the detriment of those we do not love and are thus able to view dispassionately. However, love in itself (outside of objective judgments concerning others) does not blind, but opens our eyes, gives us sight, for the first time. By revealing to us "thou" in its real profound center, by revealing "thou" as a *person*, love makes us accessible for the first time to the revelation of the *holiness* of the person, a holiness we cannot keep from loving reverently even in the most hideous, perverted, and monstrous criminal.

Furthermore, all the words with which we attempt to conceptually describe and define the miracle of love are inadequate to its mysterious, supra-rational nature. Love is *union*, being in *unity*, with "another." It would appear that nothing could be simpler and more understandable than this phenomenon. But if we reflect on it, this formula gives an indication of the unknowable, mysterious essence of love. For abstract thought, *two* is precisely *two*, and can be *one* no more than a square can be a circle. But here *two* do become *one*, or *one* becomes *one* plus *another*, a *second*. Having attained this transrational sphere of reality in its full living concreteness, I perceive that in my ultimate depth I am nevertheless not unique, not alone. My "aloneness," without ceasing to be a separate, unique being, is also revealed as a "two-ness." (Nietzsche uses the terms *Einsamkeit* and *Zweisamkeit* to describe this.) The incomparable, absolutely unique reality that I call "I" experiences itself, has itself, also as a component and particular element of a larger whole that is identical to "I" in makeup and character of being. Only here the inner essence of the total unity of being is revealed as the inwardly separated totality of immediate self-being. It is revealed that every *one* is also *one* of *two*, a member of a set of *two* (or many), and that these *two* (or many) are *one* in their ultimate depth. True transcending to "thou" as a genuine, "me-like" reality therefore presupposes the primordial being of my selfhood in the sphere of "I–thou" being, in the sphere of the living total unity that is existent for itself. This is, as it were, an attempt to reunite that which is primordially *one* in the ultimate depths of reality.

Furthermore, we are not dealing here with an exceptional phenomenon. It is a question neither of "ideal," "romantic" love in the erotic sense (*le grand amour*, as the French say) nor of religiously illuminated, profound love for one's fellow man in the sense of the Christian commandment to love one's neighbor (*agape*) in contrast to all other, "earthly" love. It is rather a question of a universal fundamental phenomenon that regulates all of human life, for in some sense the perception and acceptance of "thou" as a reality that is equivalent and kindred to me forms the foundation of all human life as immediate self-being. In this its essence, love is revealed not only in erotic and marital love, not only in maternal love, not only in love for parents, brothers, and sisters, not only in true intimate friendship, but also in every relation to "thou" as a genuine reality kindred to me, in every relation to "thou" as my "neighbor." All "sympathy"—in good and in bad, however superficial and fleeting, and even a simple smile of greeting, and ultimately even mere politeness if it is not artificial but originates in genuine respect for another's person—is a manifestation of love in its metaphysical essence. But on the other hand there is no "perfect" love, there is no "I–thou" relation that is "pure" love in the metaphysical sense (if we set aside religiously grounded love, which we shall discuss in another connection). This is the case because the element of "thou's" "alienness," "thou's" heterogeneity and strangeness with respect to me, or my "possession" of "thou" as only a necessary, useful, or even hostile dynamic entity within my self-being—is always present in every concrete human love. Every concrete "I–thou" relation is an oscillation between two poles: the pole of true love as the being of "I" together with or within the reality of "thou" and the pole of the simple "possession" of "thou" as a factor of my self-being.

Thus, the "coincidence of opposites," *coincidentia oppositorum*, in its deepest essence—the ground of reality as antinomian monodualism—is revealed in a concrete-living way only in the phenomenon of love. The unknowableness of reality is revealed here in its concrete makeup beyond the difference and opposition between the "one" and the "other"—not as logical but as concretely existent contents. The coincidence of *being for another and in another* with what is, in essence, *being in itself and for itself* is revealed in the phenomenon of love. And this coincidence is such that the interconnected diversity of being in itself and for itself is not thereby eliminated but is preserved and even completed for the first time in all its fullness and depth.

6. The Being of "We"

Taken in the aspect of its unity, the "I-thou" relation is represented in the concept of "we." Only at first glance can it appear that "we" is merely another, synonymous designation for the same relation. On the contrary, our language—having created the astonishing word "we," full of the deepest content—expresses in this word a unique element of reality, a special character or form of being, which conscious thought (at least modern philosophy) has scarcely begun to investigate.

Viewed from outside, from the standpoint of the objective observer, the being of "we," being in community, appears to be something that needs no explanation. At first glance it appears to be a simple truism that the individual man (who, biologically, owes his existence to the joining of two other individuals, his parents) in his entire material, psychic, and spiritual life is a member of a society or community (be it family, nation, church, state, class, or caste). And it appears that modern thought has sufficiently understood and exposed the superficiality and falsity of the once-popular individualist doctrine that man, in his primordial nature, is an isolated, singular being—the doctrine that it is only for reasons of necessity and convenience that man enters into an "agreement" or "contract" with other people who are similar to him to found a community or society. After all, even Robinson Crusoe owes his existence on his island to society and the resources of society: what preserves his life (even apart from the tools and supplies he salvages from the ship) is his inner mastery of the abilities, knacks, and know-how that he acquired in his native land, his native society. At first glance this appears to be so unquestionable as to leave no room for a more profound philosophical examination.

But in spite of the certainty of the foregoing considerations, we must point out that in its primary, inner structure, the being of "we" cannot be an object of objective observation and knowledge, but is given to us only as an experienced, self-revealing reality. Therefore this reality is accessible only to the mode of knowing that is appropriate to it. Taken in this its makeup, *from within*, the being of "we" turns out to be a wholly special, miraculous mode or form of being. It is a form of being which usually escapes our attention, a form of being in which the primary forms of being "am" and "art" merge into a deeper unity that is essentially different from them; or rather this unity is the common root of these primary forms. Besides the form of being of "it" or "is" and the forms of being "I am" and "thou art" (even if we take the latter two in their mutual interconnectedness, their inseparableness from each other) there exists a more deeply rooted form of being: namely the being of "we." The being of "we" overcomes, even if it also conserves, (in the dual, Hegelian sense of *aufheben*), the very opposition between "I am" and "thou art," the opposition between "I" and "thou." And since "I am" can be thought and given only in the unity "we are" (which also encompasses "thou art"), it follows that, contrary to the common view, "I am" is not the primary, adequate, and all-embracing form of inner being, immediate self-being, but is only a partial and derivative element of a deeper and more primary revelation of reality in the form of the being of "we." "We" is a coincidence of opposites experienced and revealing itself in inner immediacy, a coincidence of opposites in which I perceive the inner ground of my own existence—*me*—in the unity of being "inside of me" and being "outside of me" which surpasses all rational thought. It is revealed that *I am* even where *I myself* am not, that my own being is grounded in my co-participation in being that is not mine, that *I myself am in thou art.* "We"—as a visible community or society, as the belonging-together of two or several persons, the society that "surrounds" me and to which I belong only in a sort of external way—is only the external manifestation and reflection of the "we" in which I exist in the sense that *it is in me* or in the sense that it is the primordial inner ground of "I am" itself.

An understanding of being that is guided by the perception of the genuine essence of the phenomenon of "we" is encountered in certain themes of ancient thought, e.g., Heraclitus' teaching of the inner kinship and mutual connectedness of consciousnesses through their participation in the common *logos* that permeates them; the teaching of the Stoics concerning the cosmos as the "kingdom of gods and men"; Plotinus' comparison of men with the leaves of a tree, outside separate but inside (through the branches of a common trunk) nourished and given life by a common sap that comes from the roots. This understanding of being is the basis of St. Paul's mystical teaching of the church as a living body whose members, separate persons, form an inseparable unity that embraces and permeates all of spiritual life. But modern philosophy has in general neglected this primordial perception of being. True ontology, however, is possible only in the form of the intellectual understanding of the revelation of reality in the being of "we," only in the form that we can call "sociomorphism." We distinguished above between the self-revelation of reality to its own self in immediate self-being and the revelation of "thou" that proceeds outward and is directed at the "other," namely at "me." In the being of "we," we have a more primary form of revelation that surpasses these two forms. In the experience of "we" the revelation of "thou" that is directed at me merges with the self-revelation of my own being into *a primordial unity of outer being and inner being*, which is revealed to me in such a way that this revelation is the self-revelation of the inner ground of my own being. In the revelation of "we" we are given the joyous and fortifying experience of the inner harmony and kinship of "inner" being and "outer" being, the experience of the intimate correspondence of my inner self-being with the outer being that surrounds me, the experience of the inner refuge of the soul in its own home. This is the origin of the sanctity and the immeasurable depth of such feelings as love for motherland, love for family, friendship, and communal religious faith. In "we," reality is revealed as the kingdom of spirits, and this takes place through the inner self-revelation of reality to itself. The ontological categories of "inside" and "outside" are essentially overcome in a higher unity. In other words, the unity of separateness and mutual penetration is given here for the first time in the form of self-revelation, i.e., as a genuine, absolutely primordial, self-evident unity, which does not require and does not admit further analysis.

It is clear that an adequate social philosophy can be constructed only on the basis of the intellectual understanding of this primary mode of being, i.e., the being of "we."[4] But this problem lies beyond the limits of our discussion. Here we can only briefly outline some general ideas which are closely linked to our basic theme and are able to clarify it.

If the being of "we" is, so to speak, nothing but the inner side of the "I-thou" relation, it nevertheless is a special form of being in its own right. This is concretely expressed in the fact that the being of "we" can, in some paradoxical manner, be alienated or torn away from the depths of our self-being and appear to stand *outside* the latter. This is the case precisely insofar as I can separate, in thought and even in living experience, my immediate self-being as the detached sphere of my inner life from the sphere of the being of "we." Then I have the experience that "I" stand in relation not only to "thou" but also to "we" *as such*. My life appears to be inwardly divided into two parts: first, into the detached, lonely life of "I" as such, the intimate mystery (impenetrable for others) of my inner life as a unique, unrepeatable person; and second, into a kind of socially conditioned "I," which is a member of the unity of "we." Even when it is a question of the pure "I-thou" relation (i.e., the free communion of two human beings), a *third* something arises if the "I-thou" relation is sufficiently strong and enduring. This third something is a *whole* composed of "I" and "thou," which appears to have a certain being-for-itself *in addition to* the two singular human beings who compose it. We are speaking of such phenomena as the beginning, middle, or end of a marriage or a friendship, of the bond that unites two human beings. We are conscious of our responsibilities not only in relation to the other living participant of the union but also in relation to the union, the whole itself. And the stability of a human relationship is often determined by our attention to the value of the whole, the union, the bond itself.

The unity of "we" and the relation of "I" to this unity are even more distinct and effective when the "I-thou" relation embraces not two, but three or more persons, i.e., when "thou" is given in the plural as "you." *Tres faciunt collegium.* In fact, when I have a relation to at least two "thou's," themselves connected by an "I-thou" relation, I not only have a relation to each of them as a singular being, but also a relation to the bond that unites them, to their dual-unity, to the being of "we" of both of them. Every "you" is a part of "we" that has become alienated from me and has come to stand outside of me. Therefore the unity of "we" is alive not only in the "I–thou" relation, is not only this relation itself taken as a whole (in such a way that I could be conscious of myself only as *within* it), but also comes forth to meet me as something outside of me and demands of me a relation to itself as such. When the relation embraces many people (e.g., in a labor union or a military regiment) and especially when the whole is not created by separate individuals but has a primordial existence, so that I am born into the whole already a member of it (e.g., a whole such as a nation or a political state), then the "I–thou" relation as a relation to separate persons is absolutely secondary to the relation to the "group" itself, to the collective itself as the unity of its participants. Here what is essential is not that I am one of "many" but that I belong to the unity. Only indirectly and derivatively (precisely through the whole as such) do I have a relation to separate "thou's." I have a direct and immediate relation only to the whole, to the spiritual atmosphere that lives and functions in all the members together as a unity, to the *esprit de corps*, to the living and palpably concrete "we" as such.

This *objectification* of "we"—in which we are dealing not with an illusion but with a wholly real phenomenon (its reality can be denied only by one who has a "nominalistic" or materialistic bias and therefore identifies reality with the concrete, visible, tangible existence of singular beings)—indicates that, although the being of "we" is the inner ground of the being of my "I," this does not exclude but rather presupposes a certain tension and antagonism between this inner ground and the being of "I" as a purely inner self-being. The being "we" has an unrestrainable tendency to alienate itself from me, to grow into the objective world, to confront me as an external reality existent in itself, and to *determine* and *dominate* me from outside. Furthermore, it is not (we repeat) a question of the external, corporeal reality of separate individuals who make up "society," but of the invisible, incorporeal unity of "we," which embraces us and seizes hold of us as a supra-temporal unity, not fixed to any separate, concrete human life. When I feel the enormous power of the law, of state order or authority, the enormous power of public opinion or of the prevailing mores, and the domination of this power over my life, I stand before a mystical reality that acts upon me as a real being of the objective world, before a reality that can destroy my life like a boulder that can fall on my head or like the impenetrable stone walls of a prison, which confine and constrict my life.

The mystical nature of this reality is wholly independent of its religio-ethical evaluation, but is present simply as a fact that compels us with all the necessity and inevitability of the factually given. It makes no difference if, like Hegel, we consider the state to be an "earthly god" or if, like Nietzsche, we are repelled with horror by the state as "the coldest of all cold monsters." (We shall see directly below that both of these views contain a certain amount of truth.) The mystical element in the state—namely the fact that in the state an invisible, intangible, impersonal something dominates our fate with all the power of a colossal objective reality—remains in force simply as a fact that cannot be denied.

Here "we" manifests itself as a sort of impersonal "it," which forms the ground and the primordial source of objective being. And this is more than a mere analogy. If "we" is manifested in such a form, this is because "we" originates in the "it" (clarified in Chapter V) of immediate self-being and congeals into objectivity in its revelation in the being of "we." *The social and historical element is the cosmic element in human life.* For this reason this element has for man all the terror and irrationality that characterize cosmic being. It has all the indifference and heartlessness of nature. This element discloses that we not only find ourselves and exist in the "world" but that we ourselves also belong to the "world" precisely in the sense that the "world" lives inside us, and, growing out of us into the outside, acts upon us with all the power of the cosmic element, acts upon and dominates our self-being insofar as the latter is our "personal life."

But it would be wholly one-sided to view "we" in its solidification into "it" as only a dark force of pure irrationality. Like objectivity in the external world and in nature, objectified "we" is the unity of rationality and irrationality, and therefore it is not purely irrational but is *transrational* as well. The being of "we" is not only an elementary cosmic unity of life, it is also the rational unity of a communal *order* and a communal *goal* of life. We are most subject to the enormous power of "we" in its form as "it" not when it merely dominates us as a dark, impersonal force, a blind force of nature in its anarchic manifestation (for example, in the phenomenon of a political rebellion which resembles a hurricane), but when it rules us as a conscious human design in the form of law or state order. The norm of law or state order as the universally obligatory is that in social life which corresponds to the *law of nature*. In the final analysis this norm represents the power of abstract *definiteness*, which alone constitutes being as objective being.

In spite of the fearsome nature of this objectified "we," it performs a wholly definite, purposeful function. It is the necessary crust or shell—which has solidified or crystallized by the principle of *rational universality* as it were—with which the living, primary core of the being of "we" surrounds itself in order to protect and strengthen its inner effectiveness and validity as the living ground of our personal life. There exists an unbreakable link, an intimate bond, but also a permanent antagonism, between this inner core of the being of "we" in its living metaphysical profundity which is necessary for our life and this alienated, objectified crust or shell. The living sanctity of a nation or a homeland cannot be realized without the protection of the impersonally severe, cold firmness of the state. The living sanctity of the church cannot be realized without church discipline, law, and power. Even a family or circle of friends cannot dispense with order, discipline, common norms. The holy and deepest mystery of "we" is (just as the mystery of "I–thou") the mystery of love. But the grace-giving mystery of love protects itself and realizes itself in the world through cold, rational *order*, even though the inner essence and the outer appearance are in a permanent state of immanent antagonism. In this sense the being of "we" is also subject to the universal ontological principle of antinomian monodualism, the principle of the coincidence of opposites. The task of ontologically grounded political philosophy is to find, under the given concrete (social, psychological, cultural, and historical) conditions, the most appropriate form which could to a maximal degree insure the healthy (though always unstable) equilibrium of these two elements of the being of "we." Here we can only outline a general principle: this equilibrium must transcend both pure social *rationalism* (the limitless rationalization and therefore objectification of social life) and universal, essentially anarchic, romantic *irrationalism*. For the essence of the being of "we," as of all reality in general, is precisely the essentially unknowable. Therefore the being of "we" transcends all pure rationality and all pure irrationality and has all the antinomian fullness and concreteness of the "transrational."

We have seen that the very opposition between "inner" and "outer" appears to be overcome in the being of "we." This being exhibits both "outward" transcending toward "thou" and "inward" transcending into the primordial ground and depths of immediate self-being itself. Therefore the true transcendental-metaphysical essence of the "I–thou" relation can, strictly speaking, be attained only by the clarification of the second form of transcending: *inward transcending*. This is the subject of the next chapter.

NOTES

1. For a discussion of this see my essay "I and We" in the *Collection of Essays in Honor of P.B. Struve*, Prague 1926. And for a more detailed examination see my German essay "Ich und Wir" in the journal *Der russische Gedanke*, Bonn 1928.
2. It is well-known that executioners and professional killers never look directly into the eyes of their victims or into the eyes of any other person. This is completely natural. Since the repetition of killing presupposes an orientation to other human beings in which they are treated simply as "external" objects, pure indifferent "it's," it follows that the repetition of killing requires constant practice in this orientation. But any, even the most fleeting, encounter with the living human gaze—being the mysterious revelation of "thou," a "me-like" being, a "second" "I"—immediately annihilates this purely objective orientation, transfers us to a wholly different plane of being, in which this orientation is completely impossible. It is completely natural that in such professions this kind of encounter with "thou" is avoided, and avoided instinctively.
3. The "I–thou" relation in its primary sense as the immediate experience of reality is strikingly portrayed by Turgenev in his depiction of the relationship between man and animal in his prose-poem "The Dog": "The dog sits before me and looks into my eyes. And I look into her eyes. It is as though she wants to tell me something. She is mute, wordless, does not understand herself, but I understand her. I understand that at this moment the two of us share the same feeling, that there is no difference between us. We are identical: both of us contain the same trembling flame. . . . No! It is not an animal and a man that exchange looks. It is two pairs of identical eyes directed at each other. And in each of these pairs—in the animal and in the man—one and the same life presses close to the other in fright."
4. Translator's Note: Frank considers this problem in his book *The Spiritual Foundations of Society: An Introduction to Social Philosophy (Dukhovnye Osnovy Obshchestva: Vvedenie v sotsial'nuiu filosofiiu)*, Paris 1930.

Chapter VII

Inward Transcending:
Spiritual Being

1. INWARD TRANSCENDING

We have seen that immediate self-being in its subjectivity, in its need for fulfillment and stability, transcends outward toward "thou" and finds completion for the first time in this transcending. However, experience teaches us that this does not exhaust the transcending of immediate self-being, its aspiration to find an essential ground, a solid foundation in something "other." Just as necessary and essential for immediate self-being is transcending in the opposite direction, transcending *inward* or *into the depths*, as a result of which immediate self-being attains the sphere of "spirit" and takes root in it.

Before we attempt to clarify the possibility of inward transcending and the genuine essence of what is attained thereby, let us first ask why it is that immediate self-being or (to use the common term) the "soul" cannot be satisfied with transcending to "thou," with the realization of itself in communion. We have seen that, at least in the positive "I–thou" relation, which is based on sympathy, and particularly in the potentiated transcending in genuine "love," "I" has the comforting and joyous experience of finding a ground for itself outside of itself. Why is this insufficient for the realization of the aspiration of immediate self-being to overcome its subjectivity?

The first and most immediate answer to this question is that there exists no concrete "I–thou" relation that does not contain together with the element of "kinship," the element of finding oneself in "another," also the opposite element of what is alien, unlike, and hostile in "thou." A drop of bitter disappointment is contained in the most intimate and happy "I–thou" relation. The deepest "two-ness," even if it overcomes the hard loneliness of immediate self-being (and every communion, even the most fleeting and superficial, overcomes this loneliness to some degree), leaves behind a sediment of unspoken and unspeakable loneliness that cannot be overcome. The loneliness of my immediate self-being belongs to the very essence of the latter insofar as this loneliness is nothing else but an expression of the absolute uniqueness of immediate self-being. In this sense even the most intimate love has no right to attempt to penetrate this loneliness, to intrude into it, and to overcome it by annihilating it, for this would be to annihilate the inner being of the loved one. On the contrary, love must be (as Rilke subtly points out) a gentle protection of the loneliness of the loved one. But on the other hand, this loneliness which is jealously closed in itself and cannot be overcome from outside must nevertheless be overcome in some manner, lest immediate self-being squander and exhaust itself in empty, illusory subjectivity.

But a more profound analysis clearly shows that the insufficiency of pure outward transcending has another foundation, deeper and more general. No subjectivity in general and therefore no subjectivity of "another," of "thou" (which steps forth to meet me, as it were, in the guise of objective reality), can as such save me from my own subjectivity. Therefore insofar as it is a question of the "I–thou" relation in its pure essence, distinct from all other kinds of being; insofar as it is a question of my encounter, my kinship, my bond with another subjectivity, it is true that the circle of my subjectivity is widened, but in no sense do I transcend this circle. Being together with "thou" as another subjectivity (even if we set aside the inevitable friction that accompanies this union or bond of two) does in a certain sense lead me beyond the limits of *my* subjective being, does give me the experience that the "I am" form of being is not closed but has a necessary correlative in "thou art," in the subjectivity which is given to me in the guise of external, objective reality. Nevertheless being together with "thou" does not lead to a realization of the necessary rootedness of my subjectivity in an objectivity, in a reality that because of its actuality has its own immanent validity and can be for me an unshakeably solid ground.

Thus, the being-together with "others" (for example, in the form of communion with friends or comrades) is essentially a hopeless attempt to avoid the lack of fulfillment that lies at the base of my limited nature, an attempt that involves forgetfulness, the momentary loss of self in imaginary fulfillment, and the completion of self with the dynamic, living emanations of other subjectivities. It is true that, in contrast to this, that emi-

nent "I–thou" relation which we have in *love*, the genuine transcending to
the reality of another, signifies the miracle of the genuine transcending of
my subjectivity. But to the essence of love belongs the fact that in love
"thou" is experienced not as a purely "other" subjectivity that is akin to
me, but as a genuine *reality*, which has its own immanent value and validity;
in love, "thou" is revealed and experienced as something *trans-subjective*.
But this means that a *second* kind of transcending occurs here—toward
"thou" and by means of the transcending to "thou." This second transcending is transcending of a wholly other kind, namely the transcending
of subjectivity in general. In essence, this kind of transcending coincides
with the transcending that is the topic of the present discussion, namely
inward transcending. Only here the "inner" that is being sought is found
"outside," namely in the *inner depths* of another as a loved one. It is true that
it is easy to commit an error here: to confuse pure subjectivity (imperfect,
arbitrary, purely potential, requiring completion and fulfillment) in
"thou" with genuinely valid inner being as the unshakeable ground of
objectivity. This error forms the essence of so-called "infatuation," the
romantic "falling in love," and can be compared to the short-circuiting of
an electric current on its way inward, into the ground. This error, however, does not touch the true essence of love, which consists in the living
perception, recognition, and attainment of full-fledged reality in the
depths of "another." In love we attain inner objectivity, *inward* transcending, in and through "thou." This is perhaps the easiest and most natural
way we can accomplish inward transcending, or at least understand it.
Since the inner being we are seeking is not something that belongs to my
subjectivity, to my detached self-being, but is essentially something objective and valid in itself (i.e., universal and valid for all), it is not surprising
that it can be found in transcending to "thou," that is, on the path "outward," and that it is most easily attainable precisely on this path. For we
must not forget that the terms "inward" and "outward" should not be
understood in their literal, spatial senses, in which they signify opposite
directions. If we remain in the sphere of spatial analogies, we can say that
the easiest and truest path "inward" or "into the depths" can be found at
least as naturally through another immediate self-being, outside of *me*, as
through the direct passage into myself, just as it is sometimes easier to find
water by digging on my neighbor's land than on my own. But this analogy
is insufficient, for the very transition, in *love*, to the inner "property" of my
neighbor is *already* the transcending of my subjectivity, already the begin-

ning of a transition from the surface of my being into the depths. This is why the most natural path to the transcending "inward" or "into the depths" is the path of genuine *outward* transcending in love. It is true that a straight line is always the shortest path between two points, but it is not always the fastest and easiest path to a certain point. Thus the path "outward" can also be the path "inward" and to a certain degree already is the path "inward," for the only true, actual, adequate relation to "thou" consists in the perception in its makeup of the *trans-subjective depths of reality*. And it is just as evident that the experience of the being of "we" is already— precisely in the metaphysical aspect of this being—a form of transcending of pure subjectivity, a penetration into a deeper layer or form of being.

This does not prevent us, however, from conceptually distinguishing these two types of transcending. And now we must ask how inward transcending is possible in general and what precisely is the meaning of the word "inward" in this connection?

The question concerning the possibility of such transcending is, strictly speaking, superfluous or rather falsely posed. For here we stand before a kind of primary, self-evident relationship that requires not "explanation" but only pure description. But this question acquires meaning with regard to the common view that distorts the true relationship, namely the view that the "soul" is closed up in itself. The naturalistic point of view (characteristic of all frameworks of objective cognition) represents the soul as located in some manner somewhere inside the body, i.e., confined by the body. And insofar as the "soul" has a relation to something other than itself, it requires for this relation special "apertures," which are factually given only in the "sense organs," i.e., only in the direction outward. Every "soul" is doomed to remain confined in a kind of solitary cell that has windows looking outward. Inside, in our inner being, we are all prisoners who have nothing left but to live and dream in our detached, solitary, closed psychic lives.

It is scarcely necessary to point out that this naturalistic view is refuted both by the cognitive intentionality (which in essence is transcending through thinking) and by transcending in the "I–thou" relation. This is the case because both of these forms of transcending have a non-sensational nature. And, in general, orientation according to this naturalistic scheme can lead only to absolute skepticism and subjectivism. This scheme is based on prejudiced opinion and is inadequate, as we saw above, to the general essence of immediate self-being. When viewed in a purely descriptive-phenomenological way, immediate self-being or inner being is in itself something potentially limitless, a kind of potentially infinite universe. "You will never find the limits of the soul, even if you walk all its paths, so deep is it," justly remarks Heraclitus. This potential infinitude of immediate self-being already contradicts the crude image of the "soul" locked in a narrow cell or in solitary confinement. But of course this does not yet exclude the possibility that immediate self-being is "closed" in the sense that it cannot surpass the limits of its own qualitative essence or its intrinsic kind of being.

But this hypothesis that the "soul" is closed up in itself is refuted by the primary, self-evident fact that immediate self-being is inseparable from the revelation in and through it of the "other," of that which does not belong to immediate self-being itself. This primary self-revelation of reality as such in immediate self-being is the ultimate basis of all knowledge in general, the basis of both the ideal possession of reality in the objective intentionality and, more specifically, the "I–thou" relation. Thus, we must recognize the fundamental and self-evident fact that reality as such in all its fullness and breadth somehow *shows through* immediate self-being. In other words, the "soul" is not closed but open in the direction inward, into the depths. The "soul" is boundless and potentially infinite in itself, in its own element, in its subjectivity; and this infinitude is of such a kind that in its deepest layer the soul transcends itself and touches something other than itself—or this something "other" penetrates into the soul and reveals itself to the soul. *This is the essence of inward transcending.* The question concerning the possibility of such transcending is superfluous in the light of this primary, self-evident fact, a fact that is self-evident in the eminent sense of being "unquestionable" (see Part I for clarification). The only thing that remains to be clarified is a second question: What is the meaning of "inward" or "into the depths"? What is the character of this form of transcending that distinguishes it from the other forms of transcending that we have discussed?

Real transcending, as the self-embedding of immediate self-being into something "other" or the assimilation by immediate self-being of this "other," is possible—in contrast to ideal transcending in the cognitive intentionality—only in relation to a reality that in its essence has a certain inner kinship with immediate self-being. Here, together with reality as total unity (which has that in common with immediate self-being that it is precisely a *reality*, i.e., the unknowable in itself) and together with "thou," which is precisely another, a second, subjectivity (the subjectivity of the "other" or a reality in the form of a second subjectivity, which we encounter from outside), there is yet a *third* form of reality in which there appears and becomes accessible to us something essentially kindred, but which is not "I myself", not my immediate self-being. This third form is *life*, which is also *actuality*, actual being. "Actuality" is *actual reality* in contrast to potentiality: being and validity in itself and by itself, perfect, stable, tranquil, and acting precisely as such, in contrast to what is in a state of unrest and striving, to what is imperfect and only potential in immediate self-being. "Actuality" is what we experience as "spirit" or "spiritual reality," what is essentially necessary for our subjective immediate self-being.

The transcending to this reality or its revelation to us must not be viewed as a special process that is merely *added* on to a psychic being that is closed and self-contained in all other respects. Even if this transcending often (and even typically for those of a positivist orientation) is not understood on a conscious level, even if many people do not have the slightest understanding of spiritual being, nevertheless the transcending to spiritual being, the revelation of spiritual being, belongs—in the frame of being if not in the frame of consciousness—to the very essence of immediate self-being. And up to now our analysis of immediate self-being, carried out apart from a consideration of the spiritual element, has been based on an abstraction from the connection between spirit and immediate self-being. More precisely, we must set forth the following proposition in accordance with the general principle of transcendental thinking: *in its essence and thus always, the "soul" is something other than what it is in its detached inner, logically definable makeup*. In its genuine depths, in its genuine essence, the soul itself *is* that which is revealed to it beyond its own limits. Insofar as immediate self-being is conscious of itself as subjectivity (i.e., something essentially incomplete, groundless, unstable, striving, potential, arbitrary, ungrounded), this consciousness already contains a directedness toward *actuality*, toward that which grounds psychic being, that which gives it genuine, rooted, *illuminated being*. The connecting, transcending force of "not," the consciousness of one's own limitedness and inadequacy, already contains a relation to another, the possession of another. St. Augustine's profound idea, concerning the search for God, that we would not be able to search for Him at all if we did not already *have* Him in some way, is applicable to the relation between immediate self-being as subjectivity (i.e., potentiality) and the objectivity (i.e., the actuality) of the spirit. The very consciousness of subjectivity (that is, the feeling that we lack objectivity in our pure psychic being) is already the potential possession of this objectivity, its revelation, a positive relation to it.

2. Spirit as the Illuminating Ground

The foregoing discussion has clarified the meaning of the words "inward" and "into the depths." Transcending *inward* or *into the depths* is transcending to that *ground* through which immediate self-being acquires the objectivity (i.e., actuality) that it lacks as such. Immediate self-being, directed at itself (i.e., inward) and perceiving its own essence, has the bitter, unsatisfying consciousness of its subjectivity, its groundlessness, the instability and inauthenticity of its being. But precisely in this consciousness of subjectivity immediate self-being grasps its own roots, which point to the soil in which they are trying to anchor themselves. Furthermore, a new *reality* is revealed, *from inside*, to immediate self-being. Although it is intimately close to immediate self-being, this reality emerges as a potency that dominates immediate self-being and thereby affirms its own transcendence. The intimacy of this relation is so deep that immediate self-being, in entering into communion with spiritual being, begins to resemble the latter, merges with it, and *has its own self as spiritual being.*

Immediate self-being is not a being-in-itself, is not a detached, closed sphere of being. Concretely, immediate self-being can exist only insofar as it is grounded in and depends on forces of another order, a sphere of being that transcends purely human, "subjective" being. And grounded in these forces, it is permeated by them, assimilates them. Isolated immediate self-being is a non-existent abstraction not only in the sense that immediate self-being always overflows its bounds in the "I–thou" relation but also in the sense that it is always rooted in and nourished by some higher or deeper being.

In Chapter V, we emphasized, in opposition to the prevailing view, that psychic life as immediate self-being is a whole special world and, in this sense, an immediately self-evident reality. We also pointed out that aspect of immediate self-being owing to which psychic life, as potentiality and subjectivity, is not a genuine, full-fledged reality but only a sort of "ghostly" reality: "ghostly" not in the sense of an illusion, something that does not exist at all, but in the sense of a wandering, hovering, groundless, inwardly insufficient, defective reality. And here we find that immediate self-being acquires genuine, full-fledged reality only insofar as it pushes roots into the ground of a being other than itself, into the ground of *spiritual being*. We can say that, in its most general sense, spiritual being is *the ground and the roots of the reality* of immediate self-being. When we clearly understand our immediate self-being as a deep, solid, rooted, massive reality, and as a genuine "inner being"; when we have a clear *revelation* of our own "soul" (such clarity is very rare, the most exceptional of the states of our self-awareness), psychic being is then given to us not in its isolation but precisely in its rootedness in the ground of spiritual being, in its union with and permeatedness by spiritual being. Although on the one hand immediate self-being, as detached and isolated, consists of being for itself, self-revelation to itself, on the other hand it is also a medium for *genuine revelation*, precisely the revelation, through and for immediate self-being, of spiritual being. And only in the light of this revelation does immediate self-being genuinely understand its own reality precisely *as* a reality.

Thus, spiritual being is (we repeat) the ground in which psychic being is rooted or strives to be rooted in such a way that it acquires genuine reality. But in this formulation we have only an image borrowed from spatial being that requires further clarification. In Chapter II we touched upon the problem of the *groundedness* of knowledge and therefore of being. The groundedness of being in the usual (theoretical and ontological) sense is insured by the law or principle of sufficient reason. Any conceivable content is "grounded" (i.e., perceived as existent, as the content of *being itself*) only when we establish its necessary connection to another content that we conceive beforehand to be "true," i.e., existent. Through this connection the given content finds its proper place in being as a whole, in the total unity of what exists (which, as we have seen, is a metalogical unity). This is the usual categorial meaning of what we call "ground." But here it is clear from the outset that when we speak of spiritual being as the "ground" of the reality of psychic being, we are thinking of a "ground" that is wholly different from the "ground" that "grounds" knowledge by giving conceivable content the validity of objective being, by testifying that this content belongs to objective being. Immediate self-being is not a "conceivable content" and does not wish to be enrolled in the ranks of the content of objective being. (To be so enrolled would contradict the very essence of its being.) Immediate self-being itself testifies about itself with self-evident certainty that it is a special reality, is revealed to us (or to itself) as a special form of being, namely the "I–am" form of being. (Let us recall the Augustinian–Cartesian perception of the certainty of being in "I am".) But we cannot deny that there must be some special significance pointing to a genuine connection in the fact that we use the same word "ground" in these two different respects, understanding it in both cases to mean a certain element that "grounds" a phenomenon, gives genuine reality to this phenomenon. It is not by accident that Leibniz, the author of the principle of sufficient reason or ground, used the word "ground" not only in its general, logical sense but also in another sense—namely a teleological one. The concept of "ground" appears to have two different, though closely associated meanings; and this difference appears to be determined by the fact that the idea of "genuine reality" can have two different meanings.

A brief digression may be able to clarify this as well as the second and deeper meaning of the concept of "ground." Is it not surprising that the question concerning "ground" (the question "why?") can be posed (i.e., has meaning) also in relation to reality itself as such, i.e., in relation to the all-embracing unity of all that exists? When we stand before being itself even in all its wholeness, we stand before something that appears to us as a blind, rough, "incomprehensible" *fact*. And in relation to this fact (even if all-embracing and primordial) our spirit, in its unrest, in its lack of fulfillment, can and must ask, "why does this fact exist?" and "how can it be explained?". Why does everything exist, why does *being itself* exist, why does *anything at all* exist? It is clear that these questions are meaningless insofar as they involve a search for real (or, what is the same thing, theoretical-cognitive) ground, for everything that is real is already a part of being, and real ground is precisely nothing else but a belonging to being, the possession of a place in the ranks of being. Thus, it is contradictory and absurd to seek the "ground" of *being itself*. Positivists of all schools and orientations never tire of pointing out, with a smile of triumph, the inner absurdity of the metaphysical striving to "understand" being itself as such, to perceive its "ground" or "meaning." But in spite of this cheap triumph of minds blinded by the theoretical-objective orientation of consciousness, the foregoing questions retain their meaning and rise up from the depths of our soul to trouble us. *Why is* all this? "Life, *why* art thou given to me?"[1] It follows that another sort of "why" is possible: a question concerning a different kind of "ground," which cannot simply be reduced to the perception of the place of something in the ranks of being. For the moment let us call this other kind of ground "ideal ground." We understand at once what we are speaking of: it is a question of *right* and *meaning*. To "understand" reality in the ultimate, genuine sense of the word "understand" is not simply to submissively affirm its blind, purely factual necessity, not simply to see that "this is how it is," but to perceive the *ideal, illuminated* necessity of reality. If we witness an event that appears to be meaningless, that appears to contradict the inner essence of our own reality (for example, if we witness the sudden death of a young child whom we love), we ask, "How could something like this have happened?". Dostoevsky's Ivan Karamazov, who seeks to understand the meaning of being and is shaken by the meaninglessness of the factual order of things, says: "I cannot understand anything. I do not want to understand anything. In order to understand I would have to abandon facts, but I do not want to abandon facts." "Ideal" ground, the perception of which would give us "understanding," is seen here as contradicting the purely real or cognitive ground. It is in this sense that Lev Tolstoy once spoke of capital punishment, which he considered to be something incomprehensible and therefore impossible: "Capital punishment is one of those things whose reality does not convince me of their possibility."

The question concerning "ground" in *this* sense can never refer to the objective world as such insofar as we take this world in its isolation, precisely as something rooted in itself, as being in itself. For in its very *concept* objective being has the feature of blind *factuality*. We arrive at this question only through our immediate self-being, and this question has direct reference only to the latter. Our own being (or that which is connected with it) seems to us *genuinely real* and therefore "understandable" only when we are conscious of it as *illuminated with meaning* and in this sense having a "ground."

But only that is illuminated which has its legitimacy or value in itself, which can be perceived as valid, justified in its own self. That which is valuable in its own self, i.e., the absolutely valid in itself and out of itself, has that ultimate self-evident certainty, that immanent-inner persuasiveness toward which every "why" and "for what" are directed. In itself everything that is factual is blind and dark. It is true that it has the certainty of factuality but this certainty is not transparent, does not ground itself. Only the element of *value* in the sense of what is valid in itself and valuable in itself can *illuminate with meaning* and give ultimate, genuine, completely transparent, self-evident *certainty*. This type of value must be understood in contrast to all "subjective value," which is only experienced as "desirable," i.e., as arising from our urges and therefore from our subjectivity. And in this sense only the element of inner, objective value coincides with the ultimate, genuine ground: *the primordial ground*. And since only the self-evident possesses genuine, deepest reality, in which our spirit can find ultimate peace and fulfillment, the *illuminating ground* in this sense is also the deepest ground of reality. By the way, this overcomes that concept of value which modern German philosophy, beginning with Kant, separates from being and apprehends as a detached kingdom-in-itself. In the concept of intrinsic value as the ultimate ground of reality, the element of value is extracted from its isolation and is once again brought into immediate connection with reality, which alone befits the tradition of *philosophia perennis*.

The general ontological significance of this fundamental relation and the new, deeper concept of "reality" that emanates from it will be examined by us only later, in an analysis of the sphere of being disclosed to the religious consciousness. Here it is sufficient to note that the intrinsically valuable, intrinsically valid, self-evident (in the sense of inner transparence or persuasiveness) element of the *illuminating ground* must not be understood only in the sense of ethical or moral value. Whatever may be the defining characteristic of ethical value in contradistinction to the other forms of objective value, ethical value is only one of the possible manifestations of *value as such*, of the valid in itself as the universal element that illuminates and therefore grounds reality. In the esthetic consciousness too, in the experience of beauty, empirically given reality is apprehended by us as *illuminated and valid in itself* and therefore as the revelation of the deepest primordial ground of reality. But here revelation is so immediate, higher reality is so immanently palpable in phenomena given to the senses that the question concerning "ground" or rather the very framework of *questioning* turns out to be superfluous and inappropriate—which in fact is the special nature of esthetic experience, the esthetic revelation of reality. (We shall speak in a later connection of the meaning of beauty in its relation to reality in the deepest sense of this latter concept.) In precisely the same manner all *creativity* in general, in all its forms, signifies an intrusion into our immediate self-being, into our subjective life, of transcendent, intrinsically valid, and therefore genuine reality.

Even more essential in this connection, insofar as we are considering spiritual being as such, is the fact that the dark and dangerous forces of evil also belong to the sphere of *spiritual* being when they are experienced precisely as transcendent forces that dominate our subjective self-being. That is, in their action upon us, these forces are *objective* and *valid in themselves*: they are something to which we are subordinate not in the sphere of blind, factual necessity but in the ideal sphere, something which brings *meaning* into our subjectivity and gives it the character of genuine reality. As *dark* forces, they are of course not self-evident, not transparent, not illuminated by their own inner light as everything is that is valuable and valid in itself. But insofar as we are subordinate to these forces, this subordination is determined by the consciousness of that immediate, inner, autonomous validity with which they intrude into us and act in us. In contrast to passions that are experienced as purely subjective urges of our immediate self-being, every dark passion, manifested in us precisely as a force of a higher, superhuman order, has for us the aura of a higher, autonomous value, which does not admit questions concerning its meaning and ground, its justification. The "evil spirit" is precisely a spirit of deceit, which seduces us with its "charm," with the deceiving likeness of autonomous value. Once we have succumbed, we experience our subordination to this spirit not merely in the form of being tyrannized by a blind force, but also in the form of the awareness that we "must," that we are "obliged" to obey this spirit because of its unquestionable self-evident certainty and value. And in this subordination, in this meek, voluntary obedience, we experience (in spite of the terror that embraces us, a terror that reminds us of the deceitfulness of this force) the meaning and the real ground of our immediate self-being, even if we are aware that this ground and reality are such that they are dragging us into the abyss. This contains the deeper, genuine relationship, discovered by Socrates, between the "good" and the "true," as well as between "evil" and "error." Dark, evil forces possess only a seeming, imaginary, illegitimate self-evident certainty with which they seduce us and lead us away from the path of truth. But insofar as these forces claim to possess such certainty, they belong to the sphere of the spirit, for they are experienced as an element that illuminates our immediate self-being and gives it genuine, intrinsically valid reality. Spiritual being can be disclosed to us in various forms of revelation and action, and any concept of spiritual being that is defined too narrowly, that assumes a definite qualitative content in spiritual being, distorts the true essence of this being. For spiritual being (in complete analogy with immediate self-being) is not a *domain* of being that can be qualitatively defined in terms of its content. It is only a special *kind* or *mode* of being, a special *modal form* of being. This is the form of being of "inner objectivity" in the sense of *trans-subjective being*, perceived through the depths of immediate self-being: the form of the revelation and action of reality in which the latter emerges as something that illuminates and actualizes in immediate self-being— something that dominates immediate self-being with its authority, its inner persuasiveness, precisely because in the form or mode of its being it surpasses purely subjective being.

Spiritual being, which is not a domain but a mode or form of being (analogous to being as such), is therefore definable and describable only in its significance for us or its action upon us, but not in terms of its content. And precisely for this reason it is essentially unknowable. When we encounter spiritual being in our experience, we stand before an indefinable "something," which is indefinable not only in the sense that it is unknown or insufficiently known by us, but also in the sense that in its essence it is not something that can be defined in terms of content, is not some "this" or "that," but is simply the revelation of being as such in all the transrationality and unknowableness of this concept or, more precisely, in all the identity between being and the essentially unknowable. Therefore anyone who has the slightest experience of the reality of spiritual being has the experience of seeing certain bottomless depths that logical thinking cannot penetrate, though these depths are transparently clear and self-evident precisely in their impenetrability. And spiritual being—which is living being, the being of life—has all the transdefiniteness and transfiniteness (explained in Chapters II and III) of that which is concrete, living, existent through becoming and freedom. In other words anyone who has living experience of spiritual being knows with certainty (apart from all abstract speculation) that being is not exhausted by its logically definable, objective content but has another dimension as well—the dimension *inward, into the depths*, which transcends the logically knowable and reveals the inner unknowableness of the latter. The experience of inward transcending to spiritual being teaches us (to an even greater degree than the experience of outward transcending, to "thou") to tremble with awe before being, reveals being to us as the unity of *mysterium tremendum* and *mysterium fascinosum*.

3. "Spirit" and "Soul"

This preliminary clarification of the transrationality and unknowableness of spiritual being is insufficient. We can penetrate more deeply into the essence of spiritual being if we turn to a more precise examination of those two kinds or levels of being which we can now designate as "spirit" and "soul."

Since the time when mankind attained the concept of spirit, the perception of spiritual reality (attained partially and embryonically by Heraclitus and the Indian mystics and with greater clarity in Greek philosophy and Christian thought), no one has been able to define the difference between spirit and soul so clearly and univocally as to establish precise limits between these two spheres. Where does the "soul" end and where does the "spirit" begin? Another, closely related, question also remains unanswered: is spirit something that belongs to me, to my own inner life as an immanent part of the latter; or is it something numerically different, something transcendent in relation to me? Do I myself have spirit in the sense that I *am* spirit (and not only soul) or do I have spirit in the sense that I stand in a relation to it as to a reality outside of me (outside of my soul)? Does spirit belong to me in the sense that it is *mine* or does it belong to me only like other things in which I only share? Or perhaps we should say that both the one and the other are simultaneously valid, that on the one hand I have spirit as an element of my psychic life, and on the other hand through spirit I touch upon spiritual realities, which transcend my "I." There is much to favor this latter assumption. Above all and most immediately, I have experience of spiritual reality in the form of "my spiritual life" as the deepest and most essential element of my immediate self-being, but this experience also contains an awareness of the fact that I touch upon spiritual realities that surpass me—for example, the awareness that I "serve" the truth, the good, beauty, or God, that I obey the "call" of higher forces. Philosophical thought goes out to meet this experience and establishes a difference between the "subjective" spirit and the "objective" spirit. However, this assumption too does not aid us significantly, for the same difficulty necessarily arises when we try to determine the genuine difference between these two forms of the life and action of the spirit and the genuine relation between them. This indefiniteness arises not from the weakness of previous philosophical thought (we certainly are not so arrogant as to claim that we are more perceptive in this respect than all the thinkers who have preceded us) but lies in the very essence of the problem. And this alone we shall attempt to demonstrate now, using the general methodology that we have developed.

First of all, we can affirm that there indeed exists no precise, univocal boundary between soul and spirit. If we return to the image of the spirit as a "ground" in which the soul is rooted, we shall see that this analogy is a feeble one. This image does indeed approximately capture something essential in the difference between spirit and soul and their interrelationship, but in order for this image to be valid both the "roots" and the "ground" must somehow merge into each other at their boundary or even at the regions adjacent to the boundary. That is, the deepest part of the roots must somehow acquire the character of the ground, and the ground must not only nourish the roots with its juices but also permeate them. The deepest layer of psychic being (i.e., of immediate self-being) that reveals itself to our self-awareness is already spiritual. Thus, the layer of spirit closest to us or spirit in its immediate action on the soul's being is already "soul-like" in a certain sense, i.e., is experienced as an element or aspect of immediate self-being itself. In the light of our definition of spirit as the element that gives full, actual reality to psychic being in its subjectivity and potentiality, we must say that the soul in the direction *inward* or *into the depths* gradually becomes more and more real, comes to possess more and more autonomous, "objective" (i.e., actual) reality, while spirit in its action on the soul assumes (in the region near the boundary) the form of "potentiality," the form of "subjective life." We must not forget that in general the idea of a "precise boundary," borrowed directly from the sphere of spatial relations and fully applicable as well to the domain of purely logical relations (relations between concepts as determinations), is not applicable, without appropriate qualifications, to anything concretely real and living. And therefore it is not applicable to the realities of soul and spirit.

But precisely this discloses to us the *transrationality* of the relation between soul and spirit. This relation (just like the "I–thou" relation) is subordinate to the fundamental principle that forms the very essence of concrete reality: the principle of *antinomian monodualism*, the principle of *the unity of separateness and mutual penetration*. Here again we stand before a duality that is also a primordially inseparable unity or before a unity that reveals itself as a concrete, genuinely inner all-permeating unity precisely in the inseparable belonging-together, the irresistible mutual merging, of the *two* into which the unity is *separated*.

But in essence this already contains the only possible answer to the question concerning the "transcendence" or "immanence" of the spirit in relation to the soul. According to the principle of antinomian monodualism, this answer can only be transrational. In relation to the soul the spirit is *both* transcendent and immanent. And this is the case not in the sense of a simple addition of these two relations but in the sense of their inner, essential unity, owing to which we can say that neither of these definitions adequately expresses the essence of the relation. That is, the spirit is *neither* transcendent *nor* immanent in relation to the soul but stands in some other, ineffable, relation to it. Here once again we must recognize the inadequacy, the approximate character, of all logical definitions (in this case, the inadequacy of the categories of transcendence and immanence) and instead feel and wordlessly experience the ineffable character of this relation. We can capture it adequately only insofar as we are bold enough to *hover* above both of these logical definitions, precisely in the sphere of the "non-excluded middle."

It is extremely important not only to recognize in principle the necessity of this ineffable, transrational synthesis but also to clearly see it in all its unknowableness or, more precisely, to receive into oneself the revelation of this synthesis in an unfettered and undistorted manner. In wholly illuminating and understanding our psychic life, our immediate self-being (i.e., in having it as a *genuine*, albeit special, reality), we transcend the bounds of subjectivity, the bounds of immediate self-being in its isolation, and find ourselves in the sphere of *spiritual* being. In having ourselves as a *genuine reality*, in being conscious of the deepest roots of our subjective self-being, we have in ourselves, together with ourselves, something *greater and other* than only we ourselves in our subjectivity, in the groundlessness that forms the essence of our being, in the potentiality of our purely psychic being. Here we stand before a paradox that cannot and must not be removed and overcome but that must be submissively accepted as such: the paradox that what is *immanent* in the deepest sense, what is disclosed to us through the deep inner penetration into ourselves and the deep understanding of ourselves is thereby already *transcendent*. We can express this paradox by the following spatial metaphor: the ultimate, most intimate, and most "inner" *depth* of the human soul is located not *inside* the soul but *outside* it, is a sphere into which we penetrate only after crossing the bounds of our subjective "I" as such. The element "am" of the self-consciousness "I am," the revelation of oneself to oneself, only appears to be pure immanence, only appears to be a detached being-in-itself. But actually this "am" is—precisely where it reveals itself with ultimate certainty and validity as an objective reality—the revelation of a reality that surpasses me and is transcendent in relation to me. "Am" is not an "inner state" of myself but a "thread" that connects me to the superhuman, trans-subjective depths of reality. This is true for the relation of "I am" to reality as total unity as well as for the relation of "I am" to "thou art." And it is also true for my relation to that modal form of being which, as "spiritual reality," is the inner ground of my "am," gives my "am" actual reality, objectivity in the sense of "validity." Here one can justly affirm that life is only in the "spirit" (in *logos*) and that the essence of life is "light."

This transrational relationship is revealed in experience in the fact that (Dostoevsky showed this convincingly) whenever a man attempts to close himself off from transcendent reality and live in and from himself by the force of his subjective will alone, he perishes because he becomes the slave and plaything of transcendent forces, namely the dark forces of destruction. Furthermore, it is precisely in this sort of situation, in the experience of enslavement by and subordination to *alien* forces, that the pure transcendence, the superhumanness and inhumanness, of these forces makes itself known with particular morbidity and horror. For when transcendence forcibly breaks into the seemingly closed inner world of pure subjectivity, it breaks in as an alien, hostile, wholly transcendent force of enslavement, which completely lacks the comforting element of immanence to me myself, kinship to me, the element of belonging to the deepest center of my personal being. On the contrary, when my soul is voluntarily open to peaceful contact with the transcendent (precisely in the normal revelation of spiritual forces in psychic being), I experience spiritual being as deeply immanent, I experience its peaceful and unhindered penetration into my soul and its merging with my soul as a result of the deepest inner kinship between them and the natural "belonging-together" of the two. But when the spiritual element forcibly breaks into me with explosive force, the tranquil, life-giving light of the spirit is transformed into a hell-fire that in wild fury destroys my life. Spiritual reality can of course be revealed to us or penetrate into us simultaneously in both of these forms, and we then experience in ourselves the struggle between the powers of "light" and the powers of "darkness." According to Dostoevsky, the human heart becomes the "field of battle between God and the devil."

The characteristic form of *revelation* of spiritual being is closely linked to this transcendent–immanent relation between spirit and soul. It is self-evident that the reality of the spirit is accessible to us only through its *revelation*. After all, it is not a question of an objective reality, of the possession, by means of the subject's cognitive gaze, of some reality that is present before the subject. Transcendence in this case is rather the penetration (given in the experience itself, from within) into us of reality itself: reality's self-disclosure of its action upon us, the revelation of reality's own attractive force, or reality's "call" addressed to us. But this revelation is neither the purely immanent revelation of oneself to oneself as it forms the essence of immediate self-being nor the univocally clear and distinct revelation of purely transcendent reality to the *other* (namely to "me") as it is given in the revelation of "thou." The mode of the revelation of spiritual being stands "midway," in the transrational gap, between these two forms of revelation. This mode is *both* the revelation of oneself to oneself *and* the revelation of transcendent reality to me; or (as we have just pointed out) it is *neither* the one *nor* the other. (In this respect it resembles the experience of the being of "we," which also combines these two modes of revelation or forms a kind of single ground for the two.) Precisely for this reason spiritual reality is not "I am" for us with univocal certainty, though it is experienced in the most intimate closeness to "I" as if in the depths of the latter, and merges with "I" into a single whole. On the other hand, spiritual reality does not have the distinct character of a "thou," though it is experienced as a "voice" inside me, as a "call" addressed to me, and is sometimes perceived in the form of something "thou-like." (Socrates' *daimon* and my "guardian angel" are examples.) But neither is spiritual reality a pure "it" in the sense of an impersonal depth or "womb" of unconditional being. Language has not found the appropriate verbal expression for the categorial form of the revelation of spiritual reality. Here we appear to suffer from the lack of a "fourth person" that should be present somewhere among "I," "thou," and "it" ("he," as we know, is "thou" immersed in the element of "it"), just as the conventional musical scale does not have names for intervals less than a half tone. Of course this lack of a grammatical form must not confuse us. On the contrary, we must maintain with phenomenological accuracy a clear understanding of this verbally inexpressible, special character of the form of reality and revelation of the spiritual element. As we have pointed out, this special character is determined by the transcendent–immanent relationship between spirit and immediate self-being.

4. THE MYSTERY OF THE PERSON

The relationship between spirit and soul can be clarified in yet another way. We perceived in immediate self-being the primordially inseparable dual-unity of immediacy and selfhood. But what is essential now is that the relation of soul (as immediate self-being) to spirit *passes through* that central element in immediate being which we call selfhood. It passes through "I myself." Spiritual reality acts precisely on the center or apex or deepest depth of immediate self-being—i.e., on selfhood—and is revealed as a force that attracts our selfhood and acts in or through it. By extending my selfhood toward spirit, holding it open for spirit, and experiencing this selfhood (i.e., me my*self*) as already "spiritual" or "spirit-like" in some sense, I discover the possibility of the penetration of spirit into soul and the merging of the one into the other. True, I can close myself off, close off my selfhood from the peaceful penetration into it of spiritual reality as an autonomous, valid element. But then this spiritual reality becomes a dark, hostile power that forcibly possesses my life. This relationship, which we described above, is now enriched by the clarification of the role of selfhood. Selfhood is, so to speak, a "door" through which spirit can enter into immediate self-being. The astonishingly profound New Testament parable (John 10) of the true shepherd who enters the sheepfold by the door opened for him by the porter comes to mind. The sheep follow him because they recognize his voice, whereas the false shepherd steals into the fold like a thief and is a stranger to the sheep. But the dark power that steals into us attains its dominion over us only because it gains control (even if forcibly) over our selfhood.

Thus, the element of selfhood essentially always stands on the threshold between psychic being and spiritual being. It is the place where the spiritual penetrates into the soul, the place where the spiritual merges with the psychic into unity. This monodualism is usually reflected in our consciousness in the fact that we feel compelled to distinguish a certain duality in the simple unity of selfhood. Selfhood as the "door" to intrinsically valid, spiritual being, as the carrier and fully empowered representative of spirit, manifests itself as the "higher, spiritual I," as something contrary to selfhood in its function as the self-willed dictator of our subjectivity, our pure "soulness." And when we look at this purely "psychic" selfhood from this higher point of view, it appears to us just as blind and ungrounded, just as groundless and inwardly unjustified as the element of immediate self-being itself. This is the basis of man's mysterious ability (the only feature that genuinely distinguishes him from the animals) to separate himself from himself, to judge his immediate selfhood at a higher court, to evaluate this selfhood and all its purposes.

It is this higher, spiritual selfhood which constitutes what we call the person. The person is selfhood as it stands before higher, spiritual, objectively valid forces and is permeated by and represents these forces. The person is supra-natural being as it is manifested in immediate self-being itself.

Every man has this higher selfhood, and therefore the element of personality, and he has this higher selfhood in all of his spiritual states. For the very groundlessness and subjectivity of his immediate self-being, his pure "soulness," is direct evidence of the true ground, of what is objectively legitimate and valid in itself. Even the emptiest and most spiritually insignificant man has some sense of the intrinsically valid (i.e., spiritual) ground of his being, some aspiration, even if latent, to this ground. Even a man possessed by dark forces feels the reality of spiritual being and therefore possesses spiritual selfhood or personality.

The mystery of the soul as a person consists precisely in this ability to rise above its own self, to transcend itself, to transcend all of its factual states and even its factual *general* nature. Here we see once again, in another form, the action of the transrational principle of antinomian monodualism. The "person," that which makes up the ultimate, primordial *unity* of my psychic life, its substantial form as it were, is given to me only through *duality*, a duality that even such a naturalistically inclined thinker as Freud had to recognize when in the structure of "I" he distinguished the simple "ego" from the "super-ego" or the "ideal I." That which is most inner in my inner life, that which is most immanent in me, consists in *immanent transcending through purely immanent soulness*.

This is the genuine inner ground of what we experience as "I." We have already described how "I" arises only in the "I–thou" relation and we have examined those objections which arise naturally against this proposition. To what was said above we can add one more source for our unshakeable certainty that "I" has a purely "inner," autonomous character. "I" really is the "inner" element of our life, but this is the case only insofar as "I" is a "person," i.e., insofar as, transcending inward, it participates in the spirit. Even if spiritual being is not "thou," it is nevertheless the revelation of something "other," something transcendent, in the dimension of our "depth," our "inner" dimension. And immediate self-being is constituted as "I" precisely in this encounter with and this belonging to the transrational element. Furthermore, the "being in one's own self" that forms the essence of true freedom is realized for the first time in its full validity only when selfhood abandons itself and becomes rooted in something other, higher. For here it is no longer a question of the freedom of pure immediacy or of freedom through self-overcoming, which always presupposes inner struggle and therefore unfreedom, but of true, conclusive liberation, which consists in the fact that selfhood wholly sacrifices itself in the plane of its subjectivity, is dissolved in the autonomously valid and only thereby becomes a participant in the force of genuinely valid being that gives genuine reality; and only in this way does selfhood find for itself unshakeably solid ground. "And ye shall know the truth, and the truth shall make you free" (John 8:32).

Nevertheless this intimate immanence of the spiritual potency does not eliminate in us the transcendence of spiritual reality but rather conserves it together with the immanence and is conceivable only with regard to what is transcendent in relation to our selfhood. And our selfhood would stop being itself (that is, an element of immediate self-being) if it did not have the transcendent *outside* of itself. The higher spiritual selfhood is the representative in us of spiritual reality, to which we stand in relation as to a reality outside of us. This representative, being *in us* a higher element, is itself responsible before transcendent reality. The higher selfhood is not infallible, does not have autonomous validity; its authority has only a derivative nature. Here unity does not destroy duality but is fully realized for the first time in the latter. The relation that predominates here is (to use a favorite image of the mystics) the relation between a pure flame and red-hot iron. It is true that spiritual life is autonomous, occurs in the form of self-definition; but this very autonomy is a form of expression and action of higher *heteronymy*. What is immanent here is an expression of the transcendent, which acts *on, in,* and *through* us ourselves. Or to put it differently and more precisely, this very opposition between autonomy and heteronymy is inadequate to the essence of the relation, for the rational-categorial relation of difference and opposition between "the one" and "the other" is overcome through their transrational unity. Therefore it is correct to say (we have encountered this type of formulation more than once) that spiritual life is simultaneously *both* autonomous *and* heteronomous, and that it is *neither* autonomous *nor* heteronomous. This is the case because—in accordance with its antinomian transrationality—spiritual life is essentially and primordially *monodualistic*, so that what is autonomous in it is heteronomous and what is heteronomous in it is autonomous.

Thus, the "person" can be known only in a transrationally monodualistic manner as *the unity of separateness and mutual penetration*, as a unity whose essence consists in its *unknowableness*. That which was revealed to us as the essential feature of all concrete reality in general has particular validity with regard to man as a *person*: man as a person is always and essentially something *greater and other* than all we can perceive in him as a finished determination constituting his being. That is to say, he is a kind of infinitude, so that he has an inner bond to the infinitude of the *spiritual kingdom*. But the unity of separateness and mutual penetration that defines the person as the unknowable also has a wholly special character. It is the unity of higher and subordinate elements, the unity of the autonomously valid ground and that which is groundless and needs grounding. It is the unity of two *layers* of being that are wholly different in modality, the deeper and more fundamental layer being immeasurably, infinitely deep. Precisely for this reason, every person, every spiritual being, is a kind of primordial mystery, not only in the sense that we cannot exhaust the concrete makeup of the person by any logical analysis, but also in the sense that the very form of the person's reality is, in its general essence, a kind of *miracle* that surpasses our understanding. This is the basis for an attitude of reverence toward the person, the consciousness that in the person something divine, "the image and likeness of God," is revealed. And this miraculous, primordial mystery is revealed to us precisely in all its unknowableness, is immediately given to wise ignorance. In the face of this mystery all attempts to *rationally* understand spiritual being and the person inevitably fail, for they are attempts to deny the essentially unknowable in spiritual reality, to blindly pass by this most essential element, which constitutes precisely what the person is. All such attempts are always inadequate to the unknowable unity of separateness and mutual penetration that forms the very *essence* of the person. There are two ways in which the genuine essence of the person can be distorted. It is distorted *psychologistically* if it is taken purely immanently, as a fact, as a reality that simply in itself is some "this thing," something that does not have a relation to transcendent spiritual being—whereas, on the contrary, personal spiritual being is first constituted precisely by its participation in transcendent spiritual being. And it is distorted in a *rational-theological* way (or in a *rational-philosophical* way, which is a typical tendency of idealism) if the element of the spiritual or intrinsically valid is taken only in the aspect of its transcendence, and the person becomes only a blind tool, vessel, or medium for higher forces, becomes something that in itself is only nothing or only blind passivity. Both of these points of view remove the element of *freedom* through which the transrational merging or fusion of the transcendent and the immanent occurs and which is therefore the genuine center of spiritual life and of the person. Finally, there is a third point of view: when the transcendent itself is completely transferred into subjective self-being, and freedom, inner spontaneity, autonomy, is therefore understood rationally as a certain being in itself and from itself; it is then that the objectivity of the spiritual as the intrinsically valid vanishes and that which has autonomous, objective value is subjectified, which again distorts the genuine antinomian essence of the person. All such attempts to rationally understand the mystery of spiritual and personal being tend to *profane* this mystery. But the aura of unknowableness belongs precisely to the very essence of this being. We adequately attain this being only when in wise ignorance we apprehend it transrationally as the coincidence of opposites, as the unity of the subjective *and* the objective, the immanent *and* the transcendent. This can be expressed only in that categorial form which makes up the essence of all concrete being as the unknowable: in the form of the rationally unknowable but clearly revealed unity of separateness and mutual penetration that is the antinomian unity of the higher and that which is subordinate to the higher, of objective spirituality and subjective spiritual life.

This can be shown another way. Insofar as spiritual being constitutes the person, *individuality* belongs to the essence of this being. For the person is always an individuality, which is expressed in the absolute uniqueness, irreplaceableness, and unrepeatableness of the former. At first glance it might appear that this uniqueness is equivalent to inner isolation, absolute subjectivity, the being that is closed in itself. However, a man is factually a "person" and "individual" (with all the above-mentioned characteristics of individuality) only insofar as he "means" something for *others*, only insofar as he can give them something, while genuine isolation, absolute subjectivity, constitutes insanity, madness, *the loss of personality*. Thus, the element of autonomous validity, i.e., the element of the universally valid, attains expression precisely in individuality in all its uniqueness, while pure subjectivity in its universality (common to all people) is that which isolates and separates people, that which constitutes the isolating element of immediate self-being. The mystery of the person as an individuality therefore consists precisely in the fact that what is *universally valid* is expressed in the deepest *singularity* that defines the essence of the person. This universal validity is the all-embracing infinitude of transcendent spiritual being, common to all people, touching all equally, so that precisely this uniqueness, this singularity, is the form that is permeated by the transcendent that is common to all people. On the other hand, what is objectively valid fully and adequately reveals its genuine essence and effect only in concretely individual, personal being and not, for example, in the form of rationally expressible general content, propositions, and norms. The *infinite* can be expressed with maximal adequacy only in the concrete *point*: in the monad with its uniqueness and absolute singularity. On the other hand only that which can be recognized as a genuine personal *being-for-itself*, as a monad, can perceive and express the infinite. The essence of total unity as spirit, as the reality of intrinsically valuable and intrinsically valid being, acquires ultimate *definiteness* only in concrete individuality, in contrast to the definiteness of objective being, which is always abstract and general. *Genuinely concrete universality coincides with the genuine concreteness of the individual; genuine universal truth coincides with life.* This absolutely transrational relation discloses for us once again the transrational unity of subjectivity and objectivity.

NOTES

1. Translator's note: A line from one of Pushkin's poems.

Part III

The Absolutely Unknowable: Holiness or Divinity

> *The most divine knowledge of God is that which is acquired through ignorance.*
>
> DIONYSIUS THE AREOPAGITE

> *Der Abgrund meines Geistes ruft immer mit Geschrei Den Abgrund Gottes an: sag, welcher tiefer sei?*
>
> ANGELUS SILESIUS

> *Viderim me—viderim te.*
>
> ST. AUGUSTINE

Chapter VIII

Holiness (Divinity)

1. The Opposition between the Outer World and the Inner World and the Problem of Their Inner Unity

We have investigated the unknowable in two dimensions of being: in objective being whose primordial ground is revealed to us as unconditional being and in reality which is known through self-revelation as it is manifested in our immediate self-being and realized in transcending to "thou" and to spiritual being. Both the outer world and the inner world have turned out to be, in their deepest essence, forms of revelation of the unknowable. But now several questions arise. What is the relationship between these two forms of the manifestation of the unknowable in two different dimensions of being? Does there exist a unity that embraces the two, a single reality from which both of these forms emanate; and if so, what is the nature of this reality?

This is not an "idle" theoretical question, but an excruciating fundamental problem of man's being, a problem that is inexorably posed by man's fate. Insofar as man's being is conscious of itself, of its own immediate self-being, in all its singularity as a unique being and a self-being that extends to the "I–thou" relation and to spiritual life; and insofar as, on the other hand, it is conscious of itself as existing in an alien, objective world, as though cast into this world and abandoned, it feels the tragic nature of this duality and disharmony, and seeks a way out.

It is true that this tragic nature often remains unnoticed. We have already mentioned that there is a natural tendency not to notice immediate self-being as such in all its singularity and uniqueness and to recognize objective being as the only reality there is. Such is the natural life-feeling of anyone who has not been tempered by the bitter *experience* of the hopeless collision between these two worlds, the life-feeling of most people in youth or of people who are "successful" in life and who derive inner contentment from this success, of people who have never experienced with sufficient force and depth such facts as the shattering of youth's dreams, the perversity of fate, the loss of dear ones, and the inevitability of one's own death. In such a life-feeling one attempts somehow to dissolve oneself in objective being, to comfortably "adjust" oneself to it, to find a complete and conclusive "accommodation" to it. Less frequent but still possible is the opposite orientation, which also attempts to evade the tragic collision of the two worlds. Egocentric natures are capable of apprehending all of being, all that happens to them and in which they participate, as an "experience," i.e., as something that is a part of their own "inner" self-being. As an "image" or "impression," all that is experienced by us or touches us enters into us in some way, grows into our inner world, becomes its content. All being that is accessible to us in any form is capable of becoming for us something like a dream; and all our life is then capable of becoming like a dream. Abstract thought sanctions this life-feeling in the theory of "subjective idealism," just as it sanctions the opposite life-feeling in the theory of "positivism" or "empirical realism."

However, because they are expressions of simple blindness or of an instinctive concealing of the truth from oneself, both of these orientations are in the final analysis powerless to withstand the reality of the tragic duality of our life. One does not have to be a philosopher to be shaken sooner or later by the collision of these two worlds. When this collision is strong enough to deliver a blow to our inner essence, then even the eyes of the inveterate "realist," normally directed toward objective being alone, will be opened to the uneliminable reality of his inner life, which reveals itself in suffering and anguish. Even rougher is the awakening of the idealist from the dream of his life. He sees then with full clarity that the objective world is something greater than his own experience, than the dream of his soul. The objective world reveals itself to be an inexorably alien, hostile, cruel reality. Goethe's joke that the rocks thrown by the Jena students at the windows of Fichte's house were the best proof of the being of "the non-I" has a completely serious meaning. The experience of the collision (which shakes our inner life) between objective being and our immediate self-being can be tolerated neither by empirical realism nor by dreamy idealism. Both orientations then "come to their senses" and confront the *metaphysical* problem in all its livingness and seriousness. Then it is revealed that the "world" is neither the natural home of the soul nor its "experience"; and that "being-in-the-world" is the harsh, bitter *fate* of the soul. In confusion, alarm, and anguish, we stand before the unshakeable fact that our self-being—in all the immediacy of its reality, in its irrepress-

ible claim to infinitude and absolute validity—is only an orphan, a lonely
exile in the objective world, which threatens and hampers it on all sides.
And then there arises the most crucial problem of our life, the fundamental
problem which constitutes the final goal of all human thought: Is reconciliation possible? Is there a place in reality where our immediate self-being in
its desperate position in the world can go to be saved, where it can find
solid ground and true protection? Is the antagonistic duality of these two
worlds an *ultimate* and *uneliminable* fact before which we must humble ourselves in stoical resignation or in despair, or is there a depth of being in
which this opposition is overcome and in which the mysterious, comforting unity of the two worlds is revealed to us?

Anticipating a later discussion, let us briefly note that the religious problem of the disharmony between "faith" and "unfaith" is reducible to the
problem of the disharmony between these two worlds. If we neglect unfaith taken as pure *indifferentism*, a spiritual state that corresponds to the
orientation of blindness described above, to the unawareness of the problem itself, then the disharmony between faith and unfaith cannot be reduced to the fact that unfaith simply denies what is "blindly" accepted by
faith. On the contrary, faith and unfaith are both positive *metaphysical affirmations* or (in a certain sense) two different *religious orientations*. Unfaith is
precisely the affirmation of absolute metaphysical dualism, of the complete and profound opposition between our inner life and the objective
world, the affirmation of the presence of an absolutely impassable abyss
between the two. Faith, on the other hand, is the affirmation of the metaphysical *monism* of being, the conviction that these two worlds, in spite of
their heterogeneity and opposition, are both rooted in some common
ground, arise from some common primordial source, and that the path to
the ultimate unity in which our inner being finds its homeland is not closed
but can be found by us.

The fact that unfaith is a special metaphysical and (in a certain general
sense) even "religious" orientation is usually concealed by two circumstances. First, people come to unfaith guided by pure "reason" as the highest agency, i.e., guided by a consciousness that is oriented toward "facts"
and that generalizes them into rational "concepts." From this point of
view the opposition between the two worlds is an uneliminable and logically clearly fixable fact, in contrast to the arbitrary "presuppositions"
and "inventions" of faith. Furthermore, insofar as we take as our starting
point the consciousness of the singular nature of our immediate self-being
as pure *subjectivity* (see Chapter V, 3), i.e., as some inauthentic, ghostly,

defective reality, then the central fact of our being, which alone has genuinely objective reality, becomes the alienness and meaninglessness of being precisely as the objective world—which is alien and meaningless precisely in relation to the needs of our subjective human life. Then man feels
himself in the hopeless position of a warrior surrounded by an immeasurably superior enemy; or he feels himself to be an impotent "thinking reed,"
and, dying, has the consciousness that he alone courageously and soberly
takes account of his true position and does not succumb to the "illusions"
with which timid souls tend to comfort themselves. The fact that things are
not so simple and that unfaith is essentially a special religious-metaphysical
orientation (namely the orientation of religious-metaphysical *dualism*) is
easy to show using particular examples from the history of human thought.
Insofar as man attains the awareness that his inner life, his immediate self-
being, is, in spite of all its "subjectivity," a reality in its ultimate depth, i.e.,
the revelation of some special form of *being*, then his unfaith is expressed
openly in some religious dualism of the gnostic type: some homeland, some
ontological primordial ground of the soul does exist but only in isolation as
a distant, "unknown" God the father or God the good; and together with
this isolated unknown God there exists the demonic power that created the
world and against which our God is as powerless as we ourselves. This most
natural (in a certain sense) and simple religious orientation, which easily
forces itself upon us is essentially (if we examine it closely) the "faith" of
contemporary unfaith and is just as widespread and favored in the modern
world as it was in the twilight of the ancient world.

In our discussion, which is neither an apologia for anything or an attack
on anything but only an attempt to see in an unprejudiced way and to
describe the truth in all its fullness, we do not intend to "refute" unfaith in
its religious-metaphysical affirmation in the sense of dismissing it as a simple error. On the contrary, we recognized at the starting point of our
discussion that the orientation of religious-metaphysical dualism contains a
certain amount of unquestionable truth. The opposition between the inner
world of immediate self-being and the outer world of objective being, the
tragic dependence of the former on the latter and the outer powerlessness
of the former in the face of the onslaughts of the latter, the cleavage of
being into two heterogeneous parts, is a real *fact* that cannot be denied.
Nothing has caused so much harm to philosophical thought and religion as
the powerless, inconsistent attempt to reject this fact or to camouflage or
conceal it in some way. The fundamental ontological position of antinomian monodualism demands from us that we accept beforehand the truth

of this dualism even in the most essential meaning (which we are considering now) of this orientation. But this position also demands that we apprehend that this dualism is compatible with monism, that we seek and perceive the unity in the depths of this duality.

The particular manifestations, symptoms, or hints of this unity are essentially just as immediately evident to the attentive mind as is the fact of the duality or cleavage of being. We have experience in different forms that absolutely contradicts this simple resolution of our despair. This includes first of all the purely intellecttual self-consciousness, if it is sufficiently deep. The mere fact that we are *conscious* of this tragic duality points to some universal unity that embraces it. The unity of consciousness—in which the duality reveals itself, is perceived, and becomes distinct—presupposes a unity of being whose reflection or correlative point consciousness is. The unity of consciousness is already a unified reality that includes both the inner world and the outer world, and to the unity of consciousness corresponds the unity of unconditional being, the unity of the reality in which all consciousness is rooted (see Chapter III, 4). Both consciousness in its indefinite commonality and consciousness in its rational self-fulfillment in *knowledge* point to some all-embracing unity of being. For the fundamental fact that human thought is capable of "knowing" being (i.e., ideally possessing it, having it "for itself") would be inconceivable if not for the essential kinship of human subjectivity to cosmic or objective being. The primordial, irreducible "light" that flares up in us and illuminates objective being must somehow correspond to the essence of being itself, otherwise it could not illuminate the latter. In some sense the laws of "reason" coincide with the laws of being, and it would be too easy and illegitimate a solution to this riddle to call (as Kant did) this coincidence an illusion, to suppose that genuine being as a "thing in itself" is outside of knowledge, while the known world is nothing else but our "idea." On the contrary, the unprejudiced view must affirm that the "light" of thought that flares up in knowledge emanates from being itself. And if thanks to this light a dismembered being is revealed that is represented in the dismembered system of our concepts, this shows that our subjectivity is inwardly "adapted" to the structure of being, has roots in common with being. Insofar as philosophy is a "theory of knowledge" in the only true and legitimate sense, namely an ontology of knowledge, the affirmation of the cognitive relation as an *essential* relation between two correlative elements of reality, i.e., subject and object, the affirmation that these two elements have an inner kinship, is a simple, primordial affirmation that philosophy must accept as self-evident. In knowledge, in the successful perception of being with irrefutable, ultimate certainty, it is revealed that subjectivity and objectivity are somehow compatible, are matched to each other; and this matching has as its ground the commonality of the element of *rationality, logos.*

Another element, correlative to the element of rationality, is revealed with equal certainty in both of these parts of being: the element of irrationality. We discovered this element in the pure immediacy of immediate self-being and perceived its essential kinship with the irrational element of cosmic being. In the revelation of "thou" (insofar as "thou" is revealed to me as something alien and hostile) we encountered something frightening, which we felt to be kindred to the alienness and frightfulness of the foundation of objective being. And in the being of "we" we encountered the cosmic element in human life. Although the irrational element is experienced by us as something alien and hostile, i.e., as an indication of the duality that permeates all our being, nevertheless this duality does not coincide with the duality between the inner world and the outer world, but intersects it—which once again allows us to feel the deep unity of these two worlds. Irrationality, which forms the very essence of immediate self-being, the very essence of our life, defines (together with rationality and in inseparable connection with the latter) the essence of the outer world. The forms of being of potentiality, freedom, becoming, and time dominate both of these "worlds" or participate in both, though the particular manifestations of these forms differ in the two worlds. We have only to keep our eyes open to see with maximal clarity that all being as a whole is surrounded by the atmosphere of the incomprehensible, the irrational, and is immersed in this atmosphere.

If these two fundamental elements—rationality and irrationality belong, in inseparable unity, to both parts of being, to both "worlds", then in this sense every absolute dualism that claims to be the ultimate metaphysical truth turns out to be theoretically false and inconsistent, an internally contradictory point of view. In rationality as well as in irrationality, being in its very *concept* coincides with unity. Every duality, even the most acute and hopeless one, is nevertheless only a duality *within the limits of unity,* which embraces and permeates this duality. If we explore this idea further, we arrive (on the basis of the foregoing arguments) at the consciousness that in the final analysis all being as a whole is nevertheless rooted in the total unity of *the unknowable qua transrational,* is the revelation and the form of manifestation of the essentially unknowable. It is true that in some incomprehensible manner the unknowable splits for us into two heterogeneous worlds of phenomena, into two halves as it were. However, in the course of this process there is conserved that unity owing to which both of the halves are nonetheless parts of a whole—which means (as we already know) that they have their ultimate common ground in the unknowable. In spite of all the mutual antagonism of these two parts, the duality is a *dual-unity*.

However, this unity (which in the final analysis is reducible to the common rootedness in the essentially unknowable in its universality) cannot satisfy us, is not the unity we seek. Although the element of rationality takes the forms of "reason" and "knowing subject" in the makeup of subjectivity, it does not (as we have shown) coincide with subjectivity taken as an essential element of immediate self-being. Furthermore, insofar as rationality is expressed in pure consciousness and knowledge, in the pure light of the theoretical illumination of being, it does not save us from the blind meaninglessness of the objective world and does not change anything in this meaninglessness. After all, it is not so great a comfort to be a dying "thinking reed." As far as irrationality *qua* pure immediacy is concerned, we have seen that immediacy as such is opposed to our selfhood, that is, to the element that, *par excellence*, constitutes the special character of immediate self-being. We have also seen that in its essence immediate self-being (*my* life as it is for *me* from inside or for itself) is opposed to its own dissolution in unconditional being (in all-embracing unity insofar as this unity coincides with all-embracing and all-dissolving unconditional being) and jealously proects its *own* being precisely as *self*-being. The solution offered by Indian philosophy, namely the replacement of *my* selfhood by the indifferent totality (in "*tat twam asi*," in the consciousness that "this is thou" or "thou art in all"), the loss of my selfhood by its dissolution in all-embracing unity, in that which is "all or nothing," and the finding of final peace and salvation in this "all or nothing," this solution does not reveal to us that total unity which we seek, toward which we genuinely strive. For in the *genuine* total unity precisely *all* must be preserved, including and primarily my own self-being in all its fullness and metaphysical depth.

Is it possible to find in immediate experience a hint of the reality of such a genuinely satisfactory inner unity of the inner world and the outer world, a unity in which would be preserved all the intimacy, all the inexpressible but inalienably primary value for us of our own inner self-being?

We have such a hint, first of all, in the phenomenon of beauty.

2. BEAUTY

We cannot (and it is not necessary to) develop here a general theory of beauty. Our aim is rather to outline in a concise form those aspects of beauty or the beautiful which are directly related to the main theme of our discussion.

Without attempting to define what we mean in general by beauty or the beautiful, let us first of all note two elements that are present in what we are conscious of as the beautiful, in what we apprehend "esthetically." The first of these elements is necessarily present in all things that we apprehend esthetically and experience as beautiful. This is the element that constitutes esthetic perception as such. The second element is the necessary element of the beautiful as it is given in works of art, the element of the beautiful as the object of art.

All that is beautiful, all that is apprehended esthetically, is, first of all, a certain continuous whole permeated by inner unity. It can and even must have a diverse composition, but the members or parts of this diversity (e.g., the distinct features of a beautiful face, or the mountains, houses, vegetation, light, and air of a beautiful landscape, etc.) have force and significance not in themselves but precisely as integral, inseparably connected elements of a whole, which is a continuous, inwardly fused whole, the object not of analytical, decomposing thought but of pure sensuous contemplation. (This is most evident in the beauty that is given visually, in the form of nature, a painting, a sculpture, a beautiful face, but it is also applicable to the beautiful in music and poetry) Reducing this to concepts clarified in Part I, we can say that in this sense the beautiful is a metalogical unity insofar as it is given distinctly and apprehended by contemplation in or through its sensationally given structure. And whenever and wherever we are capable of freeing ourselves from the habitual orientation of the *objective interpretation* of reality, from the non-arbitrary perception of indications of objective reality in images, which reality falls apart into separate things and qualities expressible in concepts; whenever we are capable of concentrating on the simple contemplation of reality in its immediate concreteness; whenever we are capable—like children who without thinking greedily devour the images of being—of having pure experience of reality apart from all conceptual analysis of the latter, we apprehend reality as the beautiful. And the authentic artist has the gift of showing us reality in this its distinct immediacy, thus making us feel the novelty, the significance, the *beauty*, of even the most everyday, prosaic, familiar things.

To this is added the second element. The character of the indivisible, integral, undecomposable, all-permeating unity of the beautiful (which makes the beautiful resemble an organic unity) is intensified and becomes particularly distinct when it is expressed in the inner agreement and commensurability of the separate parts of the whole, i.e., when the unity is experienced as a *harmony*. This element of harmony gives to the beautiful a certain inner completion, a certain tranquil self-sufficiency, and therefore a certain inner absolute value. As a result of this element of harmony (which is absolutely necessary in all works of art, i.e., in all beauty that is created by man precisely with the intent of reproducing the impression of the beautiful), the beautiful is extracted from the objective world (which contains no self-sufficient parts, nothing perfect in itself; in which everything is a fragment that acquires its fullness from its connection with all other things, from its dependence upon all else) and becomes something in its own self, independent of all else: an expression of the ultimate, deepest, all-permeating primordial unity of being. In this sense beauty (embodied in the image of a beautiful woman) is adequately described by Pushkin:

> In her all things are *harmony* and *marvel*,
> *Higher than the world* and its passions.
> Her *solemn beauty* is a refuge
> For her *tranquil* shyness.[1]

These two elements taken together extract the beautiful from the objective world, free it on the one hand from the partialness, unfullness, incompletion, and imperfection that characterize all particular things, while freeing it on the other hand from the rough, blind, inwardly unilluminated and senseless factuality with which objective being is given to us. The beautiful becomes an expression of self-sufficient value, of the self-groundedness of being, of its inner validity, and therefore its "spiritualness" (see Chapter VII). *The immanent essence of beauty consists in the fact that in it we apprehend and experience immediately and explicitly in the most outer aspect of being the absolute value of being, its meaningfulness and inner groundedness.* Therefore, the beautiful is unproblematic, "questionless" being. The questions "why" and "on what ground" (with "ground" understood in its deepest sense) are inappropriate where inner groundedness is immanently disclosed in the phenomenon itself, is already contained in the phenomenon.

Another way of saying the same thing is that the beautiful is *expressive*. All that is experienced as beautiful is not simply a rough, blind *fact* which gives us nothing besides itself and (unilluminated by any higher, reasonable necessity, any inner meaningfulness) brazenly and illegitimately forces itself upon us, demands of us recognition of it, without possessing any inner persuasiveness and authority. On the contrary, the beautiful is that which inwardly "charms" and "bewitches" us, that which gains our recognition because of its inner persuasiveness and meaningfulness. In the beautiful we are inwardly *reconciled* with being, because it reveals to us what it immanently carries within itself: the ultimate depth, the ultimate, inwardly self-evident, "transparent" ground of being.

If we ask what precisely does the beautiful express, what does it reveal to us, what does it speak to us about, we find that it is essential for the nature of the beautiful that this "what" cannot be expressed in any concept. A reader who is esthetically perceptive and able to understand his esthetic experience will make it unnecessary to refute the absurd notion (which contradicts the very essence of esthetic experience) that the beautiful (e.g., in a work of art) expresses some conceptually expressible abstract thought, has some prosaically, verbally expressible "content" (independent as such from its artistic form), gives us some practically useful "principle" or teaches us some "moral." On the contrary, what the beautiful expresses is simply *reality itself* in its abstractly inexpressible concreteness, in its essential unknowableness. To experience reality esthetically, even in its smallest particular manifestation, is precisely to have living, directly persuasive experience of its unknowableness, of its coincidence with the unknowable. What we have been attempting to do in the entire course of this work through arduous and complex abstract argumentation—namely to direct the reader's attention to the unknowableness of reality or the coincidence of *the very concepts* of concrete living reality and the unknowable—is given with full immediacy in every esthetic experience, which as such immerses us into the atmosphere of the unknowable, compels us to feel all the meaning of the latter, all its coincidence with the genuine concrete fullness of reality. In this sense there is no better and simpler refutation of the opinion that identifies reality with objective reality (with that picture of being which is revealed to us by the intellectual-logical interpretation of reality and its reduction to a dry *system* of conceptually expressible determinations) than a simple reference to that image and character of reality which is given in esthetic experience.

There is no need to develop this in greater detail. Instead let us refer to our analysis (see Chapter III, 4) of the concept of reality in all its depth and fullness, in contradistinction not only to objective being but also to unconditional being. In that analysis we used examples from the esthetic sphere of experience to illustrate this concept of reality as a unity embracing the inner life of the knowing subject together with what is known, as the all-embracing fullness of concreteness. Reality in its immediate concrete fullness, depth, and livingness coincides, in a certain sense, with the reality that is revealed to us in esthetic experience. (We shall not examine the details of this relationship.)

This leads directly to the goal we set out to reach in our consideration of the phenomenon of beauty. Beauty is the immediate and most directly convincing proof that there is some mysterious kinship between the inner world and the outer world, between immediate self-being and the ground of the outer, objective world. This unity is revealed to us directly (or rather we have a kind of external revelation of it) in all esthetic experience. Esthetic experience persuades us that such a unity exists and must and can be discovered despite the obvious uneliminable *factual* disharmony and antagonism between these two worlds.

Let us return to the fundamental fact that beauty (in nature as well as in art) is necessarily *expressive*, expresses something. And we now know that this "something" is reality in its unknowableness, in some one of its concrete aspects. The expressiveness of beauty signifies (see Chapter VI, 1) that in beauty something inner (that which is expressed) in reality is revealed in the outer (in that which expresses). This expressiveness signifies the same primordial, irreducible relation between the inner and outer layers of reality which we found in the revelation of "thou." Whatever is beautiful, whatever is revealed in esthetic experience, is experienced as something akin in this sense to a living, animate being, as something akin to our own inner self-being. It is something "soul-like," something with some sort of "inner content," "inner reality," which expresses or reveals itself in outer appearance, just as our "soul" or a "thou" directed at us expresses itself in gesture, gaze, smile, or word. The beautiful (in nature and in art) "tells" us something, "gives us knowledge" of something, brings us a sign of mysterious, hidden, living depths of reality. And in this sense we "commune" with the beautiful (with the beauty of a landscape or a beautiful face; the beauty of a painting, sculpture, cathedral, or symphony) as with a close friend. We perceive in external reality something akin to our most intimate depth, our inner self-being, and at the moment of esthetic enjoyment we stop feeling alone and find in the surrounding external reality the primordial "homeland" of our soul, that lonely pilgrim in the objective world.

Of course, the positivistically inclined reader (i.e., the reader oriented toward the recognition of objective reality alone) will make the usual hackneyed objection to our theory. He will tell us that in esthetic experience we are beguiled by a kind of illusion. We non-arbitrarily "transfer" our own feelings or moods to an object, to nature or a work of art. We place our feelings into the object, thus "animating" it. Thus, art and artistic creation as well as the perception of beauty are something like a child's game, the game of transferring oneself into an imaginary world. In order to bolster this hackneyed common-sense objection, obliging philosophical thought (especially German thought at the end of the 19th century) developed the theory of *Einfühlung*. There is no need for us to carry out a detailed examination of this common-sense objection and of the corresponding esthetic theory (which has many variants, none of which, however, touches upon the essence of the problem). It is sufficient to note that this objection (in analogy to materialism, for example) simply "invents" an *ad hoc* explanation to justify the limited and blind nature of the basic instinctive orientation, without considering real facts, that is, without considering what is really given in esthetic experience. No one has ever been able to show how this subtle self-deception is supposed to occur. The structure of esthetic experience contains not the slightest indication that man takes his own feelings and transfers them to an object so as to have them "given" in the object. All this is pure "mythology," fabricated by positivism and materialism. An unprejudiced, purely descriptive phenomenological analysis of esthetic experience tells us something wholly different. It tells us that in esthetic experience the human spirit finds already "finished" and immediately given the feature of *expressiveness*, which immediately reveals the inner meaningfulness and "soul-likeness" of reality. It is not man who "transfers" something of his own to reality or forces upon it something alien; rather it is reality that forces upon *us* its special structure, infects us with it. All our activity in this regard is constrained by the fact that we have the choice of either artificially closing ourselves off from the action upon us of reality or freely opening our consciousness to the action of reality and developing a sensitivity to it.

Of course, by this we do not mean to say that the nature of a work of art really has something that is essentially identical to the human soul or spirit or to deny the role of imagination or invention (more precisely, of metaphorical thinking) in expressing esthetic experience. What is given in the esthetic object is precisely only something "soul-like" or "spirit-like." The real makeup of this experience cannot be expressed except in analogies or metaphors that compare it (in poetry and mythology) with phenomena of human psychic and spiritual life. (Directly below we shall point out the genuine meaning of the "illusory" nature of esthetic experience.) But metaphors that compare the objective to the subjective (not to mention *Einfühlung*, the "transference" to an object of what is conceivable only as a subjective experience) would be impossible and inconceivable if they were not rooted in some *objective resemblance*. No one can "liken" a circle to a triangle or (even less so) one's joy or woe to the square root of two. But when we say that a landscape is sad or happy, that the succession of sounds in Beethoven's Third Symphony conveys the heroic struggle of the human spirit, while the sounds of the last part of the Ninth Symphony convey infinite triumphant joy, or that the alternation of light and shadow in Rembrandt's paintings lets us feel the metaphysical spiritual depth of being, we are conscious with extreme certainty that the ground of such, only metaphorically expressible, analogies is contained in the real object itself. What especially merits attention is that "metaphor" (literally "transference") can also proceed in the opposite direction: from categories of sensationally perceived, externally spatial being to the characterization of human psychic or spiritual states. How are we able to understand such metaphors as, for example, the "fall" or "ascent" of a human soul, its "emptiness" or "fullness," the "blossoming" or "withering" of a soul, the "surface" or the "depths" of a soul, the "flow" of life, and even the "influence" of the human soul (the literal meaning of "influence" being "inflow")? Generally speaking, since human words in their primordial meaning signify something clearly spatial, the very possibility of their use in the metaphorical, psychological sense presupposes some deep, real resemblance or kinship between outer being and inner being. Of course, here too the theory that attempts to appease our prejudices obligingly offers the simple (too simple, for it simplifies by distorting) explanation that the analogy here lies in the human "feelings" that accompany the perception of the external reality. We respond to this theory by citing Bergson's wise objection: "Let us not be deceived by illusion. There are times when it is metaphorical language that conveys the heart of the matter, while the language of abstract concepts is glued to the surface appearance of things."

Let us summarize. The fact of beauty or esthetic experience is irrefutable proof of a *deep, inner kinship in the very structure* of the objects of inner and outer experience, the proof of a certain unity between outer objective being and inner self-being. Furthermore, esthetic experience itself is a kind of special state of being in which the very boundary between objective being and inner, subjective being is erased. In spite of all the infinite variety of objects and forms of esthetic experience, all the themes and styles of artistic creativity, esthetic experience opens our eyes to that dimension or layer of reality about which it is impossible to say whether it is "objective" or "subjective," but where it is only possible to say (and we already know the significance of this logical form) that this reality is simultaneously *both* objective and subjective or *neither* objective *nor* subjective. The experience of beauty reveals to us the essentially unknowable *unity* of reality as such beyond the limits of categories of inner and outer, objective and subjective. In other words, a deep, mysterious kinship ("prosaically" unexplainable but self-evident in all its mystery) is revealed between the intimate world of the human soul and the ground of what stands before us as the external world of objective reality.

It might appear on the basis of the foregoing discussion (and it has appeared thus more than once to the human spirit) that the phenomenon of beauty contains the solution to the tragic riddle that torments the heart of man, opens a way out of the duality, the ontological disharmony, that forms the essence of the tragic nature of human existence. Alas, this is not so. And here, not theory but life itself makes us discover the amount of truth that is contained in the feeling that what is revealed to us as esthetic experience is somehow "illusory," lacks seriousness, and sufficient ontological ground. A certain genuine reality is unquestionably revealed in esthetic experience, but this reality is in some way only "superficial," does not wholly embrace all the depths of reality. Beauty refers only to the "appearance" of reality: it does not form the genuine essence or roots of reality and therefore it does not determine the entire structure of the latter. It is true that beauty points to a certain deep mystery of being, to a certain feature of its ultimate depth; but it is only a hint, a sign of this depth, and is itself a riddle. Beauty does not tell us how to harmonize what it makes manifest with the structure of reality. For example, how often it happens that the "divine" beauty of a woman's face conceals an empty, insignificant, vain, "prosaic" soul. How often it happens that what we call the "beauty of the soul" does not reach the ultimate depths of the human spirit but conceals profound disharmony, formlessness, even ugliness. And consider the beauty of nature (whether it be the beauty of a powerful wild beast or the beauty of the ocean that threatens the seafarer with death, or the beauty of a tropical landscape beneath which lurk the terrors of a possible earthquake), often concealing the chaos of destruction, disharmony, struggle, and death. And the artist, the human being who lives in the element of beauty and is inebriated by it, is only rarely and never fully inwardly illuminated by it. As a rule, there remains in the artist—in his genuine integral self-being as it is expressed in his personal life and outer life—the same dark, unilluminated, inwardly insignificant reality that is in other people. "Of all the insignificant children of the world, he is perhaps the most insignificant" (Pushkin). Beauty as such does not save him from the destructive forces of evil or from the tragic nature of human life. Beauty as such is neutral. In a sense it is indifferent to good and evil. Symbolizing some potential harmony of being, it peacefully co-exists with actual disharmony. Furthermore, according to Dostoevsky's profound insight, beauty combines in itself the "divine" and the "demonic," for wherever we are seduced by deceitful appearances, there we have dealings with the demonic. This lack of concord between beauty—*esthetic* harmony—and the genuine reconciling, redeeming *essential* harmony of being was manifested concretely with astonishing persuasive force in the tragic life-experiences of such artists as Botticelli, Gogol, and Tolstoy. We can say that beauty is a sign of the potential harmony of being, of the possibility of actual, fully realized harmony. And if the world were perfectly beautiful, it would be perfectly harmonious, in inner accord, free of tragic duality. Therefore the dream of the ultimate transfiguration of the world is a dream of the complete triumph of beauty in the world. But it is precisely only a dream, which is opposed by the bitter reality of the inner discord and duality of being. Beauty is only a reflection of "paradise," of the ontological rootedness of all reality in divine total unity. This reflection charms us in our sinful, fallen, "earthly" being, which is torn by inner antagonism. It gives us a comforting hint of the possibility of an entirely different kind of being and therefore a hint of the ontological primordial ground of this possibility. But beauty as such is not the primordial, ontologically stable and deep unity that we are seeking.

3. Primordial Unity as the Primordial Ground of Being

All the paths to the total unity of being that we have tried until now—all the paths to inner harmony and inner kinship between the intimate world of our inner life and the indifferent, frightening objective world of outer reality—turn out to be narrow, shaky bridges over an abyss that continues to yawn beneath us. And when we glance into the depths of this abyss we are overcome with fear and vertigo. The fact that the total unity of being is a fractured, bifurcated, internally contradictory *dual*-unity; the fact that without ceasing to be a unity it splits into two heterogeneous, antagonistic halves, is precisely a *fact* and cannot be removed by any theoretical considerations. Insofar as it is a question of a purely theoretical explanation of the world, facts are facts and cannot be reasoned away. We can conceive of grasping unity precisely as genuine total unity only in a wholly different perspective, which in a sense surpasses all factuality as such. Most immediately we can conceive this unity only as the unity of the *root* or primordial ground—the unity of a "point" toward which these two worlds converge in their ultimate depth, in spite of all their disharmony.

The most proximal possibility of such a point of convergence, even for what is most heterogeneous in being, is given in the *depth* dimension of being, in the infinitude of this dimension. All being that is accessible to us (in spite of the fact that in this accessibility it is immanent to us and explicit) is always something *greater and other* than all that we can grasp in it, and also something *infinitely other* and therefore something potentially *wholly other*. This being is also all that it is in that part of its reality which is hidden from us. This is what we mean by the hidden "depth" of being. Everything that is immanent is also transcendent. And the transcendent in the immanent is, in turn, immanent. The hidden and unknown is revealed as such (i.e., in its reality) with total self-evident truth. Behind every thing and phenomenon lie infinite, inaccessible depths and distances, which, as such, are given to us with total immediacy. *"Alles ist weit und nirgends schliesst sich der Kreis"* (Rilke). The immediate vision of this contains a metaphysical consciousness compared to which all empirical-rational knowledge, all intellectual possession of something as definite, delimited being, is only a derivative, fragmentary, particular segment. This circumstance coincides with the fact that being in its ground and in the all-embracing fullness of its makeup always and everywhere coincides with the *unknowable*.

But in the unknowable—in the infinite depths that are inaccessible to us in their definiteness, in depths that essentially transcend all that is definite—all in general is possible. Truly wise and far-seeing (even purely scientific) minds have always been conscious of this. The great French physicist Arago said: "Beyond the limits of mathematics [let us add, beyond the limits of pure rationality as such] I would hesitate to use the word 'impossible'." Furthermore, not only is all in general possible in the infinite, transcendent depths of being, but these depths themselves are the womb of the all-embracing existent possibility or potency that transcends all definite being. It would be absolutely wrong and indicative of spiritual limitation for us to identify even the most general feature of all accessible being with its deepest structure, with its structure that penetrates to the ultimate depths. This is in fact the constant error of all rational metaphysics (which Kant called "dogmatic"). This alone would make it premature and unjustifiable to attribute absolute, unlimited significance to the fact that conditions our entire life: the fact of the bifurcation of being into two heterogeneous, antagonistic worlds.

But it is easy to get lost in the unknowable and infinite. In its immediate aspect the unknowable is a dark abyss before which we stand in impotent uncertainty. What path should we take, what direction should we choose, to find the unity we seek, the possible point of convergence of the inner world and the outer world? There is no need to repeat that no inquiries along the paths of "objective" knowledge can lead us to the goal, for on such paths, even if we succeed in encompassing infinitude, we would remain in only *one* of the two worlds and would not be able to go beyond its limits. Even if we think that we have attained the ultimate, absolute primordial ground (what the language of faith calls "God") on the path of objective knowledge, it is easy to see that this is an illusion and error—for the deep claims of our immediate self-being and personal life would remain unsatisfied by the blind, dark factuality that essentially characterizes objective being as such. The cleavage that passes through our entire life would remain unhealed. This is why all the attempts (even the deepest and most penetrating) of metaphysics to "rationally" ground the "objective" being of God, the soul, etc., can never satisfy religious thought, the religious longings of man, and are even felt to be a kind of mockery and sacrilege with regard to the holiness of the "heart." And it is also clear that all deep penetration into our immediate self-being, into our "inner life," insofar as we remain within the limits of its "subjectivity," can only take us away from the reconciling unity we seek. One can "hide" in one's shell from the tragic nature of life but one cannot overcome it in one's shell. Sooner or later it will overtake one even there.

But if it is contradictory and therefore vain to seek the ultimate unity of being within the limits of the subjective world, we nevertheless have a vague feeling (but a feeling that is persuasive in its vagueness) that the only path to this ultimate, reconciling unity leads *through* immediate self-being, through deep penetration into the world of inner life. In this sense one can ascribe general and fundamental significance to Augustine's command: "Go not outward but inward; the truth is within man; and where you find yourself limited, there (*within yourself!*) transcend yourself" (*transcende te ipsum*). In fact this path is indicated beforehand by the very quarry we seek. But what do we seek? We seek that ultimate *depth* of being, that ground of absolute reality in which our inner being (in all its uniqueness, with all its needs and claims) could find a stable refuge, its genuine *homeland*, could feel itself secure against the indifferent, threatening, alien world of objective reality. But if we seek the "homeland" of the soul, it can obviously be sought (or remembered) only on the paths of the soul itself.

There is no need (or any possibility) to seek somewhere infinitely far from us this homeland, which (as it is prescribed beforehand) must coincide with the primordial reality of being. It is sufficient to distinctly feel for one instant that our "I," the world of our inner life, our immediate self-being (in spite of all its "subjectivity," instability, immediate groundlessness), genuinely *is* with ultimate self-evident truth—that it is a *genuine* reality. But "to be a reality" is to emanate from or to be rooted in some *absolute reality*. Even what is most insignificant and unstable could not *be* in general if it were not rooted in some way in the ultimate depth of absolute reality. The remembrance of this self-evident truth, which, strangely, is so rarely accessible to us produces a sudden miraculous transformation of the entire situation. The tragic nature of our intimate, immediate metaphysical life-feeling consists, after all, in the consciousness that we stand at the edge of an abyss that is ready to engulf us at any moment or even that we are suspended above this abyss. What we call "being" or "reality" appears to us as such an abyss. Why? Evidently because we are conscious of ourselves as something wholly other than this "being." We are conscious of ourselves as something that, because of an incomprehensible accident, came from some place other than the abyss of being and therefore stands—*for the time being*—on the edge of this abyss or hovers above it. In other words, being is an abyss *outside* of us, ready to engulf us, only because we *exclude* ourselves from being.

Our metaphysical life-feeling will be utterly transformed if we become conscious that this abyss is *being* and remember that we ourselves (since we "are") also belong to and are rooted in (primordially, as though from inside) being. If we ourselves are rooted in being, we cannot "fall through" into it and perish in it. There is simply nowhere to "fall through." The consciousness of our self-being *precisely as authentic being* (insofar as this consciousness is sufficiently acute and clear) is already sufficient to reveal to us that *primordial unity* which we immediately lack and which we often seek with insatiable and excruciating longing. Anyone who has ever grasped, if only once, if only in a dim feeling, this self-evident truth is astonished not by this truth but by the impotent blindness of our usual, "enlightened" consciousness, by that naive, limited stubbornness with which this consciousness affirms as something undeniable the position of "unfaith," the position (as we now know) of absolute metaphysical dualism which cannot be overcome. The consciousness that imagines itself to be "enlightened" and "scientific" does not want to take anything on faith, seeks an explanation for everything, asks in relation to everything the questions "why" and "where did this come from." But with regard to one thing, the most important thing, it never asks questions concerning cause, ground, or source, but calmly and confidently considers it the result of pure, unexplained, and unexplainable chance. The "enlightened" consciousness calmly reconciles itself to the fact that our "I," our "person," our inner life with all its needs, hopes, and dreams, is something that somehow from somewhere got into the world by some unknowable chance and finds itself in this world a wholly foreign, lonely, homeless being, doomed to destruction and death. But is not our *person*, in spite of all its "foreignness" with regard to the "world," *also* a reality, which, like all realities, has its "cause," i.e., an ontological ground or source of its being? The "scientific" consciousness does not even dream of posing this question. Or insofar as it does pose it, it distorts the immediate meaning of the question by replacing man's being as an inner world of immediate revelation (the world of immediate self-being) with man's being as a "natural" being, i.e., as a particular object in the makeup of the objective world. And the only answer it knows, even to this distorted question, is the comically impotent answer of so-called "evolutionism," according to which man with his soul, intelligence, and person "evolved"—"gradually," "step by step"—from some blind, unconscious "amoeba" or "protoplasm." This would be tantamount to, say, a circle "evolving"—gradually, in the course of an immeasurably long period of time—into a triangle or a geometrical point. The "enlightened" consciousness speaks with contemptuous irony of the "anthropomorphism" of the "believing consciousness." But do we not have the right to direct this irony back at the "enlightened" consciousness and to speak of its enslavement by the naive mythology of "pragmomorphism" and "cosmomorphism."

Despite the stubbornness of the "scientific" consciousness in its limitation, we have the right to affirm the following self-evident truth: If we as persons, as carriers of the inner reality of immediate self-being, are alone in the face of the cold, soulless, impersonal, indifferent objective world, if we are impotent, defenseless exiles and wanderers in this world, *it is because we have a homeland in another sphere of reality*. Being a reality ourselves, we originate in some reality and are rooted in its womb. However far away this primordial homeland, this primordial metaphysical refuge of our soul may be from the alien world of external objective reality, both of these worlds—in the capacity of being in general—evidently have a certain common root, a certain primordial unity that is hidden from us. Therefore that which in its immediacy appears to us as a terrible, threatening abyss, now (owing to the imperceptible but decisive shift in our self-consciousness that reveals to us our own being as a genuine reality) is revealed to us in its deepest aspect as something also rooted in our native soil of primordial reality, turns out to be not an abyss but a solid ground that is inseparably (though invisibly) connected to the ground on which we ourselves stand. Whatever terms we use to express the metaphysical consciousness that is thus revealed to us, its essence is the same. It is the self-evident life-feeling of the security and stability of our inner self-being in its native soil of *primordial reality*.

One doubt, however, is unresolved. As we know, primordial reality, the primordial ground of being, is revealed to us in two opposite, antagonistic worlds: in the world of our inner life (our immediate self-being) and in the objective world of outer reality. We have become convinced that the first of these worlds—our own essence and self-being—has ontological roots, a genuine homeland, in the primordial ground of being. But the second world, the alien and hostile world of objective being, emanates from the same place, is also rooted in the primordial ground of being. It is not enough to have a homeland. In order to feel secure, one must be certain that this homeland is *more powerful* than the forces that are alien and hostile to it. Insofar as we do not have this solid certainty, the monistic consciousness that we ourselves somehow invisibly and incomprehensibly have a certain primordial ground in common with the objective being that is alien to us is not yet sufficient to save us from the religious-metaphysical dualism about which we spoke above. For the metaphysical homeland or ground of our soul could nonetheless turn out to be relatively weak and powerless in the face of the forces of primordial reality as they are manifested in the impersonal, non-human, and therefore inhuman appearance of the objective world. We must have the guarantee that the aspect of primordial reality in which it is *the primordial homeland of the soul is deeper, more powerful, more fundamental, more ontologically primary* than the other aspect in which it is the womb and ground of objective being. We must have the guarantee that the precious, inalienable special character of that which composes the intimate essence of our immediate self-being is *closer* to primordial reality and more adequate to it than the special character of the objective world which is hostile to us. But how can we prove something like this? And is not the very search for this proof an expression of the need for consolation in the face of the bitter fact that the truth is contrary to our hopes? Is it not the case, as the Germans say, of *der Wunsch der Vater des Gedankens?* And once again we encounter the mockingly triumphant Mephistophelean smile of a consciousness oriented toward objective reality, toward the sober affirmation of facts. For it would appear that facts are incontrovertible evidence of the opposite of our hopes, evidence of the enslavement of our soul (however ontologically deep and primordial its roots may be) by the forces of the objective world, by cosmic forces.

We can overcome this very difficult temptation if we remember the third kind of being that was revealed to us earlier in our discussion: namely the world of *spiritual* being. If we remember that spiritual being is not only the external, transcendent ground of psychic being but also the element that constitutes psychic being as genuine reality (see Chapter VII, 3), we shall understand that in our meditation on the primordial ground of immediate self-being (insofar as we were guided by the consciousness of the genuine reality of immediate self-being) we found ourselves, without thinking about it, in the sphere of *spiritual* being.

4. THE PRIMORDIAL GROUND AS THE PRIMORDIAL FOUNDATION, LIGHT, AND LIFE

In Chapter VIII, we saw that on the one hand spiritual being has a profound and intimately inner essential kinship with immediate self-being and forms the genuine ground of the latter (a ground in which immediate self-being finds its realization). And on the other hand, spiritual being points beyond the limits of immediate self-being and, as *objectivity*, opposes the latter. Thus, we have here the only sphere of being that, combining features of objectivity and inwardly self-revealing being, transcends the opposition between objective being and inner self-being. The essence of this objectivity consists in the fact that spiritual being, insofar as that which is valid and valuable in itself is revealed in it, is the soil or ground through which the subjectivity and groundlessness of immediate self-being are overcome. What is valid in itself is also the self-evident in the sense of inner persuasiveness and transparency. For this reason what is valid in itself provides the ultimate ground for all knowledge in general and in this sense can be understood as the ultimate ground of being itself. If, pursuing in the sphere of spiritual being that which is valid and valuable in itself and that which therefore performs the function of the *illuminating* ground with regard to our consciousness of life, we were to reach on this path the ultimate depths, we would reach the concept of the all-grounding and all-embracing *primordial foundation.*

This *primordial foundation* is not only absolutely self-evident (whatever is valid in itself and inwardly persuasive is self-evident) but is *self-evidence itself,* truth itself. Further, the concept of self-evidence and truth is taken here not in its ordinary meaning but in its eminent, potentiated meaning. Truth is the truth of knowledge only derivatively, whether this be the truth of objective knowledge as the correspondence of our representations and thoughts with reality itself, or truth as revealed presence, as the self-disclosure, the self-revelation of reality. In itself, truth is *Truth, the self-illuminating light.*[2] If previously we found in spiritual being that which is true in itself, inwardly persuasive, completely transparent, this inner illuminatedness or radiance presupposes *light itself* as the principle of illumination. The true presupposes truth itself. For in the ultimate sense, truth as light presupposes outside of itself the dark factuality (which grounds nothing) of what it illuminates. If "light" (like everything else) emanates from being, it nevertheless reaches only the outside of the reality of what is known and illuminates this reality only on the outside, leaving the interior unilluminated. Truth in this latter sense is therefore not the genuine *primordial foundation.* On the contrary, the integral truth or *Truth* is the genuine primordial foundation. Since it is the illuminating ground of being, the meaning of being, *Truth* is the unity of being and right, the foundation of being that grounds being by disclosing the inner legitimacy of the latter. But since this *Truth* is pure *Truth,* i.e., reality, in it we have the deepest, the most primary, or rather the absolutely primary reality. In this reality there is no blind necessity or factuality. There is nothing that illegitimately forces itself upon us and forces out of us its recognition or acceptance. On the contrary, the *Truth* is that which in its own self is genuine and rightful, that which carries in itself its own self-evidently valid foundation, or rather coincides with this foundation. In this its deepest, primordial sense, the truth is not some purely theoretico-philosophical "limiting concept." The wisdom of the simple Russian word *pravda (Truth)* in the dual sense of truth and justice is witness to the fact that truth in this sense is that which every act of our life serves insofar as we are moved from our ultimate depth. This truth is that to which all our aspirations are dedicated insofar as we are conscious of their ultimate, deepest essence. For in the final analysis what we seek in life is precisely this living *Truth*—something valuable-in-itself which is genuine, rightful, true being. Thus, attaining the ultimate foundation as *Truth,* we have in it the true, deepest primordial ground of all that exists.

The primordial ground of being which we sought here is therefore not some purely factual force of being, not simply the deepest, real primordial soil of being. It is rather the primordial foundation that illuminates with meaning: that which in itself is *Truth*. And now we find the solution to the doubt that came to us. The primordial reality or primordial ground of being—since it is the primordial foundation, the meaning of being—is something greater and other than the impersonal, dark, inwardly unilluminated womb of objective being. Since it is the *light of Truth* (that which is the inner foundation of being), since it is the unity of the real ground and the ideal ground, the primordial ground is more powerful, deeper, and more significant than whatever is factual. Therefore the primordial ground is more kindred to us, to our self-being (in spite of all its instability) than to impersonal, unilluminated objective being. The fact that our immediate subjective self-being is for us the only door to spiritual being, in the depth of which we acquire the primordial ground as the primordial foundation that illuminates with meaning, is evidence of the unquestionable ontological priority of our inner self-being (in spite of all its weakness) with respect to all purely factual, objective being. We shall see below that the real enigma is not how the inner essence of our life can be kindred to the primordial ground of being but rather how the objective world, with all that terrifies and repels us, can arise from this primordial ground.

We have the same thing in mind when we call primordial ground "primordial life," the living primordial source of life. It is obvious that this is not a definition of its essence ("definition" in the precise, logical sense is absolutely impossible here) but only a kind of hint with which we can characterize the paths that lead to the primordial ground or the claims that we set before it. We penetrate into the primordial ground precisely through spiritual being. As something valid in itself or rather as validity as such, as the *Truth*, the primordial ground is the ultimate foundation and meaning of our whole life. The primordial ground has a certain essential kinship, a certain most intimate closeness to the ineffable essence of our life. Being value and truth, the primordial ground must also be understood not abstractly but as a concrete reality, which is not blindly necessary being, factually present in a finished form, but something that grounds itself, i.e., something that somehow creates itself. For this we have no word but "life," which we take to mean reality as creativity and self-grounding. Since immediate self-being is precisely "life" in this sense and since the primordial ground must be understood as something inwardly kindred to immediate self-being, we come to understand the primordial ground itself in analogy to life and to call it "primordial life," the living primordial source of life. That this primordial ground is the point to which converges and from which emanates all being in general is immanent evidence of the fact that the primordial ground of both objective being and unconditional being is the primordial source of life or primordial life. That which had appeared to be an unresolvable contradiction between immediate self-being and objective being, between the turbulent, tortured movement of our inner life and the cold, rigid fixity of objective being, is now revealed as ineffable unity in what we call the living primordial source of life. Primordial life—as the valid and persuasive in itself or as the light of *Truth* itself—is the ultimate completion and ground of immediate self-being. As the unity of first and last things, as *causa sui*, primordial life is the primordial ground of absolute all-embracing fullness, of all reality in general and therefore of objective being as well. Since the living primordial source of life is the primordial foundation and the primordial *Truth*, the ground of all things, it follows that it is the primordial source and primordial unity of all. The primordial ground is precisely nothing else but the ineffable ultimate depth, the ultimate foundation, the ultimate reason why anything at all exists.

The primordial ground (or primordial foundation) is the center at which all things converge and from which all things emanate. In relation to this center all else is only the periphery, something ungrounded, rootless, unindependent, which would come to ruin if it did not stand in relation to the primordial ground; if it did not derive its being, stability, and validity from the primordial ground; if it were not created, preserved, and grounded by the primordial ground. In itself the primordial ground or primordial foundation is not "being." Since it is the primordial foundation, the first principle which, in giving meaning, values, foundation, first grounds and calls into being all else, the primordial ground (like Plato's "good") transcends being in terms of power, importance, and perfection. Or as Plotinus expresses it, the primordial ground is that which takes upon itself the task of being the being and ground of all. The primordial ground is greater than being. It is primordial reality, compared to which all being is something derivative, subject to grounding and realization. In spite of all the divergence and heterogeneity between immediate self-being and objective being, in spite of the fact that we are fated to live simultaneously in these two mutually antagonistic worlds, we feel the ultimate, unknowable unity of these two worlds, we possess this unity, even though this possession is somehow at a remove from us and reaches full realization only with difficulty. *This* unity is therefore the true point of convergence (lying in infinite depths) of these two heterogeneous layers of being, which compose being as a whole.

But when we say "point of convergence" we imagine something like a spatial point that lies "somewhere" and has all the infinitude of space outside of it. In the face of the cleavage of all empirical being into two parts, we feel that this ultimate primordial unity of being lies somehow in the ultimate depths. But once we have found this primordial unity, we become conscious of the fact that the primordial unity also reigns over all of being, embraces and permeates all of being. As Nicholas of Cusa said of God, not only does the primordial ground have its center everywhere and its circumference nowhere, but it is also a kind of omnipresent atmosphere, which is just as inseparable from the primordial ground as its center—as light (which embraces, fills, and permeates space) is inseparable from the sun. Therefore the primordial ground is the total unity or the all-one.

This fundamental relation confirms once again the all-embracing nature of the principle of antinomian (antagonistic in the given case) monodualism. We have already pointed out that the antagonistic duality between inner self-being and outer objective being cannot simply be excluded from being, declared to be non-existent. This duality is a fact which our thought is obliged to accept honestly as such. But this factual duality does not put an end to the matter. What is *two* from outside is revealed from inside (in the ultimate depths) as *one* or as what emanates from one.

5. The Primordial Ground as Holiness (Divinity)

The primordial ground as integral, living *Truth*, as the pure creative meaning and absolute primordial source of being, cannot be known of course in the ordinary sense of knowing. And in no sense is it the "object" of knowledge, the content of which could be "discovered" or "revealed." We have already seen that the primordial ground of being is itself not *being*—in the sense that the primordial ground is free of the dark, impenetrable element of factuality, the element of blind necessity that belongs to being. And on the other hand the primordial ground does not coincide with the light of consciousness or knowledge that flares up in the self-consciousness. There is only one way in which we can make the primordial ground somehow cognitively visible; or more precisely, there is only one way in which we can help our spirit become open to grasp the primordial ground. If we remember the principle of transcendental thinking, we are conscious of the fact that the absolutely uneliminable difference (theoretical and real) between value (or "meaning") which is valid in itself and crude factuality is nevertheless a *relation* and therefore a *connection* between the two terms, even if an antagonistic one within the limits of reality. And since it is a connection it evinces the transrational *unity* of the two terms. And this kind of transcendental thinking emanates from the living, deep penetration of our spirit into this transrational unity, into this genuinely first and last thing in which all reality is rooted and upon which it is ultimately founded.

This is that profound consolation (not a consolation which we must seek in excruciating concentration or which we can gain only through great labor or pain, but consolation which is given to us openly and with full self-evident truth) which we find in all deep penetration into the spirit and therefore in the transcendental thinking that emanates from this penetration. Insofar as it is a question of ultimate, all-embracing, unknowable reality it is in general unnatural and contradictory to be satisfied with pure negation, with "no" or "not" as such. For every "no" or "not" already presupposes that unity within which and on the basis of which it has meaning. In the domain of spiritual and absolute reality we *also have all that we lack*, for if we did not have it we could not be conscious of its absence. In the final analysis, all the tragedy of loss or lack arises from invisible, unconscious, hidden possession. For even Kant's famous "hundred thalers," which are easy to imagine and conceive even if we do not have them in our pocket, must exist somewhere, for otherwise I would not be able to disappointedly confirm their absence in *my* pocket. But when it is a question not of a hundred thalers but of primordial reality, which in essence is accessible to all and gives itself to all directly, then all consciousness of absence is also solid possession, guaranteed by omnipresent revelation.

But in the final analysis this means that the primordial ground as *Truth* and life (which was previously revealed to us through reflection, through complex and difficult reasoning) is revealed as itself precisely in the form of immediate *revelation*. Here we understand "revelation" not in the narrow theological sense but in the sense (outlined by us earlier) of a special kind of self-disclosure or self-communication, which we take to be different from all "knowing" or "cognition." For it is not we who by our own activity come to possess through our cognitive gaze the primordial ground and penetrate into it. Rather, it is the primordial ground itself that possesses us, penetrates into us, and reveals itself to us in this way. Moreover, it is a question of the very essence of revelation as such, of its transcendental principle as it were. For in the final analysis, all revelation is illuminatedness or self-disclosure in the light. It is a question of the light that illuminates itself, thereby illuminating everything else as well. There is no need to seek this light at length. There is in fact no way in which it can be sought, for how can we err in darkness if we are in the light, and how can we seek "clarification" of self-evident truth as such?

We have seen above that it takes but one slight, imperceptible shift in the soul, one instantaneous self-disclosure of the soul, for that which had appeared to us as a dark abyss whose otherness and meaninglessness terrified us to be revealed to us now as the primordial homeland and solid soil of our soul, to be revealed as the very light or inner Truth that we seek outside of us by the force of its presence within us.

This revelation of the primordial ground, like all revelations, scarcely signifies a logically clear perception of the composition or content of what is revealed, that is, it scarcely signifies that unknowableness is overcome. On the contrary, in contradistinction to objective knowing, all revelation is essentially the revelation of the unknowable as such. On the other hand, the light of the primordial ground shines to us from out of an infinite depth, for it is screened by the presence of objective being and can reach us only after being filtered through the latter. *Hiddenness* belongs to the essence of the primordial ground, and the revelation of the latter is the revelation of the hidden as such. It is not a question of something standing before us openly, of something that is self-evidently present to us, of something that forces itself inexorably upon the dispassionate gaze of the observer. Rather, what occurs here through living concentration and deep penetration into the self is the flaring up of light, which presupposes the exertion of seeking, the living directedness toward the light. Therefore the primordial ground is first of all (in a certain sense) *the unknowable for us*; and being the end point of some infinite path into the depths, it is *the absolutely unknowable for us*.

On the other hand the primordial ground in general is not some "something" but is precisely nothing but the primordial ground and primordial source of *all*, the creative, illuminating, and grounding *potency of all*. Therefore all questions concerning the "essence" (insofar as this category is in general applicable here) of the primordial ground can be answered only by the affirmation that the primordial ground is the absolute unity and coincidence of all opposites: *coincidentia oppositorum*. The coincidence of opposites in unconditional being (see Chapter III) and the transrational antinomian character of reality as the unknowable (see Chapter IV) are only reflections or derivative manifestations of the coincidence of opposites in the primordial ground. In the primordial ground this coincidence is much deeper, has a more deeply rooted and absolute nature. In the primordial ground this coincidence embraces and permeates the fundamental forms or modes of being as well. This coincidence therefore has a *modal* character. On the one hand it embraces in unity all the different categorial connections or relations: In the primordial ground "essence" coincides with "existence"; the "ideal" coincides with the "real"; cause coincides with ground; both ground and cause coincide with consequent or effect, and all of them taken together coincide with simple presence; unity coincides with multiplicity; quality coincides with the carrier of quality; relation to the other coincides with inner essence; negative relation coincides with positive relation; being coincides with non-being. All questions concerning the primordial ground merge into a *single* question. But this question is such that it is also its own answer, for the primordial ground is the condition of the question itself. On the other hand this coincidence of opposites also embraces the two opposite concrete forms of the manifestation of being (i.e., inner and outer) that we have considered, and it is precisely in this aspect that the coincidence of opposites has fundamental significance for us. In this coincidence the most intimate depth of immediate self-being manifests its unity with the hard crust of being in its aspect as the objective world. Spiritual being—as that which has self-sufficient value and validity, as the native soil and goal of our inner life—coincides in the primordial ground with the terrifyingly alien essence of the world of cosmic reality, indifferent to value and immediately unilluminated.

Thus, the primordial ground in its essence is something absolutely paradoxical, improbable, rationally unknowable: namely antinomian. In this respect the primordial ground is essentially unknowable; furthermore, it is maximally unknowable. In this unity of insuperable hiddenness and inwardly essential, deepest transrationality, the primordial ground is absolutely unknowable or the unknowable at its highest conceivable potency: the deep point at which the unknowable converges in all its unknowableness and from which it emanates. The primordial ground is the principle that forms *the essence of the unknowable as such*. The primordial ground is the deepest *primordial mystery* of reality as such: a mystery which, in spite of its unattainability, incomprehensibility, and unsolvability, is nevertheless revealed with full self-evidence to the spirit that penetrates into its own depths; or rather is revealed to the spirit as self-evidence itself, as absolute *Truth* itself.

In relation to this deep, all-embracing reality of the primordial ground which transcends being, all words, all names, are really (as Faust says) "*Schall und Rauch*," "noise and smoke." Whatever word or name we use, it would be inadequate to the mysterious, unknowable profundity and all-embracing fullness of what we have in mind. It would distort and narrow, would replace the ineffable essence of the primordial ground (as the primordial source of reality which transcends being) with the inadequate aspect of something objectively existent and having definite "content." It is in this sense that the contemporary mystical poet Rilke speaks of the primordial ground of being: "Thou has such a quiet kind of being that those who give thee loud names are already deprived of thy nearness."[3]

Nevertheless the human word had to make the bold attempt to approach the primordial ground, in order somehow to capture and to fix for itself this ultimate reality. Some call it *God*. We are reluctant, however, to apply to it this holy name (so often misused) in its full and strict sense, though later, for the sake of brevity and accommodating ourselves to the conventional usage, we shall be forced to employ it. The most accurate expression for this ineffable reality is the Latin term *numen*. One of the most subtle contemporary German investigators of the religious consciousness, Rudolf Otto, has formed from this root the concept of "das Numinose," "the numinous." In the Russian language this can be approximately expressed by the terms *Sviatynia* (Holiness) or *Bozhestvennoye* (the Divine) or, referring to Meister Eckhart's term *die Gottheit*, by *Bozhestvo* (Divinity) in contradistinction to *Bog* (God). Depending on the context, we shall call this primordial reality either Holiness or Divinity, while remaining aware of the inevitable inadequacy of all verbal designation. What is of importance for us here is that what the language of religious life calls "God" is, as we shall see later, a completely definite form of manifestation or revelation of Holiness or Divinity.

All human language should grow silent before Holiness. To speak directly about Holiness itself is vain and blasphemous. The only thing that is adequate to this reality is silence: the quiet, unheard, unexpressed, inexpressible enjoyment of its presence in us and for us. This is aptly expressed in the Upanishads: The disciple repeatedly asks, What is Brahman? and the sage's answer is silence. The sage then explains his answer by saying that precisely with this silence he has communicated to the questioner the very essence, inexpressible in words, of what the question was about. Similarly, Plato says in his famous Letter VII that there is and will be no work in which he reveals or will reveal his final purpose, the ultimate objective of his thought, "for it cannot be expressed in words the way other objects of teaching can be; but when you engage in a long struggle in behalf of what is essential and you live in it, suddenly it is born of itself in your soul like the light lit by a wandering spark and feeds its flame out of itself." Similarly, Gregory of Nazianzus exclaims in his hymn to God: "Thou art the goal of all. Thou art all and nothing, not one of the beings and not all being. The All-Named, how shall I call Thee, the Unique Ineffable?" And St. John of the Cross says: "Even the angels perceive the utter unknowableness of God the more clearly, the more deeply they come to grasp His essence." The only direct speech possible and appropriate in relation to Holiness is speech not *about* but *to* it (we shall discuss this later). Philosophizing about Divinity itself, which would have Divinity as the direct "object" of its reflection, is possible neither in the form of objective knowledge nor in the form of self-consciousness.

Having come to this ultimate primordial ground, we find that there is only one way (assuming the necessary condition of the real directedness of our spirit toward the primordial ground) to avoid having to lay down our pen and keep absolute silence in relation to it: Without making the vain, intellectually and spiritually improper attempt to penetrate in our thought into the unknowable essence of Holiness or Divinity, we can nevertheless circle about Holiness, we can let our thought revolve about it. This is the meaning of all speculative mysticism. As Gregory the Great says, "*balbutiendo ut possumus excelsa Dei resonamus*": in babbling as we can, we produce an echo of the mysteries of Divinity which surpass us.

In essence, this "babbling" can be as infinite as Divinity itself. But in its structure we can nevertheless delineate three fundamental problems. First, once the certainty of Holiness or Divinity has been revealed to us in living experience, in its universal revelation, we can attempt to bring this certainty closer to our thought, i.e., we can attempt to apprehend with our thought not the "what," not the "content" of Divinity as the unknowable absolute primordial ground (such apprehension is impossible because it is contradictory), but rather the reality of Divinity, the sense in which Divinity *is*. Second, we can attempt to take intellectual account of the *essential* relation of Divinity to all else, to take account of that which in the domain of the rationally knowable corresponds to the logically stipulable relationship among the contents of concepts. Third, we can attempt to somehow understand more precisely the relation of Divinity to all else, which in the domain of the rationally knowable corresponds to the *real* connectedness of phenomena, i.e., we can attempt to take some account of the forms of the action and manifestation of Holiness or Divinity in us and in the objective world. Since different and opposite things coincide in Holiness or Divinity, it is obvious that the very distinction between these three problems or themes is conditional in some sense, is a kind of transposition of the unknowable simple essence of Holiness or Divinity to the plane of our human intellectual horizon.

6. The Certainty of Holiness (Divinity)

The distinctive character of the "certainty" of Divinity, which emanates from the very form of its reality that transcends being and from the form of its self-revelation—a distinctive character that is due to the combination of absolute self-evident truth with hiddenness, "non-givenness," non-objectivity—became clear to us above when we examined the very "idea" of Holiness or Divinity. It is useful, however, to supplement or clarify what was revealed to us. We shall accomplish this by briefly analyzing the relation of this transrational certainty to certainty of the usual sort, i.e., to that ideal of groundedness and self-evident truth by which purely intellectual knowledge, knowledge through thinking, is guided. The best way to accomplish this may be a critical examination of what are called proofs of the existence of God. After all we have said above, we must expect to find all sorts of misunderstandings and ambiguities in attempted proofs of this type, and this in a two-fold respect: both in the thesis that is posited and is to be proved, and in the construction of the proof itself.

As far as the thesis is concerned, we can boldly ask: In what sense is it in general possible to speak of the "existence" of God? What does it really mean to say that "God" (or, keeping to our own terminology, Divinity) "is"? The *supra-existent* character of the reality of Divinity became clear to us above. Only the "singularly existent" "is" (or "exists") in the usual sense of the word, for "to be" means to "belong to being," "to enter into the makeup of being." We have already seen that in this sense even being itself—unconditional being—cannot, strictly speaking, be characterized as something existent. This is the kind of contradiction that arises when we attempt to subordinate a categorial form *to itself*. One cannot speak of the "cause" of causality itself or of the "quality" of the very character of qualitativeness. Similarly, one cannot say that being itself "is." One can only say that being "performs the function of being," and, as a result of this, all else "is." The word "is" is even more dubious and ambiguous when one attempts to apply it to Divinity, which surpasses all being and is the condition and source of all being.

Insofar as we take the word "is" (or "exists") to mean the belonging to objective being, we must have the courage to assert that God does not "exist." Even if we risk being misunderstood and even if we seem to be in agreement with the atheists, this assertion must be made in full awareness of the higher, absolute self-evident truth of Divinity and with awe and reverence before the omnipresence of Divinity. This assertion (utterly false and evidence of spiritual blindness in another connection) signifies for us something wholly self-evident and indubitable: God is not a part or piece of objective being. (In the next chapter we shall give another reason why the idea expressed by the word "is" is inapplicable to God) However subtle the forms in which they express their thesis, in the final analysis all atheists coincide with the not very bright Soviet propagandist of atheism who attempted to prove to his listeners that God does not exist by reference to the fact that although he has frequently flown in airplanes he has not once seen God in the sky. The very possibility of accepting such nonsense as proof of the non-existence of God is determined by the conventional view according to which the reality of God must be demonstrated in the same way as the reality of an individual fact. Or insofar as the atheist's thesis is formulated in such verbal expressions as, for example, the German *es gibt* or the French *il y a*, in which case the atheist says *es gibt keinen Gott* or *il n'y a pas de Dieu*, [4] the relative truth of this thought can be seen in connection with the exact, literal sense of these expressions (see Chapter III, 3). In reality there is no "*es*" or "*il*" that could "give" or "have" God, for this "*es*" or "*il*" itself emanates from God and is grounded in Him. And "*es*" or "*il*" does not give us God. Only God can give Himself to us. For God is not only not a part or element of objective being. He is also not a particular content of unconditional being. Thus, *God does not exist*, not in the sense that He is an illusion and must be excluded from genuine being, but only in the sense that His reality (which is the reality of the absolute primordial ground or primordial source of being) surpasses all being. It is not God who is in being, but it is all being that is in and from God. Just as being does not exist but "performs the function of being," so Divinity does not exist but "performs the function of Divinity," i.e., sanctifies and creates being itself.

Even if the assertion of atheism that "God does not exist" contains a certain amount of bitter disappointment, the loss of hope that one will ever meet God "face to face," that one will ever discern His living, tangible, "incarnate" presence in the real world; that is, even if this assertion emanates from a kind of religious hunger, from a quest for God, nevertheless it is essential to clarify that this quest involves a blinding temptation, a distortion of the very idea of Divinity. This is what Rilke has in mind when he says: "All who seek Thee, tempt Thee" (*Alle, die dich suchen, versuchen dich*). Divinity as such is not only hidden from us factually, but it is also hidden in its essence. And this is the case not only in the sense that since Divinity transcends the senses it cannot be "given" through the senses (which would be a simple truism) but also in the sense that Divinity cannot be "seen" in a "trans-sensational" way either ("nobody has ever seen God") but reveals itself only in living experience. Divinity does not stand before our gaze like objective being, and it does not even embrace us like unconditional being (which can be understood in a purely theoretical way, can be disclosed to our mind's gaze). Divinity is revealed to us as absolutely self-evident in its absolute hiddenness; and this only insofar as we attain the depths of the absolute primordial ground through unconditional being by means of immediate self-being.

The same relationship can be clarified in yet another way. Doubting the existence of God is equivalent to doubting whether there is some objective reality that corresponds to our idea or consciousness of God. Cannot this consciousness, this seeming revelation, turn out to be nothing but a self-deception, an illusion, a confusion of the subjective reality of experience itself with the objective reality of its (seeming) object? This doubt, however, is founded on a misunderstanding: namely, on the essentially inappropriate, contradictory application of the measure of "pure," "objective" *knowledge* to the content of revelation (in the above-clarified sense of this concept). Seeming revelations are indeed possible, namely, in the sense of incorrect interpretations of the content or meaning of what is "revealed." But revelation as such is not the revelation of some particular content. It is rather the revelation of reality itself as such. Furthermore, it is a question of the revelation of the primordial ground of reality itself, i.e., the revelation of that which coincides with self-evident truth—with absolute self-evident truth. It is meaningless to ask whether what we are thinking of here "really" exists or whether it is only an illusion. This is the case, first of all, because no distinction is made here between "thought" (or "concept" or "idea") and the transcendent reality of the "object" of thought. On the contrary, the experience of revelation signifies the real presence of the revealed reality. Secondly, the above question is meaningless because the very notion of verifying the self-evident (of verifying the very "light" of self-evident truth) is wholly absurd. What we perceived earlier in relation to unconditional being is *a fortiori* valid in relation to

Divinity as the primordial source and primordial ground of all being. As the condition that makes all questions possible and meaningful, that makes the very framework of questioning possible, Divinity is absolutely unquestionable. In relation to Divinity, the very idea of questioning is excluded, turns out to be meaningless and internally contradictory. Therefore, if doubts and questions do arise here, this is an indication of a (psychologically completely natural) slipping away from the position of the total possession of the self-evident meaning of revelation, a slipping away to our usual position, conditioned by our spiritual insularity and blindness.

In essence this also exhausts the second question concerning the proof of the existence of God, namely, the fact that such a proof is attempted at all. If we take proof to mean a process of thought in which something is apprehended by means of a convincing argument, then all proof of the existence (or rather of the self-evident truth) of Divinity is impossible and superfluous. It is superfluous because the self-evident truth of Divinity (in spite of the fact that it ever threatens to elude us) is, in its immediacy in living experience, much more convincing and distinct than any proof could be. The persuasive force of a proof is based on the logical necessity of a connection of thoughts. However persuasive it may be, logical necessity is not the ultimate, deepest, completely "transparent" necessity. Logical necessity refers to the domain of pure "cognitive light." It is based on the principle of sufficient reason, a purely theoretical reason, and reveals to us only theoretical truth—the relatedness of things that constrains and compels us. Meanwhile, the aspiration of our spirit to the living truth, to the *Truth*, as that which is absolutely valid in the sense of inner legitimacy, remains unsatisfied. On the other hand the necessity of the self-evident truth of Divinity is absolute necessity, the persuasiveness of which is founded on itself and which embraces the deepest depth of our life. It is also the inner persuasiveness of the living, integral *Truth*.

But proof here is also impossible. Obviously there can be no question of "deductive" proof, i.e., of inference from ground to consequent, for what we seek is the primordial ground of all else. "Inductive" proof, i.e., inference from consequent to ground (e.g., from the existence and specific structure of the world to the existence of Divinity), is also impossible, and this for two reasons. The first reason is the absolute otherness of Divinity in relation to the world (we shall discuss this in greater detail below), which is most clearly manifested in the imperfection and disharmony of the world. Without belittling in the slightest the significance of the features of harmony and rational order in the composition of the world, one must

nevertheless say that, even if the whole world were found to contain only a
single, small occurrence of evil, irrationality, unjustified suffering, then
the whole "inductive" argument would lose its power to persuade. The
second reason is that the search for the ground (theoretical or real) of being
as a whole is internally contradictory, for "ground" in this sense is nothing
but the rootedness of a particular phenomenon in the whole of being.
Theoretically (i.e., purely ontologically), this explanation finds its ultimate realization in the reduction of all that is problematic to the makeup of
being as a whole. Therefore, nothing prevents a purely theoretical orientation from affirming the world's being (more precisely, all-embracing unconditional being) as ultimate reality, grounded in itself. Such an affirmation could be the only possible premise for this orientation. Furthermore,
all attempts to theoretically prove the existence of God distort the very
idea of Divinity. All theoretical arguments, whatever their nature, presuppose relatedness and affirm that the content of this relatedness is subordinate to something else. Thus, to think about God inferentially, to deduce
His existence, is to think Him as subordinate to the relatedness of being, to
determine His place, as a particular content of being, in the makeup of
being—which, of course, is absurd and contradictory.

Thus, "proof" in the form of an inference based on certain assumptions
is utterly impossible here. Here it is neither possible nor impossible to
prove anything. The only thing that is possible is *to show*: to point the way
to the direct discernment of what is sought, the processes of thought performing only the negative function of eliminating false views that prevent
thought from freely following the ascent of the "soul" to "God." Such is
the true intent of the "ontological proof"; and therefore this "proof"
(which, remarkably, has been the subject of more attempts at refutation
than any other proof) is the only philosophical argument that at least moves
on the right path to the goal. The true meaning of the "ontological proof"
has been essentially distorted by all its foes and critics, who (starting with
Gaunilo, a comtemporary of Anselm of Canterbury, and culminating with
Kant) have made, in essence, one and the same objection against it. All the
opponents of the ontological proof start from the same assumption (which
seems to be self-evident), namely, that God is a special, existent "object"
of thought. But this is precisely what the ontological proof denies. (It is
only in its less successful and therefore more popular formulations that the
proof is made to start from this assumption, which is to be refuted later.)
The true meaning of the ontological proof is not that one can "deduce" (by
inference) *the real being* of God from the pure *idea* of God as a hypothetical

content of a concept (which is indeed absolutely impossible, and the triumph of the opponents of the proof consists in a cheap victory over this formulation). On the contrary, its true meaning is that it shows that Divinity is a reality which cannot be given as a pure idea but is always directly revealed to us as a full-fledged, concrete reality; in other words, the "idea" as only a content of thought cannot be meaningfully separated here from reality and taken abstractly as such (just as in Descartes' "*cogito ergo sum*" the content of "*cogito*" is given not as a hypothetical idea but immediately reveals itself as a reality, as "*sum*"). This "proof" is adequately formulated not only by Anselm, but also, for example, by Bonaventura, Nicholas of Cusa, and Malebranche. As an example, let us consider some of the formulations of Nicholas of Cusa: The negation of the being of a particular object presupposes the very being from which, by means of this negation, the object is excluded. Therefore, negation is inapplicable to being itself. God is not something that can "be" or "not be," but is Himself the existent possibility of all that is and is not. It is therefore contradictory to think that He "can" not be, for this "can" presupposes the existent possibility of His being. Finally, negation and affirmation signify a choice between "the one" and "the other." Therefore that whole from which the choice itself originates cannot be negated.[5]

The true and instructive inadequacy of the ontological proof consists not in the fact that it is unable to prove its thesis convincingly but in the fact that the thesis itself is ambiguous. Attempting to prove the existence of God, the proof only attains unconditional being and must somehow identify God with the latter. Here one risks not capturing the living, unknowable depth of reality, which is immeasurably greater and other than being (even in its absoluteness) and which is accessible only to the gaze directed from the inner depths of our own life. The ontological proof is, so to speak, a schematic projection of the full, living self-evident truth of Divinity onto the plane of thought.

Since Divinity as the primordial unity of value and reality, as the living primordial source of life, is absolutely transrational, its self-evident truth is also transrational. The primordial ground of total unity, Divinity is revealed only to the total unity of our inner being, to the unfragmented wholeness of our life, to that childlike "innocence" in us compared to which all that is "wise" and "sophisticated" in us signifies that our essence is fragmented and defective and thus cannot apprehend the reality of Divinity. The reality of Divinity is hidden from the "prudent" and "wise" and is revealed to "babes." This living, intimately inner total unity of the soul to which is revealed the reality of the primordial source of *Truth* and life is what Plotinus had in mind when he said: "What bold leap shall allow us to reach that unspeakable which surpasses the essence of our reason? Our answer is: by means of that which in us resembles it" (Enn. III: 8, 9). This is what is meant by "heart," and in this sense Divinity is accessible only to the "heart." "Blessed are the pure in heart: for they shall see God." But the "heart" is not, as is usually thought, something that is separate from and opposed to "reason." The "heart" is precisely the "core" of whole, all-embracing inner being, one of whose emanations can be "reason." The "heart" as an all-embracing unity is opposed only to the "pure" reason which has torn itself away from the inner "core." The reality of Divinity is inaccessible to "pure" reason, which is unnaturally closed up in itself. Insofar as the "reason" draws its force and light from the potentiality of the "heart" and thus acquires the possibility of transcending itself; insofar as it thereby fulfills itself in transcendental and transcending thought, it can accompany the living apprehension of Divinity, can participate in it, and thereby impart to this apprehension a greater clarity. Reason has performed this function since the time of the Upanishads, Heraclitus, Socrates, and Plato. And it will not stop performing this function, however much this may appall both the philosophical and the theological obscurantists of all epochs.

7. The Essential Relation of Divinity to All Else

In the domain of the rationally conceivable the "essence" of something is determined by its "place" among all else and its relation to all else. By analogy (inevitably inadequate and only metaphorical), this also applies to Holiness or Divinity. We now present a concise examination of the essential relation of Divinity to all else. Since Divinity is unknowable, its relation to all else must also be unknowable, and its intellectual apprehension must be confined to an apprehension of the transrationality of this relation. Furthermore, in relation to Divinity the extratemporal "essence" is inseparable from the fullness of concrete reality, so that what is most significant in our theme can become clear only through an examination of the *real* connections or relations that play an effective role here.

Since Divinity as the primordial ground transcends, both in essence and in reality, all that exists; and since the essence of Divinity is expressible only in the coincidence of opposites even in the deepest and most primordial categorial forms of being, Divinity must appear to us most immediately as something *wholly different* from all that we can conceive and know, wholly different from all that is habitual and familiar for us. It must appear as something *wholly other*. The feeling of the complete otherness of Divinity must be present in all religious experience; otherwise it would not be religious experience. In some vague way we feel the truth of this consciousness. Contemporary theologians) particularly Rudolf Otto) have emphasized this nature of God as "wholly other" (*der ganz Andere*). But this is easier to say than to understand. We must beware that, through the intellectualization and abstract determination of the transrationality and transcendence of Divinity, we do not once again fall into the snare of wily rationality. When we say "wholly other" or "opposite," we usually have in mind the oppositeness of contraries, such as light and darkness, good and evil, eternity and time. But precisely this sort of oppositeness lies within the confines of a common "genus," is a distinction between the most mutually remote species of the common genus. Therefore, insofar as we conceive Divinity as something "wholly other" (in the sense explained above) in relation to all else, we thereby unconsciously posit something *common* between Divinity and all else, something common which consists of belonging to the same "genus." But our genuine intent is unsatisfied. Furthermore, we commit a crude error when we *subordinate* Divinity, the all-embracing and all-grounding primordial ground, to a definite "genus." If we have in mind something wholly disparate and heterogeneous, that which in general has no connection to the other thing being considered, (e.g., consider the relation between an apple and virtue), then (setting aside the fact that the notion of a relation which consists of the absence of all relation is devoid of meaning and is only a sort of joke) we find that we contradict the meaning of Divinity as the primordial ground and primordial essence of all that exists, as the point of convergence of what is most heterogeneous. Moreover, we commit once again the crude error of subordinating Divinity to a definite genus, this time to the genus of the "wholly other."

After all we have said above it is quite clear that the relation of Divinity to all else cannot be adequately expressed in any of the usual categorial forms, for they themselves originate from the primordial ground and their very meaning presupposes the reality of the primordial ground. In other words the true path here can be disclosed only through transcendental thinking, which investigates the essence of the logical-categorial connections themselves and therefore surpasses them. If we want to adequately define Divinity as something "wholly other than all else," this very "otherness" must be "wholly other" than ordinary otherness. In any case, this is not *that* otherness which is conceived to be in opposition to identity, homogeneity, resemblance. After all we have said above, particularly after the methodological discussion in Chapter IV, it is sufficient here to briefly note that what we are dealing with is that transrational, logically indefinable otherness which is revealed only to a *wholly other* spiritual orientation, to an orientation wholly other than abstract thought: namely, to the orientation of the transcendental *hovering above* opposites. Divinity is really something "wholly other" compared to and in relation to all else precisely because it transcends the opposition (which embraces all else) between "otherness" and "non-otherness." In accordance with what was clarified above, we can say that Divinity is simultaneously *both* other *and* non-other in relation to all else, or that it is *neither* other *nor* non-other in relation to all else. And in the final analysis even these broad forms of judgment (i.e., both–and, neither–nor), precisely as forms of judgment, only approximately convey the genuine transrationality of the relation, which can be captured only in the bold hovering (not expressible in any judgment) above all opposites, in the transrational synthesis of all that is opposite.

If we must add anything at all to this general truth, it is the discernment, acquired from this truth, of the onesidedness of the idea of Divinity as something "wholly other." It follows from the transrationality of the relation that the deepest, most radical otherness is combined here with the deepest, most intimate inner kinship or resemblance. Therefore, in spite of the fact that Divinity cannot be compared to and does not resemble anything else, *everything else resembles Divinity in some sense*. Of course, this resemblance must not be understood in the logically definable and analyzable sense (see our discussion of metalogical unity) in which the resemblance can be divided into partial identity and difference. It must not be understood to mean that Divinity is identical to all else in some of its aspects or features and different from all else in other aspects or features. Divinity has no "aspects" or "features" and can be apprehended only as a whole, as a simple, indivisible unity. This is the resemblance between a symbol and what it symbolizes. This is the *shining* of the Unknowable and Incomparable through the concrete guise of all phenomena and aspects of being—an ineffable hint of the Invisible and Ungraspable through the visible and graspable. One who does not feel the otherness and transcendence of Divinity in relation to all else does not have Divinity. But one who does not feel its presence in everything, its mysterious resemblance to everything, does not have it either.

This ineffable, logically indefinable resemblance between all that exists and Divinity is applicable, above all, to being as a whole. In its infinitude, concreteness, transrationality, and unity, unconditional being is the image and symbol of the primordial source, of Divinity, and is embraced and permeated by Divinity. In the final analysis this is the basis of the possibility of grasping being in its ultimate depth precisely as unconditional being or (what is even deeper) as reality in the sense of the all-embracing absolute whole. Our present discussion indicates that genuine absoluteness belongs neither to pure being as such precisely in its blind, eminently non-self-evident, essentially non-convincing factuality nor even to reality as the unity of being and self-revelation. Ultimate, true absoluteness belongs only to Divinity as the primordial source or primordial ground, which alone grounds itself and all else. But this absoluteness shines through being as such; and in some derivative manner, in some non-genuine, merely analogical sense, belongs to the latter.

This also holds in relation to that segment of unconditional being which stands before us as "objective reality" or the "world." We have said much, and much remains to be said, about the imperfection of the "world," about those of its aspects in which it does not satisfy the demand of inner self-evident truth and persuasiveness, but, on the contrary, appears as a dark, incomprehensible, terrible reality of crude factuality. However, this must not prevent us from seeing the other side, which was so evident to the ancient and medieval consciousness, but which is largely and illegitimately unperceived in modern times. World reality, the "cosmos," is not only a blind, chaotic, disharmonious force. The cosmos also contains traces of inner unity, inner harmony, the organic and therefore teleological belonging-together and relatedness of its parts to one another. The "beauty" of the world is evidence of this. In this way the "world" is the image and symbol of the absolute unity and illumination of Divinity. We shall speak about this later.

But within the limits of being as a whole and of the world as a whole, everything resembles Divinity in some sense. It is true that not everything has the same degree of this resemblance. This is the basis of the profound meaning of the method of analogy, *analogia entis*, as it was first expressed by Dionysius the Areopagite and systematically developed by Thomas Aquinas: All that exists is ordered hierarchically according to the depth it attains, according to how close its form or mode of being approaches Divinity. All that exists is a symbol of Divinity and approaches to a varying degree that which it symbolizes, is adequate to it in a varying degree, in spite of the fact that all that exists is absolutely inadequate to Divinity in the detached "otherness" of the latter. In developing this thought we must avoid the two extremes: arrogant, unloving ontological *aristocratism*, for which only the lofty or "high-born" is worthy of being an image of Divinity, whereas all that is low is only the blind, meaningless material of being; and vulgar ontological *democratism*, which denies all hierarchy in being and, in the idea of evolutionism, in effect lowers the highest down to the level of the lowest. Hierarchy must be harmonized with the total unity, the belonging-together, the inner solidarity, the homogeneity, in the sense of a common origination, of all that exists. With this qualification the idea of hierarchy has a general significance. We have already seen that in a certain sense the world of our inner life is essentially closer to the primordial ground, to Divinity, than is the world of objective being. Expanding this, we can say that the domain of spiritual being and man as its representative and carrier in the world (i.e., man as a person) stand closest of all to Divinity. The world of immediate self-being stands closer to Divinity than does cosmic being. Rational being stands closer to Divinity than does irrational, unilluminated being. The living stands closer to Divinity than does the dead. The good stands closer to it than does evil. Unknowable, ineffable Divinity shines through, to a varying degree, everything that exists, but nevertheless it remains something absolutely other in relation to everything that exists.

Thus, the absolutely unknowable essence of Divinity becomes accessible to us also from the side of its essential relation to all else. But this occurs without our attaining its essence, without our penetrating into it; on the contrary, Divinity precisely retains all its unknowableness, around which our mind now circles. *Attingitur inattingibile inattingibiliter*: "the unattainable is attained through its unattainment" (Nicholas of Cusa). We attain it because, shining in its infinite unattainable depth, it shines through—in the closest proximity to us—all that is visible and familiar to us. The unattainable becomes graspable precisely *as* infinitely distant and unattainable. As the "wholly other," it has its likeness in all things without exception. As Tolstoy said, "We know God the way a new-born infant that has not yet awakened to full consciousness knows its mother, in whose arms it reposes and whose warmth it feels." Or to cite a more authoritative source, we see God as "through a glass, darkly."

With this we approach the *third* path of our mind's circling about the absolutely unknowable: the path of the understanding of the forms of its *real* manifestation and action in all else. All the paths of the mind's circling intersect here and are mutually tangential. This final understanding will now be developed systematically in two separate discussions: on the relation of Divinity to *me* and on the relation of Divinity to the *world*.

NOTES

1. Translator's note: The italics are Frank's.
2. Translator's note: Frank distinguishes between *istina* (ordinary truth, which is rendered as the lower-case "truth") and *pravda* (fundamental or integral truth, truth as the genuine primordial foundation, which is rendered as the upper-case, italicized *Truth*).
3. *Du hast so eine leise Art zu sein; Und jene, die dir laute Namen geben, Sind schon vergessen deiner Nachbarschaft.* (from *Stundenbuch*)
4. Translator's note: Frank uses foreign expressions as examples because there is no comparable expression in Russian.
5. It is in this sense that Plotinus uses the ontological proof (Enn. IV: 7, 9). Even Plato has the same thing in mind in the final, decisive proof of the immortality of the soul in the *Phaedo*. See the appendix to my book *The Object of Knowledge*: "On the History of the Ontological Proof."

Chapter IX

God and I

1. Divinity as "Thou"

Turning now to the *real* relation between Holiness (or Divinity) and all else, we feel that we are dealing with the most essential element in the clarification of what we have come to know as Holiness or Divinity. In spite of all its grandeur and magnificence, the idea of this primordial source of *Truth* and reality still remains unclear and indefinite for our religious consciousness. And this is the case not only in the sense (adequate to the very essence of Divinity) that this idea in itself transcends all definiteness, but also in the sense that we ourselves do not yet have it as intimately and therefore as clearly and concretely as we require. Insofar as it is directed only at Divinity as such and in spite of all attempts to acquire ultimate, genuinely concrete reality, philosophical reflection (even when it transcends pure thinking in transcendental thinking) cannot go further than something artificially isolated and therefore abstract in a certain sense. But Divinity as the primordial source or primordial ground of *all* reality cannot, in the final analysis, be separated from the rest of reality. Indeed, the essence of Divinity consists precisely in the generation and grounding of all reality. The absolute primordial ground reveals itself in its concreteness only in connection with the rest of reality. Even though the absolute primordial ground posits the rest of reality *outside* of itself, it has the rest of reality *in* and *through* itself. Leaving a detailed analysis of this problem for a later discussion, we can say now that Divinity—in its genuine absoluteness, as all-embracing and all-permeating unity—is perceived only in connection with the rest of reality.

Since Divinity reveals itself to me, above all, through the directedness of *my* being at it, through the inner apprehension of that reality which is the ultimate ground of my psychic and spiritual life—that is, only through religious experience—the first thing we must enquire about, and the thing we constantly enquire about, is the relation between Divinity and *me*.

It is easy to see that, strictly speaking, it is impossible to conceive—or, more precisely, to experience—Divinity outside of or independently of its relation to *me*. What we have in mind is not the abstract aspect of its relation to man in general, but the living, concrete, incomparable, unique aspect of its relation to *me*, to me who "am," myself, also unique and unrepeatable; or, more precisely, we have in mind the aspect of *my* relation to Divinity. This relation is not only the unique path on which I can attain or approach Divinity. It is also the only "medium" in which Divinity reveals itself and which therefore in some sense *belongs to the very essence and being of Divinity*. For Divinity is not an "object," whose being is independent of whether or not my cognitive gaze encounters it. Further, it is not at all a question of the "cognitive gaze," but rather a question of the directedness of my being as the condition of the revelation of Divinity. But this revelation belongs to the essence and being of Divinity. And if on the one hand Divinity in its essence is hidden, on the other hand it is, in its essence, self-revealing: revealing itself precisely in its hiddenness and unknowableness. But revelation is revelation *to me*, is directed immediately *at me*; otherwise it would be not revelation but only hearsay knowledge about something the meaning of which I cannot even understand. Therefore the "idea" of Divinity cannot be separated from the living, concrete experience of Divinity, from *my* experience of Divinity. Not only does the light of this idea first flare up in this experience but the idea belongs, in essence, to the experience. Or the experience belongs, in essence, to the idea. In its essence Divinity is always "God with us" (Emmanuel) and, in the final analysis, "God with me." "God without me" is a kind of limiting concept, which is necessary for religious experience (God would not be *for me* if I could conceive of Him *as such*). But this limiting concept does not fully and concretely convey what is revealed to me here. For what is revealed to me is not only God "as such" but precisely "God with me," the concrete fullness of the inseparable and unmerged dual-unity of "God and I." It is for this reason that there could have arisen, out of the ultimate depths of the mystical consciousness of God, the bold word whose true meaning is not self-elevating pride but precisely fear and trembling before the fullness of what reveals itself here: "I know that God cannot live without me for a moment. My death would cause God to die from need of me" (Angelus Silesius).*

The holy name "God" arises for the first time in this directedness of my being at the primordial ground and primordial source, which emanates from out of the depths of my subjectivity, my groundlessness, and which, strictly speaking, is present from the very beginning in the depths of my being, i.e., is given together with my being. And that great Nameless or All-Named which we conditionally designated as Holiness or Divinity becomes *God—my God*. God is Divinity as it is revealed to me and experienced by me in complete otherness, in relation to me, and in inseparable unity with me. We shall understand what this means if we remember what we said in Chapter VI about the revelation of "thou." This means that Divinity becomes "Thou" for me, reveals itself as "Thou"; and only as "Thou" is it God. Nameless or all-named Divinity, in directing itself at me, acquires a name for the first time: the name *God*. Its directedness at me or the directedness of my being at it is the place where its name is born, just as "names" in general are born from the self-revelation and evocation of reality.

God is the unconditionally unknowable, absolute primordial ground, experienced and revealed in experience as "Thou." And His "Thouness" is experienced as somehow belonging to His essence and mode of being. To speak of God in the third person, to call Him "Him," is blasphemy from the purely religious point of view, for this assumes that God is absent, does not hear me, is not directed at me, but is something objectively existent. The profound religious philosopher Ferdinand Ebner aptly states in *Das Wort und die geistigen Realitäten* that the use of the third person, which was created for the designation of what is absent, implies lack of faith in the omnipresence of God, i.e., lack of faith in God Himself. The religious consciousness of God is directly expressed not in speeches *about* God but in words directed *to* God (in prayer) and in God's word *to me*. In this sense Goethe is completely right when he remarks that "strictly speaking, one can talk about God only with God Himself." God is always with me. He always sees and hears me, and if I lose sight of God, I lose God. This does not mean, of course, that this relationship cannot become an object of reflection, of philosophical thought, thus requiring the use of the third person. It is not really a question of grammatical form but rather of the *meaning* of what is expressed. When we think "about" God and speak "about" Him with others, we refer to Him as "Him," but we must never forget that behind "Him" stands "Thou" (or, rather, *stand* "Thou") as "His" foundation. "Thou" must resound in "Him" and in the derivative reflection about "Him." Primordial directedness *to* God, speech *to* Him, must be alive in our soul as the ground of all our thinking about Him. Otherwise this speech would be empty, vain, and therefore blasphemous words.

The manifestation of Divinity as "my God," as a being who encounters me, who is connected to me by the relation of "Thou" to "I," appears to be deeply paradoxical. It appears to be immediately incompatible with the essence of Divinity as the unconditionally all-embracing and all-grounding primordial ground. But before examining this problem, let us examine the true meaning of this mode of manifestation and its consequences.

We have already seen what the meaning of the usual "thou" is, the meaning of the "thou" of a human being or, more generally, of a living being, who co-exists with us. This "thou" is "the other," an alien but "me-like" reality that encounters me from "outside" and stands before me as an objective reality. However, this "thou" is not the object of my knowledge but rather a reality that reveals itself to me. Furthermore, in "thou" is realized the genuine, actualized essence of revelation as the active self-disclosure of "the other," directed toward "me" and revealing itself through its possession of me or through my transcending to it. Strictly speaking, "thou" is nothing but that form of givenness or disclosure of reality which we call revelation. It follows that the genuine, actual revelation of Divinity (here revelation is to be understood in its general sense, clarified above)—in contrast to the general, relationless self-disclosure of reality and self-revelation to itself of immediate self-being—occurs in the "thou" form and even coincides with the "thou art" form of being.

Let us note something very important. It is self-evident that Divinity cannot be some "thou," one of many "thou's," i.e., a particular case of some universal phenomenon. The obvious reason for this is that Divinity does not belong to any particular "genus" and is not even subordinate to the special "genus" that we can call *being and disclosure*. Thus the mode of being and disclosure expressed in "thou" is not a feature of God. On the contrary, this relationship can be understood only in such a way that Divinity, as the primordial ground and primordial source of all things, is the foundation, the transcendental condition, of the possibility of the "thou" form of being. It can be understood only in such a way that the revelation of Divinity as *my* God, as *God with me*, makes possible for the first time all revelation of reality in the form of "thou," just as the illuminating light of Divinity as the *Truth* itself is the foundation of the clarity, illuminatedness, and self-evidence of every particular truth. Divinity as my God or God-with-me is therefore the "primordial Thou," the prototype or idea (in the Platonic sense) of every particular "thou," the prototype without which no concrete "thou" would be possible. It is self-evident that this affirmation must not be understood in a psychological way. We can unquestionably enter into communion with some "thou," participate in the "I–thou" relation, without conscious experience of God's "Thou." But the "thou" form as such is the condition of every particular experience of encounter with "thou." And this "thou" form as such not only emanates from Divinity as the primordial ground (from which all in general emanates) but also coincides with the manifestation of the primordial ground as "Thou," with the revelation of Divinity as *my* God, as God-with-me.

We saw above (Chapter VI, 6) that outward transcending, in the direction to "thou," already presupposes and contains inward transcending, to spiritual being. Now we see that it also presupposes that potentiated, fully realized transcending into the depths which culminates in the revelation for us of Divinity—in revelation in the form of *my God*, this form of revelation being our participation in the most primordial form of the being of "thou." This is clearly disclosed in the fully realized "I–thou" relation as the relation of *love*. Every true, free, intimate relation of love; every genuine feeling that one has one's inner homeland or native soil in "we" is already a religious experience, the revelation of Divinity. This inner connection is already contained in living experience, even if we are not clearly conscious of it. This is the basis of the indivisible essential-ontological connection between *love of God* and *love of one's neighbor*, the latter of these relations being the best psychological indicator and mode of manifestation of the former. "Everyone that loveth is born of God, and knoweth God. He that loveth not knoweth not God" (The First Epistle of John 4: 7, 8). This means that the self-revelation of my immediate self-being inward, into the depths, in the direction of the primordial ground (i.e., the revelation of Divinity as "Thou") is the ontological primordial condition of my self-revelation in the direction of human (or, more generally, in the direction of limited, creatural) "thou." All human communion, all inward togetherness of life, is, in the final analysis, only a manifestation (always limited, imperfect, inadequate, burdened with reservations) of the primordial communion, the primordial unknowable togetherness of God and me. The very form of the being of "thou art" and "we are" (regardless of the domain of being and the degree of depth in which it is manifested) is—as the unity of subjectivity and objectivity, and as the unity of being and value—a kind of emanation and manifestation (in this its transrational essence) of those primordial "thou" and "we" that coincide with the revelation of Divinity as God-with-me.

We saw in Chapter VI that "thou art" is inseparable from "I am," that "am" itself (as "I") is formed for the first time under the influence of "art." Now we can affirm that this holds *a fortiori* also in relation to the

most primordial form of "art," as it is given in God revealed as "Thou."
My inseparable togetherness with God is precisely a primordial ground
insofar as it constitutes, forms, creates *me myself*. Franz Baader is perfectly
right when he replaces Descartes' "*cogito ergo sum*" with the formula "*cogi-
tor ergo sum.*" God's gaze is always directed at me. It is an eternal gaze that is
directed at me and contemplates me. If it were possible for this gaze to turn
away from me for a moment, I would not exist that moment. This gaze of
God, directed at me, penetrating me (God as "Thou" or God as *my* God), is
the absolute, all-powerful force that constitutes and conserves my being,
the essential medium in and through which I exist. For my being as immediate being and as selfhood is only a reflection of this gaze or light, only a
spark of light lit from this primordial light. I arise as "I" for the first time
only under the pressure of this gaze. Therefore, "I am" is not only an
isolated, self-contained "spark" of self-being or self-consciousness; it is
not only a being-for-itself. We see now that "I am" not only presupposes
an inner connection with something or someone other than "only I myself"
but that it is founded on the solid possession of the primordial ground as it is
revealed in the "thou art" form of being, that it is based on the indestructible connection with God as *my God*. All being-for-itself in its very concept
is being-with-God, being-for-God, regardless to what extent we are conscious of this or to what extent we consciously realize this in our practical
experience. My deepest aloneness among other beings, unrepeatable and
incomparable, the uniqueness of my mode of being, expressed in the "am
form," precisely this metaphysical uniqueness of my being, is nothing else
but my indivisible "two-ness" or "*Zweisamkeit*" (to use Nietzsche's term
again), my inner, mutually revealed *dual-unity* with the eternal "Thou" of
God.

Two things follow from this: first, the unique absolute self-evident certainty of God and, second, the inner security and assuredness of *my* being.
As to the former: I can doubt the "existence" (or, more precisely, the
certainty) of God as little as I can doubt my own existence (or as St. Augustine says, I can doubt God's existence even less). This is the case because my
"am" is founded upon God's "art"; or, from the point of view of God
Himself, i.e., in the correct and primordial ontological order, my "am" is
constituted precisely by the fact that God tells me "thou art" or "be!".
Between the "is" form in which God's existence is abstractly expressed
and the "art" form which is concretely revealed to me, there lies an abyss
which separates that which is doubtful and uncertain from that which is
absolutely self-evident, from that which fills and constitutes with its self-

evidence my whole being. Let an atheist be right (in the sense discussed above) in his assertion that "there is no God," this understood to mean that God does not "exist," "is" not. But Thou, my God, Thou *art*! And what concern of mine is this "is," this sober "statement of fact," when I stand before this intimate, grace-giving, living "art," which inwardly grasps me?

The second thing, which is inseparably connected with the first, i.e., the consciousness of the inner security and assuredness of my own being through this inseparable bond with the eternal "Thou" of God, this second thing is the genuine ground and unknowable self-evident certainty of what I feel to be my "immortality." Philosophy as transcendental thinking cannot solve the riddles of being (see Chapter IV, 2) and, unlike so-called occult wisdom, does not pretend to be a guide through the wilderness of the soul's fate after death. The only thing that philosophy can and must give is a clear account of those perspectives and relations, immanently revealed to us but not noticed by most people, which constitute the transrational, unknowable essence of reality. In regard to this we must say the following. The isolated "I am," insofar as it is conceivable in general and is conceived precisely as such, is in itself not so self-evident as idealism tries to convince us. And this is the case if only because immediate self-being as my own concrete being does not coincide at all with the supra-temporal, abstract being of "I" as the knowing subject. If "I am" were isolated, nothing would prevent the "light" of consciousness or knowledge from fading in me and being embodied in someone else, in another point of being. If I am really nothing else but a separate, self-contained monad "without windows," nothing prevents me from becoming nothing, from ceasing to be. In this aspect, my "am" is not at all an eternal, indestructible property but only a random and therefore unstable fact owing to which I exist and with which I can perish or rather must perish.

And even the consciousness of my inner bond with the reality that, in its absoluteness and eternity, transcends me does not ensure my being. We have already seen that this reality immediately appears to me as an abyss that can engulf me. Indeed, this is the basis of the maniacal fear of death, the fear of my *not-being*, this horrible, incomprehensible but logically conceivable disappearance or dissolution in the abyss of common, impersonal being. In the previous chapter, to this natural and primordial life-feeling we were able to oppose the deeper, more profoundly penetrating life-feeling of my inner kinship and bond with reality as such, as a result of which the abyss becomes for me a solid ground in which I am unshakeably rooted. Now we perceive this situation in a more profound way. Insofar as the primordial ground of reality, Divinity, is revealed to me as an essentially eternal "my-God-with-me," this directly gives me the certainty of the eternal being of God-with-me. All the instability and insignificance of my subjective self-being is overcome here by my eternal assuredness and security in God and together with God. The form of being in which I "shall exist" "after my death" and whether it is possible in general to speak of "life after death" in temporal terms—these are things that remain for us an unknowable, unsolvable riddle which at best can be fathomed only by "concrete-positive revelation" (we shall show directly below what this means) and become an object of faith in the proper, specific sense of this word.

Nevertheless it is absolutely self-evident (though unknowable) that I am eternal. And I am eternal because of my inner bond with God which constitutes my essence and being as "I-with-God." I am eternal now and for ever. Here my essentially rootless, unstable, ungrounded immediate self-being, which lacks genuine reality, turns out to be a participant in the absoluteness and eternity of God as God-with-me. If we reflect on the matter more deeply, it becomes clear that the true meaning of cares concerning the security and assuredness of my being consists not in whether I shall continue to exist after my body dies but in whether I now already possess authentic being or only ghostly, inauthentic being. My "am" acquires stability and even its genuine essence and being only in dual-unity with God's "art," and this dual-unity, this intimacy, depends to a certain degree on me myself, on my own spiritual intensity. It follows that this my true and eternal being is always threatened by the possibility of slipping into detached, ghostly being, being that is dying and death. My being as "I-with-God" can always regress to the ghostly, illusory, non-existent being of "I-without-God." The consciousness of the eternity of the genuine "am" in its transrational-antinomian essence is a kind of *hovering* between stability and instability, and is inconceivable outside of the tragic nature of such antinomian dualism. But in the final analysis the transrational self-evident certainty of my eternity is given in the confident belief (which continually reasserts itself) that "I" in the ultimate, deepest ground of my being maintain an eternal and indestructible bond with God—in the confident belief that even if I abandon God, He does not abandon me; that even *my being without God is God's being with me.*

2. THE GENERAL REVELATION OF GOD AND CONCRETE-POSITIVE REVELATION

The progress of our thought, namely the clarification of the essence of the reality of God-with-me or (what is the same thing) of the general revelation of Divinity, now compels us to touch upon a more general question, which essentially goes beyond the scope of our theme. In order to more clearly understand what we mean by general revelation, we must clarify its relation to what religious consciousness and theology mean by revelation. In this sense we distinguish general revelation (usually called natural revelation, a term we prefer not to use because of the many misunderstandings associated with it) from concrete-positive revelation.

When we examined the "I–thou" relation, we saw that every revelation of "thou," though it is essentially a disclosure of reality as such, nevertheless always includes a partial apprehension of the concrete content or makeup of "thou." If we keep from confusing concrete content or makeup (*Gehalt*) with abstract content (*Inhalt*) that is logically definable in concepts, we can say that completely contentless (in the sense of *concrete* content), indefinite, empty reality is impossible. Reality is always concrete fullness; it contains something, has content. The reality of "thou" "gives me knowledge" of itself insofar as it "expresses" itself (in gaze, gesture, word, smile, etc.) and thereby reveals for me, at least partially, its qualitative content at a given moment. Conscious that it *is*, I simultaneously find out (even if only partially and dimly) *what* it is. The same situation holds for the revelation of Divinity as "Thou." When Divinity, the absolute primordial ground of all reality and value, reveals itself to me, "gives me knowledge" of its presence, this revelation is inseparably connected with the living, concrete revelation (though usually only in the form of an obscure feeling) of its content, of *what* or *who* is revealed to me. In no wise does this contradict the absolute unknowableness of God's essence, because that which is revealed to me here is revealed precisely as *the absolutely unknowable*, as bottomless depth or unencompassable fullness (for even the fullness of the concrete content of every "thou" is unknowable). But this unknowableness does not prevent us from more or less clearly (or obscurely) perceiving the expression of certain positive elements of the concrete content of this unknowable reality. When God reveals Himself to us, he "gives us knowledge" not only of His presence but also of His essence, for His presence or being coincides with His essence. He "speaks" to us, "expresses" Himself, "addresses" us, "acts" upon us in such a way that beyond His absoluteness and unknowableness we apprehend (dimly or more or less clearly), if not His general concrete-positive essence, at least His "voice" and "word" addressed to us, that which He wants or demands of us, that to which He calls us, His "attitude" towards us. This is precisely concrete-positive revelation, that which theology usually means by the word "revelation."

But concrete-positive revelation must not be taken in too narrow a sense. Even if it consists in God's "speaking" with us, His giving us an "understanding" of Himself and His Will, this Word of God must not be simply identified with the ordinary human word, not even with that word in which the divinely inspired man fixes and expresses (in the Bible, for example) the Word of God. Even when the Old Testament prophet conveyed to his people what God Himself told him, he heard the voice of God saying: " . . . my thoughts are not your thoughts . . . For as the heavens are higher than the earth, so are my ways higher than your ways, and my thoughts than your thoughts."[2]

Here, we approach *the mystery of the Word* and must briefly touch upon it because it is directly connected with our basic theme. There has been much argument about whether the primordial essence of the word consists in its function of designating objects or in its function of expressing feeling. We are not concerned with the question of the "origin" of language. In essence, the answer to this question lies in the fact that here too the divisive "either–or" must be overcome by the connecting "both-the-one-and-the-other" or by the even more profound unity of "neither–nor." In its essence the word is neither concept nor interjection, for it is the indivisible unity of both the one and the other. Primordially, the word expresses *neither* objective being as such in its mute, cold objective content *nor* my subjective impression, my emotional state upon encountering an object. What the word expresses is unknowable reality in its absoluteness (in one of its particular manifestations), which lies *deeper* than all division into subject and object or subjectivity and objectivity (see Chapter III, 4). Primordially, the word does not speak *about* anything, and it does not express the "subjective" human essence. Reality itself acquires a voice in the word and speaks about itself, expresses itself.

The unfathomable mystery of the word is the mystery of the unknowable itself as such. The unknowable cannot be known, is not subject to cognition, but it not only stands distinctly before us in its unknowableness, it not only reveals itself to us as such—it also has a "voice," it "speaks," it "expresses" itself in all its unknowableness *in the word*. This means that the Word is essentially revelation and the human word is thus also revelation.

This is why all vain babbling and all careless words are blasphemous. The human word emanates from the Word of God, from the Word (Logos) which "in the beginning was with God and was God." Thus, the human word is a reflection, albeit imperfect, of the Word of God. Evidence of this is poetry, that form of the human word in which it reaches its fullest value. In its essence poetry is neither abstract, conceptual determination nor the objective description of objective reality nor purely subjective self-expression (the lyrical confession of the poet) but rather the human revelation of the mystery of primordial reality in all its depth and significance which escapes the "prosaic" word. Poetry is the "angelic song" about reality which the poet has managed to hear and convey. It is the voice of reality speaking about itself. Human revelation in the word differs, however, from divine revelation in that man himself as such is not a primordial reality but stands in his being on the threshold between subjectivity and objectivity (i.e., objective reality) and is encompassed by the conflict between the two. Therefore, in some sense the human word is always "subjective," evidence of which is the multitude of existing languages and dialects, the imperfection of all of them, and even the ideolectical differences among speakers of the same language with respect to the living form of speech, the style of language. On the other hand the human word always has the tendency to narrow itself, solidify and crystallize into the pure designation of abstract concepts: a tendency to acquire exact, limited, "literal" meaning—which even enhances its value from the point of view of "objective," "scientific," "pure" knowledge. But precisely for this reason it is essentially inadequate to the Word of God. And the concrete revelation of God, His "Word," is expressed, from the human point of view, in "unspeakable words, which it is not lawful for a man to utter" (II Corinthians 12, 4).

Moreover, all particular "words of God," as they are conveyed in the Bible or as they may be "heard" by every man (if he is worthy), are particular manifestations of the Word, Logos, as the expression of the very essence of God, an expression in which His essence acquires for us a living image and likeness (without thereby ceasing to be unknowable). This expression of God—as the Word, in a living image—is that highest and most adequate concrete-positive revelation in which "the Word was made flesh" in the human figure of Jesus Christ.

In concrete-positive revelation, God's "Thou" enters into earthly, temporal being. The interpretation of this positive revelation is the task of theology. This is the limit to all philosophy, the point at which it separates itself from theology. For philosophy can orient itself and has the right to orient itself only with respect to general, eternal revelation. Furthermore, philosophy in its essence is nothing but such orientation through spiritual self-revelation and penetration into itself, which finds expression in potentiated, transcendental thinking.

This distinction must not be understood, however, as an absolutely divisive logical distinction but rather as a transrational distinction in which division is also connection and therefore antinomian unity. If general, eternal revelation (the revelation of the primordial ground of reality as such) is inseparable from concrete-positive revelation, the latter is also inseparable from the former. Therefore, both theology and philosophy are based on general, eternal revelation, for all concrete revelation already presupposes our sensitivity to it, our sensitivity to the voice and manifestation of God. It presupposes our ability to understand every concrete revelation precisely as *the revelation of God*. But this means that the *general nature* of revelation—the reality of God as "Thou" in its general, eternal essence (and this is precisely general, eternal revelation)—logically precedes all particular concrete revelation. Thus, we would have an utterly false understanding of revelation if we thought (as many do) that revelation *as such* can be wholly exhausted by some particular, single concrete case of revelation that has occurred in time. Every full-fledged, living religious consciousness is perfectly right in protesting against this understanding. If it is absurd and blasphemous (following the example of ecstatic sects and all kinds of vain easy-believers) to ignore the fullness of an already-given revelation, to thirst after new revelations and to find them where they are not, it is just as blasphemous to think that revelation has been completely exhausted in the "letter" of recorded revelation and that there can be no new revelations. On the contrary, in the concrete revelation of Jesus Christ this inexhaustedness and inexhaustibility of revelation is unambiguously expressed in the idea of the Holy Spirit, in the Spirit of Truth which "God giveth not . . . by measure," which "bloweth where it listeth," and which "will guide you into all truth." The Holy Spirit—God as God-with-me and God-in-me—is precisely the eternal unbreakable bond between concrete revelation and general revelation.

The same bond is also revealed from the point of view of philosophy, i.e., thought oriented toward general revelation. For general revelation is also precisely *revelation*. Here, unknowable Divinity clearly reveals itself; moreover, it reveals itself as God-with-me (or God-with-us, i.e., God-with-the-world, which we shall discuss later). In some sense, Divinity as-

sumes a concrete form. To what degree this concretization approaches
concrete revelation (it can never attain it and coincide with it) cannot be
accurately and univocally determined beforehand. Although great care
must be taken to avoid the temptation of self-glorification, it is necessary
to affirm that the philosopher (as a man who in his limited, human way
interprets and describes reality in its primordial ground, i.e., the general
revelation of Divinity) cannot be distinguished, with sharp, univocal definiteness, on the basis of some external characteristic, from the seer, the
prophet, or the mystic, who experiences the action of the Holy Spirit.

The fundamental unity of general revelation and concrete revelation,
upon which their differentiation is based, is revealed in experience in the
fact that both of them, in their ultimate fullness and highest potency,
merge into inseparable unity in speculative religious mysticism. In the *unio
mystica* of the human soul with God, general revelation and concrete revelation (and therefore philosophy and religion) are bonded together in *gnosis*, in deep penetration into the inexhaustible depths of God, in the attainment of divine wisdom and its enjoyment. But this does not signify the
brazen and blasphemous intent to fully understand the mystery of God.
This participation in divine wisdom and in the divine essence can never
(even in the most fiery concrete religious experience) be such as to exhaust
and overcome the inexhaustibleness and unknowableness of God, i.e., the
general revelation of God. Even when God reveals His most profound
mysteries, He does not cease being the unknowable God, He does not cease
being the God who reveals Himself precisely in all the unknowableness of
His reality.

Together with the unity of the forms of revelation (as it is clearly disclosed in the mystical speculation of the fathers and teachers of the Church
and the great mystics, in the thought of Origen, Augustine, Dionysius the
Areopagite, Maximus the Confessor, Nicholas of Cusa, Jacob Boehme)
there also exists an antinomian conflict between them, which is manifested
in the eternal conflict between philosophy and religion. In its genuine and
deepest essence this conflict between philosophy and religion should not be
reduced (as it often is) to the crude and awkward formulation that philosophy, guided by the aspiration to pure objective knowledge, exposes the
illusory nature of the achievements of the religious consciousness, while
religion as "blind faith" rises up against the pretensions of reason and
simply rejects them. In this crude, simple form of purely rational and therefore unresolvable contradiction, the relationship between philosophy and

religion is expressed only in impoverished, defective, inadequate forms of both philosophy and religion. The genuine essence of the conflict (as it is expressed in the ancient philosophy of Heraclitus, Xenophon, and Plato, and in the modern philosophy in Pascal's inner struggle and in Kierkegaard's attack against Hegel) consists in something else altogether. Although both philosophy and religion are founded on religious experience (on revelation), philosophy has the immanent tendency to emphasize general, eternal revelation at the expense of concrete-positive revelation, thereby "purifying" if not altogether eliminating the latter and taking it in the aspect of its fundamental general meaning. On the other hand concrete religious consciousness and theology which is based on this consciousness have the opposite tendency to emphasize the concrete side of positive revelation at the expense of general, eternal revelation, to prevent concrete revelation from dissolving in general revelation and slipping away from the spiritual gaze. The total truth lies in transrational antinomian synthesis, in free *hovering* in the sphere of higher unity, which embraces and permeates the conflict. The philosopher, if he wishes to be a genuine philosopher (i.e., if, following the example of Socrates, he wishes to take account of the unknowable, to have *wise ignorance*), must recognize with complete humility that in all concrete forms of religious experience, where God Himself possesses us and gives us living revelation of Himself, the Unknowable becomes visible, palpable, close in a different way than in the most profound philosophical speculation. But on the other hand the religious man who has come to understand the whole depth and meaning of that positive revelation in which he participates must be aware that behind this concrete revelation one can see horizons of fundamental general, eternal revelation, which, as such, is the mystical ground of the intellectual intuition of philosophy and which can be expressed most clearly by philosophical thought. By the way, this is why Christianity's use of the concepts of ancient philosophy to interpret its positive revelation is not, as Protestantism tends to believe, a sign of decay and distortion but rather a sign of blossoming and adequate self-disclosure.

3. God as "Thou" and Divinity

In the foregoing discussion we were compelled to wander far from our basic theme and to explore a region that transcends all philosophy in general. The transrational unity of general revelation and concrete-positive revelation which we outlined in that discussion should not tempt us, however, to go beyond the limits of general revelation, and thus beyond the limits of philosophy, and to enter the domain of dogmatic theology. With conscious self-limitation we remain within the limits of what is given to us in general revelation—in the revelation of Divinity as "my God" or as "Thou" in its general essence. We return now to our basic theme.

Here a doubt arises. Can the all-embracing Absolute, the all-embracing primordial ground that in essence has no name and that, in its all-embracing essence and meaning can only be grasped by some general feeling (and which of necessity was expressed by us not in reverent silence but instead in the name "Holiness" or "Divinity")—can this ineffable primordial ground be adequately apprehended as "Thou"? Although we have been guided from the very beginning by the feeling that concrete religious experience is somehow more reliable in this connection than all reflection and abstract reasoning, we do not have the right to avoid the attempt to harmonize what is immediately given in living experience with *the conditions of the conceivability* of the reality of "Thou." A two-fold problem arises. First, how can we apprehend Divinity itself (in spite of its absoluteness) as "Thou"? And, second, how can we understand this "Thou" in its essential and necessary *relation to me*? How can Divinity be a "Thou" if it is the Absolute and the Primordial Ground? And how can Divinity be for me a genuine "Thou," so that I do not disappear before it, do not dissolve in it, but retain in relation to it (as this is necessary in relation to every "thou") my autonomous, self-grounded being? These two questions cannot, strictly speaking, be separated from each other. Nevertheless, because of the discursive nature of our presentation we are compelled to discuss them separately. Let us address the first of these questions.

In any "I–thou" relation of some intensity (and especially in that potentiated, eminent "I–thou" relation we call love) "thou" is apprehended as a *person*, having with respect to me a specific "I–thou" relation. And intense, living religious consciousness always apprehends God as a *person*, as a *personal* God. But to what degree can God really be conceived as a person? Doubt first arises here because of the undeniable truth that is revealed here to transcendental thinking (the only kind of thinking that is appropriate here): namely, the truth of the general *transrationality* of Divinity. Since Divinity cannot be subsumed under any category, cannot be referred to any "genus," it follows that Divinity cannot be subsumed under the concept of "the person," cannot be conceived as one of many possible persons. From this point of view we can consider God not as a person but as the primordial ground or principle that determines the very possibility of personal being. In other words Divinity in this sense can be considered as a *supra-personal* principle. But even apart from this purely formal-ontological consideration, there is another difficulty.

What we call the "person" in man (see Chapter VII, 4) is the unity of his subjective, inwardly groundless selfhood with the objectivity of intrinsically valid, spiritual being. The "person" is the mode of man's being in its necessary transcending inward, into the depths, into the deep layer of reality that surpasses man's being. Divinity obviously cannot be a "person" in this precise sense of the word. Unlike us, Divinity in itself is not groundless, does not need fulfillment and support, does not have that which forms the purely subjective, psychological element of our inner immediate self-being. Divinity is not a "derivative" reality. It cannot, nor does it need to, transcend into a sphere of reality that is higher or deeper than it, into the reality of what is valid and valuable in itself, for Divinity is the primordial ground or primordial source of this very reality. The human person is grounded in spirit, and only in this sense is it itself spirit; whereas Divinity is spirit because spirit originates from Divinity. In other words, Divinity as the Absolute and the absolute primordial ground is not a person. Goethe's riposte to abstract theism illustrates this with perfect justice and murderous irony: "*Der Professor is eine Person, Gott ist keine.*" But Divinity is *not* a person only in the sense that it is *more than* a person or in the sense that one can say of it that it is *also* a person but that one cannot say of it that it is *only* a person—just as, in general, everything we can say about Divinity is valid only in the context of transrational unity, in the context of "both the one and the other," with the added qualification of "neither the one nor the other." We can express this in the following way: Divinity in its essence is *supra-personal* and is not a person in this eminent sense. But insofar as Divinity reveals itself to me as "my God," as "God-with-me," it appears to me as a person. The concept of "to appear" must be understood here not in the subjective sense of "to seem" but in the objective sense. Divinity turns to me that side of itself from which it is indeed a person (precisely *also* a person). Divinity "faces" me with its *personal* side.

In this sense the personal character of Divinity (which reveals itself directly in religious experience, in general revelation) is not an illusion, not a self-deception, but precisely an immanently and immediately self-evident side of its reality. And since Divinity reveals itself with complete actuality precisely as "my God," as "God-with-me," it follows that the element of the *person* belongs to the complete actuality of Divinity. Let us dispell a very crude misunderstanding. The usual debate between the mystical-philosophical and purely religious ideas of God about whether Divinity is an impersonal "it" or a living personal God, a "He," is evidence of the utter helplessness and poverty of abstract thought when this thought stays at the surface of the rational element and is incapable of rising or plunging to the level of transcendental thought (which alone is adequate to the transrationality of the matter at hand). Human thought becomes helplessly ensnared in a net of cliches, of commonplace verbal expressions. Since grammar knows only the distinction between masculine and neuter genders (why not feminine as well?), between "he" and "it," between personal being and impersonal being, it is thought necessary to subsume Divinity under one of these two forms. And the only argument is whether Divinity is an "it" (the Absolute, for example) or a living being, a "He," a personal God. In particular, naive philosophical thought thinks (with naive, humiliating futility) that just by calling ineffable reality the "Absolute," "Total Unity," or the "Primordial Ground," it can define the type or character of this reality. But the Absolute, the all-embracing whole and the all-determining primordial ground, is sufficiently rich so that one may speak of it simultaneously in the masculine and neuter genders. In Russian these forms are *"Absolutnyi"* (the masculine) and *"Absolutnoye"* (the neuter). The masculine and neuter genders, indices of personal and impersonal being, do not determine the Absolute in such a way that It (He) must be subordinated to one of them. On the contrary, both of these genders emanate from the Absolute and are subordinated to It (He). The "Unknowable" must also be understood as simultaneously neuter and masculine: *"Nepostizhimoye"* (neuter) and *"Nepostizhimyi"* (masculine). And only the poverty of our language, which does not have a special form for the all-embracing and all-grounding character of the reality we have in mind, makes us choose between the masculine and neuter forms. Insofar as this verbal paucity determines the content of our thought, the wise philosopher finds himself on the mental level (but with an opposite sign as it were) of the savage, for whom all objects designated by nouns of masculine gender are thereby felt to be animate male beings, "spirits" of a sort.

However, by declining to choose between masculine and neuter genders, between personal and impersonal principles, between "He" and "It" in relation to Divinity, we have not yet exhausted all that can be said in this connection. Without daring to make a self-contradictory and even blasphemous attempt to define the nature of Divinity (i.e., all the while strictly observing the essential unknowableness of Divinity), we nevertheless have the right to say that the element of *personal* being is—in some metalogical, metaphysical sense—closer and more adequate to the unknowable, ineffable essence of Divinity than the element of *impersonal* being. This is the case not only because impersonal being, compared to personal being, signifies deprivation, the absence of something, whereas Divinity as the absolute primordial ground and all-embracing unity is not deprivation and absence but fullness and abundance (although in essence this consideration alone would be sufficient). Insofar as philosophical thought has the immanent tendency to subordinate Divinity to the neuter gender, to conceive Him as impersonal, it is guilty of the primordial fallacy that, in conceiving Divinity, it treats Him as an "object," that is, conceives Him as a part of objective reality. In contradistinction to this, we must re-emphasize that Divinity is not something that is *objectively existent* but rather is the primordial source of reality and surpasses all objective being. Furthermore, since we penetrate to Divinity and Divinity reveals itself to us only on the path inward into our immediate self-being and through the sphere of spiritual being; since the reality of Divinity is for us, first of all, the reality of the native soil and homeland, the primordial ground, of our inner personal life; and since it is the transformation of the impersonal "abyss" (which threatens to engulf us) of being into the self-evidently stable, inwardly kindred refuge of our soul (see Chapter VIII, 3-5), it follows that precisely this element of Divinity (i.e., its personal being) penetrates more deeply into the essence of Divinity (without being its logically defining "characteristic") than that aspect in which it appears to resemble impersonal being of the cosmic order. We arrive at the same conclusion if we base our reasoning on the method of analogy (see Chapter VIII, 7). Using this method and the idea that Divinity, although remaining heterogeneous to everything, shines through (in varying degrees of symbolic or metaphorical correspondence or resemblance) everything that exists, I see that I as a *person*—as the form of existence that is maximally concrete and full (see Chapter VII, 4)—stand closer to Divinity than any "it." I stand closer to Divinity than some rock that can crush my skull at any moment, I even stand closer to Divinity than some blind, wild, impersonal passion (my own or someone else's) whose victim I can become. Therefore, when I am conscious of Divinity as a person, when I enter into personal communion with Him, I perceive His essence (without thereby penetrating directly into His unknowableness) more deeply than when I am shaken by some incomprehensible act of His in a blind "it," in an earthquake, storm, or flood, or in an explosion of human passions.

However, it is essential that this comforting view not block the other side of Divinity from our gaze. God as a person, God as the absolute "Thou" before whose gaze I stand, God as "Father," as "my eternal neighbor in need" (Rilke), God who cannot be conceived outside of the form of being "Thou art" (even if this form is used only metaphorically), this "my God" is also Divinity, the all-embracing Primordial Foundation, the point of coincidence of my inner immediate self-being, my soul, with objective reality which is immediately alien to me. This "my God" is also the primordial ground of unconditional being in its totality. Therefore, being conscious of and feeling "my God," I cannot and do not have the right to lose sight of that depth of His in which He is the unspeakable, unknowable, and terrible (in His unknowableness) Divinity, which essentially transcends all definition and therefore transcends the "thou art" form of being as well. It is precisely the full-fledged, full-valued religious consciousness that has Divinity in these two aspects: as a personal God, a divine "Thou" who abides with me in all the intimacy of trust, kinship, and love that is possible between "I" and "thou," or rather in an intimacy that infinitely surpasses all human communion; and as Divinity, the unknowable, all-embracing Primordial Foundation of all, the ultimate, only dimly felt depth of reality, which inspires in us unspeakable metaphysical fear and trembling. This is the concrete content of general revelation, and it must be taken as it is, without any reinterpretation.

It would therefore be erroneous to seek here some intellectual compromise in the form of a self-consistent, uncontradictory *concept*. It would be totally incorrect to understand the foregoing discussion to mean that God is a kind of indifferent, neutral mixture of personality and impersonal absoluteness. On the contrary, according to the principle of antinomian monodualism, God is *the simple transrational unity of opposite and conflicting determinations, both of which are conserved in Him in all their force.* Here too, the true and necessary synthesis is not rational synthesis, it is not synthesis accessible to the "pure" reason. Rather, it is synthesis accessible only in the form of the rationally inexpressible *hovering* above or between opposites, which (see Chapter IV, 3) is essentially different from the helpless oscillation between two mutually contradictory concepts. Psychologically (in the concrete experience of piety), this transrational hovering corresponds to the mystical feeling of fear and trembling, in which the opposition between love and fear, trust and trembling, is both conserved and overcome.

4. God's Absoluteness and "I" as a Reality

This does not yet exhaust the problem of the transrational unity of God as "Thou" and Divinity. As we have already noted, this problem has another side, which consists in the question, How can God's "Thou" be harmonized with the absoluteness of God in such a way that God remains a genuine "Thou" in relation to me, i.e., in such a way that He is a reality correlative to me, which leaves me room for my free existence, *independent of Him*. If "thou" is the condition of the actualized being of "I" itself (see Chapter VI, 2), it is obvious that "thou" on its part presupposes "I" as a reality correlative to itself. Every "thou" is precisely "thou" *in relation to me, in connection with that "my own being" for which it is "thou."* Thus, our question means: How can God in His absoluteness also be conceived as a *member of a relationship*: namely as a reality which *outside of itself* presupposes me?

The "Thou" that stands before me here and that, like all "thou's," is *in relation to me, for me*, is also (as the absolute primordial ground and total unity) such that in some way it embraces and includes *me* into itself. It is "Thou," but it is also the source, condition, and place of being of "I." Thus, it is a question not only of the usual unity of separateness and mutual penetration as it forms the essence of the usual, typical "I–thou" relation (see Chapter VI, 4). It is also a question of *the unity of separateness and the creation* of the one by the other; and the "creature" is completely permeated and encompassed by the "Creator." We are then confronted with the following question in all its force: Am I a being that is *separate* from God and *autonomous in its existence*, or not? Are God and I *two* beings or *one*? If we are one, then it would appear that there could be no relation between me and Him. Only two possibilities would then remain. Either *I myself*—in all my ungroundedness, rootlessness, instability—*am God*; and this is a meaningless and monstrous assertion (which has not prevented it from arising repeatedly in the human consciousness) that contradicts the fundamental meaning not only of all religious experience (for this would destroy the meaning of the idea of God) but also of the healthy ontological self-awareness of man. Or *I do not exist at all*, and there is nothing but God. This latter conception is somewhat unnatural, tortured, artificial, but it is nevertheless somehow closer to the truth. For example, Spinoza's pantheism is, as Hegel pointed out, wholly unlike atheism. But this conception too contradicts the obvious content of religious experience. If I disappear, God, precisely as "God-with-me," also disappears, and there remains at best only a Divinity that engulfs everything and therefore determines and grounds nothing: Brahman coincides with Nirvana.

Therefore, religion must always insist on duality in this particular context. But the difficulty here is that duality conceived rationally (i.e., in a logical-mathematical manner) presupposes the mutually independent beings of precisely *two*, i.e., a certain "equivalence" of the two, if only in a general logical-ontological sense. But this is what must be necessarily avoided here. This difficulty is manifested concretely first of all in the necessity, and impossibility, of preserving my "freedom" in the face of God, i.e., it is manifested in the antinomy between human "freedom" and the all-powerfulness of God. If I have being that is separate from God and "independent" of Him at least *in this sense*, the essence of this being is precisely freedom—*my* freedom. This is the only condition in which I can be a "responsible" being, responsible for my sins and errors. But more importantly, only in this condition can I "seek" and encounter God, and only in this condition can He "reveal" Himself to me. Furthermore, this means that even though I am a being that is conscious of myself as God's creature, as a being that is obliged to God for its existence, nevertheless once my existence has begun, I can be and act independently of God as though there were no God. Then I am conscious of myself as a being that exists and acts "out of itself." But this would seem to mean that God is not all-powerful, is not the all-determining absolute primordial ground, and that His action is, at best, adventitious to my being, comes to me from outside in the form of grace and helps me—despite the fact that I first received being and the possibility of action from God, and hence the very possibility of "having" God. But with this orientation we have fallen into a kind of "Pelagian heresy," which in the final analysis must lose all consciousness of God as the creative, all-determining, all-embracing, all-permeating primordial ground. This consciousness of being with God but independently of Him leads in the final analysis (as this is concretely illustrated in the history of thought by the natural transition from deism to atheism) to the consciousness of being *without* God.

Thus, if within the framework of rationality, we understand the problem of the freedom and action of God in terms of determining the modes of *interaction* between God and me as two beings autonomous in their existence, then the problem is absolutely unsolvable. Either my being takes away from the absoluteness and all-powerfulness of God or God engulfs and annihilates me precisely in that element of freedom, or primordiality, that forms the very essence of my "I." *Tertium non datur.* God's all-powerfulness and my freedom are in absolute disharmony. It is well known with what intellectual sharpness and religious intensity various attempts have been made to find a rational resolution to this antinomy in the dogmatic development of the Christian consciousness as well as in other faiths. We do not intend to offer a novel solution with novel content. On the contrary, our intent is to apprehend, by transcendental thinking, the transrationality of the relationship and thereby to clarify the true *meaning* of the problem.

Let us formulate the antinomy in its most general form: *the reality of God in its absoluteness and my being which is autonomous in relation to God are absolutely rationally incompatible.* Nevertheless we must be *two* different, separate entities in our being. Otherwise that which I mean by "God" loses all meaning. After all we have said above, it is not difficult to "resolve" (at least in principle) this antinomy in the only way genuine antinomies can be resolved: namely by not attempting to establish new concepts in which the antinomy could disappear and be extinguished, but by achieving transrational synthesis in which it would be overcome yet be conserved. The dual-unity of God and me, which rationally can be conceived without contradiction *neither* as a unity *nor* as a duality, can be apprehended only in the form of antinomian monodualism. Only insofar as I conceive the relationship between God's being and my being as simultaneously *both* genuine duality and deepest unity, and only insofar as I hover above this contradiction, do I grasp the true relationship in this transrational synthesis, in this wise ignorance. The religious consciousness is usually interested in conserving this duality. But a deeper religious reflection shows that it is just as important to emphasize the unity based on the all-reality and all-powerfulness of God, the unity from which it follows that I am nothing before God, for I am obliged to God for my whole being—not only for its creation, but for every moment of its continued existence and active manifestation. The general resolution of this antinomy can consist only in the fact that "both the one and the other"—both duality and unity—are affirmed in their antinomian coincidence.

Let us attempt to clarify more precisely this transrational relationship. Our starting point is the absoluteness of God. Before this absoluteness, I am precisely *nothing.* But what does this mean? "Nothing" in the absolute sense (i.e., in the sense of not being a component of any relationship) is nonsense,

is something that, according to Parmenides, "cannot be thought or expressed." "Nothing" acquires meaning only as a component of a relation
to something, as a term of a relation. But this means that the meaning of the
concept of "nothing" is in general first realized only in transcendental
thinking. When applied to our problem, this means that I am not a "pure
nothing" (we repeat: a concept that is impossible because it is nonsense)
but precisely a "nothing before God," a nothing in the makeup of the
dual-unity of "I–God." But no rational interpretation of this concept can
satisfy us. If here I must think of myself as something akin to an empty
vessel or an absolutely contentless something, with all the content poured
into me by God, this would simultaneously affirm too much and too little
about my reality: too much because my being as such, as a "form" or
"carrier," would be absolutely autonomous, "out of itself," before God;
and too little because all the concrete content and essence of my being,
including my will, would only be placed or poured into me from outside
without being mine or from me. (This is the error comitted by the thought
of Luther and Calvin, which was religiously zealous and truthful but philosophically helpless and one-sided.) On the other hand this must not mean
that I am obliged to God *only for my existence* but that I can independently
create the content of my life out of myself, so that in relation to this content
God would not be the all-powerful lord and guide of my whole concrete
life. The only possible interpretation here is the transcendental and, hence,
transrational interpretation. The bond between God and me must be
considered to be not an external relation but a transcendental, essentially
monodualistic unity. This means that "am" itself (both in the sense of
autonomous *being* and in the sense of concrete *content* that originates from
this autonomous being, from my freedom) exists only before God, not only
originates from God but exists always through Him. At every moment of
my existence, in every content and event of my life, I am in some sense
created by God, receive my reality from Him. And precisely in this sense I
am a "nothing" which He fills with content. Or more precisely, I have my
"I am" in all the autonomy of its being, in all the fullness of its content,
only as God's gift and not as something primordially independent of Him.
Insofar as God is the absolute primordial ground and all-embracing total
unity, I am *nothing*. But insofar as He is *my* primordial ground, which
creates and determines *me*, I *am*. Precisely for this reason I am an *existent
nothing*. It is not a question of dual-unity in its usual sense of simple correlatedness, and it is not even a question of metalogical unity in the usual
sense, as it was revealed to us in Chapter II as the primordial ground of

every connection between contents of concepts. It is rather a question of antinomian dual-unity and precisely in the form of this dual-unity that is valid in the relation between the Absolute and everything else.

If we attempt to express this in the aspect of duality, we can say that in relation to God I am unquestionably someone *other*, not God Himself and not a part of God. But this "being-as-other-than-God," this "being-as-not-God," not only originates from God but continues to abide in Him and has its essence in Him. No one else but God Himself not only creates me as something other than He but also grounds this uniqueness of my being. Even though I am "other" than God and exist "alongside" Him as an autonomous being, this otherness, this "being-alongside-Him," is only from and in God. And on the other hand this my complete subordination to God, my complete determination by Him, this being in and from Him, does not reduce but rather grounds the autonomy of my being just as it grounds my freedom, the primordiality of the creativity of my life. God creates me, has me, embraces me in Himself—not as a non-autonomous, intrinsically insignificant, passive particle of Himself, but precisely as a full-valued "I am," with all the primordiality and autonomy of my being and self-disclosure (though in a deeper sense this independence is derivative). I am a genuinely autonomous, primordial, free, creative being. In other words I am a being that has the right to say of itself: "I am" and "I act of my own free will." This is so precisely because I am not only the "image and like-ness of God," but also a being in my own right that wholly exists in and through Him. God and I are *two* only in the ground of a deeper-lying primordial transrational *unity*. And my unity with God is such that it is manifested in the form of a genuinely real and full-valued *duality*.

It follows that the all-powerfulness of God and of His grace, which rationally is utterly incompatible with my freedom, in a transrationally antinomian manner forms with my freedom a primordial inseparable (though "unmerged") unity. The total unity of God does not contradict the autonomy of my being. The all-powerfulness of God and His predetermination of everything do not contradict my freedom, for this total unity and all-powerfulness antinomianly abide in *two different layers* of being: in and through the layer of my freedom and primordiality, originating from God, grounded in Him, and abiding in Him; and in the layer of interaction with my freedom. In this second, derivative layer, God's action (precisely His action upon me, which presupposes my independent, separate being and my freedom) becomes what is usually and *par excellence* experienced and designated as "grace"—namely *gratia concomitans*. However, everything that is positive, valid, ontologically real in my own being and in my own freedom is also experienced as a manifestation of *grace of a more primary order*, as grace which it is not sufficient to call "precedent" or "preparatory" but which can only be understood as creative, absolute grace, knowable only transrationally. Given this dual-unity of "God-with-me," inseparable and acting in two layers as it were, how is it that I can *fall away* from God, how is it that I can enter into a being *without* God and even *against* God? This is a special problem which we shall address in another connection.

5. GOD-WITH-ME AS LOVE

If we wish to grasp the transrational nature of this relationship in a simple, concrete, living idea, there is only one word that is able to describe it. This word is *love*. Taking human relationships first, let us recall what we mean by love.

As we have shown (see Chapter VI, 5), the ultimate and deepest essence of the "I–thou" relation, in which this relation fully realizes itself for the first time, is precisely the "I–thou" form of *being*. In itself love is already a mystery. The lover, giving himself in self-forgetfulness and self-denial to the loved one, transfers the center of his being (without ceasing to be himself) to the loved one and abides in the loved one just as the loved one abides in the lover. *I* lose myself in *thou* and thus acquire *myself*, enriched by the gift of *thou*. He who gives and squanders becomes (precisely because of this giving and squandering) the one who acquires. This relationship is completely evident in living experience, though it contradicts the most elementary axioms of logical thinking. It turns out that a definite quantity, when it has subtracted from it a quantity almost equal to it, does not approach zero but, on the contrary, becomes *greater*. Mathematically, this theorem can be roughly expressed in the formula: $A - A + A = B$. It is true that in this form the formula is not completely adequate to the relationship. What occurs here does not completely coincide with the relation $A - A$. Such isolated annihilation of a quantity by the subtraction from it of itself would correspond in living experience only to suicide and not to self-sacrifice and self-denial. Insofar as the self-giving or self-denial occurs in relation to another, toward "thou" and transcending to "thou," the subtraction is balanced by a unique form of addition. Mathematically, the quantity obtained would have to be roughly expressed by the formula $A - A + B$. Nevertheless there remains the contradiction that $A - A + B$ yields not simply B but precisely $A + B$. Furthermore, A itself as such becomes (through the subtraction from it of itself in the presence of B) an A raised to a higher power, a kind of A^2; the plus sign here indicates not simple addition, but the *inner* enrichment of A itself as such through the penetration of B into A. In other words, it is not possible to express this relationship mathematically (or logically)—not only because it is not quantitative but rather qualitative in nature but also because it is constituted by the living transrational unity of separateness and mutual penetration, which transcends the sphere of abstract thinking.

In every genuine relation of "thou," the beloved "thou" appears to us as *infinitely valuable*. And since value and being coincide in the final analysis in the idea of *foundation* or *fundamental being* (see Chapter VII, 2), it follows that love also appears to us as infinitely full of being. After all, love is precisely the apprehension of the genuine reality and, hence, the infinite, inexhaustible depth of being of another soul. But in relation to the infinite, everything that is finite becomes a vanishing quantity, seems to be a kind of "nothing." Therefore it follows from the essence of all true love that I am as nothing, count myself as nothing, in relation to the beloved "thou." It follows that my closed, self-contained self-being vanishes from my gaze and is replaced by my being *for* and *in* another soul. But being in another soul, in "thou," nevertheless continues to remain being in the form of "I am," the being of "I," and even appears to me as the genuine being of "I" acquired for the first time—precisely as being enriched through the possession of "thou." It is as if that "thou" which I have gained through self-sacrifice gives me my own "I" for the first time, awakens my "I" to truly grounded, positive, and therefore infinitely rich and abundant being. When I love, when I give myself in self-forgetfulness and stop caring about my closed, self-contained "I," I "blossom," become "enriched," become "deeper," attain "authentic" being for the first time in the sense of experientially apprehended inner being. This is the essence of the mystery or miracle of love, which—in spite of all its unknowableness and incomprehensibility for my "reason"—is self-evident to immediate, living experience.

Let us now imagine that the beloved "thou" is completely free of the subjectivity, imperfection, and limitation that are characteristic of every human being and that, in one way or another, are taken into account by the lover. This is precisely the way in which we experience the "Thou" of the absolute primordial ground, the "Thou" of Divinity. This is precisely the way in which I experience "my God," i.e., I experience "my God" as a reality of genuinely infinite value and infinite depth and fullness. Compared to Him, I appear to myself as an absolute "nothing." The grounding

and enrichment that I receive from this "Thou" which fills me are experienced as infinite. I experience Him as the creation of me, as the giving of
life to me, as the awakening of me to life. Furthermore, this "Thou" appears to me not as some closed being that gives birth to me or creates me
accidentally, by chance. On the contrary, His very essence is a creative
overflowing of His bounds, a giving of Himself. This "Thou" is not an
"object," is not egocentrically closed in Himself. It is not a being that is
only directed toward me by chance in a "thou-like" form of being. On the
contrary, it is a flow of life that rushes onto me and gives birth to me or
calls me to life. It is not only the "loved one" and not only the "lover"; it is
love, creative love itself. "God is love."

But the appearance, manifestation, or revelation is equivalent here to
the reality itself. The reality of what is given in living experience is *revealed*
precisely in this experience. Therefore, the loved one is revealed here not
only as the lover but also as the source of love, as love itself. God as God-
with-me is precisely creative love, a flow that constantly spills over the
bounds of itself, a reality that is always greater than only itself, precisely a
reality that, beyond the bounds of itself, embraces *me* as well—me, whom
it creates. Not being God or being not God, a being other than God, I as
such am therefore "God's other," a "non-God" that in essence belongs to
God. Therefore, my love of God is only a reflection of His love of me or,
more precisely, the reflection and revelation of God Himself as love. Even
my obscure search for God and my helpless longing for Him are the revelation of the power of His love over me, for the search already presupposes
the possession of what is sought—just as my rejection of God, my denial of
Him, like all the forms and contents of my inner being and consciousness, is
a revelation of the characteristic form of His presence and action in me.
(Thus, an atheist, who exists—just like everything else—only by the grace
of God, is, in this sense, a "living calembour" as someone has aptly said.)
My love of God, my aspiration to Him, arise out of my "encounter" with
Him, which in turn is a kind of potential possession of Him, a kind of
presence and action of Him in me. My love and aspiration arise through a
kind of "infection" from Him or the way in which a flame flares up from
the spark of an enormous fire.

6. THE PARADOXICALITY OF LIFE AS THE BEING OF "I-WITH-GOD"

We have just noted the paradoxicality of the relation of love, particularly of that fundamental form of this relation in which it is my love of God
and God's love of me—love as the revelation and action in me of God

Himself. This conclusion can be generalized: *All* life as the being of "I-with-God" is essentially paradoxical—i.e., it has a structure and a governing principle that contradict all we know from external experience and all that logical thought considers to be certain. In my life as being-with-God, not only the universal transrationality of all concrete reality as such (the coincidence of reality with what we call the essentially unknowable) is revealed but also that potentiated transrationality which belongs precisely to Divinity, the absolute primordial ground or source of being owing to which God (in the potentiated sense) is a reality of a "wholly other" order than everything else in the world. This "complete otherness" of God, His essential "paradoxicality," shines through all being in its totality and distinctly illuminates in colors of improbability and paradoxicality that concrete being of *Godmanhood* which we have in our inner life as the being of "I-with-God." Compared to all our being and to the rest of being in its totality (insofar as we apprehend this being outside of any relation to God, as a kind of self-sufficient being and, therefore, insofar as we apprehend it rationally—in concepts and legitimate connections of scientific thought or abstract, rational morality), the genuine essence of my inner being as "I-with-God" or "God-with-me" appears to be something that contradicts common sense and accepted rules of behavior. It is always "unto the Jews a stumblingblock, and unto the Greeks foolishness." It is necessary to have spiritual courage and a gaze completely open to the perception of the ultimate depths, the ultimate truth, of reality in order not to recoil from this paradoxicality, not to be frightened by it, not to consider it a sign of the impossibility of that being to which it belongs, but, on the contrary, to see in it a sign of *genuine, deep reality*, genuine truth, evident precisely as a result of its potentiated transrationality, its "incomprehensibility" and "unnaturalness." Genuine reality and truth as the being of "I-with-God" acquire their fundamental, essential paradoxicality from the very essence of God. This paradoxicality contradicts all the measures and laws that operate in the other, "earthly," aspect of being, which is apprehended in external experience and interpreted rationally. Measures and laws of a wholly other, opposite kind operate in this paradoxicality. Here, everything that is "right" from the human point of view is not right in this paradoxicality, and vice versa; everything that is right in this being, which has a deep connection to the primordial source, is absurd, unnatural, improbable, irrational from the point of view of the external, "rational" apprehension and understanding of being.

In essence, all the world religions have this consciousness to a greater or lesser degree, feel more or less obscurely that the religious life, the being-with-God, is something wholly special, not resembling in its structure and laws purely utilitarian, "rational" human (or even cosmic) life. This consciousness is inseparably connected with the very essence of religious life—the consciousness of God. But in no religion is this consciousness expressed so clearly, vividly, and boldly, so without compromise with the human "mind" and usual human moral measures as in the revelation given in the words, figure, and life of Jesus Christ, and in the Christian teaching founded upon Him. This is due to the fact that the Christian religion is precisely the religion not only of God in general but especially the religion of God as my "Father," as God-with-me or God-with-us (*Emmanuel*). This paradoxicality of the Christian truth, of the truth of life as "I-with-God," is expressed with particular distinctness in Tertullian's well-known paradoxes.

Consider several examples of this paradoxicality of life as the being of I-with-God: Those who are "first" in earthly life (first not only in the sense of wealth, fame, and power but also in the sense of moral and intellectual level, and even "piety") are "last" before God, while the "last" are "first." In contradiction to all natural justice, those who have receive even more, while those who have not have it taken away from them. Reward is not proportional to labor but is a pure gift, which depends on the will of the giver. The greatest sinner—insofar as, in the act of repentance, he demonstrates that he is with God—pleases God more, is valued more, than a virtuous and righteous man who does not have the consciousness of being with God; and there is more joy in heaven for the sinner than for ninety-nine righteous men. The "prodigal" is dearer to his father than the son who toils virtuously at home. Strength is weakness and weakness is strength. Poverty is wealth and wealth is poverty. Suffering is the joyous way to bliss, while success is the way to perdition. Those who cry are comforted, while those who rejoice are doomed to torment. The "poor in spirit" possess all the fullness of spiritual wealth in the kingdom of heaven. And what is hidden from sages and seers is revealed to innocent children. There is no essential difference between a murderer and a man who bears rage and malice in his heart against his neighbor. There is no difference between an adulterer and a man who only looks at a woman with lust in his heart. A stranger can turn out to be one's closest friend, while one's closest friend can turn out to be a stranger. You must "rejoice and be exceeding glad" when "men shall revile you and persecute you, and say all manner of evil against you falsely." But we would have to cite nearly all the Gospel parables and teachings and nearly all the Epistles in order to give a good picture of all the indications in the New Testament of the paradoxicality of the true life as being-with-God.

All these things are not merely pious precepts, they are not even only indications of a high "ideal" which is essentially unattainable for human powers. This usual interpretation only indicates that the inner meaning of these ideas is hidden from us, has not reached that organ of apprehension and knowledge to which this meaning can be revealed. On the contrary, in their special way these ideas are a purely objective, utterly "sober," i.e., precise, distinct, and adequate description of a certain *ontological* content: a description of the uneliminable, *genuinely* existent, peculiar structure of the ultimate deep layer of human being in which this being is the being of *I-with-God*. These paradoxes are the "axioms" of a certain exact "science" (which does not allow any arbitrariness) of spiritual being as being-with God.

To give a systematic explanation of this paradoxicality of being-with-God would be to develop a theory of the general nature and structure of religious life, to develop a system of science concerning spiritual being as being-with-God. This goes far beyond the scope of our theme. We must limit ourselves here to a simple affirmation of the paradoxicality of the life of "I-with-God." All we can add to this affirmation is an indication of the two fundamental elements of this paradoxicality and a brief clarification of the essence of the latter, of its place in being as a whole.

In the foregoing examples of the paradoxicality of my life with God, it is easy to notice *two fundamental features* which determine the nature of this paradoxicality. First of all, my life with God is a kind of *inner, deep, hidden* life that is inaccessible to observation or perception from outside. Since all external expression of this life is at best imperfect and distorted, and since, in its essence, this life shyly hides from alien gazes, is conscious of its own ineffableness, and wishes to remain ineffable, it follows that it is open only to *itself*: i.e., only to its two participants, God and me (insofar as I am spiritually mature enough to consciously apprehend and understand it). To the observer's gaze which is directed at objective being, at "facts" which admit "objective affirmation," my being with God is as hidden and inaccessible as God Himself. Like the reality of God, this being cannot be "objectively disclosed" or "proved" in its genuine essence. In its essence this being is only the inner life, the inner state or structure, of the soul, and not some objectively definable "behavior," "life-order," or combination of acts. This is why all human judgments about this being—if it is not *my* judgment about *me*, i.e., if it is expressed not in the form "am" but in the form "is"—are not only arbitrary in their content, pure guesswork, and not objective knowledge, but—in their form, the form of judgment about objective content—are inadequate to the reality they try to capture. My being-with-God *can reveal itself only from within, can illuminate itself only with its own inner light*. Insofar as we attempt to illuminate it from outside, to project on it a beam of light from the "lamp" of external, "objective" observation, its genuine essence eludes us. This explains one aspect of the paradoxicality of my being with God. Neither in content nor in form is this being as it *appears* on the basis of externally observable features. This is the ontological-epistemological basis of the commandment not to judge one's neighbor but only to judge oneself.

The *second* aspect is closely linked to the first. We have seen above (Chapter II, 2b) that even in objective being everything that exists is individual, unique, singular in its concrete nature. This is even more applicable to "me," both as a pure *selfhood* (that absolutely unique point which, as the center of my immediate self-being, is the place through which my link to being passes and in which the flame of being-for-itself first flares up in me) and as a *person*. But this uniqueness of me myself is manifested in maximal measure in my being with the One who by His very essence is the Unique One, but who nevertheless is Special for everyone, Other, "only mine," ineffable for others in the way He reveals Himself to me. My being with God (let us repeat Plotinus's phrase) is "the flight of the solitary one (the unique one) to the unique one." For this reason this being cannot be explained by any general rules or laws. In essence every human being has his own special being-with-God, his own special God who cannot be communicated to others, his own "religion" in spite of all the universality of religious experience, rooted in the universal nature of man and in the absolutely all-embracing "nature" of God.

In the most adequate expression of the religious consciousness, the Christian teaching, this aspect is disclosed in the fact that the "law" is overcome and completed by "grace," which essentially is always individual. The "law" in the sense of universal norms or rules of behavior normalizes precisely the external behavior, the external life, of people, be it the norm of right (even "natural right") or the norm of morality. "Norms " "rules," and "principles" of life in the domain of obligatory behavior correspond to the "laws of nature," to mathematical-logical connections or to "empirical" or "ideal" necessity in the domain of objective being. Like laws of nature and mathematical-logical connections, norms are expressions of the rational element of being, the element owing to which the singular is identified with much else that has with it a "common" content (i.e., a content that is fixed in its qualitative definiteness). The recognition of such norms in the external aspect of the life of people is just as necessary as the recognition of the fundamental laws governing objective being. But life and being have another aspect: namely, reality as it inwardly reveals itself to itself. In this reality the total unity that encompasses and permeates everything that concretely exists does not have abstract-universal features and therefore cannot be expressed in concepts or therefore in laws or norms. *Concrete universality as the inner kinship and unity of everything that exists* leaves all that is uniquely concrete strictly individual, completely unrepeatable; and this concrete universality is even adequately expressed for the first time in the concretely individual, the unrepeatable, the unique. Such precisely is my reality as my being-with-God. Here only one rule operates, which consists precisely in the denial of the adequacy of all universal rules. Here only one principle operates: *si duo faciunt idem, non est idem*. This is the second of the determining elements of the paradoxicality of life as being-with-God: the element of *irrationality*.

As the deepest layer of reality, this life is colored and determined in maximal measure by that irrationality which lies at the base of all being (see Chapter II, 2). Here everything contains those aspects of irrationality which we discussed in a previous chapter: the irrationality of the substratum of being, its transdefiniteness and transfiniteness, its quality of constant "becoming," its dynamicity, potentiality, freedom. Here being is not definite, finished being, but living becoming or *life* in the most profound and intimate sense of this word. God is *life*, and therefore my being with God is essentially *life*: living, indeterminate, and essentially *indeterminable*, being created and creating, eternally moving, plastic, dramatic, in spite of all its inner repose. "God is the God of the living." In this aspect the qualitative content of my being-with-God cannot be defined (except in a negative way, which we shall discuss below); surpasses all that is generally known, familiar, repetitive; remains essentially unknowable, a permanent mystery or miracle that transcends all our concepts.

If in these two fundamental features of my being-with-God (its hidden intimacy and its irrational individuality or uniqueness) being-with-God is revealed, like God Himself, to be "wholly other" than all our familiar, habitual, rationally definable life, we must not forget what we learned earlier about the "complete otherness" of Divinity. We have seen (Chapter VIII, 7) that this otherness is categorially *other* than usual otherness, than logical difference or logical otherness or heterogeneity. The complete otherness of Divinity does not prevent Divinity from *shining* in or through everything that exists, does not prevent everything that exists from having a certain kinship with or resemblance to Divinity. The same transrationality operates in my being-with-God and is revealed in its relation to my entire life. As something wholly other, objectively ungraspable, hidden, absolutely singular, my being-with-God is not an absurd, meaningless paradoxicality which is detached from the rest of my life. On the contrary, it is the soil and living roots that nourish all of life, filling life with its forces, illuminating and transfiguring life. It is true that the outer expression or manifestation of this hidden, indescribable life with God never coincides with the inner essence of this life, is never adequate to the inner essence, but tends to have features that contradict it. But even though the outer expression is inadequate to and opposed to the inner essence, the "inner" shines through the "outer." In spite of—or rather because of—its detached character, being-with-God is a creative, formative force. One Apostle teaches us that the essence of this being consists in pure "faith" and not in "works" or the "law," while another Apostle tells us that "faith without works is dead." And they are both right. On the one hand what is important is not our outer behavior, but only our inner state, the inner structure of our soul. But on the other hand this hidden, inner state is "known by its fruits." Thus, the grace-giving life-with-God is not life *without* the law but life *above* the law, the life through whose force the law can be genuinely carried out for the first time. The detached hiddenness, ineffableness, unrepeatable and indescribable uniqueness of my life-with-God is combined here with the dynamic, formative, creative directedness toward all life in all its fullness. Therefore this life-with-God also finds expression in the rational side of life, for this life is not exhausted by pure irrationality but is full of the transrationality to which the very relation between the rational and the irrational is subordinate. Even external, objective observation of life (of individual life as well as of collective-historical life) must affirm that the hidden life of man with God, inaccessible and incomprehensible to such observation, this hidden life which is called "religion" or "faith," is the most powerful, influential, and decisive factor in all of human life. In this combination of transcendence and immanence, detached hiddenness and omnipresence and omnipotence, *my* being-with-God reflects the absolutely transrational essence of God Himself.

7. GOD-WITH-ME AS "GOD-MAN" BEING

Something new was revealed in the foregoing discussion: namely, that the dual-unity of "I-with-God" is not only love, not only a relationship (mine with God or His with me) but also something more intimate—a special, inwardly undivided and inseparable being. "I-with-God" or "God-with-me" is not only a relationship, but also a special *being* which, like all being, is fundamentally a *unity*. If love is an expression of *the unity of two* (even if the second of these two— "I"—is experienced as originating from the first, God), this unity has another aspect in which it is not the unity of *two*, but the primordial, "dual-nature" unity of *one*, namely of "me myself." Let us examine this point in greater detail.

We already know that the way from me to God passes through spiritual life, through the domain of the spirit. But we have seen (Chapter VII, 3) that this domain is a kind of intermediate layer between being that is purely transcendent and being that is immanent in relation to me. This domain is the "soil" of my self-being, which in turn is the "roots" of my person. Or this domain is the "roots" of my self-being, which imperceptibly merge with the "soil" in which they are anchored. Spirit stands on the threshold between "me" and all that appears to me as "thou" and "he." But insofar as God appears to me as the end point on the path through the domain of spiritual life and therefore belongs to this domain in some way, it follows that the revelation of God as "Thou"—as God-with-me or I-with-God— is complemented by another, much more immanent form of being which we can call "God-in-me" or "I-in-God." The element of mutual penetration (which, however, does not exclude the element of separateness) turns out to be even more intimate and profound here than in the "I–thou" relation. We have already mentioned that the "Thou art" of God is the foundation of "I am." But this leads us to the fact that God's "art" is in a certain sense already contained in the depths of my own "am," or that my "am" is somehow rooted in the "am" of God Himself. It is true that we must distinguish here between the isolated "I am" as such as it is fixed by abstract thinking and the eminent self-transcending "I am" in which both "I" and my "am" are precisely greater and other than the pure closed, self-contained "I am." If we did not make this distinction we would commit the error of self-deification and completely distort the true relationship. If we observe this distinction, the supra-rational self-evident truth of my rootedness in God or my inner, immanent possession by God is revealed— which of course does not eliminate His essential transcendence. This relationship (at the highest and most explicit level of its revelation) is recognized by the mysticism of the Eastern Orthodox Church as the "deification" of man. In its *general* form this consciousness of the inner unity of man and God can be called the "God-man" being of man. And insofar as this unity is connected with the consciousness of the rootedness of "I" in "we" (see Chapter VI,6), we have the revelation of what may be called "Godmanhood."

"Godmanhood" is a fundamental *form of being* based on the merging of the reality of God with the form of being of "I am" (or "we are") or, more precisely, on their original, primordial unity. This "Godmanhood" does not coincide of course with what the Christian teaching (on the basis of concrete-positive revelation) perceives to be the unique "dual-nature" "God-man" essence of Jesus, the *God-man as such*. But if this teaching considers Jesus to be the founder of the Godmanhood of all people who perceive His essence,[3] then, from the point of view of the general and eternal revelation contained herein, this presupposes the very idea (and therefore the eternal reality in the form of pure possibility) of "Godsonhood" as a universal principle of being. This Godsonhood signifies that man is not only "created" by God, not only exists by the force of God's reality, but is also "born of God," "from above," has "heaven" as his birthplace. This is the specifically mystical feeling of unity with God which genuinely grounds the consciousness of God as "Father," the consciousness that I, despite my "creatural" nature, am nevertheless *descended from God*, somehow participate in God's reality. Insofar as I experience myself as a *person* (i.e., a being to whom the spiritual element is immanent or who is inseparably rooted in the domain of the spirit) my *eternity* is given to me in the temporal dimension not only with respect to the future but also with respect to the past: my being is revealed to me as essentially *eternal*, i.e., as originating in eternity and having eternity within it.

Furthermore, my Godsonhood has a deeper, more intimate aspect, in which not only am *I* born of God but also (as many mystics say) *God Himself* is born *in me* in my limitation, subjectivity, and imperfection, so that I carry God within myself. In its ultimate depth my being is revealed to me not only as *my being in God* but also as *God's being in me*. The consciousness of this relation is a false invention of human pride only if its content is rationally fixed and isolated (that is, conceived as logically opposed to my origination in God and my creation by Him) and excludes the consciousness of my absolute "nothingness" (in the literal sense of being as "nothing") before the absolute, all-embracing, eternal primordial ground of all being—before God. But if this consciousness is understood *transrationally*, i.e., in inseparable antinomian unity with the elements that are opposed to it, if the God "being born in me" remains my eternal Father and Creator, then this living consciousness is a true, self-evident revelation. Only Godmanhood reveals the true concrete fullness of both manhood and Godhood. Just like "I," manhood (being as human being) does not exist as an absolutely self-contained, self-sufficient, autonomous being. And our Godmanhood is not a being that is adventitious to our "purely human" being. It is not an appendix we can easily dispense with. The basic idea of profane, worldly, non-religious humanism is revealed to be illusory and internally contradictory. What is human in man is not his purely human essence but precisely his "God-man" essence. Once Divinity is grasped in living experience not only as God-*with*-me but also as God-*in*-me or I-*in*-God, the manhood of man is revealed as his primordial Godmanhood. Of course, God is not man and man is not God. But here too, the separateness or difference that determines the isolated, self-sufficient being of the separately existent is revealed (from the point of view of its transcendent ground) as connection or unity realized by the coupling element "not." *Man is a being rooted in superhuman soil*; this is the only valid definition of man's being. He is this kind of being whether he likes it or not. What depends on him is only the layers of superhuman soil that he touches and the manner in which the force of the soil, Godmanhood, is manifested in him. Man is man, a human person with all the associated freedom and primordiality of being, only insofar as he is greater and other than only man as a limited, self-contained, closed phenomenon of nature. And in the final analysis he is man only insofar as Godmanhood is realized in him, only insofar as he is in God and has God in himself.

But Divinity as "my" and "our" God, as God-with-me or God-with-us, is greater and other than just an isolated, self-contained, closed reality. The old classical definition of "substance" as that which "is in itself" and is "known independently of everything else"—this definition, which is inapplicable to any particular existent because it is contradicted by the all-permeating, essential, total unity of being, is *inapplicable even to God*. God too is not a "substance" in this sense. He is not self-contained, isolated, and logically graspable in this isolation. We have already seen this in a general form in Chapter VIII. Here only one thing is essential for us. As we pointed out above, God as love is not a closed being but a *flow* of love that creates and grounds *me* in its movement. As such, He contains me in Himself from the very beginning in transrational unity with His pure "Divinity" as such. He contains the element or potentiality of "manhood." His essence is kindred to mine. Only this relationship can ground my being as the "image and likeness" of God. As the true, all-embracing, all-determining God, He is precisely not "only God and nothing else." Rather, in His very essence He is "God *and* I" (the conjunction "and" indicating not the addition of something other and heterogeneous, something adventitious and separately existent, but the same thing as the prepositions "with" and "in"). He is God-with-me and even God *in* whom I am and who is *in* me. He is the true God precisely as *God-man*—not only in His revelation and appearance on earth and in His relation to me, but also *essentially*, i.e., in His "heavenly" being. If we use A and B to represent the two realities of God and me, respectively, we have the theorem A = A + B. We can see from this formula that on the one hand B compared to A (which is an infinite quantity) must be equal to "zero," "nothing," since it can add nothing to the value of A. On the other hand, B—since it belongs to A—must be infinite itself and therefore eternal. This leads us to the primordial idea, encountered in all of the more profound religions, of the "Eternal" or "Heavenly" "Man." This was what Nicholas of Cusa had in mind when he affirmed that only by apprehending the Creator in the unity of Creator and creation (a unity which does not exclude their difference and opposition) do we come to know the genuine essence of God; and our thought, leaping over the "wall of opposites," enters into the "heaven of the coincidence of opposites." Anyone who suspects this view to be "pantheism" only reveals his ignorance in this matter.

But insofar as "manhood" means not only "my" or "our" inner self-being but, as "man" and "mankind," must be necessarily thought as a part of the "world," we have already broached the topic of "God and the World."

Notes

1. *Ich weiss, dass ohne mich Gott nicht ein Nu kann leben; Werd ich zu nichts, er muss von Not den Geist aufgeben.*
2. (Isaiah. 55: 8, 9.)
3. " . . . but as many as received him, to them gave he power to become the sons of God . . . which were born . . . of God." (John I, 12–13).

Chapter X

God and the World

1. THE CONCEPT OF THE "WORLD" AND THE PROBLEMATIC NATURE OF THE "WORLD"

The meaning, the ground of being, and the genuine realization of my immediate self-being, my "I am," lie in the reality of "God and I." However intense and tragic the conflicts and struggles which we sometimes experience in this connection and which determine the inner dramatic nature of our being as spiritual being (let us recall the struggles of Kierkegaard and Dostoevsky), in the final analysis they are nevertheless resolved in the intimate primordial unity of "God-with-me," which immediately reveals itself to me. This transrational unity which embraces and permeates all antagonism and all conflict, this unity as inner essential kinship and inseparable belonging-together, is the absolute ground of my "I am," the deepest essence of my "I am" insofar as it has attained maximal transparence.

But something else also participates in my being, something which embraces and entraps me with such force that I usually do not even remark this absolute, self-evident primordial ground of my being. This something else is my being *in the world*. To the primordial, unknowable, self-evident (in this unknowableness) unity of "God and I" a *third* element is added: the "world." Let us recall that our search for the absolute primordial ground or primordial source of all being was determined by the direct opposition between "my inner world" as immediate self-being and the "outer world" as objective being. And this primordial ground was revealed to us as the deepest primordial unity of these two worlds, so opposite and heterogeneous in their immediate manifestation, the manifestation most evident to our gaze. As precisely such a primordial unity of this antagonistic duality, as the point of convergence of two heterogeneous worlds, the primordial ground of being was revealed to us as that Absolute which in itself is unconditionally unknowable and ineffable and which only conditionally and of necessity we called "Holiness" or "Divinity." And only as we came to a greater understanding of this primordial ground did it reveal itself to us in its side that is closest to us and also in its most intimate side as God-with-me. Thus, despite all of the essential intimacy and immediacy of the unity of God-with-me, the path on which this unity was revealed to us was from the very beginning determined by and oriented toward the reality of the "world" in all its problematic nature. But let us now note the other side of this relation. After the path to the primordial ground as Divinity and as God-with-me has been completed (or, more precisely, after this reality has revealed itself to us), the concept and problem of the "world" assume for us a different aspect than was the case at the starting point of our spiritual movement toward this reality.

First of all, the concept of the "world" in the aspect in which it is now revealed to us does not coincide with the aspect in which it was revealed as "objective reality" or "objective being" but is only tangential to the latter. In our discussion of the general concept of "ground" and its deep, eminent meaning (see Chapter VII, 2), we had occasion to note that from the purely "scientific" point of view (i.e., for a consciousness directed at a purely "theoretical" orientation in being) the concept of the "ground" of objective being itself as a whole (or, in this sense, of the ground of the "world") is meaningless because it is internally contradictory and acquires meaning only for the consciousness that transcends "scientific" thought. Therefore, the "world" in this connection is already something other for the consciousness that rises above the "world" and views it as a part or element of some wider and more all-embracing whole than it is for the consciousness that orients itself only within the limits of the "world" itself.

On the other hand, when we first posed the problem of the unity of our inner life or self-being with the external world, we immediately noticed two things: First of all, such a unity unquestionably exists and expresses itself in the fact that the rational and irrational elements are common to both worlds. And, second, this tormenting, tragic disharmony of the two worlds (let us recall Tyutchev's verse: "Where and how did this disharmony arise? And why is it the soul does not sing like the sea in the common choir and the thinking reed complains?") does not coincide with the duality of immediate self-being and objective being, but goes in another direction and intersects this duality (see Chapter VIII, 1). Finally, in the phenomenon of beauty we encountered a certain reality that transcends the difference between my inner self-being and the outer objective world, and that consists in the revelation of a primordial unity that surpasses this duality. Nevertheless, beauty is the beauty of that which for us is, in some sense, the real, "objective" world. Thus, in this respect the "world" does not coincide with what from the point of view of scientific (i.e., rational) consciousness is "objective reality" or "objective being."

Let us generalize these separate considerations. If previously the concept of the world as objective being was determined for us by the element of rationality and logical definiteness, precisely as the element that "objectifies" being, that makes being stand before us as a fixed, frozen picture of being that is at rest in itself (which, however, did not prevent us from apprehending the secret womb of irrationality which gives rise to the world), now the concept of the world signifies for us a kind of transrational being which stands in opposition to my selfhood or to me as a *free person who exists immediately out of its own self*. First of all and most proximally the world is, of course, the immediate *environment*, the totality of all that I encounter and all that has an external effect upon me, the totality of all that I perceive with my senses or my mind. In this sense the world is "objective," merges for me with what philosophically must be conceived as objective being. But the world also acts upon me through my relations with other people as well as through me myself in the form of every blind passion or purely factual psychic force whose power over me I experience. We can define the world as the unity or totality of all that I experience as *inwardly non-transparent* and therefore alien and incomprehensible for "me myself"—as the totality of everything that is either given to me objectively or is experienced by me inwardly in such a way that it has the character of a factual reality that forces itself upon me and compels me. In other words the world is the unity or totality of *impersonal being*—a reality that in its enormous, all-embracing totality as well as in its separate parts and forces stands before me and acts upon me as some "It." There is no need to stress that this world includes many living, animate beings (even those who in another aspect of their being are "persons"), that the "monadic" structure of total unity which is manifested in the world allows us to see in the world a kind of kingdom of spirits, and finally that even the world itself as a whole sometimes appears (often not without reason) to human thought as a kind of living, animate being. This does not in the slightest contradict the fundamental, constitutive element of the world, the element that constitutes the very concept of the world: namely, the fact that it is an impersonal, factual reality—something that is a kind of "It," something that is the womb and source of all that appears to us as "it."

Furthermore, at this level of thought or spiritual perception it is not a question of some abstract construction (e.g., the idea of objective being) but rather a question of *concrete reality*, revealing itself to living spiritual experience. As we have pointed out, this living spiritual experience is forced to take account of the fact that—together with "me" and "God," together with the intimate dual-unity of "God-with-me"—there is a third element, the world, which intrudes, as it were, into this intimate, transparently self-evident dual-unity. And the participation of this third element in reality determines the tragic nature of my own being, determines the obscurity and incomprehensibility for me of "me myself" as well as of Divinity and being or reality in general.

This is an outline of the basic problem of the world. In its general form this problem is reducible to the difficulties we encounter when we attempt to understand the *real relation* between Divinity (in particular, Divinity when it reveals itself as the primordial ground and homeland of my "person," Divinity as God-with-me) and that which stands before us as the world, as the unity of factual, impersonal being. Not having the opportunity to survey and resolve this problem in all the fullness of its separate elements, we confine ourselves to an examination of its fundamental aspects.

First of all, if we can keep from confusing the world in its living, concretely transrational essence with the rationalized picture of objective reality or objective being as it is delineated "theoretically" by "scientific" reflection, the world astonishes us with its inner, immanent *significance*. This significance is characteristic of the world in *both* of its fundamental elements: in the element of *rationality* and in the element of *irrationality*. The world is "significant." It amazes and astonishes us both as *cosmos* and as *chaos*. The dominant consciousness (or what was until but recently the dominant consciousness, for the scientific achievements of the last few decades have shaken this consciousness and have begun to prepare something new) of modern times views the world as completely rational and rationalized in terms of form, as something expressible in mathematical formulas. But in terms of content or essence this consciousness views the world as completely blind, meaningless, chaotic—as the formless result of the random, irrational collisions of blind forces of dead matter. That which in itself is chaos is, in some incomprehensible manner, formulated by the human mind in mathematical laws, i.e., in the form of logical rationality. The world appears to this consciousness as an utter chaos that is completely subject to rational knowledge. And the overwhelming majority of people never even bother to think about this paradox. Kant, the only thinker who was astonished by this paradox, could find a solution only by means of an artificial construction: human thought is supposed to cast the shadow of its own rationality upon the chaos of the world and thus only *appears* to discover this rationality in the world itself. But we have already pointed out that the unprejudiced mind must consider rationality to be a constitutive element of world being itself, while realizing that the essential irrationality of objective being and therefore of the world itself in its dark depths sets a *limit* to all rational apprehension of the world. The world is not a rationally knowable chaos. On the contrary, it is simultaneously *inwardly illuminated* and *unknowably miraculous* and *incomprehensible*; and this is the basis of the immanent validity of the world. This validity was apprehended by men of antiquity, of the Middle Ages, and of the Renaissance. For them the world was a kind of cosmos, a harmonious whole, and even a living divine being, while at the same time being a terrible domain of maniacal and demonic forces. Precisely this aspect of the world in its dual and ambiguous significance is now gradually being disclosed in the natural sciences (including psychology).

But despite its significance, despite everything in the world that produces in us a *religious* impression, draws us to pantheism (in the inevitable ambiguity of this religious orientation), and precisely because of its immanent, purely "worldly" significance, the world does not completely satisfy us, remains for us something alien and incomprehensible. The peculiar form of unknowableness that constitutes the very essence of the world's being as such is precisely its incomprehensibility. This leads to the question: How can the world somehow co-exist alongside and together with God as the primordial ground and homeland of my soul, as the most intimate essence of my inner self-being? And also to the question: What is the *meaning* of the world's being? These questions pertain to the ground or "origin" of the world.

But secondly (and this is the second fundamental aspect of the problem of the world), the world is not only incomprehensible in its immanent significance, in the pure *factuality* of its being. It also involves another, even more disturbing and tormenting, riddle for our religious consciousness, i.e., for our self-consciousness as "I-with-God." The world is incomprehensible, non-transparent, inwardly ungrounded in its factuality, in its purely "worldly" significance (see Chapter VII, 2). And the world is also indifferent to that which is revealed to our inner self-being in its deepest, precisely spiritual ground as the difference between "good" and "evil," the difference between "truth" and "untruth." This neutrality of the world in relation to "truth" and "untruth," this sovereign indifference to these principles, i.e., to the illuminating ground of our being and of all being, is already experienced by us as a kind of fundamental *defect*, as a "bad" or "evil" element in the world. But the world is not only indifferent or neutral in relation to good and evil. In the dominant trend of its being, in its dominant structure, the world itself appears to be full of evil. It even appears to take the side of evil in the struggle with good, thus assuring the triumph of evil. The world as such appears to be hostile to good and truth, to that ultimate ideal toward which our "soul" aspires. In other words the world appears to be hostile to that primordial reality which was revealed to us in Divinity and God-with-me as the ontologically primordial home-land of my soul. Precisely this is the problem of the *evil* that is immanently present in the world's being: How can the reality of Divinity (and especially the reality of Divinity as God-with-me) be reconciled with the *evil of the world*?

These two problems—the problem of the ground or "origin" of the world as an inwardly non-transparent, impersonal, factual reality and the problem of the nature or "origin" of evil—must be examined by us separately. Only after taking account of the meaning of these two problems and of the form in which they can be solved, shall we attain transrational knowledge—in the form of wise ignorance—of Divinity in that aspect in which it is revealed to us in the dual-unity of "God-and-the-world" (or in the tri-unity of "God, I, and the world").

2. The Problem of the Ground or Origin of the World

Let us once again consider the *meaning* of this problem. We repeat that as a "metaphysical" problem (i.e., as a problem of the theoretical-objective understanding of the world) the problem concerning the cause or ground of the world's being is completely meaningless. It is true that, in principle, cosmogony does have the possibility of clarifying the *genetic origin* of the world, i.e., of understanding how the world in its present structure arose from some not yet fully formed and, in this sense, "primordial" state. But this "primordial" state is nonetheless a state of the *world*, i.e., it presupposes the existence of the world itself as such. To pose the problem of the "first cause" or "origin" (in the absolute sense) of the world would be to illegitimately and unnaturally apply to the world as a whole a category which can be meaningfully applied only to the relationship among the elements or parts of the world. As soon as we pose this theme objectively, we encounter an unending darkness and our topic becomes a phantom that eludes us.

But, as is evident from the foregoing discussion, the meaningful and essential problem of the "origin" or (more precisely) "ground" of the world has nothing in common with the objective-metaphysical formulation of the problem, with the attempt to understand the world's being by reducing it to a state that is more primary yet just as objective and factual, i.e., "worldly." As we have indicated, it is a question of the *meaning* of the world's being, i.e., of the explanation of how its being *as* the world (as the totality of factual, impersonal being) can be harmonized with the reality of Divinity. It is a question of the genuine relation between God and the world.

In such a formulation there is no way to avoid this problem, regardless of to what extent and in what form it is solvable. Once it is established that the constitutive feature of the world is its factuality, its non-transparence, the absence in its being of inner persuasiveness and ultimate self-evidence, it follows that the world in its immanent essence is *groundless*, does not have the *ground* of its own being in itself, is not *causa sui*. Thus, concerning the world we can (and therefore must) ask: *Why* does it "exist"? Why does the world have being and not *non-being*? But this can be reduced to the question: What is the *meaning* of the world's being as such?

In its general, essential form, i.e., in the form that follows from the nature of transcendental thinking, (the only kind of thinking that is applicable here), the very posing of the problem contains the solution. Based on the transcendent, *linking* significance of negation, the affirmation that the ground of the world's being is not present in the very essence of the world, the affirmation that the world is different from that which is inwardly self-evident and persuasive in itself, is immanent evidence of the world's *antinomian bond* with what carries its own ground within itself, evidence of the world's transcendent "origination" from what is not the world, evidence of the world's origination from the Primordial Ground as Divinity.

However incomprehensible and unknowable for us this bond, its very presence, the fact that it exists, is immanently given to deep-penetrating transcendental thinking in its affirmation of the incomprehensibility, un-persuasiveness, non-self-evidence of the reality of the world as such. Since the world in itself does not contain the ultimate truth of its own being, and since the truth as such cannot, without contradiction, be denied in relation to any reality, this means that the world's being is determined by *supra-worldly* truth—by the *Truth* itself as such.

It follows that this bond is absolutely *transrational*, the bond of two essentially opposite, logically incompatible realities. The world has its origin in a reality of another order than itself. The world—as a being that is impersonal, factual, and devoid of inner truth in itself—originates from what in itself is existent or, more precisely, supra-existent *Truth*.

This opposition between the world and its genuine primordial ground, this transrationality of the relation between the two, this antinomian monodualism which is the governing principle here, is why no philosophical theories of "emanation" are applicable here, and why the genuine philosophical consciousness that apprehends the full depth of the unknowable must perceive the transrational truth contained in the religious idea of the "creation" of the world. Every point of view that considers the world to be a kind of essentially unchanged "emanation" from God or the self-disclosure of God Himself presupposes the *essential identity* of God and the world; and either God is "secularized" or the world is "deified." Either case obliterates the essential difference or opposition between the two which is at the base of the very problem of the relation; in either case the transrational is illegitimately rationalized. The relation between God and the world is neither a causal-temporal relation nor a supratemporal-logical relation (as between an ordinary "ground" and "consequent"). On the contrary, this relation is something essentially other, the essence of which is characterized by transrationality and unknowableness and which can be apprehended only through wise ignorance (*docta ignorantia*). This contains the philosophically true and unquestionable element of the idea of the "creation" of the world by God. And in this sense the mystery that is concealed in the idea of "creation" is revealed in its self-evident truth on the foundation of *general, eternal revelation*.

Taking general revelation as our starting point, we cannot accept the traditional, popular teaching of the "creation of the world" in its literal sense. That is, we cannot accept it as an account of some causal, albeit miraculous, relation between God and the "origin" of the world. The fact that the world and all the things and creatures in the world "came into being" from nothing by the command (the commanding word) of God is inconceivable in this form for two reasons: first, because the "nothing" from which the world is supposed to have originated, i.e., "nothing" as some absolute state or reality, is a mere word that means *nothing* (as we have already had occasion to point out); and, second, the "origin" that is supposed here already presupposes *time*, while time itself can be meaningfully conceived only as an element or dimension of the world's being. We are not concerned here with the problem of the correct theological interpretation of the Biblical tale of the creation of the world. We stand by the meaning of the idea of "creation" which we clarified above: This idea combines the consciousness of the inner, immanent *groundlessness* of the world itself as such with the consciousness of the transrationality of the relation owing to which the world has the genuine ground of its being in God (i.e., the consciousness that this relation is essentially different from all causal and logical relations). What is unknowable here is that God—as the primordial ground, the unity of being and value—is the living integral *Truth*, so that the "creation" of the world by Him, His command that the world *be*, coincides with *the giving of ground and value, with illumination.*

If we speak of the "Word" of God through which the world is created, this is not a distinct word of command spoken at some definite moment (what moment and the moment of what time?) but rather the *eternal Word of God*, the *Word* as *Logos* or *Meaning*, eternally "spoken" by Him and through the force of which the world *is* and *is grounded*. In its essence and being the world is, on the one hand, groundless in itself; and on the other hand, it has its real ground and ideal foundation in God. This and nothing else is the "createdness," the "creatureliness," of the world. We cannot say that the world "was created" by God nor that it is continuously "being created" by Him (the latter idea is at best only an inadequate reflection—in the world's being itself and from the point of view of this being as it were—of the true ontological relationship), for both of these ideas subordinate God Himself (both in the "act" of creation and in the grounding of the world) to time— which is impermissible. On the contrary, the world is supra-temporal, a living unity that embraces *being* and *meaning*. In all its boundless and immeasurable extension and duration, the world *is* "created," "creatural" being and essence. The world has infinite duration in time, for it is of the essence of the world that it is the infinite, uninterrupted connection between the moments of "before" and "after." Nevertheless, the world does have an absolute "beginning"[1]—precisely in that which is not the world itself but is absolutely other. This "beginning" of the world lies in a dimension of being that is wholly other than all "origination" in time. It lies in a kind of "vertical" dimension, i.e., a dimension "perpendicular" to the horizontal line of the infinite stream of time.

The entire makeup and being of the world are grounded in something "wholly other," "supra-worldly," and emanate from this something "wholly other" as from their "beginning" or "principle." In this sense the world only has infinite and immeasurable duration in time (in both directions of time) but it is not eternal, for it does not issue from itself, is not *causa sui*. If the world has an absolute "beginning" in the sense of an abso-

lute ground, it also has an absolute "end"—not in time but *together with time*.
All that has duration in time cannot "end" (for time and duration are
precisely one and the same), but time itself can and even must "end." The
world has an absolute *final goal*, an absolute *limit*, which will not be attained
"some time" but is attained beyond all time. Both the "beginning" and the
"end" of the world lie beyond all time. In this sense "beginning" and
"end" signify precisely something wholly other than coming into being
and disappearance, for the two are conceivable only as events or processes
in time. Here it is rather a question of the absolute, living, illuminating
"groundedness" of time, which is essentially the bi-dimensional unity of
"whence" and "whereto," "from what" and "for what," "alpha" and
"omega."

On the other hand this living supra-temporal groundedness must not be
rationalistically identified with extratemporal, i.e., purely logical, connection, such that the world (to cite Spinoza) may "follow from God as the
equality of the angles of a triangle to two right angles follows from the
nature of the triangle." For it is a question not of abstract, *extra*-temporal
connection but of concrete, *supra*-temporal connection, which (from the
point of view of the world itself) includes *time*. In other words, the world's
being is a temporal process; the fact that it occurs in time belongs to its
essence. And if this connection is broader and more encompassing than
logical connection, it is also deeper; to "ground" here means to give legitimacy, to ground in the dimension of *value*. Only in this logically unfathomable integral sense does the world "follow" from God, "is" through
Him, "is created" by Him—God being not the "substance" or "substrate"
of the world but something "wholly other" than the world.

There is another, more essential, difficulty or insufficiency in the idea of
"creation." If the idea of "creation" is true insofar as it denies the identity
of God and the world and affirms a relation of heterogeneity or otherness
between them, we must nevertheless recall what we said above (see Chapter VIII, 7) about the genuine nature of the otherness of Divinity. It was
revealed to us by transcendental thinking (which penetrates into the very
depths of categorial relations) that this otherness is not ordinary otherness
but a "wholly other" kind of otherness. It was revealed to us that otherness
in the transrational sense is more than separation and division, that it is also
a positive relation which unites and makes kindred—a relation that emanates from higher transrational unity and expresses this unity. God as the
absolute primordial ground is the total unity outside of which nothing is
conceivable. If, compared to God, the world is something wholly other

than God, we must not forget that the world is precisely "God's other." If we say of the world's being that the world possesses being that is different from God's being and in this sense is autonomous, we must not forget that this difference, this autonomy, is itself a relationship that emanates from and abides *in God*. Even if we say that the world does not issue *out of* God but that it only arises *from* God, we must not forget that this very "from" issues "out of" God and is in God. All the categorial forms we use to define even the most drastic opposition between God and the world have their roots in the primordial unity that lies beyond the duality of "God and the world" and is more profound and primordial that this duality.

But this signifies that once the world is apprehended by us in its connection and unity with the primordial ground or Divinity, it becomes for us something greater and other than "only the world." For precisely in this way the specific "worldly" character of the world is overcome without the world itself being "removed" or "eliminated." The meaninglessness of the world, its pure factuality and impersonality, its indifference to the *Truth*, are overcome. The world in unity with God, the world as the world-in-God, is something other than the world "in itself" (just as, once we have attained the depths of Divine reality, objective being is transformed for us from a terrifying dark abyss into our solid native soil: see Chapter VII, 3). If previously, in the face of the unknowable transrationality of the relation between God and the world, we were obliged to reject the rationalistically understood idea of "emanation," we are now obliged to take into account the partial truth of this idea: i.e., precisely insofar as the reverse side of this *transrationality* is expressed in this idea. The world is not identical or kindred to God, but neither can it be something wholly other and alien in relation to God in the abstract-logical sense of such difference, which would exclude inner unity and kinship. The genuine relation between God and the world (like the relation between God and "me") can be understood only in the form of transrational-antinomian monodualism as the inner *unity of two* or the *duality of one*. This applies to the essence of the world as well as to its being.

As far as the essence of the world is concerned, it is sufficient to briefly recall what we clarified in Chapter VIII, 7. The otherness of the world in relation to God does not exclude kinship or resemblance. But, admittedly, this resemblance is not ordinary resemblance. Even though God is a principle of "complete otherness," He symbolically "shines through" the world as "through a glass, darkly." If the world precisely in its "worldly" nature drastically differs from all that is "illuminated" (i.e., from the Primordial

Ground as *Meaning*) precisely because of its meaninglessness, its indifference to Value and Truth; if *in this sense* it is not the "image and likeness" of God and opposes the inner essence of "manhood"—nevertheless, in its other aspect, in its connection with God, in its reflection of God and therefore in its kinship with *me* (I, who in some sense belong to the world, forming with it a certain unity, having with it a point of convergence), i.e., in its harmony and in the organic unity of its structure, the world is a kind of distant likeness of God. We feel this immediately every time we apprehend the *beauty* of the world (this indeed is the meaning of beauty: see Chapter VIII, 2), every time we apprehend the world in the living experience of *integral reality* as such (see Chapter III, 4). Just as time is (according to Plato) "the moving image of eternity which is at rest," so the moving, changing, unilluminated, inwardly antagonistic, motley, manifold diversity of the world is also a harmonious organic unity, an illuminated order. In this sense the world is a "reflection" of God's glory; and the ancient world-view that considers the world to be a cosmos, a divine being, is completely legitimate insofar as it does not eliminate our awareness of the true God who is wholly other than the world. In spite of all the opposition between God and the world, the world in some sense (precisely in the eminently transrational sense) bears an essential likeness to God. And all total rejection of the world as completely evil, all rejection of its divine roots and therefore of its "likeness" to God, leads in the final analysis to the loss of the religious consciousness and to blindness in relation to the supra-existent reality of God—which was already made clear in our foregoing discussion of absolute dualism (see Chapter VIII, 1, 3).

But "essence" and "being" coincide in the primordial ground. Or, more precisely, the primordial ground is the higher unity from which both essence and being simultaneously emanate. Therefore, the eminent metaphorical essential resemblance between the world and God is also the eminent unity of their being, in relation to which the separateness in being is only the self-disclosure of the latter. By this we do not mean *numerical* unity or the essential-*qualitative* identity of God and the world. We mean precisely transrational monodualistic unity, the depths of which already contain duality. God is not a "whole" in relation to the world, and the world is not a "part" of God. But as the absolute primordial ground, God is also total unity. And He is total unity in the sense that all separation, all being outside of Him, is conserved but is conserved precisely *inside total unity*. The very "being-outside-of-God," the very elements of "outside" and "separately," exist *in* God, like all else in general. Let us recall Nicholas of

Cusa's profound affirmation that the unknowable unity of God is fully revealed only in the (antinomian) unity of "Creator" and "creation."

This will become concretely clear to us if we recall the results reached in our discussion in Chapter III. The world in the sense considered here does not coincide, of course, with the concepts of objective reality and objective being described in that chapter. In contrast to these concepts, the world is a reality given in living integral experience. Nevertheless the concept of the world has this in common with the concepts of objective reality and objective being that it is the unity of the factually "given" or "present," that it is the unity of the inwardly non-transparent reality that forces itself upon us from outside and surrounds us as it were. In this sense we can say about the world what we said about objective reality and objective being—with the difference that what was abstractly disclosed in Chapter III is now felt in immediate experience as immanently present in the world's being itself. That is, we can say about the world that the world's being is rooted in supra-temporal being, i.e., in unconditional and therefore all-embracing reality. But this supra-temporal, ideal–real being from which the world's being arises and in which it is grounded already stands in some way on the very threshold of the primordial ground or Divinity. It stands midway, as it were, between God and the world.

The endless argument (proceeding from the time of Plato and Aristotle to the ontology of our own time) about the theory of "ideas" is precisely an argument about whether the "ideal" world belongs to God or to the world's being, whether the "ideal" world is transcendent or immanent in relation to the world. This argument can be adequately resolved only in a transrational-monodualistic manner: the "world of ideas" is simultaneously "both the one and the other" or it is simultaneously "neither the one nor the other." In its ultimate depths or in its primordial essence, the "world of ideas" coincides with absolute Meaning and absolute Truth, belongs in some way to God Himself in the capacity of His self-disclosure in *Logos*. But in its concrete manifestation and action, the "world of ideas" is not *causa sui*, is not "self-evident" in the above-clarified eminent sense and therefore approaches "created," "worldly" being. Here too it is a question of a kind of creative, inwardly transfiguring self-transformation of "soil" into "roots." Reality in its absoluteness as eternal and all-embracing unity from which the world's being first arises or emanates stands "midway" between "emanation" from and "creation" by Divinity. This reality is simultaneously the divine element in the world's being and the eternally primordial element of the world's being in Divinity itself. Or, as we have already stated, it is the absolutely ineffable "neither-the-one-nor-the-other."

This contains the mysterious, absolutely unknowable essence (which is explicit and distinct in its unknowableness) of the "transition" from God to the world. This transition from God to "what is other than God" occurs through a kind of solidification, through the generation of the "palpable," "visible," "factual" being of the world from the womb of transparent spiritual, supra-temporal, ideal reality. We may call this a kind of incarnation of the invisible God, His investment in an outer flesh, which, like everything else, is created by the inner force or potency of God Himself, but precisely as something "other" than He. The world is neither God Himself nor something *logically* other than God and alien to Him in this sense. The world is the "vestment" or "flesh" of God, "the other of God Himself," or (to cite Nicholas of Cusa) the *explicatio Dei*. The world is that "other of God" in which God is "disclosed" or "expressed." Here we have the deepest analogy (which is, of course, transrational) to the relation between spirit and the fleshly shell in which spirit is expressed—the analogy between the act of "expression" (in all its primordiality: see Chapter VI, 1) and the "revelation" of what is expressed in the alien medium, in that which expresses. There is the difference, however, that the invisible core of Divinity which expresses itself in the world "creates" the medium of its expression—the "vestment" or "flesh" in which it is expressed.

The same antinomian-dualistic unity of God and the world can be expressed another way. If the abyss between God and the world is filled in some way by positive reality in the form of supra-temporal ideal–real total unity, the very *negativeness* that constitutes the essence of the world must be "transcendentally" apprehended as the world's *positive connection* with God. In itself the world is groundless, not *causa sui*, hovers above an abyss, is suspended above "nothing" (and in this sense is really "created from nothing"). But in order to avoid the meaningless hypostatization of this "nothing" and the dualistic opposition of this "nothing" to God (as if outside of and alongside God there could exist something of autonomous origin and being, be it only empty "nothing"), it must be understood only as the manifestation of the element of "non" or "not" in the depths of God Himself. This is only another expression of the fact that the otherness of the world in relation to God (just as everything categorial in general) issues from God. Like man, the world is an "other of God," and as such it is based on the element of "non" or "not" which belongs to the essence of God.

There is no need to repeat that the essence of God is not something definite which is constituted by the negation of the "other." Rather, the essence of God is absolutely transdefinite and transfinite, i.e., it includes all that is other as well as the very categorial element of "not" which constitutes all otherness. If all concrete reality is something greater and other than all that forms its intrinsic content, it follows *a fortiori* (that is, in such a way that this relation encompasses the modal-categorial forms of being) that this is the only way in which we can conceive God. The Kabbalah myth of the creation of the world represents graphically and strikingly this generation of the world from the womb of God's "not." The myth relates how God (initially all-embracing, infinite fullness) compresses Himself and folds up into the very depths of Himself, with an empty "space" formed about Him. This empty space is a kind of divine "not" upon which God projects His own essence, namely the image of the "heavenly man," and thereby "creates" the "world." In this antinomian-dualistic unity with God, the world—retaining all its opposition to God, its being "alongside" God—is nevertheless a manifestation of God, a *theophany*.

In conclusion, let us recall that this whole problem of the relation between God and the world, the origin of the world from or through God, has genuine meaning for us not as a theoretical construction, not as an object of idle curiosity, but solely in its living significance—solely in its significance *for me*, its significance for the relation between the world and the primordial unity of "God and me." *I myself* as a human being, i.e., as a spiritual being, in all the uniqueness of my essence and being, am, in the final analysis, *the only key that opens the door to the mystery of the relation between God and the world*. This relation passes through the ultimate depths of me myself.

But this means that, together with and through *Godmanhood* as an inseparable-unmerged unity, there is revealed "God-world" being, the "theocosmism" of the world. If previously we saw that there must exist a point of being at which my immediate self-being and objective being converge, now this relationship is disclosed to us as "reconciliation" between *me* and the *world* in Divinity (which was foreshadowed by us in the very concept of the primordial ground as Divinity: see Chapter VIII). In this ultimate depth, whose beams of "light" penetrate and envelop all that arises from it, I am in primordial unity with the world. And I am conscious of the fact that I am not only an exile cast into an alien world; I am conscious of the fact that I myself belong to this world, *because it belongs to me*. To cite Vladimir Soloviev, "beneath the rough crust of things," we see "the undecaying porphyry of Divinity." Despite its appearance of factuality and impersonality, the world is *potentially human*, for through its groundedness in God it is connected with the *human* element and even coincides with this element. All of creation, including *me*, becomes—in God or before God—a harmonious inner unity. And since the world's being coincides here in its nature with what I experience as the ultimate essence of my "I," all of creation becomes a grand holy "we," a "creatural" total unity which is wholly a *total unity existent for itself*. All of creation is revealed to be a harmonious "choir" that surrounds God and praises Him and has its being, its life, in God Himself. What from the point of view of empirical knowledge seems only an infinitely distant ideal, a dream of the "new heaven" and "new earth," which are to be attained only in some uncertain future time, is revealed in the ultimate depth of being to be an *eternal reality*. And it could not be otherwise, for all that "should be," all value, in the primordial ground of being, coincides with *reality* itself.

3. THE PROBLEM OF THE ORIGIN OR GROUND OF EVIL (THE PROBLEM OF THEODICY)

But the full unknowableness of this relation will become clear to us only if we take account of this opposition between the outer aspect, the empirical picture, of the world's being and its deep inner essence. And here once again we must avoid the dreamy romantic attitude and the tendentious apologetics, which, attempting to see in reality only what is desirable, simplify reality and ignore its incomprehensibility, thus artificially rationalizing it. On the contrary, we must deal in complete seriousness and truthfulness with reality in its concrete wholeness. The deeper understanding of the world attained by us, wherein the world's being is illuminated, nevertheless does not transform the severe reality of the outer aspect of the world into a pure "illusion," into something imaginary that has no "objective" existence. On the contrary, a dualistic understanding of the world corresponds in some sense to the dualistic essence and being of the world; the world as the "creation," "vestment," or even "manifestation" of God cannot be identified without qualification with the world as it is empirically given to us. A question inevitably arises: Why is the permeatedness of the world by God or the rootedness of the world in God not seen as completely self-evident? Why does this permeatedness or rootedness not determine with complete explicitness the *entire* nature of the world's being? Or why does God require as His "vestment" not transparent being through which He could always be visible with full clarity but rather a dark "veil" which by its nature is something *other* than He: namely, something inwardly *unilluminated*, impersonal, purely "factual"—precisely that which constitutes the essence of "worldly" being? We have already seen that this pure impersonal factuality is, in its indifference to truth and value, a kind of *defect* in being, a kind of *evil*. And the indifference and unilluminatedness of the world make room in the world for the hegemony of all kinds of evil. The fact that "God's world," the world which is divine in its deepest essence, is also a world dominated by all kinds of evil is the greatest and most incomprehensible of all mysteries. When we examine this mystery the essence of reality as the unknowable is revealed to us in a new aspect and in its ultimate depth. This brings us to the problem of *the ground or origin of evil*, to the problem of *theodicy*. We shall, however, examine this unencompassable theme only insofar as it touches upon the basic topic of our discussion.

a. The Limits of the Validity and Solvability of the Problem of Theodicy

Nothing is so widespread in the contemporary consciousness as the use of the difficulties associated with theodicy to lay a facile and seemingly convincing foundation for unfaith or atheism. "Since there is evil in the world and since this evil is incompatible with the 'all-goodness' and 'all-powerfulness' of God, it follows that there is no God"—this is the facile conclusion that can be reached by any adolescent armed with the ability to "reason." Indeed, this conclusion is so facile that one begins to suspect that it serves only as a convenient pretext for atheism whose true source lies elsewhere. The very fact that people who are not persuaded by this conclusion are called hopeless fools or hypocrites is enough to make one wonder.

Meanwhile, the reverse argument, based on the same premise as its counterpart, is also very widespread. "Since the reality of evil in the world is incompatible with the existence of God and since God exists, it follows that evil does not really exist, and apparent evil must be explained in such a way that it becomes a direct manifestation of the goodness and wisdom of God." This is a sample of the typical reasoning of "believers."

In opposition to these two equally *rationalistic* points of view, we must decisively affirm two things. First, however disturbing the problem of evil may be for our religious consciousness and however difficult it may be for our religious thought to harmonize the reality of evil with the reality of God, these doubts do not shake in the slightest the self-evident truth of God. For this self-evident truth is wholly *immediate* (in the sense clarified in

Chapter VIII, 6), is grounded in itself, and is not the result of any inference. Furthermore, as we have already shown, the reality of God has
a greater self-evident truth than that of a fact, for His reality coincides
with self-evident truth itself or Truth and is the condition without which
nothing could be self-evident or true. As such, the reality of God has incontestable priority over whatever is self-evident only factually, regardless of
the crude compelling force of this factuality. But even if we set aside this
latter consideration, even if it were only a question of two equivalent
truths lying on the same plane of certainty, our spiritual point of view in
relation to theodicy could be compared to the point of view of the scientific consciousness when it confronts two incontestable and certain facts,
whose connection and compatibility are unexplainable and perhaps seemingly even impossible (given the present state of our knowledge). This
excruciating theoretical difficulty does not give the scientific consciousness the right to reject either of the facts, insofar as both of them, as facts,
are certain. Anyone who has but once experienced the immediate self-
evident truth of God (despite His "invisibleness") finds himself, in the
worst case, in the same sort of predicament. He can agonize over the fact
that the compatibility of God's reality with the presence of evil in the
world is incomprehensible for him, but he cannot reject or doubt the self-
evident truth of God that was once revealed to him. This is the unshakeably
firm limit to the validity of the problem of theodicy, a validity that is so
often exaggerated. The reality of God is self-evident "despite everything." Furthermore, we are concerned here with His *full* reality as the
absolute primordial ground of all being, all value, and all truth, i.e., (putting it in traditional theological terms) the reality of God in His "all-
powerfulness" and "all-goodness."

The inner connection between God and the "evil" empirical world is
precisely an antinomian-transrational connection and self-evident only in
its unknowableness. This means (and this is the *second* thing we wish to
emphasize) that *the problem of theodicy is absolutely unsolvable in a rational way*.
Furthermore, this unsolvability is not only factual unsolvability, i.e., it is
not only determined by the weakness of our cognitive ability. Rather, it is a
fundamental, essential, necessary unsolvability which can be demonstrated
or perceived with certainty in much the same way that the impossibility of
squaring a circle can be mathematically demonstrated.

Speaking metaphorically, evil as darkness, as that which is opposed to
the light of truth, is opposed thereby to the mind's light and cannot be
clarified. The darkness itself, as such, eludes all light and cannot be illumi-

nated by it. Let us express ourselves more precisely, in philosophical terms. What does it really mean to "explain" the reality of evil? It means to find the *ground* of this reality or (what is the same thing) to perceive its appropriate, *legitimate* place in the total unity of being. We know that *real* ground must coincide in its ultimate depths with *ideal* ground, with *meaning*, and, in the final analysis, with the primordial ground itself, with Truth itself as the primordial source of all validity. To "explain" evil would be to "ground" it and therefore to "justify" it. *But this contradicts the very essence of evil as that which is illegitimate, as that which should not be.* The French proverb says, "To understand is to forgive." This should be made even stronger: "To understand everything is to justify everything." Thus, any solution of the problem of theodicy is a conscious or unconscious denial that evil is evil—an impossible and illegitimate attempt to perceive or understand evil as good, to perceive the meaning of that whose essence is meaninglessness. On the contrary, evil lacks ground precisely as that which is illegitimate. As that which should not be, evil is a reality for which there is no place in the total unity of being, a reality which is not a constituent of *what truly exists.* The only legitimate attitude towards evil is to reject it, to cast it off, but not to explain and thus to legitimize and justify it. Thus, in general, the problem of theodicy can never be "solved," i.e., the problematic nature of evil can never be "eliminated." All that is possible here is to capture this problematic nature of evil (which belongs to the very concept of evil and constitutes its essence) indirectly in some sense, through what Plato called "illegitimate speculation."

As a reality that absolutely lacks ground and in this sense lacks *genuine* being, evil must be confused neither with the transrational "nothing" or "not" of God Himself (which is also everything and the primordial ground of everything) nor with the "existent nothing" of my "I" before God. On the contrary, evil is something wholly other than these "nothings." The existent "nothing" of my "I" before God is an element of being that, through the medium of "nothing," rises from seeming, illusory reality to genuine and complete reality. The *non-existent* reality of evil, however, is a problematic "something" which constitutes itself as a reality precisely through its detachment from true, grounded, legitimate reality and thus becomes a seeming, illusory, illegitimate, deceitful reality. If previously we spoke about a "groundless" being which sought, and found, its ground in another, more solid being, in a kind of "soil," now we speak of a reality which desires to be groundless and makes itself groundless, which affirms itself precisely in its groundlessness. In one case being is attained through "nothing"; in the other case, being is lost. In one case the path leads upward, to reunification or the re-establishment of primordial unity; in the other case, the path leads downward, into the abyss of separation and dismemberment. In one case it is a question of the creation and completion of reality; in the other case, it is a question of falling away, death, annihilation.

Non-existent in the genuine ontological sense, not rooted in absolute reality, consisting precisely in the falling away from or the falling out of being—this problematic entity of evil nevertheless factually exists in the world. It is an empirical reality with tremendous force in the empirical world which even seems to triumph over good, over the truly existent. There is something in the world which is a kind of phantom, an existent illusion or mirage, but which nevertheless exists in and rules the world. This is an undeniable bitter fact which we cannot deny and do not have the right to deny. Deep cracks pass through the harmonious divine total unity of being. Abysses of non-being, abysses of evil, appear in this unity. In its empirical aspect, total unity is a "fractured" unity. Philosophical thought, whose intent is precisely to "explain" or to find the ultimate ground and therefore the *unity* of being, is subject (even if it is not occupied consciously with the problem of theodicy) to the constant temptation of mistaking this its ideal goal for a truthful integral reproduction of reality as a whole—the temptation of simply not noticing and denying the cracks in total unity. In a certain sense the fact of evil is the absolute limit to all philosophy. When philosophy recognizes this fact it must admit that it is powerless to explain being in its totality. *Philosophy has an immanent tendency to optimism*, a tendency to deny the reality of evil. In its metaphysical aspect, this is equivalent to a tendency to *pantheism*, to the unqualified acceptance of the divinity of being. But the irrationality of the divinity of being in all its concreteness, in which it also includes all the meaninglessness of the empirical world, takes revenge. Alongside the aspect of being as *deus sive natura* there appears—without explanation, as "contraband"—all the changeable, motley irrationality of *natura naturata* (Spinoza). Alongside being as "absolute spirit" or "universal reason" there appears all the unilluminated randomness of the empirical world, which Hegel contemptuously rejects because philosophy is not competent to deal with the unconditionally irrational (Hegel's celebrated "so much the worse for facts"). Furthermore, even the most profound and genuinely instructive attempts at a theodicy or an explanation of evil (including the attempts of Boehme and Schelling) cannot defend themselves against the reproach that in some sense they "justify" evil, i.e., attempt with philosophical argument to "whitewash" evil in its groundlessness and illegitimacy.

b. *The Essence of Evil*

In attempting to understand in some way the essence and possibility of evil without committing the error discussed above, we must consider, first of all, the following question: What is the meaning of evil as a reality that has fallen away from being and is in this sense *non-existent*? Or, to pose the question in another way, how can one explain evil in its essential *groundlessness* without attempting to "ground" it, i.e., taking into account its groundlessness? The first, most general and indefinite answer to this question is that reality has depths which are infinite, immeasurable and therefore absolutely inaccessible and dark for us, and that in some sense absolutely *everything* is possible in these depths—including what is logically and metaphysically *inconceivable*. This is simply a reference to wise, knowing ignorance (*docta ignorantia*), which coincides here with Plato's *logismos nothos*, the mind's perception of the absolutely incomprehensible, the logically impossible. If you like, this is simply the recognition that philosophical thought is powerless to solve this problem. But one must not forget that the very recognition of one's powerlessness to know some reality indicates a positive, if only indirect, apprehension of the peculiar nature of this reality. True, it could appear that this representation of the origin (even if incomprehensible for us) of evil in the depths of reality itself is *already* the positing of a certain, though completely indefinite, "ground" for evil. But this must be understood to mean that evil (precisely insofar as it "is" in some sense) is also really rooted in being and has its foundation in being. And this agrees with the idea (expressed in the unquestionably true ancient teachings and evident for all points of view except absolute and hopeless dualism) that, insofar as it *is*, evil is also good. (According to a whole series of teachers and fathers of the Church, from Makarius the Great to Thomas Aquinas, even the devil is good precisely insofar as he *is*.) But evil *as such* is *non-being*, reality as the falling away from being. And our problem is focused in the question: How can we conceive of something existent, i.e., something rooted in the depths of being, in such a way that its content (*what it is*) is groundlessness and non-being? The general answer to this question, an answer that is not the solution to the riddle but only a description of its meaning, consists in the fact that in being a kind of *spoilage*, a kind of *perversion*, occurs, through which the positive, i.e., the existent, acquires negative content, unnaturally and contradictorily becomes the carrier of the force or potency of *non-being*. We find ourselves here at the ultimate limit of the conceivable. But we can take one more step and look even more closely at this essentially "impossible" process which nevertheless factually occurs. In order to take this additional step, we must use what was revealed to us in the element of negation, in the element of "not" and "nothing."

We have already seen that "nothing" taken in the absolute sense as something existent in itself is inconceivable and meaningless. However, we have also seen that "not" is the fundamental transrational element that constitutes reality in its transrationality and that therefore enters into the makeup of reality itself. "Not" as the element of the separation or dismemberment of being constitutes precisely the connectedness, the belonging together, the total unity, of being. "Not" constitutes total unity precisely as the unity of many, the universal unity of all singular things, existent and grounded in themselves. In other words, "not" simultaneously affirms both the unity and the separateness of *all*, it affirms *all as each in separateness*. "Not" is a principle which *individualizes and unites at the same time*. But this "not" which constitutes every separate being in its separateness as well as in its connectedness with everything else, this "not" as an element of total unity, must not only *outwardly* embrace and determine everything that is singular but must also be *inwardly* present in everything that is singular. This means that "not" is concealed or slumbers, as it were, in the depths of every singular being and belongs to the substrate or "substance" of the latter. Every singular existent is not only an existent but also an existent "not." Precisely this "not" as an element of reality in everything that exists makes up the deepest essence of what we call *freedom*. The immediate meaning, emanating from the ultimate depths, of this "not" and of "freedom" consists not in limitation, separation, diminution, but rather in an *individualization* which is simultaneously a *transcending* through everything that is limited and positive; an individualization which is the capacity to have also that (or to be also that) which the given singular thing, as such, is actually *not*. "Not," the element of freedom in the depths of life, is simultaneously our solid ground (the force affirming our individuality, that which constitutes us in our own, special, separate being) and the force of attraction between us and total unity or the primordial source of total unity—the force owing to which we have our center not only *inside* but also *outside* ourselves; or, more precisely, we have our center inside ourselves precisely because this "inside" has its point of reference outside itself, in its connection with *everything*, with *total unity*.

In these ultimate depths, something wholly unknowable and unexplainable occurs, something that does not emanate from any "ground." The invisible thread of this positive, transcendent "not" cannot be completely broken but it can become so frayed and attenuated as to slip away from us. Then the connective, transcendent, positively individualizing "not" is transformed into a "not" which closes off and isolates absolutely—into "not" as absolute separation. Precisely in this way is the paradox of real, existent non-being realized. Limitation, an essential and necessary characteristic of everything that is particular as such, and fulfilled at once as it were by the belonging of everything that is particular to total unity, this limitation is thus transformed into absolute lack, defect, insufficiency. A reality that closes up into itself thus falls out of the general connectedness of being, out of total unity, and mistakes its own inner center (which as such can exist only through its connection with everything else) in its isolation for the absolute foundation of reality. This is the perversion which constitutes the essence of evil as existent non-being.

When through the absolutization of "not" which constitutes its essence, the particular, the singularly existent, asserts itself as closed, as absolutely existent in and by itself, it becomes a seeming absolute for itself, a kind of pseudo-divinity. But since actually, existentially, it is not All but needs an infinitely great number of things, needs all else, its seeming all-being can be realized only in the form of infinite indefatigable striving to acquire all, to engulf all. *Self-assertion* (what the language of morality calls pride) corresponds to endless greed or lust. And since all separation is essentially *mutual* (by separating ourselves from others, we have these others as beings separate from us), this leads to a metaphysical state of the world which is endless war of all against all, a world dominated by pillage and murder. Here it is not only the case that *homo homini lupus* (man is a wolf to man) but also that *ens enti lupus*—every being is a wolf to every other being. This war is endless and absolutely hopeless. Since every particular and singular being is connected with other beings, needs other beings, and has the foundation of its being in other beings, it follows that this war is endless *self*-annihilation, *self*-torture, and suicide—which indeed is the hell-torment of earthly existence.

As we have indicated, this is the all-embracing metaphysical and therefore cosmic condition. It determines not only moral evil but also evil as metaphysical and physical calamity. Above all, it determines the central and fundamental metaphysical evil—*death*. At the present time even the positive biological sciences are coming to the awareness that there is no such thing as a "natural" death, that in the final analysis every death is an imposition, a murder, the survival of some beings by the destruction of others. Every death is an expression of existence as a condition of universal, pervasive "civil war" among human beings. This also determines such calamities as need, sickness, suffering, and deprivations of all kinds. And all this is the consequence of cosmic civil war, emanating from the self-isolation and self-assertion of particular elements of reality, from a kind of decay or degradation of total unity. The fate of the whole world is to participate jointly in evil and to suffer from it.

This condition of cosmic being finds its deepest and most all-encompassing expression in the essence of *time* as *earthly* time. Being in God, in the primordial ground and total unity, is being in eternity, the joint being of all things in unity, the peaceful co-existence of all things together with and in all things, without anything excluding any other thing. It is true that eternity is not dead fixity but precisely eternal life, eternal creative activity. But creativity occurs in repose, and what is created does not "arise" in time but is itself eternal createdness. And createdness is accompanied by spontaneous dynamicity, by creative force, which is derivatively introduced into created being, is given to this being. This leads to eternal becoming, the tireless generation of the new, a kind of blossoming and fructification of being and, consequently, of *time*. However paradoxical this may seem from the point of view of abstract thinking, the new must not exclude the old. It must not arise at the expense of the old. The new can be pure *enrichment* without loss. In our earthly life only those new things are truly solid and fruitful which are rooted in the old, which live by the forces of the old and protect the old. Thus, one may think of time as submerged and rooted in eternity.

On the other hand, the falling out of eternity, the falling out of total being (insofar as such falling out is conceivable), signifies the origination of "earthly" temporality as the permanent exclusion of one thing by another, the generation and evolution of one thing at the expense of the decay and destruction of another. As the *external* relation among the elements of being, the essence of earthly time is precisely the struggle for existence, the rising of one thing to the light of being at the expense of the submergence of another thing in the dark night of non-being, birth at the expense of death. And this gives rise to the changeableness, the appearance and disappearance, the insolidity and instability, which characterize the "flow" of time. To this corresponds the eternal inner condition of being, restlessness, unquiet, care, bother. Restlessness, endless dissatisfaction, the endless and hopeless chase for the will-o'-the-wisp that ever eludes us—this is the adequate condition of closed, fallen, non-existent being. This is the condition of the human soul when it is possessed by evil and this is the condition of the world's being when it has fallen apart and fallen away. This is the world as the "blind will to life" of Schopenhauer or the "restlessness-in-itself" of Hegel. This is being which—conscious of its emptiness, its irreality—realizes itself in endless striving, in insatiable hunger for fulfillment, stability, genuine support. This is being which realizes itself in vanity, worry, care. This earthly temporality is the expression of the falling out of being, whereas "genuine," existent time is the self-disclosure of eternity in the process of creation.

The restlessness which forms the concrete content of the entire "worldly" mode of being, the insatiable hunger and hopeless self-torture of the world, is precisely an expression of the living inner contradiction and conflict which form the very essence of evil: namely the fact that *non-being asserts itself as being*, the fact that what by its content has fallen out of genuine reality, out of total being, desires to be a reality precisely in its fallen state. If we consider the Biblical tale of Adam's fall (and the fall with or in him of all mankind and all creatures) to be only a "myth," a depiction of something in the form of a temporal event which by its nature could not have occurred in time (if only because time in its earthly sense is a product of this "event"); and if we set aside the problem of responsibility for the fall and not ask whether this responsibility is to be borne by Adam himself, by all mankind, by the tempting serpent, or by God Himself, who allowed the possibility of the fall—then we can say that the "fall" of the world is not a theological dogma and not a metaphysical "theory" or "hypothesis" by which one can "explain" the appearance of evil in the world, but rather a simple statement or phenomenological description of the state of the world's being. Factually, the world is not as it is in its deep primordial ground, in its being which is determined by Divinity. Factually, the world is not as it is as the creation and "vestment" of God. The essence of the difference lies in the fact that the world undergoes a kind of degeneration which fractures the all-permeating harmonious total unity of being. In other words, the world's being has *fallen out* of the harmonious total unity of Divinity. Let us repeat, this is a simple statement of a bitter but inexorably certain *fact*, which retains all its force regardless of whether we can understand how it is possible, regardless of whether we can "explain" it.

c. The Problem of Responsibility for Evil

But the following question arises in us with insuperable force: Who is to blame for this condition of the world, which we can call its "fallen state"? Who is responsible for it? It is true that in a certain sense this question can signify a surrender to the temptation of a rational "explanation" of evil, a rational disclosure of its genuine "ground." Our foregoing discussion, however, leads us to anticipate that in *this* sense the question has no answer. And we must then reject as contradictory the very posing of the question in this sense; theodicy in a rational form is impossible, and the very attempt to construct it is indefensible and impermissible—not only logically but morally and spiritually as well. But some very powerful and uneliminable feeling in us protests against such a simple evasion of the question. If we cannot and do not have the right to rationally "explain" the fact of evil, neither do we have the right to become "reconciled" to it. The fact of evil *must* disturb and torment us. The truth of the matter is that the fact of evil is inextricably linked with the idea of "guilt" or "responsibility." In the face of evil there inexorably arises, and *must* arise, the question: Who is responsible for evil? Who is to blame for evil?

We can look for responsibility in three areas: (1) the primordial ground of all being—God; (2) the objective carrier of evil, or evil itself as such, or the "spirit of evil"; and finally (3) *I myself*. Let us for the moment set aside God and the problem of His responsibility. The problem then assumes the character of a question concerning the relative responsibility for evil of *the force of evil itself* and of *me myself*.

Let us first try to clarify the meaning of the question. The existence "in evil" of every separate being, of every "soul," is its co-participation in the perverse, "fallen" state of the world, the fact of its being "possessed" by demonic cosmic forces, its enslavement by the "prince of this world." We have already seen (Chapter VII, 3) that precisely the assertion of the autonomy, the unconditional "being-out-of-itself-alone," the unlimited freedom of my selfhood leads to my enslavement by evil, hostile forces. But who is to blame for this: "I myself" or the "forces of evil"? In other words, where is the source of evil—in the "spiritual world," transcendent in relation to me, in which I only participate and to which I am subordinated, or in "me myself"? To one who is not experienced in the spiritual life and who lacks an organ for the perception of the spiritual as such in the ontological objectivity of its being, this question may seem utterly absurd and even an attempt to confuse and darken the conscience with theological fantasy. In contrast to this naive view, it is necessary to emphasize that there is a deep metaphysical truth in the idea that evil as a spiritual potency of being or as the "spirit of evil" seduces man, leads him into sin. Insofar as man is spiritual in his deep essence (and, hence, insofar as he has a relation to the spirit as a special domain of being, insofar as he transcends into the kingdom of the spirit), he has a relation—both in good and in evil—to the objective spiritual element and depends on the latter. In the final analysis, all evil has a spiritual nature and a spiritual origin. When man "falls" into evil, he becomes subordinate to the forces of evil, which enslave him. In this sense man himself is not the original source of evil but only its instrument or obedient slave, the one who executes the will of evil. On the other hand, this view is questionable and unacceptable insofar as my consciousness of my participation in evil, in that which "should not be," is inseparable from my responsibility for it.

Of course, the common simplistic "explanation" which affirms that evil arises from human "freedom," from the ability of every man to choose between good and evil, is a wholly illusory explanation. First of all, the very existence of evil as such, the thing that must be explained, is tacitly assumed. Furthermore, this explanation distorts the content of the factual experience of "falling" into evil. Evil is never chosen freely. On the contrary, we are involuntarily pulled, drawn, or chased to evil. The very nature of this "attraction" to evil means that in experiencing it we lose our freedom. Only good is chosen freely, for good alone, coinciding in the depths of reality with *being*, forms the genuine inner ground of our being. We set aside for the moment the most difficult and tormenting aspect of the problem; namely, whether we are to blame for the fact that God has provided us with a freedom so dubious and unstable that it can lead us to evil when it would have cost Him nothing (it seems) to give us, His "image and likeness," the freedom that essentially coincides with *saintliness*, with the free adherence to good alone. We shall return to this aspect of the problem later.

Thus, there is a certain antinomy between my responsibility for evil and the responsibility of the force of evil that acts upon me. But we already know how to "resolve" antinomies: not through their elimination in new rational concepts but only through their courageous transrational acceptance. In the present case we can apply the antinomian relation we discovered between the psychic nature of man and the reality of the spirit (see Chapter VII, 3). Since my self-being and spiritual being form a dual-unity, inseparable yet unmerged, mutually intermingling, undivided yet clearly distinct in their duality, it follows that in this dual-unity the *one* cannot be opposed (either temporally or logically) to the *other*, the one cannot precede and determine the other. The two stand in a relation of inseparable belonging-together and mutual determination, not in the form of an external interaction between two separate, heterogeneous entities but in the form of inseparable, antinomian dual-unity. We can also apply this to the relation between "me" and the "forces of evil" or the "prince of this world." For I am not only a small particle of the universal whole and subordinate to the forces of this whole. I am also the center of the universal whole or the infinite place where the whole is *wholly* present, just as I am the point through which the connection between the world and God passes, the point of encounter between the world and God. Therefore the fall of the world is my fall, and my fall is the fall of the whole world. It is not by blind natural necessity that I am subordinate to the fall and that the fall is reflected in me. This would be a great injustice, removing from me all responsibility and making me an innocent victim. Furthermore, such an affirmation is utterly absurd because blind natural necessity is itself an expression and result of this fall. On the contrary, I as such, from the depths of my own being, continuously take part in the fall. We already know that I am always something greater than only I alone, that I am "I am" precisely because I transcend and embrace everything else as well. I am subordinate to the demonism of the world, but all the demonism of the world also exists *inside me.* The "outside" itself turns out to be "inside." The outer foe turns out to be an inner foe. If I surrender to him and he takes me prisoner, it is only because I gave birth to this foe and nurtured him in myself and because we are both equally responsible for evil. Or (what is the same thing) neither of us is responsible separately, and therefore we are not responsible together. Rather, the responsibility is borne by that point of being (simultaneously my being and a being that transcends me) in which I coincide with my foe in inseparable-unmerged dual-unity. The total unity of being, owing to which everything that is particular and singular is not only a part of the whole but also carries the whole in itself, also retains its force (though in a distorted way) in the mode of being as evil. Evil reigns as a universal, all-pervading "atmosphere" over all of the world's being, but in such a way that its center and source is located in everything and, consequently, *in my own being* as well.

But if evil in me coincides with the enormous, all-embracing demonism of the whole world, where then is the omnipresent, all-emcompassing and all-permeating unity of God as the all-powerful and all-good God? If God Himself creates or merely voluntarily allows evil, where is His all-goodness, His essence as the homeland of my soul in its deepest hope, His essence as the Light of Truth which makes up His absolute self-evident truth? And if He is only forced to tolerate evil, where then is His all-powerfulness, His absolute all-creating, all-permeating reality, owing to which He is God as the absolute primordial ground of all? Our thought seems to have no way out except to deny either the all-goodness of God or His all-powerfulness. In the former case we are forced to place the final responsibility for evil upon God. In the latter case He does not bear responsibility (responsibility is borne by the foe, the force of evil), but is powerless to help us. In both cases the very idea of God is destroyed—the idea of God as Divinity and of God as God-with-me.

However, if the idea or, more precisely, the very reality of God has for us an ultimate and utterly immediate self-evident truth, and its perception and acceptance therefore cannot be shaken by any doubts relating to the problem of evil, we must honestly admit that we confront an *absolutely unsolvable riddle*, a riddle we must and can only simply pose or perceive (but not solve) as such in all its *unknowableness*. But this does not prevent us from clarifying (even here, at the limits of all human thought) the nature of this unknowableness (without attempting to "solve" the riddle) and thereby understanding more deeply the compatibility of this riddle with the correctly understood recognition of the reality of God.

First of all, let us recall that these two equally necessary aspects of universal being are certain in wholly different ways. And the true state of affairs is not the one conceived by the "sober," "common-sense" consciousness for which raw facts, unilluminated but visible, possess ultimate, triumphant certainty. The empirical certainty of evil is not only not "self-evident," not "inwardly persuasive" in the higher, ultimate sense, but is even something opposed to self-evidence—i.e., this empirical certainty is precisely an absurdity, a kind of impossible reality, an *untruth*. On the other hand, the Divine aspect of universal being is absolutely primary, absolutely inwardly persuasive—for it is the *Light of Truth*. The inner absurdity of the denial of God consists in the fact that even this denial itself is accomplished by the force of and in the name of the *Truth* (even though the Truth is ill-applied here). Although incorrectly expressed and understood by us, this denial is the action of the existent Truth in us, just as our very being is a manifestation of the Truth. This is not empty abstract sophistry or illusory self-consolation. This is manifested wholly concretely and tangibly in the fundamental fact that evil, though it is the decay and annihilation of being, does not have the power to destroy the world's being. Evil can act only

within the limits of the world's being, only on the unshakeably firm surface
of being as total unity, but cannot penetrate into the depths of this being.
However much truth they may have in relation to the empirical world,
i.e., in relation to the *surface* of being, all complaints concerning the all-
powerfulness of evil, its triumph over good, contain an evident internal
contradiction: If the destructive force of evil were not confined by absolute, inviolable limits, all would have been destroyed long ago and *there
would be nobody to complain about evil*. We return to the obvious but paradoxical proposition that evil as such is not something existent. Only individual
"evil" things exist or have genuine being. And insofar as these things *exist*,
they are good. The devil himself is good insofar as he *is*. But even this is not
enough. Insofar as evil is nonetheless a reality, a kind of cosmic force, it
does not have the power to triumph completely and to rejoice in its triumph. Since it is isolation, separation, a closing-up-into-itself, since it is
therefore forced to engulf, kill, destroy everything around itself, evil is
also self-destruction. Evil leads not only to the suffering and destruction of
the victim of evil but also to the suffering and destruction of the *carrier of
evil*. And this is so precisely because of the inviolableness and unshakeable-
ness, the inner solidarity, of the total unity of being. The non-existent
reality of evil is a kind of reflection, in the abyss of being, of the supra-
existent reality of God, precisely as the uniting and all-permeating total
unity. The mode and character of the action of evil imply the absolute
all-powerfulness of God. Therefore, evil carries within itself its own immanent punishment. As Jacob Boehme says, this punishment is "God's
wrath" as the revelation of God's love in the abyss of evil, as the devouring
flame into which the light of God is transformed in the element of non-
being. And whoever "falls" into evil thereby falls into "the hands of the
living God." God does not attack and destroy from outside. He forces evil
to die from inside, to destroy itself. To consider evil an absolutely primary,
unconditionally autonomous force, a reality opposite to good in its ontological ground, and to base the struggle against evil on this nearsighted
rationalistic dualism—is to fall into spiritual ignorance.

In no sense is this the "solution" to the problem of theodicy. On the
contrary, it brings us face to face with the most terrifying idea that has ever
arisen in the human mind, an idea that has arisen in only the most spiritually
courageous minds: namely, the idea that in some ultimate, deepest sense,
the primordial source of evil (if not evil itself in all its explicitness) is
concealed in the unknowable depths of God Himself. This theme is present
in the profound meditations on evil of Boehme and Schelling. And we
cannot deny that this view contains a certain amount of truth, precisely

insofar as it perceives and overcomes the falseness and superficiality of the *rationalized* concept of all-goodness, the incompatibility of this concept with the unknowable depths of God's reality. Just as God is not "all-powerful" in the manner of a despot who fills his prisons with disobedient subjects, so He is not "all-good" in the manner of a good old grandfather, who caresses his grandchildren with worn, wrinkled hands and gives them sweets. The all-good God the Father is also the God who inspires in us ineffable fear and trembling.

Nevertheless, the idea of God as the primordial source of evil, even if only in some remote and indirect way, is unbearable and inconsistent—for it destroys the very idea of God, the self-evident truth of which emanates from His being as absolute Truth and, consequently, absolute Good. In this sense, the ancient gnostic who said, "I would rather admit anything at all than that God is not good," is perfectly right. But how can we harmonize this necessary all-goodness with the all-powerfulness or, more precisely, the *all-reality* of God, owing to which He is the primordial source of all things? And if He is the primordial source of all things, it appears that He would also have to be, directly or indirectly, the primordial source of evil.

Let us repeat, it is absolutely impossible to logically harmonize these things; and the first thing we are obliged to do is to admit this impossibility honestly and without qualification. But we must also repeat something else. The impossibility of *logical* harmonization here is based on the essential *transrationality* of God, and in the very apprehension of this impossibility we acquire a deeper *positive knowledge*. The difficulty here is that our concepts are inevitably inadequate to the transrational reality of God, that it is impossible to subsume the reality of God under the *form of a concept*, under the form of a "determination." In posing the question concerning the responsibility of God for evil, we conceive God as a certain *particular entity*, for we can conceive of something only in the form of a particular "definite object." But God is more than "something" or "someone" for us. He is also total unity, the all-encompassing fullness of all things without exception. God as a reality is also all that which "He Himself" is not. Perhaps we can attempt to "babble out" the solution to the riddle of responsibility for evil: The responsibility for evil is borne by that primordial and primary reality which though *in God* (for all things without exception are *in* God) is not God Himself or is something opposite to God Himself. *The place of the groundless birth of evil* is that place in reality where evil, born of God and abiding in God, *ceases to be God*. Evil is generated from the ineffable abyss which lies, as it were, on the threshold between God and "not-God."

There is no need to search long for this bottomless, essentially indefinite place or to construct abstract hypotheses concerning it. It is given to me in living experience as *I myself*, as the bottomless depth which connects me with God and separates me from Him. *There is only one possibility of apprehending in living concreteness the absolutely unknowable "origin" of evil.* This possibility is contained in the consciousness of *my responsibility, in the experience of "guilt."* This is why the true question concerning the "origin" of evil is really a question concerning the "responsibility" for evil. To be "responsible" for something is not to be its "cause" (in the theoretical-ontological sense). Responsibility is a category that is wholly other than the objective-ontological category of cause. The "guilty" one is responsible, not the "cause." On the contrary, the cause is never responsible, for it is necessary. Only in the primordial, logically indivisible experience of "guilt" do I have living transrational knowledge of the true essence of evil—namely, its *groundless* origination as the incomprehensible *falling out of* being, as "non-being" in me, as the existent reality of the abyss, full of being but opposed to being.

The consciousness of guilt is more than the recognition of the non-transparent *fact* of the occurrence of something bad, something that should not be. Guilt in living experience is equivalent to *sin*. Guilt is precisely the experience of the unknowable transformation of my true, God-grounded, free being and essence into a chaotic and rebellious pseudo-freedom in which I become a carrier of non-being, a prisoner of the dark force of non-being which I myself produce. To ask how God could have "given" to me or "permitted" in me this possibility of ontological perversion is to lose the depth and primordiality of the experience of guilt. It is to evade responsibility and to turn aside from the only path on which real, living knowledge of evil is possible. It follows from the metaphysical essence of the matter that guilt can be experienced only in me myself, only as *my* guilt. Only *in myself alone* can I come to know with certainty that guilt is sin, that it is an unfathomable violation, a defect, of the ineffable essence of being. Compared to this, all guilt attributed to others is, at best, an affirmation of the illegitimacy of their actions and a protest against this illegitimacy; it is a framework relating to law and morality, and does not involve metaphysical perception. Only to the extent that I embrace another person in love, disclose in him my own reality, can I apprehend his guilt as sin. But then I feel myself co-responsible for *his* sin, experience his guilt as *our* sin and therefore as *my* sin. This is the more profound and primordial basis of the commandment to seek only one's own responsibility, not another's (see Chapter IX, 7).

When evil is objectively perceived as a fact of the world's being which is external and incomprehensible to me, when the unsolvable problem of theodicy is posed, it is easy and costs nothing to judge the whole world and even God, to become a *judge of being*. It is easy to base one's perception of evil on the hatred of evil and to place the responsibility for evil on someone else. But then one is utterly blind to the true, irrational metaphysical essence of evil—for one fails to notice that, in this hatred as well as in the arrogance of the accusatory posture, the judge himself is seduced and captivated by the perversity of evil. This blocks the only path to genuine knowledge of the unknowable essence of evil, the path into one's own depths, the only path on which, through the consciousness of *my responsibility*, the unknowable becomes visible. In this perception of evil as guilt and sin (as *my* sin) lies the only possible form of the "knowledge" or "explanation" of evil which is not its "justification," which is not an attempt to find the "ground" of evil, an attempt which contradicts the essential groundlessness of evil. In the consciousness of guilt and sin, which is nothing else but the living concrete perception of the *illegitimacy of evil, the absolutely unknowable is known in an unknowable manner in all its self-evidence*. And since all knowledge is, in the final analysis, the perception of a relation with the primordial ground, with God, it is precisely by this knowledge that one can overcome evil as groundlessness and non-being and re-establish the unity with God. *The only way we can know evil is by overcoming it and extinguishing it through the consciousness of guilt*. Rational, abstract theodicy is impossible, but living theodicy, attainable not through thought but in living experience, is possible in all its unknowableness and transrationality. When the gentle, consoling, and reconciling light of God shines through the terrible pain of the awareness of sin, that which is experienced as incomprehensible separation, isolation, perversion, is also experienced as undamaged and inviolable being with and in God. That which is in irreconcilable conflict is perceived as being in primordial harmony. In this form the fundamental principle of antinomian monodualism reveals its action in relation to the problem of evil and in the living victory over evil.

d. The Meaning of Suffering

The same thing becomes clear in another aspect (which leads, moreover, to the enrichment of our wise ignorance) when we examine evil in the phenomenon of *suffering*. Suffering is a kind of universal, all-embracing aspect of the imperfection and inner defectiveness of being. Moral evil in its *effect* consists in the experience of suffering by the carrier of evil. Even metaphysical evil—death—would not be experienced as evil if it were not associated with suffering, with the torments of dying and the fear of death for the dying one and the suffering of loss for his dear ones. We would not attain the depths of the problem of evil if we did not consider evil in that aspect in which it is suffering.

It is true that, from the purely metaphysical or causal point of view, suffering is simply the consequence of evil, the consequence of the falling apart of total unity into separate, mutually antagonistic parts, each of which must live at the expense of the others. Without the "struggle for existence," the suicidal universal civil war, there would be no suffering in the world. But this purely theoretical explanation is insufficient for our purposes. If we consider how much innocent suffering there is in the world (recall Dostoevsky and his "infant's tear"), this causal relationship between suffering and guilt seems to us a monstrous absurdity and injustice, and we are ready to exclaim along with Ivan Karamazov: "Why then do we need this satanic good and evil?"

We do not intend to raise once again the problem of theodicy after "solving" it in the only way it can be solved—through the perception of the transrational ground of its rational unsolvability. Nevertheless, the universal fact of world suffering, which bears witness to a kind of fateful meaninglessness of the world's being, cannot fail to confound our thought. In this fact we confront the necessity of accepting blind, bare factuality as something ultimate. If suffering has neither meaning nor justification (and, in contradistinction to moral evil, suffering at least admits the possibility of seeking the meaning of evil), our whole being is meaningless, even in spite of the self-evidence of its divine primordial ground.

In perceiving evil in suffering, we silently take as our starting point the belief that perfection or the good coincides with *bliss* in the sense of pure unclouded happiness, perfect joy and enjoyment. It would appear that our entire life ought to be *bliss* insofar as it really emanates from God and is in Him—for God, the all-grounding and all-illuminating primordial ground, is absolutely perfect and is the primordial source of all perfection. It seems natural for us to view God as absolutely blissful or as absolute bliss. However, in this popular representation we rationalize and therefore narrow and distort that transrational and therefore antinomian unity which is the only form in which we can adequately conceive reality and its primordial source. What makes us so sure that the ineffable and unnameable, yet all-named, essence of the One we call God is exhausted by the feature which we conceive as untroubled bliss? The very fact that suffering (in spite of all the obviously sophistic and unconvincing attempts to describe it as a "lessening of pleasure") is something with *positive content*, the fact that pain is not a "lesser pleasure" but a great *real* torment, should be enough to make us stop and think. Unlike moral evil, suffering is not a phantom, not an existent illusion, not a reality in the form of a deception. Suffering is a genuine, though severe, *reality*. And unlike moral evil which, empty and groundless, seeks wih meaningless stubbornness to affirm itself as a reality, suffering is a kind of reality that is aware that it should not be and seeks to conquer or overcome itself. Nietzsche puts this in a lapidary aphorism: "*Weh spricht: vergeh!*" ("Pain tells itself: Go away!"). It is true that precisely in suffering as something which should not be but nevertheless is a reality we once again seem to encounter something that contradicts the fundamental religious intuition of the coincidence of reality and value in the primordial ground. But here too we must not forget that mystery, unknowableness, and transrationality form the very essence of reality and that we can acquire positive knowledge or understanding through the perception of this transrationality.

Arising from evil, suffering shares the groundlessness and meaninglessness of evil. In this respect suffering itself is evil which can never be so "explained" as to be justified. But containing in itself the tendency to overcome itself, suffering is also the movement of *return to reality*, and in this sense it is not evil but genuine reality or genuine good. The element of hopeless, meaningless torment—torment to the point of despair—lies not in suffering itself but in that worry, disgust, and struggle with which we experience suffering, i.e., it lies in the attempt to get rid of suffering by external "mechanical" means, to simply annihilate suffering, to submit it to the absolute divisive and annihilating action of "no" or "not." The pure essence of suffering is disclosed to us in the spiritual acceptance of suffering, in our ability to endure and withstand it. Suffering is then experienced by us not as meaningless evil, not as something that absolutely should not be, not even as an externally imposed punishment, but as a *healing* from evil and calamity, a God-sanctioned and divine path of return to the homeland, to the perfection of reality. One of the most evident laws of the spiritual life is that without suffering there is no perfection, no complete, unshakeably stable bliss. "Blessed are those who cry, for they will be comforted"; "strait is the gate, and narrow is the way which leadeth unto life"; and "through many sorrows do we enter the Kingdom of God." Or, as Meister Eckhart puts it: "The fastest horse to perfection is suffering." Suffering is like a hot probe that cleans and expands our respiratory paths, thereby for the first time opening for us free access to the blissful depths of genuine reality. There is no need to emphasize that suffering reveals its deepest essence only when endured in *my* deep inner experience and only in its aspect as *my* suffering. And only as *my* suffering does it find meaning and justification. But because of the total unity of being, *my* suffering becomes suffering for the universal sin, for sin *as such*. This discloses the genuine meaning (the meaning disclosed in general, eternal revelation) not only of the Christian idea of redemption but also of the idea of sacrifice as it is encountered in almost all religions.

Insofar as essentially antinomian reality is a *living* reality and, as a fallen and decaying reality, is marked by non-being, bears within itself the sting of non-being, it is therefore *antagonistic* reality in its inner essence. Precisely as a reality, it is *ant-agonia*, with *agonia* taken in the ancient sense of this word, the inner struggle against self, self-recovery and self-healing through self-overcoming or self-conquest, through deprivation and sacrifice, i.e., through tragedy and suffering. Only to the soul that is closed up in itself is suffering hellish torment, leading to despair, the meaningless agony in the devouring flame. But to the soul opened into its own depths, suffering is difficult ascent to heavenly bliss, the miracle of participation in the ineffable and unfathomable mystery of divine life. And here the *true* all-powerfulness and the *true* all-goodness of God are revealed in their unknowableness in the fact that God never annihilates suffering in an external or mechanical manner, in the fact that he never destroys it with a bolt of lightning from the blue as it were. Instead God grants the victory of genuine reality through our endurance of suffering on this necessarily antinomian and antagonistic inner path.

But this understanding is justified and makes the reality of total being transparent and inwardly persuasive for us only if we refrain from conceiving the absolute perfection and absolute bliss of God in the vulgar, rationalistically distorted sense of infinite self-enjoyment and monotonous, untroubled tranquility. The absolute perfection of God can be conceived (or rather felt) only in the form of the fullness of all-embracing (i.e., embracing also all opposites), boundlessly profound and illuminated life. And insofar as we can adequately grasp this fullness, this ultimate unity of God only in the unity of Creator and creation, we do not have the right to affirm that God remains in a state of undisturbed, blissful tranquility in the face of the world's suffering. Everything that is positive belongs to God, comes from God, occurs in God. Consequently, the good that is in the endurance of suffering also comes from God. The return of creation to God through suffering occurs (like everything else) *in God Himself.* This is the general, eternal revelation contained in the concrete-positive Christian revelation of the suffering of the God-man who offers himself in redeeming sacrifice for the sin of the world. It is evident that this too must not be understood as a rational definition of the essence and life of God, as an adequate and exhaustive disclosure of His infinite mystery. And of all the rational theological "theories," perhaps the most pitiful, the most helpless, and the most blasphemous is the rational theory of "redemption." Here it is sufficient to note that, insofar as we are in general capable of intellectually taking account of this unknowable reality, we must conceive it according to the principle of antinomian monodualism. God abides in eternally detached, transcendent, blissful tranquility (or, rather, He *is* this tranquility), but *at the same time* He also participates in the world's suffering, "takes" this suffering "upon Himself," co-experiences the whole tragedy of the world's being, and precisely thereby manifests His essence as the illuminating primordial ground of all being. Or, more precisely, "in Himself" God is "neither the one nor the other" (just as in general He can never be a "one" or an "other") and only in our human approximation is He the antinomian unity of the one and the other. Only in this unknowable and ineffable form is He absolute perfection, and only in this form do we find in Him the eternal blissful homeland of our "I" and of the world's being.

e. Summary of Our Examination of the Problem of Evil

This reveals the relationship between the knowledge of the rootedness of all being in God and that "illegitimate speculation" (Plato's *logismos nothos*) by means of which we apprehend the essence and origin of evil. The overcoming of evil in the awareness of guilt and the overcoming of evil in the endurance of suffering are both based on our being in God, are both a return to God. Insofar as we see guilt and suffering in the light of God Himself, in the light of absolute love, the impossible occurs: all evil is really overcome and exposed as a deceitful illusion. *Evil ceases to exist.* If I myself and the world in our autonomous being in relation to God are nonetheless only *from, with,* and *in* God, it follows that the potentiation and degeneration of this autonomy in the "falling away" from being, i.e., from God, are somehow healed at the very moment of the fall, are overcome by the omnipresent, all-reconciling force of God's reality. The total unity cannot be fractured in such a way as to break into separate pieces; and insofar as it is fractured, it is such only in our human aspect. In the divine aspect, it remains eternally whole, for all its cracks are immediately filled with positive being from the primordial ground itself, and Truth merges into absolute harmonious total unity, to which alone belongs ultimate, absolutely self-evident, inwardly persuasive reality. For us this awareness is like the awakening from a nightmare.

In the final analysis, *our very knowledge of good and evil* is revealed to be inadequate. Furthermore, in accordance with the wise Biblical tale, this knowledge turns out to be a result of the "fall." Genuine Truth, heavenly Truth, Truth as unknowable, living divine reality, *lies beyond the knowledge of good and evil.* Even though this knowledge is a necessary corrective to the fall, the "working hypothesis" of our earthly human existence, it is not the ultimate and absolute truth. But insofar as ultimate Divine truth is revealed to us, the absolutely Unknowable as such (even as the absolutely incomprehensible) is revealed to us with self-evidence. The heavens are infinitely above the earth and are unattainable if our starting point is the earth. But we ourselves are always in heaven. We have been given the ability to survey the totality of being from the point of view of "heaven," and this heavenly point of view is the point of view of all-embracing, absolute *love.* The loving perception that penetrates into the depths of the world does not know evil, for all evil manifests itself here as the illusory mask of good, and love is the only force that can genuinely overcome evil. Everything that appears to us in its *crude factuality* as non-divine and anti-divine turns out here to be Divine. And the only reason God must and can be revealed to us as "all in all" (as the old promise says) or become such for us is that He really is *all in all.* In spite of the problem of evil, the world—in its ultimate ground and truth—is "transfigured" being, the Kingdom of Heaven.

This too must not be understood as a solution to the problem of theodicy, the problem of evil. On the contrary, even this higher truth would become a lie if it claimed to be an absolute, exhaustive truth, if it claimed that the problematic reality of evil could be completely removed by this higher optimism, that it could be "reasoned away" (*hinwegdeduziert* as the Germans say). We must not forget that the troubling problem of evil retains all its force even from the "point of view of heaven"—even if evil is perceived from there to be on a lower, subordinate, less real level of being. On the one hand, in the ultimate depth of being, the Light of God dissipates and annihilates the darkness by illuminating it. But on the other hand that terrifying, incomprehensible relation expressed in St. John's Gospel retains relative validity and reality: "And the light shineth in darkness; and the darkness comprehended it not.''[2] Light is surrounded by darkness, which remains stubborn in its dark being and does not receive the rays of light, does not disappear. Even the ultimate overcoming (from the point of view of God Himself, which is somehow accessible for us) of all crude, unilluminated, evil factuality does not completely exhaust this ineffable connection, but is valid only in antinomian unity with the opposite, human-earthly point of view, for which the incomprehensible fact of the "fall," the falling away of creation from God, remains a bitter uneliminable reality.

Only in transrational hovering *above* or *between* these two aspects of reality, in a hovering which alone is adequate to the ineffable *antinomian-monodualistic fullness of absolute reality*, is the absolute reality of Divinity—of God-with-us—as the terrifyingly sweet, mysterious essence of being revealed to us in all its unknowableness.

NOTES

1. Translator's note: The Russian word for "beginning" (*nachalo*) can also mean "principle."
2. Translator's note: Frank examines this relation in his book *The Light Shineth in Darkness: An Attempt at a Christian Ethics and Social Philosophy. (Svet vo t'me. Opyt khristianskoi etiki i sotsial'noi filosofii*), Paris 1949.

Conclusion

Our investigation is concluded. Our aim was to find out whether it is possible to justify "objectively" that perception of being for which being appears to be something unknowable, ineffable, mysterious, incomprehensible, marvelous. It is our belief that we have convincingly demonstrated this possibility. First of all, we disclosed the unknowable in the makeup of objective being, in the makeup of that aspect of being which is constituted, as we have seen, by the element of rationality. We found out that this objective being is not a self-contained, closed, autonomous being, but only a dependent and incomplete "aspect" of being that has its roots deep in supra-rational unconditional being or all-embracing reality. It was also disclosed to us that what we call "being" (in contrast to its "content") simply coincides with the element of the unknowable.

Further, we examined being in the fundamental form in which it is "given" to us not from outside but is a reality that *inwardly reveals itself to itself* and *to us* insofar as we take part in it. This is psychic being, which we examined as immediate self-being. We also examined this being in the form in which it is "my inner life" and in the form in which, transcending itself, it is life in communion (in the "I-thou" and "we" relations) and spiritual life. Looking impartially at this aspect of being, we became convinced that its very essence is transrational, i.e., unknowable, but that it is nevertheless distinctly revealed to us precisely in all its unknowableness. Finally, we penetrated to the primordial ground or source of the *unity*, hidden from our immediate knowledge, of these two worlds or aspects of being. And this primordial ground of the unity, possessing the highest degree of self-evident truth which emanates from the coincidence in this unity of reality with value or meaning—this primordial ground was revealed to us as the Holiness of Divinity. And in this its general form and in its concrete manifestation as God-with-me and God-with-the-world, this primordial ground of reality harmonizes in itself complete self-evident truth with transrationality and unknowableness.

Thus, we became convinced that the world and being, both in their concrete manifestations and in their primordial ground, are not only unknowable in general but also *coincide with the unknowable*. This result of our study does not coincide, however, with the affirmation of skepticism or absolute irrationalism. It does not lead to the teaching that all positive rational knowledge (be it scientific knowledge or knowledge pertaining to practical orientation in being) is "bankrupt." The element of rationality, which in the final analysis is the basis of this kind of spiritual position, is for us an *objectively real* element of being itself. Therefore the point of view of the sober, rational world-understanding based on the element of rationality is, as such, completely justified and appropriate. Furthermore, the *abstract irrationalism* which denies the objective validity of the rational element is even falser and more harmful than abstract rationalism. The only thing which we found to be unjustifiable in this position of rational knowledge is its claim that it is the only valid position, its claim that it leads us to absolute truth, which leaves no room for truth of any other kind. On the contrary, our investigation has shown that rationality—as a reflection of the "light," as the "visible" element of being as it were—is only one of the elements of being and is inseparably connected with the opposite element of being. Rationality directed at itself (which is what philosophy really is) necessarily discloses its own transrationality as well as the transrationality of being owing to which being is the inseparable unity of *rationality and irrationality*. Therefore, genuine knowledge is acquired only by that deep-penetrating gaze which perceives the transrationality, the *unknowable* and *unexplainable* nature, of being.

The unknowable is not a night in which "all cats are gray." It is not a night in which the clear and distinct "daytime" perception of the world loses all meaning. On the contrary, the unknowable is the unapproachable Light from which the ordinary "daytime" visibleness of the world emanates and before which the ordinary clarity of the world turns out to be dark, impenetrable, irrational. The truth of science and of the sober, rational apprehension of the world turns out to be derivative, partial, and inadequate only *in this sense*. Genuine truth is revealed to us only by philosophy, in a framework in which rationality, by directing itself at itself, transcends itself and acquires a ground in the general, eternal revelation of reality as the Transrational and Unknowable. And, in turn, philosophy postulates as its source (in which it is born and acquires its possibility and essence) the immediate religious perception of being—more precisely, the holy reality of Divinity by the force and revelation of which all things in general *are* and *are for themselves*, i.e., are revealed for knowledge.

And if the hostile reader attempts to destroy the very intent of our investigation with the mocking objection that "the Unknowable as such is unknowable," we can only answer that the truth of this objection is as unquestionable and as *dumb* as the truth contained in Kuzma Prutkov's wise teaching that "it is impossible to encompass the unencompassable."[1] Kuzma Prutkov and the hostile reader who follows his wisdom do not even suspect all the mystery and wonder contained in the very possibility of being able to say the word "unknowable" (or "unencompassable"), i.e., the possibility of having this idea or concept of the unknowable. For in saying this word and forming this idea we have already "encompassed" the "unencompassable," and captured, apprehended, and, in this sense, "known" the "unknowable."

To the seeming wisdom of Kuzma Prutkov (so influential and authoritative for most people) we have opposed, in the course of our entire investigation, the genuine wisdom of Nicholas of Cusa (which expresses the wisdom of all true philosophers): *attingitur inattingibile inattingibiliter.* The unattainable is attained through its unattainment. *The unknowable is known through knowledge of its unknowableness.* When this fundamental consciousness, illuminating our life, is lost, life becomes a meaningless, blind existence.

Notes

1. Translator's note: Kuzma Prutkov is the pseudonym of three 19th-century writers (the two Zhemchuznikovs and Alexey Tolstoy) who collaborated on absurd aphorisms and verses.

INDEX

Absolute, the, 81-82, 110, 113-114, 143, 238-240, 247, 261; as the unknowable, 86; in the Upanishads, 108; and selfhood, 112
Abstract possibility, 62
Abstract knowledge. *See* Conceptual knowledge
Adam, 285
Am-form of being, 108-110, 113, 115, 149; and the art-form of being, 131; *See also* I
Am-is unity, 73, 76
Angelus Silesius, 41, 225
Anselm of Canterbury, Saint, 216
Antinomian knowledge, 97, 118; as wise ignorance, 94
Antinomian monodualism, 110, 144, 148, 170, 185, 206, 242, 245, 268, 271, 293, 297, 299; and wise ignorance, 97; as triadism, 98; and wc, 154
Aquinas, Saint Thomas, 221, 281
Arago, Francois, 197
Aristotle, xviii, 42, 62, 89, 113, 273; on possibility, 41
Art, 191, 193; and beauty, 189
Art-form of being, 113, 149, 227-229, 242; and the am-form of being, 131; *See* Thou
Aseitas, 132
Atheism, 244; and proofs of the existence of God, 213; and theodicy, 277
Atman, 74, 111
Augustine, Saint, xiii, 71, 99, 163, 181, 198, 229, 236; *Confessions*, 40; the idea of the search for God, 161

Baader, Franz, xiii, 229
Bacon, Francis, 7
Beauty, the beautiful, xix, 166, 169, 191, 193, 195, 262-263; and art, 189; as a metalogical unity, 189; as harmony, 190, 196; and the self-groundedness of being, 190; expressiveness of, 192; and the appearance of reality, 195; of nature, 195; of the world, 221, 272; *See also* Esthetics
Becoming, 39-41, 168, 187, 255; scientific knowledge of, 40
Beethoven, Ludwig van, 194
Berdiaev, Nikolai, xi
Bergson, Henri, 40, 115; *Deux sources de la morale et de la religion,* 194
Berkeley, George, 22, 134
Bible, 233-234, 298
Boehme, Jacob, 97, 236, 280, 290; on *Ungrund*, 46
Bonaventure, Saint, 217
Both-and, both-the-one-and-the-other, 79-80, 82, 85-86, 93-94, 109, 233, 239, 245; and Divinity, 220
Botticelli, Sandro, 196
Brahman, 111, 114, 210, 244; and revelation of reality, 74
Buber, Martin: and the I-thou relation, 141
Bulgakov, Sergei, xi

Calvin, John, 246
Causal connection, 24, 42, 44
Christian teaching, 168, 252, 254, 258
Christianity, 237

Church, the 236; St. Paul's teaching of, 150

Coincidence of opposites, *coincidentia oppositorum*, 144, 154, 177, 218, 260; and unconditional being, 68; revealed in love, 148; and we, 149; and the primordial ground, 208-209

Common sense, xvi, 16

Communion, 130, 157, 228, 242, 300; in the I-thou relation, 142

Conceptual knowledge, xv-xvi, xxiii, 23, 25, 27-28, 33, 44, 66, 86, 92-95, 144, 240; and the metalogical nature of being, 28-30; and becoming, 40; true ground of, 79; and negation, 82; and thou, 128; *See also* Rational knowledge

Consciousness, 107, 111, 118, 161, 188, 193, 230; as cognitive possession, 105-106; in an infant, 133; unity of, 186

Conservation, laws of, 42

Cognitive intentionality, 104, 143, 159-160; transcending in, 120-122

Contradiction, 25, 36, 83, 93; transcending of, 83

Copernicus, Nicolas, xvii

Corinthians, 234

Cosmic being, 153, 186-187, 222; *See also* Objective being

Creation, 268-270, 275, 285, 296-297, 299; Creator and, 273; as we, 276

Creativity, 166

Dawson, Christopher, 20n

Definiteness, 59, 65, 89; as element of conceptual knowledge, 23, 25; and metalogical unity, 26, 38; and plurality, 34; and the irrational, 36-37; and total being, 38; and objects of judgment, 52

Democritus, 42

Descartes, René, xviii, xxiii, 31, 60, 103-104, 163; *cogito ergo sum*, 71, 105, 217, 229

Determinations, 21, 23, 32, 36, 43, 52-53, 84-85, 95, 191; and the laws of logic, 26-27; and the is-element, 61; and negation, 78; and thinking, 91

Devil, 281, 290

Dionysius the Areopagite, xiii, 181; *Mystical Theology*, 93; the method of analogy, 221

Divinity. *See* Holiness (Divinity)

Docta ignorantia. *See* Wise ignorance

Dogmatic metaphysics, xvii, 90, 198

Dostoevsky, Feodor, 49, 76, 116, 171-172, 196, 261; Ivan Karamazov, 165, 294

Dualism, 97, 186-187, 201, 281; and unfaith, 184-185

Eastern Orthodox Church, 258

Ebner, Ferdinand, 226

Eckhart, Meister, 80, 210, 295

Einfühlung, 126-127, 193-194

Either-or, 79, 82, 84-86, 93, 95, 233

Eleatics, 43

Empiricism: and the limitedness of consciousness, 7; sensationalistic aspect of, 8

Erotic love, xix-xx

Esthetics, the esthetic, 166, 189-196

Eternity, 219, 258, 284-285; and time, 41; of I, 231

Ethics, 166

Evil, 219, 222, 265; in spiritual being, 166-167; and beauty, 196; in the world, 266; ground or origin of, 266, 277, 279-281, 291-292, 297; as darkness, 278; essence of, 281, 285, 292-293, 297; groundlessness of, 281; and

death, 283-284, 294; responsibility for, 286-293; spirit of, 286-297; self-destruction of, 290; and guilt and sin, 292-293; and suffering, 293, 297-298; victory over, 293; *See also* Theodicy
Evolutionism, 200, 222
Excluded middle, 26, 78
Explicitly given, the, 8-10
Extratemporality, 37; and ideal being, 60-62; and ideal-realism, 63

Faith, 256; and unfaith, 184
Fall of man, the, 285, 298
Familiar elements, xv-xx, xxii, xxiv-xxv
Fear and trembling, xviii-xix, 225, 242, 291
Fichte, Johann Gottlieb, 61, 110, 125, 183
Francis of Assisi, Saint, 135
FRANK, S.L., 223n; and the flowering of Russian philosophy, xi; important works of, xi; *The Unknowable,* xi; *The Soul of Man,* 123n; "I and We," 155n; *The Spiritual Foundations of Society,* 155n; *The Light Shineth in Darkness,* 299n; *See also Object of Knowledge, The*
Freedom, 46-48, 168, 175, 187, 255, 259, 282, 286; in immediate self-being, 115-116; as self-overcoming, 117; as potentiality, 117; as center of the person, 177; of I in the face of God, 244-247; and evil, 287
Freud, Sigmund, 175
Future, the, 258, 276; and potentiality, 46; in objective reality, 54-55

Gaunilo, 216
German idealism, 71
Gnosis, 236

God, 14, 31, 73, 77, 92, 113, 169, 177, 181, 185, 198, 206, 210-211, 219, 222, 227, 230-232, 234, 244, 251, 256, 279, 284-285, 294, 296, 299; concept of, xvii; proofs of the existence of, 212-217; ontological proof of the existence of, 216-217; and I, 225, 245-249, 261; as He, 226; speech to, 226; as Thou, 226, 228-229, 235, 242-243; as my God, 229; certainty of, 229; Word of, 233; personal, 238, 240, 242; as Father, 242, 252; absoluteness of, 243, 245; as love, 250; my love of, 250; as life, 255; as God-in-me, 257-260; and the world, 267-277, 288; self-evident truth of, 277-278; and the responsibility for evil, 286, 289-291, 293; as participant in suffering, 297; as all in all, 298
God-in-me, 257-259
God-man being, 258
Godmanhood, 251, 258-259, 275
Godsonhood, 258
God-with-me, I-with-God, 225, 227-228, 232, 244, 248, 251-257, 259-262, 264-266, 289, 300; Divinity revealed as, 231, 235, 239; as love, 248, 250
God-with-the-world, 235, 300
God-with-us, 225, 235, 252, 259, 299
God-world being, 275
Goethe, Johann Wolfgang, xx, 14, 29, 33-34, 91, 117, 183, 226, 239; *Faust,* 210
Gogol, Nikolai, 196
Good, 169, 196, 219, 222, 265-266, 280, 287, 290-291, 294, 296, 298; and suffering, 295
Grace, 244, 247-248; and law, 254
Greek philosophy, 168
Gregory of Nazianzus, 211
Gregory the Great, 211

Ground, 163, 167, 174, 216, 262; ideal, 164-165; illuminating, 165-166, 203; *See also* Primordial ground

Groundedness, 163, 190, 212; in conceptual knowledge, 23-25; of time, 270

Guilt: and evil, 292-293, 297

Hallaj, al-Hussayn ibn-Mansur al, 20n

Harmony, 190, 196, 293

Hegel, Georg Wilhelm Friedrich, 40, 45, 82, 98, 114, 149, 153, 237, 244, 280, 285; on negation, 78; on freedom, 115

Heart, 218

Heraclitus, 96, 150, 160, 168, 218, 237

Hiddenness: in the primordial ground, 208-209; of Divinity, 214, 225; of my life-with-God, 256

Holiness (Divinity), 226, 236, 251, 256, 266-267, 271, 273-276, 285, 289, 299-301; in contradistinction to God, 210; certainty of, 212-218; and its essential relation to all else, 218-222; as wholly other, 219-220, 255; and unconditional being, 221; as Thou, 224, 228, 232, 238, 249; and I, 224-225; as God-with-us, 225; revealed in love, 228; as God-with-me, 231, 235, 239; as a suprapersonal principle, 239; as person, 240-241, 244; as God-in-me, 259, 262; and the world, 264

Holy Spirit, 235-236

Hovering, 110, 220, 231, 237, 299; as expression of antinomian knowledge, 94-95, 97-98

Humanism, 259

Hume, David, 24

Husserl, Edmund, 7, 57

I, 15, 106, 110-112, 124-126, 134, 136-137, 140-142, 144-149, 151-152, 156, 169, 171, 173, 199, 228-229, 231, 242-243, 245, 248-249, 257, 259, 261, 276, 279, 297; and the knowing subject, 71, 104; in immediate self-being, 104; and the encounter with thou, 131; relative sovereignty of, 132; the rootedness in unconditional being of, 132-133; the rootedness in we of, 133; the relation to God of, 133; as actualized being, 138; a second, 155n; higher, spiritual, 174; as person, 175, 241; in the world, 200, 272; as nothing, 246; as other than God, 247, 250; and the responsibility for evil, 286-288, 292-293

I-am being, 73

I-thou relation, 122, 131-132, 134, 139, 141, 151-152, 154, 155n, 156-160, 170, 175, 182, 227-228, 232, 238, 243, 248, 257, 300; two basic forms of, 137, 140; as communion, 142; as the unity of separateness and mutual penetration, 142-144; as a dual-unity, 143; as I-thou being, 144; realized in love, 144; and we, 148

I-with-God. *See* God-with-me

Ideal being, 57-60, 70; Plato on, 57-58; and negation of time, 60-62

Ideal-realism, 63

Idealism, 65-66, 177, 230; and the objective validity of knowledge, 11; as rationalism, 67; and unconditional being, 70; subjective, 134, 183

Identity, 25, 36-37, 89, 109, 220; and becoming, 42

Illegitimate speculation, *logismos nothos*, 32, 279, 281, 297

Immediate self-being, 100, 125, 128, 138, 142-145, 147, 149-150, 153-154, 160-161, 165-166, 169-174, 178, 182-185, 187-188, 192, 198, 200, 202, 205, 209, 214, 222, 227-229, 239, 241, 243, 254, 260, 262, 275, 300; and objective being, 101; and reality, 101; as psychic being, 101-102; and the knowing subject, 104; as consciousness, 105; as light and darkness, 106-107; in the form of self-revelation to itself, 107; as the unknowable in its immediacy, 107; as the am-form of being, 108; and absolute reality, 110; immediacy in, 110-112, 115-117; selfhood in, 110, 112-113; and freedom, 115; as subjectivity, 118-122; and cognitive intentionality, 120-122; as I, 124, 131; self-transcending of, 130; with thou as a center, 146; and spiritual being, 156, 162-163, 204; loneliness of, 157; and inward transcending, 162; and evil, 167; as a genuine reality, 199; rooted in the primordial ground, 201; in God-with-me, 231

Immortality, 230

Indian philosophy, 105, 168, 188; *See also* Brahman; Atman

Individuality, 33, 35-36, 282; and plurality, 34; and the person, 128

Infinite, the, 10-11, 14, 39, 178, 249; in space, 15; in time, 15-16

Intuition, 30; as primary knowledge, 27, 29

Inner world, the, 192; and the outer world, 182-188; in the unity of consciousness, 186

Inward transcending, 123, 154, 156, 158, 162, 175, 228, 239, 261; in love, 159; and the soul, 160; to spiritual being, 168

Ionian nature philosophers, 42

Irrationality, the irrational, 116, 153-154, 187, 216, 262-265, 280, 301; in psychic life, xxi; as the ground of metalogical concreteness, 30-33; and rationality, 31-32; and the metalogical nature of reality, 36, 41; as the

substrate of being, 46-47; and objective reality, 53; as the subjective, 53; in the paradoxicality of being-with-God, 255

Is-element, the, 61, 67

Isaiah, 260n

It, 173; and he, 126; and thou, 139; and we, 153; the world as, 263

James, William, 7

Jesus Christ, 234-235, 252; the God-man essence of, 258

John, First Epistle of, 228

John, Gospel of, 174-175, 260n, 299

John of the Cross, Saint, 211

Judgment, 4, 8, 24-25, 27, 59-61, 91-94; existential, 2, 11, 67; impersonal, 2; synthetic, 3; and thinking, 87; as realization of objective knowledge, 90

Kabbalah, 275

Kant, Immanuel, xix, 55, 88, 102, 134, 166, 186, 198, 207, 264; and dogmatic metaphysics, xvii; and thing-in-itself, xxiii, 18-19; and the critique of reason, 87; and transcendental logic, 87; categories of, 87, 89; and the ontological proof, 216

Kierkegaard, Soren, 237, 261

Knowing subject, 71, 103, 105, 124, 129, 188, 192, 230; as conceived by Kant, 88; and immediate self-being, 104; and I, 104

Law, 254-256; and we, 152-154; and guilt, 292

Laws of logic, 25; and determinations, 26

Leibniz, Gottfried Wilhelm, 164

Lenin, Vladimir Ilyich, 134

Lévy-Bruhl, Lucien, 134

Life, 161, 168, 171, 178, 250, 255-256; and reality, 75-76; and immediate self-being, 107; primordial, 204-205; as the being of I-with-God, 251-253

Light, 186, 214-215, 219, 227, 254, 275, 278, 290, 301; as the essence of life, 171; of spirit, 172; the self-illuminating, 203; of Truth, 204, 289; of consciousness, 206, 230; and revelation, 208; of God, 229, 298; and darkness, 298-299

Logical connections, 24-25, 27, 270

Logical realism, 63; and nominalism, 70

Logos, 150, 171, 187, 234, 269, 273

Lossky, Nicholas Onufriyevich, 57

Love, 91, 139, 141, 154, 156-159, 228, 238, 242-243, 249, 257, 292, 297-298; and realization of the I-thou relation, 144; as transcending to thou, 146; as union, 147; Divinity revealed in, 228; God-with-me as, 248, 250; paradoxicality of, 250; God as, 259; and evil, 290

Lotze, Rudolf Hermann, 103

Lucretius, 42

Luther, Martin, 246

Makarius the Great, 281

Malebranche, Nicolas, 217

Massignon, Louis, 20n

Mathematical knowledge, 27, 39, 197; the groundlessness of, 64

Maximus the Confessor, 236

Meaning of being. *See* Primordial foundation, the

Metalogical nature of being, the, 23, 41, 48, 66, 87; and the irrational, 36

Metalogical unity, 29, 37-38, 59-60, 78-80, 109, 163, 220, 246; and definiteness, 26; and the irrational, 30-32; and beauty, 189

Monism, 97, 184, 186

Mysterium tremendum, 138-139, 141, 168; *See also* Otto, Rudolf

Mystery of being, the, 76, 91, 98, 130; and unconditional being, 67-68; and beauty, 195

Mysticism, xiii, xxv, 258; speculative, 211, 236

Neither-nor, 82, 86, 93-94, 233, 274; and the unknowable, 80-81; and Divinity, 220

Negation, 9, 87, 132, 144, 207, 267, 282; and definiteness, 36-37; as differentiation, 77-80, 85, 97; negation of, 78-81, 84, 86, 94; as either-or, 79; absolute, 81; limitation as the meaning of, 84; as the rejection of what is false, 84, the overcoming of, 84, 86-87; as affirmation, 85, 93; and the ontological proof, 217

Negative theology, 92, 108

Neo-Kantianism, 71

New Testament, 252-253

Newton, Isaac, 13

Nicholas of Cusa, xiv, 56, 78, 81, 95, 206, 222, 236, 260, 273-274, 302; on the ontological proof, 217

Nietzsche, Friedrich, 50, 153, 295; *Zweisamkeit*, 147, 229

Nirvana, 244

Nominalism, 70

Non-otherness, 78, 97; and the Absolute, 81

Nothing, 80, 82, 245-246, 258, 268, 274, 279-280, 282; and the unknowable, 81

Numinous, the, 210; *See also* Otto, Rudolf

Object of Knowledge, The (S. L. Frank), xi-xii, xxiii-xxiv, 2, 8, 11-12, 17,

20n, 23, 25-26, 37, 43, 223n; on time, 39; on the ideal world, 58; on idealism, 66; on transcendence, 72

Object of knowledge, the, 21, 27, 29, 35, 127, 206; as the unknown and ungiven, 2-13

Objective being, xxv, 2, 22, 52-53, 70-71, 84, 87-89, 102-103, 109, 125, 153, 163, 178, 182-183, 186-187, 190-191, 194-195, 198, 204-206, 208, 213-214, 222, 233, 241, 253-255, 261, 273, 275, 300; transcending of, 11; and objective reality, 48-49; and ideal being, 57-65; and unconditional being, 64-65; and immediate self-being, 101; opposition to I, 137; rooted in the primordial ground, 201; and the world, 262-265, 271

Objective knowledge, xxiv, 2-4, 18-19, 90, 198, 203, 211, 214, 234, 236, 254; overcome, 73; in Kant's system, 87

Objective reality, xv, 3, 22, 48, 87, 118-119, 121, 124, 143, 146, 157, 172, 185, 189, 191, 193, 195, 199, 201-202, 214, 221, 234, 241, 264, 273; and objective being, 21; and subjective phenomena, 50-53; and the consciousness of time, 53-56; and total being, 56; and potentiality, 56; and ideal being, 57-65; and unconditional being, 64, 74; and the world, 262-263

Ontological proof, 216-217

Origen, 236

Otto, Rudolf, 138, 141, 210, 219

Outer World, the, 192, 261; and the inner world, 182-188; in the unity of consciousness, 186; *See also* Objective being

Outward transcending, 122, 124, 154, 156-157, 168, 228

Pantheism, 265, 280

Paradoxicality: of love, 250; as sign of genuine reality, 251; of life as the being of I-with-God, 251-256

Parmenides, 246

Pascal, Blaise, 15, 237

Past, the, 40, 258; as object of scientific knowledge, 45; in the makeup of objective reality, 54-55

Paul, Saint, 150

Pelagianism, 244

Person, the, 200, 222, 238, 254, 257-258, 263-264; mystery of, 91, 174; holiness of, 146; and spiritual selfhood, 174; as the primordial unity of psychic life, 175; and I, 175; as the unity of separateness and mutual penetration, 176; as revelation of the image and likeness of God, 177; as individuality, 178; in Divinity, 239-240

Phenomenology, 7; and ideal being, 60

Philosophia perennis, xiii, 166

Philosophy, 301; nature of, 88-89, 96; conflict with religion, 236-237

Plato, 32, 41, 62, 70, 205, 210-211, 218, 237, 272-273, 279-280, 297; on the world of ideas, 57-58; *Phaedo,* 223n

Platonism, xiii, 58, 60-62

Plotinus, xiii, 40, 113, 150, 205, 218, 223n, 254; and the divine spirit, 58, 62

Poetry: as the voice of reality, 234

Possession, cognitive: and immediate self-being, 105-106

Positivism, 183, 193

Potency of thought, 70-71

Potentiality, potency, 41-45, 47, 117, 119-120, 161, 170, 187, 197, 255; as primordial freedom, 46; and objective reality, 56-57; and thought, 61; in immediate self-being, 115; and the primordial ground, 208-209

Practical orientation in life, xv–xvii, 5–7

Prayer, 226

Present, the: the objective reality of, 54–55

Primordial ground, the, xxv, 197–198, 201, 203, 211, 213–215, 217–219, 221–222, 224, 226–227, 232, 234–236, 238–244, 246, 249, 251, 260, 262, 264, 267–273, 275–276, 278–279, 284, 286, 289, 293–295, 297–298, 300; as Truth, 204; 206–207; as primordial life, 204; Plotinus on, 205; revelation of, 208; as the absolutely unknowable for us, 208; as potency of all, 208; as coincidence of all opposites, 208–209; as the essence of the unknowable, 209; expressed in the human word, 210; as Holiness, 210; as Thou, 228

Primordial foundation, the, 204–205, 242; as truth itself, 203

Primordial unity, 80, 199, 206, 280; of the soul and objective reality, 201

Protestantism, 237

Prutkov, Kuzma, 302

Psychic being, psychic life, 107–108, 111, 161–162, 169–172, 174, 194, 202; as immediate self-being, 101, 300; and physical and physiological being, 102; substrate of, 116; rooted in spiritual being, 163; and the person, 175; *See also* Soul, the; Subjectivity

Psychoanalysis, xx

Pushkin, Aleksandr, 179n, 190, 196

Rational knowledge, xxii, xxiv, 40, 197, 264, 301; and ideal being, 58; and idealism, 67

Rationality, 87, 89–90, 153–154, 186–188, 219, 244, 256, 262–264, 300–301; in the world, 265

Reality, 74, 91, 95, 97, 109, 164, 166, 182, 193, 195, 199, 207, 216, 224, 226, 230, 233, 251, 264, 272–273, 276–277, 281–282, 295, 298–300; and unconditional being, 72; as unity of being and truth, 73; as the essentially unknowable, 73, 75; revelation of, 73; as concrete fullness and organic unity, 75, 232; contrasted with objective reality, 74–76; as living life, 76; triadism of, 98; and immediate self-being, 101; and we, 150; expressed in beauty, 191–192; as Truth, 203; of thou, 232

Redemption: Christian idea of, 296; rational theory of, 297

Religious consciousness, 166, 198, 224, 235–236, 238, 242, 245, 254, 272, 277

Rembrandt van Rijn, 194

Renaissance, 55, 265

Revelation, 130, 214, 234; of thou, 128–129, 227; general, 129, 232, 235–239, 242, 258, 268, 297, 301; of the unknowable, 129; of spiritual reality, 172–173; as self-disclosure in the light, 207–208; of the primordial ground, 208; of Divinity, 225; concrete-positive, 231–238, 297; of Divinity as Thou, 232; in the Word, 233; of God, 234–235

Riehl, Aloys, 43

Rilke, Rainer Maria, 19, 20n, 157, 197, 210, 214, 242

Scheler, Max, 141

Schelling, Friedrich Wilhelm Joseph von, 43, 280, 290

Schopenhauer, Arthur, 119, 285

Scientific knowledge, scientific consciousness, 38, 44–45, 200, 234, 301; and common sense, xvi; of becoming, 40; and the past, 45

Self-evident truth, self-evidence, 203,

207-208, 221, 300; of Divinity, 212-218; of God, 277-278, 289

Selfhood, 110-113, 147, 188, 229, 239, 254, 263, 286; and the absolute, 112; and spiritual reality, 173-174; constituting the person, 174; and true freedom, 175

Sensations, 22

Simmel, Georg, 141

Sin, 293; guilt as, 292; and suffering, 296; of the world, 297

Shakespeare, William, 119

Skepticism, xxi-xxii, 301; legitimate meaning of, 69

Socrates, 20n, 70, 76, 96, 167, 173, 218, 237

Socratic irony, 96

Solipsism, 134

Soloviev, Vladimir, xiii, 275

Soul, the, 161, 192-195, 201, 218, 226, 230, 236, 242, 253, 256, 262, 266, 285-286, 296; naturalistic view of, 159; in inward transcending, 160; and spirit, 168-174; homeland of, 199; enslavement by the objective world, 202; self-disclosure of, 208; *See also* Psychic being

Spinoza, Baruch, 31, 243, 270, 280

Spirits, kingdom of, 114, 133, 136, 144; and we, 263

Spiritual being, spirit, 123, 150, 156, 162, 164, 168, 175-178, 182, 193, 202-204, 206-207, 209, 222, 228, 239, 241, 257-258, 261, 274-275; and actuality, 161; and immediate self-being, 161; and psychic being, 163; and evil, 166-167, 287; and soul, 168-173; and selfhood, 173; as being-with-God, 253

Stoics, 150

Struve, Pyotr B., xi, 155n

Subjectivity, 84, 88, 159-160, 162, 166, 171-172, 174, 178-179, 184-185, 187-188, 199, 225, 228, 233-234, 258; and objective reality, 50-52; and unconditional being, 71; and immediate self-being, 118-122; transcending of, 158; kinship with cosmic being, 186

Substance, xvii, 31, 259, 282

Sufism, 20

Suffering, 216, 294; and evil, 293; as a reality, 295; as healing, 295-296; for sin, 296; of the God-man, 297; God's participation in, 297

Sufficient reason, principle of, 163-164, 215

Supratemporality, 63; and the is-element, 61-62

Tertullian, 252

Theodicy, 277, 280, 286, 290, 293, 298; validity of the problem of, 278; unsolvability of the problem of, 278-279, 294

Theology, 234-237; dogmatic, 238

Theory of knowledge, 8, 186

Thing-in-itself, xiii, 18-19, 186

Thou, 113, 131-134, 140-144, 148-151, 154, 155n, 156-160, 168, 171-173, 175, 182, 187-188, 192, 227, 248-249, 257; and the actualization of immediate self-being, 125; and he, 126; interpreted as an object of knowledge, 127; revelation of, 128-129; as revelation of the unknowable, 130; seeming revelation of, 135; as alien, 137-139; as it, 139; as thou-for-me, 145; and love, 146; as a second I, 146; Divinity revealed as, 224, 226, 232, 238; God revealed as, 229; of God, 234-235, 242-243, 250; of Divinity, 249

Time, 9, 187, 219, 268-270; and infinitude, 15-16; and becoming, 39-41; consciousness of, 53-56; and objective reality, 53-56; and ideal being,

60-62; and ideal-realism, 63; Plato on, 272; earthly, 284; genuine, 285

Tolstoy, Lev, 165, 196, 222

Total unity, xxv, 19, 36, 41, 47, 64, 76, 81, 112, 128, 132, 136, 147, 160, 187-188, 197, 206, 217, 222, 240, 243, 246, 255, 259, 263, 270, 274, 276, 279-280, 282-283, 285-286, 291, 296-298; and selfhood, 113; as the Absolute, 114; revealed as living being, 144; in concrete individuality, 178; God as, 272; degradation of, 284; the inner solidarity of, 290

Tragic nature of human existence, 290

Transcendental logic, 87-89

Transcendental thinking, 87-92, 94, 124, 132, 161, 206-207, 219, 224, 230, 235, 238, 240, 245-246, 267, 270; and knowledge of the unknowable, 92

Transcending. *See* Inward transcending; Outward transcending

Transdefiniteness, the transdefinite, 32, 107, 109, 168, 255; and definiteness, 33; and individuality, 35; and potentiality, 46; and unconditional being, 68

Transfiniteness, the transfinite, 36-39, 42-43, 48, 107, 109, 168, 255; and potentiality, 46; of unconditional being, 68

Transrational unity, 98, 176, 247, 249, 256, 259; of subjectivity and objectivity, 179; of God as Thou and Divinity, 242-243; of God-with-me, 261; and otherness, 270

Transrationality, the transrational, xxii, 23, 47, 58, 68-69, 82, 87, 89-92, 94-95, 97-98, 107, 109-110, 119, 144, 154, 168, 187, 207, 220, 240, 245, 251, 256, 268-269, 271, 282, 293, 295, 300-301; of unconditional being, 67; of relation between spirit and soul, 170;

of Divinity, 218-219, 238; of God, 291

Triadism, 98

Truth, 96, 169, 185, 204-205, 207, 209, 215, 218, 223n, 224, 227, 269, 271, 273, 278-279, 289, 291, 298, 301; as *adaequatio intellectus et rei*, 22; transrational, 94-95; and life, 178; and the primordial foundation, 203; integral, 203; spirit of, 235; and untruth, 265-266; as determining the world's being, 267-268

Turgenev, Ivan: "The Dog," 155n

Tyutchev, Feodor, 19, 111, 116, 141, 262

Unconditional being, 65, 83, 109, 112, 173, 182, 188, 191, 205, 208, 212-214, 216, 242, 300; and objective being, 64; and the transrational, 67-68; as *coincidentia oppositorum*, 68; and ideal being, 70; and transcendence, 72; and I, 133; and the unity of consciousness, 186; and the ontological proof, 217; as the image of Divinity, 221

Unity of separateness and mutual penetration, 97, 110, 118, 170, 243, 249; in immediate self-being, 114-115; and the I-thou relation, 142-144; in the form of self-revelation, 150-151; and the person, 176-178; *See also* Antinomian monodualism

Unfaith, 185, 200; as absolute metaphysical dualism, 184

Unknowable, the, xx, xxiv-xxv, 13-14, 69, 76-77, 86-87, 90-96, 100, 108, 110, 130, 135, 138, 178, 182, 188, 191, 197-198, 208, 220, 222, 233, 237, 240, 268, 277, 293, 302; concept of, xxiii; and negation, 78; as all-embracing fullness, 79; as neither-nor, 80; as nothing, 81; as the absolute, 83, 114;

as the unity of unity and diversity, 83; thinking apprehension of, 87; and immediate self-being, 107; and either-or, 109; revelation of, 129; as thou, 129; the absolutely, 298; in objective being, 300; as the unapproachable Light, 301

Unknowable, the essentially; the unknowable in itself, xxiv, 14, 33, 41, 48, 70, 75, 119, 143, 160, 168, 177, 187-188, 251; in metalogical knowledge, 29; and reality, 30, 73; and ideal being, 58; and unconditional being, 67; and we, 154; and the primordial ground, 209; and the word, 233

Unknowable for us, the, xxiv, 19, 29, 43, 208; and the knowable, 14

Unknown, the, 3-9, 11, 43, 72; identity with the known, 12; as the object of knowledge, 13-14; and the unknowable, 13-14; the infinitude of, 15

Upanishads, 96, 108, 111, 210, 218

Validity, 171, 176, 279; of knowledge, 11-12; of the problem of theodicy, 218

We, the being of we, 131, 133-134, 151, 159, 172, 187, 228, 258, 276, 300; as a self-revealing reality, 149; as a coincidence of opposites, 149; as community, 148-149; revelation of reality in, 150; objectification of, 152-154; as it, 153; as the mystery of love, 154

Wise ignorance, xxv, 69, 91, 95, 108, 115, 177, 237, 245, 268, 281, 293; as antinomian knowledge, 94; as goal of human thought, 96; and antinomian monodualism, 97

Word, the: as revelation, 233; of God, 234, 269; *See also* Logos

World, the, 5, 48, 153, 183, 201, 204, 209, 211, 215-216, 273, 286, 288, 293-294, 297, 300-301; practical orientation in, xv-xvii; transfiguration of, 196; and I, 200; as symbol of Divinity, 221; my being in, 261; concept of, 262-263; as transrational being, 263; inner significance of, 264; as chaos, 264-265; rational apprehension of, 265; ground or origin of, 265-268, 275; evil in, 266, 280; God and, 267, 269; originating in Truth, 268; creation of, 268-270; absolute beginning of, 269; end of, 270; as God's other, 271, 274; as the world-in-God, 271; as distant likeness of God, 272; as incarnation of God, 272, 274-276; as theophany, 275; restlessness in, 285; degeneration of, 285; as the kingdom of heaven, 298

Xenophon, 237

Zeno of Elea, 40